The Oxford Guide to Library Research

THOMAS MANN

The Oxford Guide to Library Research

Fourth Edition

OXFORD
UNIVERSITY PRESS

OXFORD
UNIVERSITY PRESS

Oxford University Press is a department of the
University of Oxford. It furthers the University's objective
of excellence in research, scholarship, and education
by publishing worldwide.

Oxford   New York
Auckland   Cape Town   Dar es Salaam   Hong Kong   Karachi
Kuala Lumpur   Madrid   Melbourne   Mexico City   Nairobi
New Delhi   Shanghai   Taipei   Toronto

With offices in
Argentina   Austria   Brazil   Chile   Czech Republic   France   Greece
Guatemala   Hungary   Italy   Japan   Poland   Portugal   Singapore
South Korea   Switzerland   Thailand   Turkey   Ukraine   Vietnam

Oxford is a registered trade mark of Oxford University Press
in the UK and certain other countries.

Published in the United States of America by
Oxford University Press
198 Madison Avenue, New York, NY 10016

Library of Congress Cataloging-in-Publication Data
Mann, Thomas, 1948–
The Oxford guide to library research / Thomas Mann.—Fourth edition.
pages   cm
Includes bibliographical references and index.
ISBN 978-0-19-993104-0 (hardback)—ISBN 978-0-19-993106-4 (paperback)
1. Library research—United States.   I. Title.
Z710.M23   2015
025.5'24—dc23   2014041525

9 8 7 6 5 4 3 2 1
Printed in the United States of America
on acid-free paper

For
Jack Nabholtz
(1931–2010)
The best teacher I ever had

Contents

Preface

THIS BOOK IS INTENDED TO FILL A PARTICULAR NICHE. IT WILL answer three questions: First, what is the extent of the significant research resources you will you miss if you confine your research entirely, or even primarily, to sources available on the open Internet? Second, if you are trying to get a reasonably good *overview* of the literature on a particular topic, rather than just "something quickly" on it, what are the methods of subject searching that are usually much more efficient for that purpose than typing keywords into a blank search box? And third— a concern related to the first two—how do you find the best search terms to use in the first place?

My experience in working with many thousands of researchers convinces me that most people who rely primarily on the Internet have a kind of visceral suspicion that they are not finding everything relevant to their subject interests, and maybe not even the most relevant sources, especially if their primary tools are Web search engines and Wikipedia. Their hunches are usually right if they are pursuing scholarly research rather than simply seeking quick information fixes. Even those who tap into a few popular proprietary sources such as *LexisNexis* or *JSTOR* or ProQuest for full-text journal articles are frequently left with the "unscratched itch" that there may be more, and better, information somewhere else. Professors frequently advise or require students to use sources other than just the Web, but the students, and even the professors themselves, usually lack a clear understanding of what research libraries can provide that the Web cannot, and of what steps, exactly, researchers must take to find those additional resources that lie outside the scope of the free Internet.

THE SIX BLIND MEN OF INDIA
AND THE ELEPHANT

My daily experience as a reference librarian is that most researchers, especially those moving into a new subject area, are very much in the position of the Six Blind Men of India in the fable, who were asked to describe an elephant. One grabbed a leg and said, "The elephant is like a tree"; one touched the side and said, "The elephant is like a wall"; one found the tail and said, "The elephant is like a rope"; and so on with the tusk ("like a spear"), the trunk ("like a hose"), and the ear ("like a fan"). Everyone latched on to something quickly, and each thought he was perceiving the whole animal. No one grasped the extent of the other parts, and no one perceived how the many parts fit together. Finding "something quickly" in each case proved to be seriously misleading.

This book will show you how to go about gaining an overview of the "whole elephant" of whatever your research topic may be. It will explain the variety of search mechanisms that will give you reasonable confidence that you have not overlooked something important. In presenting search mechanisms it will provide not just lists and descriptions of the databases (and other sources) themselves, but discussions of the *ways to search* within them: how to find the best search terms, how to combine the terms, and how to make the databases (and other sources) show you relevant material even when you don't know in advance what, exactly, to type in.

WHAT CANNOT BE FOUND ON THE
OPEN INTERNET

Real bricks-and-mortar research libraries contain vast ranges of printed books, copyrighted materials in a variety of other formats, and hundreds of site-licensed (or password-restricted) subscription databases that are not accessible from anywhere, at any time, by anybody on the open Internet. One can reasonably say that research libraries today routinely include the entire Internet—that is, they will customarily provide terminals allowing free access to all of the open portions of the Net—but that the Internet does not, and cannot, contain more than a small fraction of everything discoverable within a research library's walls. The major difference is caused by copyright law: in spite of much wishful thinking by Internet enthusiasts, it has not been repealed. Most of the books published in the twentieth century and after are not freely available on the Internet. Moreover, even in the areas of content overlap between the

Web and research libraries, *finding* the best material in websites is often impossible, especially when relevance-ranked keyword searching is the only avenue of access.

TRADE-OFFS BETWEEN REAL AND VIRTUAL LIBRARIES: *WHAT, WHO,* AND *WHERE* RESTRICTIONS ON FREE ACCESS

If you wish to be a good researcher you have to be aware of unavoidable trade-offs between virtual and real libraries. While the former apparently overcome the *where* restrictions of bricks-and-mortar facilities, they do so only at the unavoidable cost of imposing other significant and inescapable restrictions of *what* and *who*: Internet providers must limit *what* they make available to begin with (open source or copyright-free material); if they do mount copyrighted sources and hope to profit from them, they must then impose major access restrictions on either *who* can view them or *where* the can be viewed. The *who* are those who pay fees at the point of use or who pay special assessments or taxes to become members of password-restricted user groups. In the case of public libraries, such charges are covered by local property taxes within a defined geographic area; in academia, they are covered by tuition payments. In either case researchers outside those geographic areas or paying communities will not have the same access as those on the inside. Even for insiders the range of databases paid for by their subscription fees can itself vary greatly from one geographic community or school to the next. Further, most students in college environments will find that they lose all remote access to their school's subscription databases as soon as they graduate. When you don't pay the tuition, you no longer have the remote access.

In the overall universe of information records, three considerations are inextricably tied together: (1) copyright protection; (2) free "fair use" of the records by everyone; and (3) access limitations of *what, who,* and *where*.

It is not possible to combine (1) and (2) without restricting at least one element of (3). "Free" Internet access (that is, without point-of-use charges) usually entails barriers to either *what* is searchable to begin with (exclusively public domain material) or *who* can view it—i.e., "free" only to those with passwords or free only within the walls of libraries *where* it can be viewed. The one major exception appears in the provision of access to copyrighted material without point-of-use charges via the imposition of advertisements. This too is a limitation, however, in that it entails the required acceptance of "terms of service": if you don't put up with the ads, you don't get to view the site. This limitation, however, is largely irrelevant to the kinds of scholarly resources that are the focus of this book. These include the many hundreds of databases offered by ProQuest, EBSCOhost, Gale, Thomson Reuters, and many others—databases that are not on the open Internet—for which payment made to their providers through advertising revenues is simply not a workable business model. Advertising aside, the only way to overcome the *what* and *who* barriers of cyberspace, and to provide *free* access to copyrighted sources even to people who don't pay local taxes or tuition (and who therefore don't have passwords), is to impose a *where* restriction within library walls. Within those walls, libraries can make any information records at all, including both copyrighted print sources and expensive subscription databases, freely available to anyone who comes in the door, whether or not those people live in the immediate area and whether or not they pay any monetary support for the library's operation. Those who regard "access within walls" as the weakness of real libraries have the situation exactly backward: it is precisely this *where* restriction that *enables* libraries to make all information, both public domain *and copyrighted*, available *freely* to anyone at all who comes in the door. This is something of an oversimplification, but still mainly true: when you are on the Web, you can usually find references that point you to a library's copyrighted holdings, but Web access to the full texts themselves (especially post-1922 books, which are still protected by copyright) requires you to pull out your credit card. The provision of free access to so much copyrighted material is a genuine strength of real libraries that cannot be matched by the open Internet. (Long-term preservation is another such strength, but that is a concern beyond the scope of this book.)

Printed books and journals, as physical objects in nonbroadcastable formats, have built-in *where* restrictions that enable them to be offered for free use within library walls. This restriction itself, however, is mitigated by several additional considerations: that much printed material can be checked out and used in other locations at any time of the day or night, that materials unavailable in one library locale may often be freely borrowed from another, and that there are so many publicly accessible libraries dispersed in so many different geographic areas. You cannot get "everything" freely online from your home or office, but most readers of this book will nonetheless have convenient access to local libraries that do indeed provide free access, both onsite and via interlibrary loan, to vast stores of resources not freely accessible via Amazon, Google, Bing, or Yahoo!.

An awareness of format considerations is also necessary to an understanding of the particular function and importance of real research libraries;

this entails a further understanding of why it is not possible to convey all of the materials needed for substantive scholarship via the open Internet. Some preliminary considerations must precede this conclusion, however.

HIERARCHY OF LEVELS OF LEARNING: DATA, INFORMATION, OPINION, KNOWLEDGE, UNDERSTANDING—AND WISDOM?

The field of library and information science is obviously concerned with "information," but the discipline has traditionally made finer distinctions within its subject matter, at least roughly, according to a hierarchical ranking such as this:

1. *Data* are the unorganized, unfiltered, and unevaluated raw materials of thought, comparable to sensory experiences.
2. *Information* is data conceptually organized to the point that statements can be made about it, true or false, and coherent or incoherent with other information.
3. *Opinion* is a form of belief to which is attached an added weight of either confidence or assent (i.e., approval or disapproval) prior to or apart from objective verification. The basis of the weighting comes from the apparent coherence of the belief with one's other personal beliefs—whether or not those beliefs are themselves true—apart from confirmation mechanisms accessible to other people. What is plausible (without such confirmation) to one interlocking, internally coherent set of beliefs may therefore not be plausible to another, and opinions that are deemed irrelevant or misguided within one belief system may have consequences that are nonetheless deemed very important within another.
4. *Knowledge* reflects a still higher level of learning, to the point that truth or falsity can be judged by interlocking tests of correspondence to, and coherence with, the world of experience and of other ideas—with the further qualification that this level of learning entails discernment of patterns within information and the making of generalizations that are accessible to, and verifiable by, other people. (Note that knowledge of effects alone can be considered knowledge even without a grasp of their underlying reasons or causes—i.e., one can *know that* such and such is the case even if one does not *understand why*.)

5. *Understanding* is a higher level of thought in that it comprehends not just patterns and generalizations but the justifying causes, reasons, or narrative stories behind them. An understanding of physical causes, especially linked to mathematical patterns, gives one a measure of predictability, the hallmark of the sciences. The humanities, on the other hand, are grounded on the assumptions of the nonillusory nature of free will and the reality of consciously chosen goals (as opposed to unconscious impulses) as motivating factors in human actions. Hallmarks of humanistic learning are philosophical justification by reasons (not just physical causes) or by narrative integrations of experience in explanatory sequences of beginnings and middles leading to ends. The social sciences mix both scientific and humanistic criteria of explanation, with a particular emphasis on statistical patterns in human behavior, which form a kind of middle ground between realms of free will and determinism.

Wisdom is usually ranked as the topmost level of learning in such a traditional hierarchy; its function lies in assessing the worth of all of these other levels according to ultimate criteria of truth, goodness, and beauty. It accomplishes this assessment within overarching frameworks or philosophies of what counts as evidence, or what counts as an acceptable explanation to begin with. Such frameworks necessarily assume some ultimate stopping point or ground of explanation which, when reached, finally suffices in justifying a sequence of thought. The qualification that prevents wisdom from being considered as simply the top step on the same ladder, however, is that wisdom is not simply cognitive; it also entails ethical virtue in a way that can "surround" (or not) the other steps. (An adequate discussion of these points, however, would take us on paths beyond the present concern; see Appendix A.)

Wisdom, of course, is difficult to come by. We are on simpler and more stable ground with the more hierarchical levels of learning such as knowledge and understanding. The important point here is that these are not generally attainable in high degree by people with short attention spans, especially in the areas of the conventional academic disciplines. Achievement of these higher levels of thought usually requires written texts in narrative or expository formats that are of substantial length, spelling out both the extent of relevant considerations and the complexities of their interrelationships. One does not achieve these levels simply by finding "something quickly"—as did the Six Blind Men.

FREE ACCESS TO BOOK-LENGTH FORMATS IMPORTANT FOR HIGHER LEVELS OF LEARNING

Books—or book-length texts, whether printed or electronic—are therefore unusually important formats in facilitating learning at the higher levels. The majority of the electronic formats available today have an undeniable bias toward the pictorial, the audio, the colorful, the animated, the instantaneous connection, the quickly updated, and the short verbal text—qualities that most readily engender learning at the levels of data, information, or opinion, and (to some extent) knowledge. The level of understanding, however—which is ultimately inseparable from lengthy verbal narratives and expositions—is still conveyed, and attained, by book formats or electronic equivalents that make lengthy and complex texts comfortable to read.

UNAVOIDABLE COPYRIGHT AND OTHER LEGAL RESTRICTIONS

Contrary to a widespread popular belief, the vast majority of book-length texts in any substantial research library cannot be digitized for free distribution on the open Internet or via handheld readers. The primary reason, again, is that the copyright laws of the United States and the international community will never be repealed to allow the free distribution of protected texts to anyone, anywhere, at any time on the Web. Most of the books in any large library will have been published since 1923, the date from which copyright restrictions take effect. These terms of protection are generally "life of the author plus seventy years." There are, of course, ongoing efforts to make legally available (on the Web) "orphan" works whose post-'22 copyright status is unclear; Google Books, on its own understanding of the law, is digitizing millions of these post-'22 books along with those that are clearly in the public domain. Google, however, cannot present more than brief, disconnected snippets of the books whose copyright status is in question, and it may wind up being legally enjoined from continuing even that practice. (The courts, as of this writing, have not provided any definitive resolution of this issue.) The Internet Public Library and the Hathi Trust are similarly hamstrung by post-1922 copyright restrictions. Kindle and Nook e-books continue to proliferate, of course, but these are not freely available to anyone, anywhere—they require credit card payments.

What this boils down to is the fact that real (as opposed to virtual) research libraries remain essential to the conveyance of most of the knowledge contained in copyrighted book-length texts, especially if access to that knowledge is to be made *freely* available—albeit only to those who comes "inside the walls," even if they then borrow the free library material for use elsewhere. (The *what, who*, and *where* distinctions and trade-offs are unavoidable.) The present book will make clear, however, that such libraries make freely available much more than printed book formats alone—i.e., the vast majority of subscription databases (themselves replete with full-text content) are also made freely available only via library subscriptions. *Free* access to these, however, is itself restricted either by site licenses (a *where* limit) or by passwords registered only to those who pay (a *who* limit) to support the library via tuition or local taxes.

ALTERNATIVE METHODS OF SEARCHING NOT AVAILABLE ON THE OPEN INTERNET

If I may anticipate points that will be made throughout this book, real research libraries also offer multiple *methods of searching* that are not accessible on the open Internet; that enable researchers to recognize, in systematic ways, the range of relevant sources whose keywords cannot be specified in advance; and that enable such recognition within conceptually focused contexts that eliminate the excessive clutter of tens of thousands of "noise" or "junk" retrievals. It would profit scholarship very little to have every book in the world digitized on Kindles or Nooks or iPads if the only mechanism for *finding* what was needed within those devices were algorithmic relevance-ranked searches on uncontrolled keywords. Kindles and Nooks provide only very narrow means of gaining subject access to their contents; they are wonderful if you have a specific book in mind that you wish to view, but they preclude any ability to see "the shape of the elephant" of the overall range of literature relevant to a topic. They leave users who wish to do extensive subject searching permanently stuck in the situation of the Six Blind Men, with no remedies. (Further, access problems in the future will be greatly exacerbated if these formats cannot be preserved.)

THE ADVANTAGES OF FOCUS IN LIBRARY COLLECTIONS

One of the format peculiarities of books produced by reputable publishers (even apart from preservation advantages) is that because of their production costs (including editorial vetting as well as printing and binding), there are necessarily many fewer of them than there are websites. The comparatively smaller number of reputable (vetted) books thus enables libraries to focus cataloging efforts on them, thereby providing standardized conceptual categorizations of these texts within the two complementary systems of subject cataloging in online catalogs and classified shelving in physical bookstacks (see Chapters 2 and 3). The sheer number of websites precludes any such standardizing treatment by library catalogers.

The proliferation of self-published (and unvetted) books is also a growing problem for scholarly researchers—but one that is at least partially solved within libraries by the mechanism of selection by acquisitions professionals, a mechanism not found in Google, Bing, Yahoo!, or Amazon. These professional selection and cataloging operations applied to books provide greatly enhanced means of subject access to a pool of the very formats that most readily convey the highest levels of learning. Conceptual categorization, with search mechanisms promoting easy recognition of relevant sources (no matter what keywords their authors use), is very different from relevance-ranked displays of resources whose terminology must be specified in advance, especially when that terminology can only be guessed at. When cataloging treatment is applied to collections selected by quality considerations to begin with—and including both in- and out-of-print sources, in multiple languages, and in formats that can also be readily preserved—then researchers seeking knowledge or understanding have a powerful mechanism for solving many of the most important discovery problems encountered by the Six Blind Men of India.

Both levels of learning, on the one hand, and formats of materials, on the other, thus remain crucial considerations in justifying the maintenance of real research libraries. A concern for this maintenance is not in the least "sentimental"; rather, it reflects a justifiable and serious concern that our culture not lose its higher levels of thought. We continue to need—perhaps more than ever—free access (without point-of-use charges) to vast amounts of lengthy texts that cannot be put on the open Internet because of copyright, monopolistic, and contractual legal considerations. And we also need the variety of search mechanisms accessible via libraries that cannot be duplicated by Web or Amazon-type searches. The latter—while immensely useful within their own niches—cannot show all of the parts of "the elephant," display all of the relations of those parts, or segregate them from the clutter of too many unwanted irrelevancies.

For three decades it has been fashionable in the library profession to assert that "we need to think outside the box of brick-and-mortar libraries." While that is wholly true, it is not the whole of the truth: we equally need to think outside the box of the open Internet itself because it has major boundaries and limitations of its own.

THE ORGANIZATIONAL SCHEMA OF THIS BOOK: NINE METHODS OF SUBJECT SEARCHING

Most guides to research are organized either by subject resources (for education, for history, for nursing, and so on) or by type of literature (atlases, directories, encyclopedias, handbooks, websites, commercial databases, etc.). Such guides continue to be both important and useful. This one, however, is different. Although it makes use of both these traditional schemes, this book is primarily structured around an outline of nine different methods of subject searching:

1. Controlled vocabulary searching (Chapters 2 and 4)
2. Use of subject-classified book stacks for general or focused browsing (Chapter 3)
3. Keyword searching (whether or not relevance-ranked) (Chapter 5)
4. Citation searching (Chapter 6)
5. Related record searching (Chapter 7)
6. Use of published subject bibliographies (Chapter 9)
7. Use of truncations, Boolean combinations, and other search limitations (Chapter 10)
8. Tapping into the subject expertise of people sources (Chapter 12)
9. Type of literature searching (Chapter 15; also Chapters 1 and 8)

Each of these methods is potentially applicable in *any* subject area; each has both strengths and weaknesses, advantages and disadvantages; and each is capable of turning up information that cannot be reached by the other eight. Information that lies in a blind spot to any one method of searching, however, is usually discoverable by changing the search method. This outline forms the overall schema of this book, and I hope it will remain noticeable within the welter of specific details—and a few sidetrack excursions (Chapters 11, 13, and 14). Note especially that keyword searching, which most students resort to in most situations, is only one approach among many others; its weaknesses (and strengths) will be clearly spelled out in subsequent chapters.

I have found through experience that this scheme simply works better as an overall model than the traditional alternatives. (It does not abandon them, however; rather, it encompasses them.) A major point of this book is that since the various search techniques cannot be used simultaneously, most serious research cannot be accomplished by "one-stop shopping" via any single source or any single search box. A variety of approaches, coming at the same subject from multiple angles and providing feedback to direct necessarily subsequent search steps, usually works much better.

My own background includes work as an academic researcher at the doctoral level, as a private investigator with a detective agency, as a graduate student in library science, as a freelance researcher, as a reference librarian at two university libraries, and as a general reference librarian for more than 30 years at the largest library in the world. A second formative element derives from my having worked with and closely observed tens of thousands of other researchers pursuing their own interests in all subject areas. Taken as a whole, this experience has taught me that most people unconsciously work within a framework of very limited assumptions about the extent of information that is easily and freely available to them, especially in large research libraries; indeed, most researchers, nowadays, have only very hazy notions of anything beyond Web search engines and Wikipedia articles.

It strikes me, too, that previous writers on this "research" subject who are not librarians tend to overlook some fundamentally important steps and distinctions in telling their audiences how to proceed; many have even perpetuated harmful notions. (One such notion is that copyright law can be swept under the rug.) On the other hand, some librarians who have written on the subject have not placed the weight and emphasis on certain matters that scholars and other investigators require; indeed, many research guides offer little more than lists of individual printed and electronic sources with no overall perspective on methods or techniques of *using* them—as though there were no more to it than just typing in a few keywords in the first blank search box that comes up.

The proliferation of published guides to research as well as "information literacy" classes that are focused exclusively on the Internet also tends to dumb down the whole process by suggesting, or even stating, that "everything" is now freely available on the open Web and that the only learning required concerns how to do critical thinking about it. This view confines researchers' purview, right from the start, to only one galaxy of sources within an information universe that is truly much larger. Moreover, critical thinking about the websites does not solve the blind men problem: when the under-the-hood programming of search engines fails to disclose the remarkable range of other relevant sources that have not been found to begin with, one cannot do any critical thinking about *them*. Reliance on "black box" algorithms to decide what is relevant to begin with may be acceptable if one needs only to find something quickly, but it does not provide the overview required by scholarship (see Appendix B). In this regard, no computer program is an adequate substitute for education. And education itself is ineffective if it stays at the level of general precepts without concrete examples of what to do—or of what not to do, which may be the more instructive.

Much of what I've learned over the past few decades I have had to learn the hard way, and I especially hope to save readers from some of the more egregious mistakes and omissions I've been guilty of myself at one time or another. Although it has frequently been a humbling experience, I have had the good fortune of gaining feedback from these mistakes due to the several shifting professional perspectives I've had in repeated involvements with the same types of problems. Without that substantial feedback it would have been very easy to regard as "experience" a long continuation of making the same mistakes (and especially omissions) without ever discovering there are better ways to do things. When one does research only for oneself, there is always a tendency to be satisfied with whatever one can succeed in finding on one's own—as with the Six Blind Men. We trim our assessments of success to the level of research skills we already have, and we all too readily assume our own personal limits are shared by everyone else. Further, we especially let the tools we are familiar with—nowadays, Web engines, Wikipedia, and social media—define the boundaries of the information universe we assume to exist. The many thousands of researchers I've worked with, however, have forced me to realize that the limits I once would have accepted for myself were not adequate for answering *their* questions— i.e., I could not comfortably stop with what *I* would have accepted as sufficient for my own information needs on any particular subject when the feedback I received so often told me that my personal view of what would've been "enough" for me was *not* enough for *their* purposes.

When I got my own Ph.D. (in English) before I became a librarian, I thought I was a pretty good researcher, and so did my professors. But I thought so only because neither I nor my teachers realized how much I was missing. When I had difficult questions to pursue, I can see now that I usually fell prey to that strong human propensity toward "least effort"— I'd stop researching when I found only the few things that I *could* find on my own, and then I'd hide the problem by changing the scope of the papers I was working on: instead of discussing what I really wanted, I'd restrict the analyses to make them cover only the limited information I could actually find.

It was only when I started working as a reference librarian in university libraries that I began to see two things clearly: how vast is the range of subjects people are interested in that I would never have had any questions about myself, and how little I knew about finding anything beyond my own academic subject area. I was myself one of the blind men without realizing it. Having to help so many people whose interests lay so far outside my own personal knowledge boundaries, however, has been a genuinely stretching experience. The insight of "Oh! There's a way to do that!—I wish I'd known that before!" has come to me many times, in many unexpected ways over the decades, especially since many types of questions come back repeatedly and enable changed approaches or new resources to be tried. Such repetitions have made certain patterns in the orientations of other researchers more evident to me, specifically:

- Patterns in the types of questions they ask, and in how they ask them (or type them into search boxes)
- Patterns in the usually unconscious assumptions they hold about the range of options available to them
- Patterns in the bad advice they are sometimes given by teachers, employers, colleagues, and even librarians
- Patterns in the mistakes and omissions that routinely reduce the efficiency of their research

Viewed collectively, these patterns suggest the areas in which most people need the most help, and it is on this group of concerns that I wish to concentrate. I hope especially to give readers a sense of the principles and rules involved that are applicable in any situation, not just an annotated list of sources relevant to certain subjects. In terms of the above list of levels of learning, I hope to get readers to that of *understanding*.

PRELIMINARY ADVICE

Three overall points to keep in mind, right up front, are these:

1. There is no "one-stop" solution to research problems (including, especially, the notion that "everything" can be made accessible through under-the-hood programming behind "a single search box"). Instead there is a system of trade-offs among a variety of different search approaches. If you understand in advance what the trade-offs are, however, you can efficiently exploit them to your advantage, focusing on the best avenues of access immediately rather than on alternatives, the otherwise unperceived limitations of which would waste your time, get in the way of finding what you need, or prevent you from seeing "the whole shape" of the relevant literature.
2. Although it may be surprising to many people, the fact remains that, in most cases, you do not need prior subject expertise to do good research in unfamiliar areas if you simply know the techniques of searching (with their trade-offs) that can be used in *any* field.

3. While technological improvements continue to refine algorithms for sorting, ranking, and displaying keyword-generated search results, as well as for combining coverage of more databases and websites into "seamless" searches, it nonetheless remains true that such "black box" programming cannot possibly do all of the intellectual work needed for scholarly research. You just need to know—and understand—some things in advance, before you even touch the keyboard. (Indeed, in some cases you will be better with sources not accessible via *any* keyboard.) Again: algorithms are no substitute for education—no matter how many "developments" in information science are premised on the assumption that algorithms *are* a substitute.

Many specific sources, both electronic and print (as well as microform), will be discussed in this book, and many will probably not be locally accessible to you, even in university or research libraries themselves. Indeed, not all of the sources covered here are available even at the Library of Congress, where I work. I hope, however, that in bringing their existence to researchers' attention, more scholars will ask for—even *demand*—them at their local libraries. Collection development librarians are always on the lookout to obtain sources needed by their users; even in selecting basic library catalog systems library administrators often make decisions about which to purchase for economic or prestige reasons, in the absence of any significant personal experience in using those catalogs themselves for scholarly research. (Inadequate catalogs are then maintained because "no one has complained" about them.) If, then, your own library lacks something you believe it needs, by all means let the librarians know. Persistence on the part of researchers—especially faculty library committees—does lead to improvements in library offerings.

While there are thus implications in this book for the kind of service that I think librarians should provide, the audience I most hope to reach is that of the researchers "on the other side of the desk" who use research libraries, either professionally or for personal projects. Many, many more options exist for gaining efficient access to the stored records of our culture "than are dreamt of in their philosophy." I hope this volume will serve as a road map, a menu of options, and a catalyst for their broader, deeper, and more efficient use of those libraries.

T. M.

Acknowledgments

For this new edition I wish to thank all of my colleagues at the Library of Congress, from whom I have learned more than I can convey here. Particular thanks go to Cassy Ammen, Barbara Bair, Lee Douglas, Sheridan Harvey, Jan Herd, Emily Howie, Laura Kells, Judy Robinson, Diane Schug-O'Neill, Anne Toohey, Virginia Wood, Kathy Woodrell, and the late Bill Reitwiesner. Kristi Conkle's help with the illustrations has been especially valuable. Researchers Joel Achenbach, Jane Blevins, Ellon Carpenter, Paul Dickson, Abby Gilbert, Isabella Jackson, Ken Kitchell, Edward Luft, Joshua Nall, Martina Schlögel, Claire Sherman, and David Stewart have also provided particularly useful feedback for this edition. (Not least among such researchers are the members of The League of Extraordinary Gentlemen, a secret society of questionable characters who keep coming up with unusually interesting inquiries.) Thanks, also, to the many companies and database providers from whose promotional material and websites I have derived (sometimes with modifications of my own) descriptions of their wares. Stephen Rhind-Tutt of Alexander Street Press, Nick Galvin and Karena Donnelly from EBSCO, Alistair Morrison of LexisNexis, Eric Calaluca and Peggy Fulton from Paratext, Kristin Culp of Thomson Reuters, and Clay Boss, Catherine Jervey Johnson, and Daniel Coyle of ProQuest were particularly helpful. Any mistakes remaining in the text are entirely my own.

A very special thanks to Nancy Toff at Oxford University Press, who has been most understanding and patient in shepherding this edition into print, and Richard Johnson, senior production editor, who was most helpful during the final stages of editing.

A note to library catalogers: the first edition of this book appeared in 1987 as *A Guide to Library Research Methods*; the second and third editions (1998 and 2005) were published under the current title.

The Oxford Guide to Library Research

CHAPTER 1

Initial Overview Sources: Specialized Encyclopedias

A MAJOR PROBLEM THAT RESEARCHERS INEVITABLY HAVE WITH any Internet search engine is that finding something quickly within the first two or three screens of retrievals does nothing to give them any sense of "the shape of the elephant" of their topic. With Web search engines you can never tell what or how much you are missing, nor can you judge the importance of what is in front of you in comparison to (possibly) better retrievals from alternative sources. The best solution, or at least partial solution, to this problem provided within the Internet itself is Wikipedia. The latter, being a kind of universal encyclopedia, has the virtue of providing concise overviews of just about any subject. It's a quick way to see the basic facts about your topic—to gain what the Wikipedia contributors deem to be overview information.

I am not going to provide any elaborate criticisms of Wikipedia; I frequently use it myself in situations that do not require academic documentation or footnoting. The latter concern, however, is very important within college or professional environments: you cannot cite Wikipedia as a source in student or professional writings because its articles, being subject to continual modification, are not stable; what you cite today may not be there next week, let alone years from now. (While it is technically possible to call up earlier versions of the same article, the fact that the earlier versions had to be changed is in itself good reason to avoid citing them.) Moreover, those who make the modifications sometimes introduce particular biases for which more formal editorial procedures would compensate. Often the best experts on particular subjects simply don't bother to correct (or even notice to begin with) what Wikipedia may say on their subjects—which means that those who do bother may have peculiar interests or agendas to promote. Nonetheless, Wikipedia is indeed often a very good source for getting an initial overview of basic information on an unfamiliar topic, especially in comparison to an overwhelming retrieval of search engine hits.

STARTING POINTS BEYOND WIKIPEDIA

Other starting-point sources are available in libraries, however, that are frequently far superior. Two databases for identifying initial overview articles deserve particular emphasis:

- *Reference Universe.* This is a subscription file published by Paratext (Stone Ridge, VA) that is an index to all of the individual articles in about 45,000 specialized subject encyclopedias and other reference sources from 750 publishers; coverage extends back to 1980. This database also links directly to full texts of the articles supplied by other sources (e.g., *SAGE Knowledge, Oxford Reference, Elsevier's ScienceDirect, CREDO Reference*) if your library already has separate subscriptions to these databases.
- *Web of Science.* This is a subscription database from Thomson Reuters. It indexes high-quality journal articles from about 13,500 academic journals, worldwide, in all subject areas. (Don't be misled by the word "Science" in its title; it also covers social sciences and arts and humanities journals.) What is particularly important for initial overview purposes is that it has a search-limitation feature that enables you to zero in immediately on "literature review" articles in any subject area—those that try to present a state-of-the-art summary of current knowledge on whatever the topic may be. (This database will be discussed in greater detail in Chapters 6 and 8.)

Although *Reference Universe* indexes many kinds of reference publications (e.g., handbooks, histories, guides, and sourcebooks), it is particularly useful in indexing individual articles in specialized subject encyclopedias. Most students are familiar with a few general sets such as *Encyclopaedia Britannica, World Book,* or *Encyclopedia Americana* (and, of course, Wikipedia), but very few realize how many thousands of other encyclopedias exist.

ADVANTAGES OF SPECIALIZED ENCYCLOPEDIAS

One major advantage of specialized encyclopedias is that their articles will not change from one week to the next, and so you can cite them with confidence in scholarly papers.

A second advantage is that articles appearing in these published sets have gone through editorial vetting or peer review in ways that are more formal than those at work on the open Internet. Indeed, many of these articles are signed rather than published anonymously.

A third advantage is that if you can find articles from several different specialized encyclopedias—those that provide a depth of coverage well beyond that of the general sets—and compare them to each other, then, right there, you are beginning to get a good overview your topic in a way that solves the problem created by Internet searching and also takes you considerably beyond the reach of Wikipedia articles. For example, a student interested in "globalization" would find articles on that topic, from a wide variety of unanticipated perspectives, in all of the following sources:

Encyclopedia of Religious Revivals in America
Encyclopedia of Community
Blackwell Encyclopedia of Sociology
Encyclopedia of Communication and Information
Berkshire Encyclopedia of World History
Encyclopedia of Evolution
Encyclopedia of Clothing and Fashion
Encyclopedia of Management
Encyclopedia of Information Science and Technology
Encyclopedia of American Foreign Policy
Encyclopedia of Democracy
Globalization: Encyclopedia of Trade, Labor, and Politics
International Encyclopedia of Environmental Politics
International Encyclopedia of Political Science
Encyclopedia of African History
Routledge Encyclopedia of Philosophy
Routledge International Encyclopedia of Women
Tobacco in History and Culture: An Encyclopedia
International Encyclopedia of the Sociology of Education
Encyclopedia of the Arctic
Encyclopedia of Government and Politics
Social Science Encyclopedia

The combination of perspectives and cross-disciplinary purview available through these printed sources cannot be matched by a single website. (A few hundred of these encyclopedias are available in online versions, but they are subscription databases available exclusively through library affiliations.)

The whole purpose of any encyclopedia article is to provide a concise overview of generally "established" knowledge on its topic, written for a nonspecialist audience, with a brief bibliography of highly recommended sources for further study (rather than an indiscriminate printout of "everything"). And there are literally thousands of such encyclopedias. (Don't be misled by the word "Dictionary" in the title of many of these sets; in library terminology it refers simply to the alphabetical arrangement of articles, not to their length, and so it is frequently used synonymously with "Encyclopedia.")

SAMPLE LISTS OF ENCYCLOPEDIAS

The following sets are often considered standard sources within their fields:

International Encyclopedia of the Social & Behavioral Sciences, 26 vols. (Elsevier, 2001)

Encyclopedia of World Art, 17 vols. (McGraw-Hill, 1959–1987)

Dictionary of Art, 34 vols. (Grove, 1996; Oxford University Press, 1997) and online by subscription

New Grove Dictionary of Music and Musicians, 29 vols. (Grove, 2001) and online by subscription (Oxford University Press)

American National Biography, 24 vols. and supplements (Oxford University Press, 1999–2005) and online via subscription

Oxford Dictionary of National Biography (British), 60 vols. (Oxford University Press, 2004) and online via subscription

Dictionary of American History, 10 vols. (Scribners, 2003)

New Dictionary of Scientific Biography, 8 vols. (Scribners, 2008)

New Dictionary of the History of Ideas, 6 vols. (Scribners, 2005)

Dictionary of the Middle Ages, 13 vols. and Supplement (Scribners, 1982–2004)

Encyclopedia of Philosophy, 10 vols. (Thomson Gale, 2006)

Routledge Encyclopedia of Philosophy, 10 vols. (Routledge, 1998)

New Catholic Encyclopedia, 15 vols. (Catholic University of America Press, 2003)

New Palgrave Dictionary of Economics, 8 vols. (Palgrave Macmillan, 2008)

Encyclopedia of Psychology, 8 vols. (Oxford University Press, 2000)

Encyclopedia of Religion, 15 vols. (Macmillan, 2005)

McGraw-Hill Encyclopedia of Science and Technology, 20 vols. (McGraw-Hill, revised irregularly)

Grzimek's Animal Life Encyclopedia, 17 vols. (Gale, 2003–2004)

International Wildlife Encyclopedia, 22 vols. (Marshall Cavendish, 2002)

Blackwell Encyclopedia of Sociology, 11 vols. (Blackwell, 2007)

Although the above sets are certainly important, they by no means exhaust the field. The following is a list of selected representative titles; it only scratches the surface of the range of sources available in research libraries:

Black America: A State-By-State Historical Encyclopedia, 2 vols. (ABC-CLIO, 2011)

Dictionary of Literary Biography, 350+ vols., ongoing (Gale Research, 1978–)

Encyclopaedia Judaica, 22 vols. (Macmillan, 2007)

Encyclopaedia of Islam, 3rd edition (in progress; Brill, 2007–)

Encyclopedia of Aesthetics, 4 vols. (Oxford University Press, 1998)

Encyclopedia of African-American Culture and History, 6 vols. (Macmillan, 2006)

Encyclopedia of Aging, 2 vols. (Springer, 2006)

Encyclopedia of Agricultural Science, 4 vols. (Academic Press, 1994)

Encyclopedia of American Cultural & Intellectual History, 3 vols. (Scribners, 2001)

Encyclopedia of American Education, 3 vols. (Facts on File, 2007)

Encyclopedia of American Foreign Policy, 3 vols. (Scribners, 2002)

Encyclopedia of Anthropology, 5 vols. (Sage, 2006)

Encyclopedia of Antislavery and Abolition, 2 vols. (Greenwood, 2007)

Encyclopedia of Applied Ethics, 4 vols. (Academic Press, 1998)

Encyclopedia of Applied Plant Sciences, 3 vols. (Elsevier Academic, 2003)

Encyclopedia of Asian History, 4 vols. (Collier Macmillan, 1988)

Encyclopedia of Bilingual Education, 2 vols. (Sage, 2008)

Encyclopedia of Biodiversity, 5 vols. (Academic Press, 2001)

Encyclopedia of Bioethics, 5 vols. (Macmillan Reference, 2004)

Encyclopedia of Cancer, 4 vols. (Springer, 2009)

Encyclopedia of Criminology, 3 vols. (Routledge, 2005)

Encyclopedia of Anthropology, 5 vols. (Sage, 2006)

Encyclopedia of Drugs, Alcohol, and Addictive Behavior, 4 vols. (Macmillan Reference USA, 2009)

Encyclopedia of Educational Leadership and Administration, 2 vols. (Sage, 2006)

Encyclopedia of Environment and Society, 5 vols. (Sage, 2007)

Environment Encyclopedia, 11 vols. (Marshall Cavendish, 2001)

Encyclopedia of Ethics, 3 vols. (Routledge, 2001)

Encyclopedia of European Social History: From 1350 to 2000, 6 vols. (Scribners, 2001)

Encyclopedia of Food and Culture, 3 vols. (Scribners, 2003)

Encyclopedia of Food Science and Technology, 4 vols. (Wiley, 2000)

Encyclopedia of Forensic and Legal Medicine, 4 vols. (Elsevier Academic Press, 2005)

Encyclopedia of Forensic Sciences, 3 vols. (Academic Press, 2002)

Encyclopedia of Forest Sciences, 4 vols. (Elsevier, 2004)

Encyclopedia of Historic and Endangered Livestock and Poultry Breeds (Yale University Press, 2001)

Encyclopedia of Historical Treaties and Alliances, 2 vols. (Facts on File, 2005)

Encyclopedia of Holocaust Literature (Oryx, 2002)

Encyclopedia of Human Nutrition, 4 vols. (Elsevier/Academic, 2005)

Encyclopedia of Immigration and Migration in the American West, 2 vols. (Sage, 2006)

Encyclopedia of Journalism, 6 vols. (Sage, 2009)

Encyclopedia of Latin American History and Culture, 6 vols. (Gale, 2008)

Encyclopedia of Law Enforcement, 3 vols. (Sage, 2005)

Encyclopedia of Leadership, 4 vols. (Sage, 2004)

Encyclopedia of Mathematical Physics, 5 vols. (Elsevier, 2006)

Encyclopedia of Ocean Sciences, 6 vols. (Academic Press, 2001)

Encyclopedia of Physical Science and Technology, 18 vols. (Academic Press, 2002)

Encyclopedia of Prisons and Correctional Facilities, 2 vols. (Sage, 2005)

Encyclopedia of Psychological Assessment, 2 vols. (Sage, 2003)

Encyclopedia of Race and Crime, 2 vols. (Sage, 2009)

Encyclopedia of the Renaissance, 6 vols. (Scribners, 1999)

Encyclopedia of Rose Science, 3 vols. (Academic Press, 2003)

Encyclopedia of Special Education, 3 vols. (Wiley, 2007)

Encyclopedia of Terrorism (Facts on File, 2007)

Encyclopedia of the American Constitution, 6 vols. (Macmillan, 2000)

Encyclopedia of the Human Brain, 4 vols. (Academic Press, 2002)

Encyclopedia of the United Nations and International Agreements, 4 vols. (Routledge, 2003)

Encyclopedia of Themes and Subjects in Painting (Abrams, 1971)

Encyclopedia of Violence, Peace, & Conflict, 3 vols. (Elsevier, 2008)

Encyclopedia of White-Collar and Corporate Crime, 2 vols. (Sage, 2005)

Encyclopedia of World Geography, 24 vols. (Marshall Cavendish, 2002)

Feminist Encyclopedia of Spanish Literature, 2 vols. (Greenwood, 2002)

Food Cultures of the World, 4 vols. (Greenwood, 2011)

Gale Encyclopedia of Alternative Medicine, 4 vols. (Gale Cengage Learning, 2009)

Gale Encyclopedia of Medicine, 5 vols. (Thomson Gale 2006)

Greenwood Encyclopedia of Global Medieval Life and Culture, 3 vols. (Greenwood, 2009)

International Encyclopedia of Dance, 6 vols. (Oxford University Press, 1998)

International Encyclopedia of Political Science, 8 vols. (Sage, 2011)

International Military and Defense Encyclopedia, 6 vols. (Brassey's [US], 1993)

Legal Systems of the World: A Political, Social, and Cultural Encyclopedia, 4 vols. (ABC-CLIO, 2002)

Literature of Travel and Exploration: An Encyclopedia, 3 vols. (Fitzroy Dearborn, 2003)

Macmillan Encyclopedia of World Slavery, 2 vols. (Macmillan USA, 1998)

Mrs. Byrne's Dictionary of Unusual, Obscure, and Preposterous Words[1] (Carol Publishing Group, 1994)

New Palgrave Dictionary of Economics and the Law, 3 vols. (Stockton Press, 1998)

Oxford Encyclopedia of Ancient Egypt, 3 vols. (Oxford University Press, 2001)

Oxford Encyclopedia of Economic History, 5 vols. (Oxford, 2003)

Oxford Encyclopedia of the Reformation, 4 vols. (Oxford University Press, 1996)

Routledge Encyclopedia of Language Teaching and Learning (Routledge, 2001)

Routledge International Encyclopedia of Women, 4 vols. (Routledge, 2000)

World Education Encyclopedia: A Survey of Educational Systems Worldwide, 3 vols. (Gale, 2002)

World Encyclopedia of Peace, 8 vols. (Oceana, 1999)

Worldmark Encyclopedia of Cultures and Daily Life, 5 vols. (Gale, 2009)

Worldmark Encyclopedia of Religious Practices, 3 vols. (Thomson Gale, 2006)

None of these sources is freely available on the open Internet (sites that are available to anyone, anywhere, without requiring a password or a credit card). Many of the subjects suggested here are covered by several other specialized works, too; and thousands of additional encyclopedias exist for still other topics. (Since the year 2000 the Library of Congress has cataloged more than 8,700 such works.)

IDENTIFYING STANDARD WORKS, PROVIDING PRIMARY SOURCES, AND PROVIDING OVERVIEW LISTS OF ARTICLES

I mentioned above that one particularly useful feature of specialized encyclopedia articles is that they usually provide a brief bibliography of highly recommended sources for further study. This produces a fourth advantage: you can frequently use these selective bibliographies to identify immediately the "standard" or best books on a particular topic, which would otherwise tend to be buried in larger retrievals. For example, a student interested in "the system of tribute payments among the Greek city-states during the Peloponnesian War" identified, through *Reference Universe*, an article on "Tribute lists (Athenian)" in *The Oxford Classical Dictionary*. The source note at the end of this article says, quite explicitly, "The standard work on the tribute records is B. D. Merrit, H., T. Wade-Gery, and M. F. McGregor, *The Athenian Tribute Lists*, 4 vols. (1939–53)."

In another instance, a student writing a paper on "moonshining" found two encyclopedias in very different disciplines that had articles on the subject: the 10-volume *Dictionary of American History* (2002) and the 4-volume *Encyclopedia of Drugs, Alcohol & Addictive Behavior* (2008). The articles from both sets overlapped in recommending one particular work in their short bibliographies, Joseph Dabney's *Mountain Spirits* (1985), so that became a basic point of departure for her next step.

In the same way, another scholar trying to get oriented to the literature on the topic "Human Rights in Islam" was greatly aided by a comparison of the multiple articles supplied by the following:

- The 5-volume 2009 *Encyclopedia of Human Rights* (with a 13-page article on "Islam")
- The 6-volume *Oxford Encyclopedia of the Islamic World* (2009; 9-page article on "Human Rights")
- The 2-volume *Encyclopedia of Islam in the United States* (4-page article on "Human Rights")
- The 2-volume 2004 *Encyclopedia of Islam and the Muslim World* (2-page article on "Human Rights")
- The 3-volume 2001 *Human Rights Encyclopedia* (2-page article on "Cairo Declaration of Human Rights in Islam")

More specifically:

- The bibliographies of *all five* of these articles overlap in recommending *one* particular book, A. E. Myer's *Islam and Human Rights* (2006)
- The bibliographies of three of them overlap in recommending a second book (An-Na'im, *Toward an Islamic Reformation*)
- The bibliographies of three of them overlap in recommending a third book (Baderin, *International Human Rights and Islamic Law*)

Five additional sources were recommended by at least two of the several bibliographies.

This overlap of recommendations is important because the literature on such a subject can be overwhelming in its sheer volume. In the online catalog of the Library of Congress alone, for example, a search combining **Islam?** AND **Human rights** as subject terms produces more than 500 hits.

It is therefore extremely helpful to researchers to get multiple "takes" on the same subject for two distinct but related reasons:

1. To identify the most important *concepts* relevant to the topic— i.e., "the basic facts"—or the "what's important" ideas the absence of which might be fatal to a paper that overlooks them
2. To filter the huge mass of available material by identifying the *core literature* on the subject, segregated from indiscriminate printouts or computer retrievals of hundreds or thousands of hits

The comparative perspectives provided by multiple specialized encyclopedias thus provide an assurance of quality that does not attach to Wikipedia articles. Again, this is not to criticize the latter for what they do; it is rather to point out that other important research options for gaining overview perspectives exist "outside the box" of that one website.

A fifth advantage in using specialized encyclopedias comes from an interesting feature of very many recent sets: they often include in their last volume (after the A–Z sequence of articles) a compilation of primary source documents relevant to the subject covered by the set. For example, the 5-volume *Encyclopedia of the American Civil War* (ABC-CLIO, 2000) has 274 pages of primary sources reproduced in its final volume, including letters, proclamations, laws, ordinances, orders, and official reports. The last volume of the *Encyclopedia of Arms Control and Disarmament* (Scribners, 1993) reprints the texts of more than 140 treaties of historical interest, from the twelfth century B.C. to 1992. The final volume of the *Encyclopedia of Genocide and Crimes against Humanity* (Thomson Gale, 2005) reprints 193 pages of primary source documents including letters, laws, orders, identity cards, reports, conventions, Security Council resolutions, and judicial decisions. Students who are told to "use primary sources" in their assignments are well advised to look for these specialized subject encyclopedias. Once again, you will not find such compilations—carefully selected by experts—attached to Wikipedia articles.

A sixth advantage to these specialized sets is that, in their prefatory matter, they routinely provide an easily skimmable alphabetical list of all of their articles. Such a menu can greatly expand one's awareness of the many unanticipated aspects of the subject. The 9-page "List of Entries" in volume 1 of the 4-volume *Oxford International Encyclopedia of Peace* lists, for example, articles on "Architects for Peace," "Draft Resistance in the Soviet Union," "Gay Rights Movements," "Humor," "Japanese Peace Museums," "*Lysistrata*," "Photography," "Race and Conflict," "Spinoza's Ideas on War and Peace," "Sustainable Development," "Truth and Reconciliation Commissions," "Tibet, Resistance to China in," "War Toys and Noncompetitive Games," and hundreds of other topics that probably would not occur to students curious about this field. Skimming through such lists can open up whole new areas of awareness and focus that cannot be perceived via websites. The same lists can often suggest many unanticipated but relevant search terms that can be used in further database searching.

Specialized subject encyclopedias thus offer six major advantages over Wikipedia:

- Their articles are stable.
- They are reliably vetted (and often signed).
- They provide, when used in combination, multiple different disciplinary perspectives on the same topic.
- Their concise bibliographies are easy to compare for overlapping recommendations of unusually important sources.
- They frequently offer large compilations of primary source documents.
- They provide very helpful overview "lists of entries" that spell out unanticipated aspects of their topic and also bring to your attention good search terms for use in other sources.

HOW TO FIND ARTICLES IN SPECIALIZED ENCYCLOPEDIAS

How, then, do you find out which encyclopedias have articles specifically on your subject? The easiest (though not the only) way is through searching *Reference Universe*. While this database does not cover *all* encyclopedias—not even all of those listed above—it does provide much more extensive coverage than any other single source.

What I have found in practice is that if *Reference Universe* leads me to a particular encyclopedia on the library's shelves, then frequently there will be similar encyclopedias covering the same subject shelved right nearby, some of which are not indexed by the database. For example, I have twice helped readers who wanted information on "Montague grammar," which is a kind of formal system of analysis in linguistics. *Reference Universe* points to a 2-page article on the topic in the *International Encyclopedia of Linguistics* (4 vols., Oxford University Press, 2003), but the 14-volume *Encyclopedia of Language & Linguistics* (2nd ed., Elsevier, 2006), not covered by *Reference Universe*, was shelved right nearby. This set provided a 12-page article on the topic, plus a 3-page article on Richard Montague himself.

Similarly, a reader interested in "federalism in Argentina, Mexico, and Brazil" found, through *Reference Universe*, one article in a reference source with the call number F1401.L3253, but shelved right nearby at F1406.E53 2008 was the 6-volume *Encyclopedia of Latin American History and Culture* (2nd ed., Gale, 2008) with a 2-page article on "Federalism" in the whole region.

Other good resources for identifying specialized encyclopedias are the following:

CREDO Reference (Credo Reference) is a subscription database that provides full texts of articles from more than 600 reference sources, including many encyclopedias, from more than 70 publishers. It is not as extensive in its indexing range as *Reference Universe*, but everything in this database is full-text.

Sage Knowledge (Sage Publications) is a subscription database that offers full-text access to more than 2,700 e-books. Within this collection is the *Sage Reference* component that provides more than 450 specialized encyclopedias and subject handbooks (e.g., *Encyclopedia of African American Society, Encyclopedia of Geographic Information Science, Encyclopedia of Psychological Assessment, Handbook of Early Childhood Literacy, Handbook of Marketing Research, SAGE Handbook of Educational Leadership*); more titles are added each year.

Oxford Reference Online (Oxford University Press) provides the full texts of more than 300 dictionaries, encyclopedias, and *Oxford Companion* volumes (among many other sources).

Guide to Reference (American Library Association) is a subscription database often used by reference librarians; it is a comprehensive list of reference sources in all subject areas and languages, categorized by types of literature, including dictionaries and encyclopedias (see Chapter 15).

ARBAonline (Libraries Unlimited) and its corresponding print volumes *American Reference Books Annual*. This source provides reviews of over 60,000 reference sources, both print and online, since 1970; it has excellent indexes enabling you to identify encyclopedias in all subject areas, and its annotations provide critical evaluations (see Chapter 15).

Dictionary of Dictionaries and Eminent Encyclopedias, by Thomas Kabdebo (Bowker-Saur, 1997, 2nd ed.). This is a critical guide to more than 6,000 dictionaries and encyclopedias; works discussed can be monolingual, bilingual, or multilingual as long as English is one element. It will often tell you the *best* source in an area and compare it to other sources. It has a very good index. Although it is becoming somewhat dated, you can always check to see if a title recommended here has come out in a later edition.

Dictionaries, Encyclopedias, and Other Word-Related Books, by Annie M. Brewer, 2 vols. (Gale Research, 1988, 4th ed.). This is a large survey listing of about 30,000 works, from all time periods, arranged in the order of Library of Congress Classification numbers, with an index of subjects and titles. Entries reproduce nonevaluative library catalog records.

Catalog of Dictionaries, Word Books, and Philological Texts, 1440–1900, compiled by David E. Vancil (Greenwood Press, 1993). A good source for historical research, this is an inventory of the Cordell Collection of Dictionaries at Indiana State University; it is the world's largest, with more than 5,100 pre-1901 imprints plus several thousand more for the twentieth century. Indexes are by date, by language, and by subject. Entries are not annotated.

Anglo-American General Encyclopedias: A Historical Bibliography: 1703–1967, by S. Pedraig (James Patrick) Walsh (R. R. Bowker, 1968). This is another good source for a historical overview; its 419 entries are extensively annotated. The indexes are by editors and publishers/distributors; there is also a chronological listing of titles.

If you wish to check your own library's holdings for specialized encyclopedias, both old and new, you can usually find them under these forms of subject headings:

[Subject heading]—Dictionaries
[Subject heading]—Encyclopedias
[Subject heading]—[Geographic subdivision]—Dictionaries
[Subject heading]—[Geographic subdivision]—Encyclopedias

The important thing to note, here, is that either of the subdivisions, **Dictionaries** or **Encyclopedias,** may turn up a good source. (The several ways to find the right subject heading in the first place—especially the crucial first element in the string—will be discussed in the next chapter.)

EXAMPLES OF SEARCHES

The utility of specialized encyclopedias is often discovered by researchers writing short papers.

- A researcher interested in "the theology of humor" found a 30-page article on "Humor and Religion" in the *Encyclopedia of Religion*, 15 vols. (Thomson Gale, 2005); another of 10 pages in *Encyclopaedia Judaica*, 2nd ed., 22 vols. (Macmillan, 2007); and 8 pages in *The Anchor Bible Dictionary*, 6 vols. (Doubleday, 1992). He also discovered 2- or 3-page articles on "Humor" or "Humour" in each of the following: *Encyclopedia of Religion and Ethics*, 13 vols. (T & T Clark, 1913); *Encyclopaedia of the Qur'an*, 6 vols. (Brill, 2002); *Interpreter's Dictionary of the Bible*, 5 vols. and supplement (Abingdon Press, 1962, 1976); *Dictionnaire de Spiritualité*, 17 vols. (Beauchesne, 1969); *Encyclopedia of Mormonism*, 5 vols. (Macmillan, 1972); and *Encyclopedia of Islam and the Muslim World*, 2 vols. (Thomson Gale, 2004).
- An analyst looking for an overview of "Jimmy Carter's foreign policy" found a 4-page article in *Encyclopedia of U.S. Foreign Relations*, 4 vols. (Oxford University Press, 1997) and an 8-page article in *U.S. Presidents and Foreign Policy: From 1789 to the Present*, 1 vol. (ABC-CLIO, 2007); also multipage sections in *Encyclopedia of American Foreign Policy*, 3 vols. (Scribners/Gale Group, 2002) and *Encyclopedia of American Foreign Policy*, 1 vol. (Facts on File, 2004).
- A grad student interested in "the theory of the State" found a whole variety of sources: an 8-page article in *Encyclopedia of Philosophy*, 2nd ed., 10 vols. (Thomson Gale/Macmillan); 4 pages in *Routledge Encyclopedia of Philosophy*, 10 vols. (Routledge, 1998);

7 pages in *Dictionary of the History of Ideas*, 5 vols. (Scribners, 1973); 8 pages in *New Dictionary of the History of Ideas*, 6 vols. (Scribners/Thomson Gale, 2005); 12 pages in *New Catholic Encyclopedia*, 2nd ed., 15 vols. (Thomson Gale, 2003); and 27 pages in the "Syntopicon" introduction to *Great Books of the Western World*, 2nd ed. (Britannica, 1990).

- A social studies researcher interested in the idea of "community" in Nazi Germany found an article on precisely that topic, outlining the different concepts involved, in *The Encyclopedia of the Third Reich*, 2 vols. (Macmillan, 1991). The article included numerous cross-references within the set to other aspects of the subject ("Volk Community," "Front Experience," "Family," "Education," "Führer Principle").

- A researcher interested in "how blind people perceive colors" found that the concept of "Synaesthesia" was directly related; on that topic she found a 3-page article in the *Encyclopedia of Aesthetics*, 4 vols. (Oxford, 1998), and an 8-page article in the *Encyclopedia of Creativity*, 2 vols. (Academic Press, 1999).

- A humanities student interested in "Metaphor" could find only very brief articles in the *Britannica, Americana,* and *World Book* sets, but the *Encyclopedia of Aesthetics*, 4 vols. (Oxford, 1998) provided a 17-page article. Additional lengthy treatments could be found in several of the sources mentioned above—*Routledge Encyclopedia of Philosophy, Encyclopedia of Philosophy,* and *Dictionary of the History of Ideas*—as well as in the *International Encyclopedia of Communications*, 4 vols. (Oxford, 1989), the *New Princeton Encyclopedia of Poetry and Poetics* (Princeton, 1993), and in the various *Linguistics* encyclopedias mentioned previously.

PECULIAR STRENGTHS OF GENERAL SETS

In emphasizing specialized encyclopedias, I do not mean to suggest that the general sets are unimportant. Indeed, some surprising features within these sets are particularly useful. The *Encyclopedia Americana*, for example (unlike other encyclopedias), sometimes prints the full texts of historic documents in addition to providing information about them. When you look up "Declaration of the Rights of Man and the Citizen" or "Mayflower Compact" or "Washington's Farewell Address," for instance, you get not just summaries but actual texts. *Americana* also has articles on each individual century (e.g., on the Fifth Century or the Nineteenth

Century) that are useful; it also has articles on each book of the Bible as well as on many individual works of art, literature, and music (the *Winged Victory* statue, the novel *Middlemarch*, the ballet *The Firebird*, etc.). (Current editions of this set are now available only via an online subscription; the last printed version appeared in 2006.)

The *Encyclopaedia Britannica* (which since 2010 has been available only electronically) covers philosophy particularly well, including a book-length article "Philosophies of the Branches of Knowledge," which no other encyclopedia offers. The annual *Britannica Book of the Year* supplement (still available in print format) is very good in its presentation of statistical data on political, social, demographic, and economic conditions in the countries of the world; and it provides them in two sections, the first by country and the second by subject, so that comparisons can be readily made among countries. The *Macropaedia* (long article) section of the printed *Britannica* set also does something the other sets don't—it clusters what would otherwise be many alphabetically separated small articles within larger theme articles, often book length. Thus "Musical Instruments" gathers in one place articles on percussion, stringed, keyboard, wind, and electronic instruments; the article "Transportation" includes sections on history, motor vehicles, railroads, aircraft, ships, pipelines, urban mass transportation, traffic control and safety, and so on. The *Micropaedia* (short length) section of the set offers articles that often serve as overviews of the longer treatments in the *Macropaedia* section. The printed set's one-volume *Propaedia* is a fascinating classification of all of the articles in the entire *Britannica* in a logical order, showing relationships and linkages not apparent from the alphabetical sequence of the articles themselves. (This outline is entirely omitted from the online version of the encyclopedia. I much prefer the final 2010 printed set myself, especially since its *Macropaedia* articles are so long.)

The *World Book* is exceptionally good in providing quick, "look-it-up"-type information—on flags, state flowers, first aid, gardening instructions, symptoms of illnesses, metric conversion tables, football rules, summaries of Shakespeare's plays, and so on.

General foreign-language encyclopedias are often particularly good in turning up biographical information on obscure figures who played roles in the histories of various countries. Their illustrations are also sometimes more useful than those in the English-language sets. These sources, however, are overlooked much too often.

Many encyclopedias focus specifically on biographical information. For an overview of research options in this area, see Chapter 14.

When you need an article on a particular subject (a substantive but less than book-length source), keep in mind that you have several options beyond free websites:

- An encyclopedia article (generally written as an overview for nonspecialists)
- A "state-of-the-art" literature review article (generally written as an overview for specialists)
- A journal/periodical or newspaper article in databases (or in other formats) not freely available on the open Web
- An essay in a book anthology

Each of the latter forms is accessible through sources that will be discussed later. For an encyclopedia article, however, you should start by assuming that there are *specialized* encyclopedias covering your area of interest and then actively look for them.

CHAPTER 2

Subject Headings and the Library Catalog

W HY SHOULD YOU USE A LIBRARY CATALOG IN ADDITION TO the Internet? There are two major reasons:

1. Most of the material listed in the library's online catalog will not be available digitally. The catalog will give you a list, primarily of books, most of which are not accessible online because of copyright, site license, and other legal restrictions. And yet this material may well provide much of the best scholarship available on your topic, particularly in humanities or social sciences fields.

2. The library catalog—if it is set up properly—will provide mechanisms for subject searching that are frequently much more efficient than simple keyword searching. Catalogs can give you a systematic overview of your library's relevant book literature on your topic, enabling you to recognize whole groups of relevant sources whose keywords you could not think up in advance. Further, catalogs (if searched properly) won't overload you with a jumbled heap of thousands of irrelevant hits having the right words in the wrong contexts and whose relationships to each other are not obvious.

WHAT ONLINE PUBLIC ACCESS CATALOGS (OPACS) CONTAIN

A library's online catalog primarily lists the book holdings of the institution; in current terminology it is often referred to as an online public access catalog (OPAC). Your local OPAC may also list nonbook formats such as manuscripts, sound recordings, videos, maps, photographs, and so on; it may also provide links to e-books that your library offers. The titles of journals and magazines (e.g., *Harvard Business Review*, *Sports Illustrated*) held in physical formats (paper or microfilm) by the library will also be recorded, but, as a general rule, the catalog will not enable you to search for the individual articles that appear within the journals. (For those you will need separate databases and indexes, discussed in Chapters 4 and 5. For determining the library's holdings of journals in electronic formats, see Chapter 4.) Each entry in the catalog will provide you with a call number enabling you to locate the desired volume on the shelves.

PROBLEMS IN DETERMINING THE RIGHT SUBJECT HEADINGS

The most frequent, and most serious, problem that people have in looking for books in the catalog is the determination of the right subject headings to use. For example, if a reader wants books on morality, should she look under "Morality" or under "Ethics"? Or must she try both? Or perhaps, with a more focused topic in mind, she should look directly under "Ethical relativism"? Similarly, if another reader wants information on sentencing criminals to death, should he look under "Death penalty" or under "Capital Punishment"? And how does he know that he's thought of all of the right terms? Perhaps he should look under "Execution" or "Lethal injection" or some other terms as well.

Reference librarians routinely deal with people having problems in this regard. One student, for example, became frustrated in looking for material under "Moonshining" because it is not entered under that heading. In a standard library catalog, works on this subject are recorded under **Distilling, illicit**. The student who was researching the Huron Indians found, upon asking for help, that the preferred subject term is actually **Wyandot Indians**. (Similarly, the proper OPAC heading for Chippewa Indians is **Ojibwa Indians**.) Another researcher wanted books on "Corporate philanthropy"; before talking to a librarian she hadn't found anything on target because she was looking under "philanthropy" rather than under the proper heading **Corporations—Charitable contributions**. Researchers who want "Multinational corporations" often make the mistake of searching under that term when the proper heading is actually **International business enterprises**; those searching for

"Test tube babies" usually fail to search under the proper heading, **Fertilization in vitro, Human**.

Not only the choice of words but also their order may be confusing—for example, should one look under "Surgical diagnosis" or "Diagnosis, surgical"? under "Heavy minerals" or "Minerals, heavy"? under "Fraudulent advertising" or "Advertising, fraudulent"? Inverted forms are not used consistently, so there is much room for error unless you catch on to the easy systems for getting to the right choice. (Some OPACs solve these problems by searching for terms in any order; some do not.)

LIBRARY OF CONGRESS SUBJECT HEADINGS

You do not have to just guess—there are indeed systematic steps to take that will solve most of these problems. Specifically, there are five ways to find the right subject headings for your topic—to get *from* the terms you think of *to* the often different terms used for categorization purposes by the library catalog. Two of these ways are available through an annually revised online list called *Library of Congress Subject Headings* (*LCSH*) published by the Library of Congress; as of July 2013, it is available as a free PDF online: www.loc.gov/aba/publications/FreeLCSH/freelcsh. html. This is the standardized list of terms and phrases used by libraries throughout the English-speaking world for categorizing the books in their collections. All college, university, and research libraries use this list; so do most large public libraries. (Small neighborhood libraries may use a different one called the *Sears List of Subject Headings*; this is a much shorter one-volume roster that does not make all of the fine distinctions that are needed for categorizing really large collections.)

There is also a printed version of the *LCSH* in a 6-volume 35th edition (2013) set; it is often referred to simply as "the red books" because bright red was the color of its binding. Since 2013, however, only the online PDF version has been available, but the printed edition will still be useful for several more years, and its format makes it easier to flip through.

Apart from consulting the *LCSH* list directly (whether PDF or red books), there are three other ways to find the best subject terms for your topic just by using mechanisms within the library's online catalog itself. It must be noted, however, that many libraries have recently opted for Internet-type single search boxes that do not provide the mechanisms of access described below, a point to which I'll return. In such situations you can still use the *LCSH* system via the online catalog of the Library of Congress at catalog.loc.gov for subject access, and then check the titles discovered there to see if your local library owns them.

Before looking at all of the five ways to get from your keywords to the right *LCSH* category terms, however, it is important to consider the principles governing the compilation and use of the *Library of Congress Subject Headings* system, because these principles put catalogs into a different universe of search capabilities—more predictable and more systematic—than the realm of the open Internet. They are:

- Uniform heading
- Scope-match specificity
- Specific entry

These may sound like deadly dry irrelevancies to anyone who wants to get in and get out quickly in doing research, but an understanding of how these principles structure the catalog will actually give you the best means of doing just that—of using the OPAC quickly, with maximum efficiency, and without any wasted effort in having to sort through mounds of irrelevant or tangential hits (produced by keyword searches) that don't really provide exactly what you want. It is the combination of these three principles that enables the library OPAC to show you "the shape of the elephant" of the book literature on your topic—i.e., enabling you to see all of the relevant titles in your library (not just those whose keywords you can guess) and their relationships to each other, in ways that weed out hundreds of irrelevant works having the right keywords in the wrong contexts and that give you reasonable confidence you haven't missed something important.

UNIFORM HEADING: STANDARDIZATION OF SEARCH TERMS

"Uniform heading" is the principle that addresses the problem of synonyms, variant phrases, and different language terms being used to express the same concept (e.g., "Death penalty," "Capital punishment," or "Todesstrafe"; "Flying saucers," "Unidentified flying objects," or "UFOs"). Authors who write about any particular subject simply do not use identical terms to refer to it. Librarians who create systematic catalogs, however, solve the problem by choosing *one* of the many possible terms, in such cases, and entering all relevant records under that single category term, rather than repeating the same list of works under each of several terms. Since the full list of relevant books (or other records) appears under only one of the terms, the catalogers will insert cross-references from several of the other possible terms to steer readers to the one main grouping.

For example, books on the subject of the Cockney dialect have titles such as the following:

> *Ideolects in Dickens*
> *Bernard Shaw's Phonetics*
> *Fraffly Well Spoken*
> *The Muvver Tongue*
> *Sources of London English*
> *Zur Sprache Londons vor Chaucer*
> *The Early London Dialect*
> *Anecdotes of the English Language, Chiefly Regarding the Local Dialect*
>   *of London and Its Environs*
> *Die Londoner Vulgärsprache in Thackerays Yellowplush Papers*

No one researching this topic would be able think up all of these unusual keywords if confronted only by a blank search box, as in Web search engines. Library OPACs, however, round up all such books because the library's catalogers have artificially attached to each record the same (uniform) heading, **English language—Dialects—England—London.** When this cataloger-created heading is affixed to each different title record, the result is that all of those records then have a retrievable point of commonality that would not otherwise be present. The researcher who finds just this one common subject heading, then, can thereby round up all of the disparate title records to which it is attached, without having to guess all of their variant title (or other) keywords.

Similar scattering shows up in just about any other subject area. Here, for example, is only a brief sampling of the many variant book titles that are cataloged under the heading **Capital punishment**:

> *The Ultimate Coercive Sanction*
> *To Kill and Be Killed*
> *A Life for a Life*
> *Executing the Mentally Ill*
> *Hanging Not Punishment Enough for Murtherers*
> *Habeas Corpus Issues*
> *In Spite of Innocence*
> *The Unforgiven: Utah's Executed Men*
> *Until You are Dead*
> *Fatal Error*

Philosophy of Punishment
Death Penalty
Legal Homicide
Legal Executions in the Western Territories, 1847–1911
Death Sentences in Missouri, 1803–2005
Lethal Injection
Dokumentation über die Todesstrafe
Contre ou pour le peine du mort
Cesare Beccaria e l'abolizione della pena de morte
Contra la pena de muerte
Prăna-danda

Hundreds of other keyword-variant titles could be listed—and in scores of languages other than English. Without the creation and assignment of the artificial point of commonality (the *LCSH* term **Capital punishment**) to each record, a researcher looking for what the library has to offer on this topic would miss most of these works. Their own keyword terms are simply too diverse to be rounded up systematically by computer algorithms (which usually rank the displays of *only the exact words that have been typed in*, without noticing synonyms or variant phrases for the same concept); nor could the full variety of the books' own keywords be anticipated even by researchers having some prior expertise in the subject area.

This is an important point: *relevance ranking* of keywords by Internet search mechanisms is very different from *conceptual categorization* brought about in OPACs. The former may massage the display order of records containing the words you've typed in, but it won't bring up records having any of the other ways of articulating the same idea. (There are minor exceptions here, in that some search engines do automatic word stemming—which means that, for example, entering "homeowner" will also retrieve variant endings of the same word stem such as "homeowners" or "homeowner's.") Projected large-scale semantic Web solutions, in which computer algorithms attempt to aggregate synonyms or variant phrasings, don't work now even within English, let alone across multiple languages simultaneously. It is therefore prudent to accept only with a grain of salt claims for their future success. Moreover, the synonym linkages in semantic webs are such that you can never tell which links have *not* been made—look again at the unpredictable variety of title keywords in the examples above. Subject headings, in contrast to keywords, are *conceptual category* terms—if you find the right *LCSH* heading, you've found essentially all of the books in that category, no matter what unpredictable terms the books may use themselves. (I'll have to qualify that word "all" below.)

DISPLAYING UNANTICIPATED ASPECTS AND RELATIONSHIPS: BROWSE MENUS

A uniform heading also serves to round up the different *aspects* of a subject through the use of subdivisions of the lead term in the verbal string. (This is an area in which *LCSH* differs in an important way from other thesauri, or lists of controlled indexing terms that are used in other databases.) In the "Cockney" case, the proper heading not only indicates the subject of the books to which it is assigned, it also appears in the library catalog's *browse display* in a way that shows how it is *related to other aspects of the topic*. The following is only a brief sample of the hundreds of subdivisions that show up under **English language— Dialects**:

English language—Dialects—Africa, West
English language—Dialects—Alabama
English language—Dialects—Australia
English language—Dialects—Bahamas
English language—Dialects—Bibliography
English language—Dialects—England—Berkshire
English language—Dialects—England—Bibliography
English language—Dialects—England—Cambridge
English language—Dialects—England—Cornwall (County)
English language—Dialects—England—Dorset
English language—Dialects—England—Lake District
English language—Dialects—England—London [the
     "Cockney" heading]
English language—Dialects—England—Norfolk
English language—Dialects—England—Penrith
English language—Dialects—England—Phonology
English language—Dialects—England—Suffolk
English language—Dialects—England—Wessex
English language—Dialects—Indiana
English language—Dialects—Ireland
English language—Dialects—New England
English language—Dialects—New York (State)
English language—Dialects—Social aspects
English language—Dialects—South Africa

English language—Dialects—United States
English language—Dialects—United States—Bibliography
English language—Dialects—Wales
English language—Dialects—West (U.S.)

Sometimes people wonder why a complicated heading like **English language—Dialects—England—London** is used rather that more obvious and direct terms such as "Cockney" or "Cockney dialect." The latter forms are certainly preferable by a simple criterion of popular usage, but there's more involved in the cataloging system than just that one consideration. The reason for using the string is that, as in this example, it is crafted to draw attention to *a larger context of relationships to other relevant subject headings*. In this case, a researcher interested in the Cockney dialect may well discover, through such a browse display, several other aspects of English dialectology that might be of interest.

Browse displays of the many aspects of a topic enable researchers to recognize what they cannot or did not specify in advance; the larger a library's collection, the more readers need such *menus* to serve as road maps into the range of available, but unexpectedly relevant, resources. (Note further that semantic webs may succeed in rounding up some synonyms and variant phrasings for an idea—in one language—but they cannot bring to your attention *related ideas* that are "off to the side" and that alert you to the larger surrounding contexts of a subject. This is not to say that semantic webs are useless—far from it; it is simply to point out that there are real trade-offs involved, and that they are no substitutes for the *LCSH* system.)

The creation of browse displays of headings with subdivisions (as above) is one of the main differences between a library catalog and a mere inventory of holdings; the latter will record individual items but will not display subject categorizations of the items or show relational linkages among the categories themselves. Inventories give you lists of the items within a collection; library catalogs provide not just lists of the items themselves but higher-level subject linkages: the subject headings themselves round up keyword-variant texts on the same subject so that the variants can be seen in relationship to each other; and both cross-references and browse menus systematically map out the further, "outside" relationships *of the subject categories themselves*.

Library catalogers who create headings have to be mindful not just of the appropriateness of any individual term (that "artificial point of commonality") that they assign to an individual catalog record (for a book) to designate its conceptual grouping, but also of the "browse" position in which the chosen form of heading will appear in relation to other established headings.

DIFFERENCES FROM TAGS

This concern also points up a major difference between formal *LCSH* headings and keyword "tags" added to records by amateur enthusiasts, as in LibraryThing.com—the latter index terms are words attached to individual book records without any regard for the *uniform* application of the *same* term(s) to *all* of the other relevant books on the same subject. In other words, the consistency of tags from one record to the next is itself as unpredictable as the range of keywords in the books' titles. Tags are assigned by readers' whims, without regard to any cataloging principle of *uniform heading*. Moreover, tags are applied without any intention of placing them in a formal network of relationships that will display other concepts that may also be of interest, but which are a bit "off to the side" of the one particular book in hand—i.e., the one being tagged. Searching on the tag "Cockney," for example, will not bring to your attention other works on different dialects, such as **English language—Dialects—England—Dorset**.

LINKAGES TO CLASSIFICATION NUMBERS

The creation of uniform terms with standardized subdivisions serves yet another purpose in relating a library's books to each other. The many possible subdivisions of a single term (e.g., **Bibliography**, **History**, **Law and legislation**, **Study and teaching**) may serve to direct researchers to entirely different call number areas in the bookstacks, scattered throughout the classification scheme.

For example, works under the *LCSH* term **Small business** usually get classified and shelved in HD (Economics) or KF (U.S. law) areas, but if the books being cataloged are assigned the **Accounting** subdivision, they switch to HF (Commerce) classes instead. If they receive the **Finance** subdivision, they are usually classed in HG (Finance); if they are on the bibliographical aspect of the topic (**Small business—Bibliography**), they are classed in Z7164.C81 (Business bibliography). All of these different class designations, while scattered in the bookstacks, nevertheless appear together in the catalog under the one heading **Small business** (with its various subdivisions). Thus, catalogers who choose one heading form over another have to be thinking not just of the conceptual relevance of the verbal string to the book in hand, and not just of its contextual display in a browse list, but also of which classification number may be tied to the string that is created. (Further, they have to keep in mind the heading's position in a network of broader, related, and narrower subject relationships defined by cross-references.)

SUBJECT HEADINGS IN THE OPAC AS INDEX TO THE CLASSIFICATION SCHEME

There is not a one-to-one relationship between all *LCSH* headings and specific classification numbers, but there are so many tens of thousands of such formal linkages that the subject headings in the catalog effectively function as the index to the classification scheme in the bookstacks (see Chapter 3). Finding even slightly different subject headings in the OPAC may bring up catalog records whose call numbers point you to entirely different areas of the bookstacks if you want to browse the shelves. Good catalogers are fully aware of this linkage—which provides yet another important distinction between a library catalog and a simple inventory list. The same consideration of linkages to classification numbers also points up another substantive difference between *Library of Congress Subject Headings* and "descriptors" in conventional subject thesauri—the latter terms do not need to be linked to class numbers in a library shelving scheme. This point also applies to the application of keyword tags, by amateur contributors, to book records in LibraryThing (and elsewhere)—those tags are assigned without any regard to, or awareness of, appropriate or consistent call number linkages defining where the books will be physically shelved in relation to other books. For example, a large library cannot sanely assign all of the books on the various aspects of the subject **Afghanistan** to a single classification number; there are too many distinctions that have to be made within that large topic, without which researchers would be overwhelmed by too many irrelevancies. Distinctions must be made both within the *LCSH* headings themselves (via subdivisions) and within the class numbers that determine where the books will be shelved. Thus, specifically distinguished aspects of the subject heading in the catalog are also frequently tied to specifically distinguished classification numbers:

> **Afghanistan—Antiquities** [DS353]
> **Afghanistan—Description and travel** [DS352]
> **Afghanistan—History** [DS355-DS371.43]
> **Afghanistan—History—Soviet occupation** [DS371.2]

Without these distinctions in the OPAC subject headings, the 10,000+ books on Afghanistan at the Library of Congress would all be jumbled together incomprehensibly in the bookstacks in a single undifferentiated mass. (A similar, although lesser, problem would exist in all other research libraries. The importance of shelf-browsing capabilities within different aspects of a large subject will be discussed in Chapter 3.) Note that these class distinctions could not be designated in the first place without the corresponding *LCSH* headings being created as multiword strings—a feature of *LCSH* headings that make them unlike the single-term descriptors used in conventional thesauri. Such strings are entirely eliminated in the faceted OPACs that are now, unfortunately, used by many university libraries. (A faceted catalog breaks up subject strings into their individual component words. See the discussion of precoordination and postcoordination, below.)

Uniform headings in OPACs thus round up in one place both *variant titles* for the same subject that may be alphabetically scattered among keywords from A to Z and *variant classification numbers* for aspects of the same subject that are scattered throughout the bookstacks.

RECOGNITION ACCESS (PROVIDED BY CONCEPTUAL CATEGORIZATION RATHER THAN RELEVANCE RANKING)

The emphasis in library catalogs on collocation via uniform subject headings points up a major problem with Internet search engines, in contrast: no matter how sophisticated their relevance ranking algorithms may be, they are still ranking only the keywords that you've typed in to begin with. (Even if, in some cases, there are under-the-hood links to other terms, you still cannot tell *which* terms are linked and which are overlooked.) If those terms are not the best ones to use in the first place, manipulations of their rank-ordering will do nothing to bring about the retrieval of entirely different words for the same subject—i.e., typing in "Cockney" will not retrieve "Fraffly" or "Muvver" or "Vulgärsprache," as in the above example. (Nor will it bring to your attention the many other geographical options arrayed under **English language—Dialects**.) Typing in "death penalty" will not retrieve "ultimate coercive sanction" or "murtherers" or "unforgiven"—nor will any semantic web make such connections automatically. Nor will user-assigned tags. *Relevance ranking*, again, is not the same as *conceptual categorization*. The latter function is absent in Web searches. Internet or Amazon-type searches may provide some linkages of a very different—and often very useful—kind (e.g., "Customers who bought this book also bought these"), but that sort of linkage cannot find conceptually similar works, with variant keywords, in a systematic manner; and it usually does not notice relevant foreign-language or out-of-print works at all. *Library of Congress Subject Headings*, in contrast, round up all (or at least most) of the books in a library's collection on a given topic, no matter what keywords their authors used, in either English *or* foreign languages, and both in print and out of print—they all show up under the one *uniform heading* chosen by the catalogers. Further, all of the library's books—which have been professionally selected to begin with on the basis of quality—will appear there, even if no customer/user has yet read or recommended them.

There is thus a huge difference between online library catalogs and Internet search engines or Amazon displays. The former, constructed on the principle of uniform heading, enable you to recognize, within a retrieved subject set, a whole host of relevant titles whose variant phrasings—such as those above—you could never have specified in advance. The crucial element of serendipity or recognition at the retrieval end of library searches is a direct function of keyword-transcendent categorizations having been created by librarians at the input (cataloging) end of the operation.

Cataloging is thus not at all the same as merely transcribing existing data from title pages or tables of contents (as in an inventory), nor is it simply a matter of adding keyword tags that are not uniformly assigned to all of the conceptually relevant records (as in LibraryThing). It is a process of adding terms that are standardized "on top of," or in addition to, the words provided by the book itself, or by tags contributed unsystematically by amateurs. These standardized elements serve to collocate under one subject heading the widely varying expressions used by many different authors, worldwide, in talking about the same subject; and at the same time they function to bring to your attention a whole network of cross-references and menus of related aspects of your subject, off to the side, that you probably wouldn't think of on your own until you saw them listed for your inspection. Moreover, these category terms themselves, unlike title (or other) keywords or tags, can be identified without guesswork through predictable and systematic means (the five methods discussed below).

SCOPE-MATCH SPECIFICITY AND ITS MODIFICATIONS

"Scope-match specificity" is the second principle governing the operation of *Library of Congress Subject Headings*. Its meaning requires some understanding of library history. Prior to the advent of computer catalogs, books as a general rule were seldom assigned more than two or three standardized subject headings. This limitation was an important consideration in the era of card catalogs, because filing individual cards for each book under a half dozen or more terms at different places in the alphabet would result in a catalog that was physically very bulky. The fewer categories to which any book was assigned, in other words, the fewer cards had to be filed, and the more manageable was the size of the overall physical file—a matter of considerable importance in research libraries holding millions of books.

Another important consideration—still relevant even in the age of computer catalogs—is the volume of work that catalogers have to do. Although the number of books published every year is huge, almost all libraries are chronically underfunded, and so catalogers who have to create records for dozens of books each day don't have the time to figure out 10 or 12 headings for each one. Again, cataloging is not simply a matter of transcribing words from titles or tables of contents—nor is it simply a matter of employing existing headings from the *LCSH* list. It is also a matter of extending the list, creating new headings, and—the difficult part—integrating all of the new terms into an intricate webs of cross-references, which require the specification of hierarchical relation-ships (broader, related, narrower) to many other headings. Considerations of the best *form* of heading to create—and how that form will show up in relation to other terms in browse displays—are also important, as are considerations of how new headings may be linked to new classifica-tion numbers, which may also have to be created at the same time. The intellectual work involved, when done well, is quite intricate and chal-lenging. It's sort of like doing multidimensional crossword puzzles—you have to get words that are not just appropriate to a particular book but that also fit into several large patterns of linkages to other terms that already exist in the same system.

Considerations such as these affect scope-match specificity. In the card catalog era, the principle meant that catalogers would usually assign the minimum number of headings that indicated the subject content of a book *as a whole*—that is, catalogers would not assign a standardized term for each individual chapter or section of the book. Thus a book about **Oranges** and **Grapefruit** would have both terms assigned to its catalog record, because in combination they covered the whole scope of the work. If another book dealt with these two fruits plus **Limes**, a third subject heading would be assigned. However, if a book dealt with **Oranges**, **Grapefruit**, **Limes**, and **Lemons**, in traditional cataloging it would not receive all four headings; rather, a single generic heading representing all of the subtopics comprehensively would be assigned— in this case, **Citrus fruits**. While this is indeed a generic term, it is nevertheless the most specific one that covers the book *as a whole*. Catalogers traditionally aimed for this level of coverage in the card catalog era. If there was not a single term that expressed the subject of the book as a whole, the goal was to sum up the book in as few headings as possible—usually about three.

The advent of computer catalogs more than a generation ago eliminated the need to worry about physically bulky card catalogs bursting with too many cards in too little space to contain them, so computerized catalog records often receive more than three subject headings. Records created in earlier decades, however—especially prior to the 1980s—still reside in online catalogs with what today would be considered nearly minimal subject headings on them. So, if you need to search for early books, remember that you do not have as much leeway in your choice of headings as you may have in searching for more recent books.

The welcome development of computer catalogs—and especially of full texts of books appearing online—has led some commentators to assert that subject headings are no longer necessary at all; they say, in essence, "Why is there a need for adding any terms to catalog records when so many more searchable words have now become available through full-text search capabilities?" One major answer to this question lies in the fact that scope-match specificity in subject headings solves one of the biggest problems that researchers have in trying to find books relevant to their interests. (The other answers entail an understanding of the principles of uniform heading and specific entry; but the people who ask the question to begin with usually don't want to hear the replies.) As anyone who has ever used Web search mechanisms discovers immediately, typing keywords into a blank search box will overwhelm you with thousands, if not hundreds of thousands, of websites or e-books having those words anywhere in their texts.

SOLVING THE PROBLEM OF EXCESSIVE GRANULARITY

What researchers really want, especially when they are at the initial stages of an inquiry, is not a roster of *every* book having the right words appearing in any context, no matter how tangentially. What they want to start with is a much smaller list of *whole books* on the topic—or at least only those books having substantial sections on the desired subject. They want first to find the substantive treatments of their topic, not just tangential references to it. This is exactly what scope-match subject cataloging provides immediately and that keyword searching of full texts misses. Full-text keyword searching usually provides results that are much too granular—that is, it buries the substantive works within thousands of essentially irrelevant retrievals. (There are of course other times when very granular retrieval is highly desirable; see Chapter 5.) You cannot see "the shape of the elephant" of the book literature on a topic by doing full-text keyword searches; you will get way too many hits that have the right words in the wrong contexts, or that have only tiny sections pertinent to what you want. And the presence of so many thousands of irrelevancies serves to hide from view many of the best sources. Scope-match searching (via *LCSH* headings), in contrast, retrieves whole books on the desired subject, segregated from thousands of irrelevant retrievals.

It is perhaps ironic, but it is nonetheless true: a cataloging rule that was created to solve a different problem in the card catalog era (that of preventing catalogs from becoming too physically bulky) now serves *to directly solve one* of the most serious problems of the online age: that of excessively granular retrievals—i.e., way too many irrelevant works being brought up by full-text search capabilities. Researchers who understand the advantage of scope-match subject cataloging in OPACs thus have a major advantage over those who cannot see retrieval possibilities beyond keyword searching of full texts. Cataloging retrieval will bring up not just conceptually related works (no matter what keywords or languages their authors have used), it will also bring up only the most substantive relevant works, freed from burials within thousands or millions of irrelevancies.

The current *Subject Cataloging Manual* of the Library of Congress, which is more or less the standard for catalogers in all large libraries in the English-speaking world, allows for a "20 percent rule"—that is, a heading may be assigned for any topic that takes up 20 percent of a book's content. The manual further notes that "generally a maximum of six [headings] is appropriate. In special situations more headings may be required."

PROBLEMS WITH COPY CATALOGING

I say the *Manual* is "more or less" the standard because many libraries today have chosen to produce records at a less rigorous level, called "core cataloging" or "cataloging on receipt" (COR). At this "core" level, two subject headings per book are usually deemed appropriate.[1] Other books may receive "minimal-level cataloging," which means that their titles are recorded but they are assigned no standardized subject headings at all.

These lower levels of work are turned out by some libraries because of the huge volume of book publication coupled with the decreasing number of trained catalogers. Indeed, traditional cataloging is a subject no longer required in some library schools. Additionally, most libraries do "copy cataloging" as much as possible, which means that they strive to find within the OCLC system catalog records already created by some other library—*any* other library—and simply import them into their own catalogs, frequently with minimal review or quality control of the copied subject terms. (OCLC used to stand for "Online Computer Library Center," a network incorporating the catalogs of more than 70,000 libraries worldwide; now it's just plain OCLC.) Obviously the quality of cataloging contributed from so many sources varies a great deal—which causes the principle of *uniform heading* to be considerably undermined in all too many instances. This is a reality that researchers have to take into account: You do want to start by looking for what are presumably uniform headings, but you also have to know how to navigate through the unavoidable inconsistencies that are unfortunately becoming more common.

Here's an example of the problems that the "core" standard can create. A book published 20 years ago, in 1984, with the title *Censorship and Interpretation: The Conditions of Writing and Reading in Early Modern England*, received a generous set of headings:

Censorship—England—History—16th century
Censorship—England—History—17th century
Books and reading—England—History—16th century
Books and reading—England—History—17th century
English literature—Early modern, 1500–1700—History and
criticism
England—Intellectual life—16th century
England—Intellectual life—17th century

A similar book published in 2001, however, *Press Censorship in Jacobean England*, received only two headings:

Freedom of the press—England—History—16th century
Press—England—History—16th century

There are a couple of problems here. The first is that the person who cataloged the second work lacked sufficient subject expertise and mistakenly assigned "16th century" rather than "17th" for the Jacobean period. And here it must be admitted that library work is as much an art as a science; despite its many rules designed to bring about uniformity and standardization, they are only as good as the person using them—and good subject cataloging requires some expertise in the subject area as well as a knowledge of the cataloging rules.

The more serious problem is that the first book, *Censorship and Interpretation*, is widely considered the standard work in its field—but a researcher who looked in a library catalog under any of the headings used for that book would not have found the later 2001 work, which covers much of the same ground from a different perspective. The minimal two headings given to the later volume were simply not adequate to place it into any of the same categories in which the first book appears—and it should show up in some of those same groupings. The problem in this case was solved by a "guerrilla cataloger" who, once the difficulty was pointed out, simply ignored the core cataloging standard and added to the 2001 record several more of the *LCSH* terms that now enable researchers to find the two books under some of the same headings.

Not all such problems, however, can be solved by guerrilla catalogers who will ignore the rules they are told to work with and do better work than the core standard requires. This means, again, that the "uniform" part of the principle of uniform heading has been considerably diluted in the library profession in recent decades, and so researchers need to be aware of the ways to compensate for decreasing standardization.

SPECIFIC ENTRY

This is by far the most important principle that researchers need to be aware of. It means that, given a choice between using specific or general headings for a book, catalogers will predictably choose the most specific possible heading(s) for the book as a whole, rather than the more general headings that are also available in the *LCSH* list.

For example, if you are looking for material on nightmares, you should not look first under **Dreams** or **Sleep** but under **Nightmares** specifically. Similarly, if you want books on Siamese cats, you should look under the specific heading **Siamese cat** and *not* under the general heading **Cats**. One researcher looking for material on Jewish children mistakenly assumed the proper heading would be **Jews**. It isn't. It's **Jewish children**. Works under this more specific heading are *not also* listed under the more general heading **Jews**.

Another reader looking for information on recreation rooms searched under **Homes**. The right heading is **Recreation rooms**.

A reporter looking for material on game shows looked under **Television**. The right heading is **Game shows**.

A reader looking for information on archons (chief magistrates) in ancient Greece searched under both the keyword phrase "ancient civilizations" and the heading **Civilization, ancient**. The right heading is **Archons**.

A reader looking for information on emblem books searched under **Iconography**. The right heading is **Emblem books**.

A reader looking for information on the problems that alcoholic parents create for their children wasted a lot of time after being inundated with records under **Alcoholics**. The right heading is **Children of alcoholics**, and there is also an even more specific term, **Adult children of alcoholics**. Again, books listed under the narrower terms are *not also* listed under the general heading—you have to find the most specific headings *rather than* (not in addition to) the general terms. Still another reader interested in the effects of divorce on children made the usual mistake of looking under the general heading **Divorce** rather than under the specific heading **Children of divorced parents**. (And there is also a heading for **Adult children of divorced parents**.) The materials listed under narrower terms do not also appear under the broader term or terms; the choice of which term(s) to use, when several levels of generality are possible, is predictably made on the basis of the principle of specific entry.

This is not to say that the general headings aren't used—of course they are. If a book is about **Divorce** in general, then it will receive that heading, because in that case the general heading is indeed the tightest fit for the scope of that book.

The problem is that most people search under general headings when they really have something more specific in mind; they simply assume mistakenly that the general categories "include" the more specific topics. The rule for researchers, then, is to start with the most specific terms from the *LCSH* list and then "go general" only if you cannot find narrow terms that match your specific topic exactly.

Note that this rule runs counterintuitively against the grain of what students are usually told: "Start with a broad idea and then try to narrow it down as you go." While this may be very good advice in other situations, you should do the exact opposite when you are using a library catalog. (I dearly wish someone had pointed this out to me when I was still a student myself.)

The problem for researchers who start with general terms is that in doing so they usually do find a few sources that appear to be in the ballpark—but they simultaneously miss most of the best material without knowing it, and they usually stop with their initial pool of general sources. The researcher who looks under **Divorce**, for instance, may indeed find a few books that have sections discussing the effects of divorce on children—but if she stops there (and most people, like the Six Blind Men, do stop at the first level that seems at all relevant), she will miss all of the works under **Children of divorced parents**, which are whole books (rather than just chapters or section) on that topic. Progressively refining the wrong initial search set by adding extra keywords will not magically transform it into the right initial search set.

PREVENTING OVERLOAD IN COVERAGE

There are two good reasons for the specific entry rule. First, the segregation of different levels of specificity prevents any of them, broad or narrow, from becoming overloaded with irrelevant clutter. For example, the heading **Decoration and ornament** is quite general, but linked to it (via cross-references) are 125 narrower terms such as:

Airplanes, Military—Decoration
Antiques
Balloon decorations
Bars (Drinking establishments)—Decoration
Book covers
Bronzes
Cattle—Housing—Decoration
Church decoration and ornament
Decoupage
Driftwood arrangement
Embroidery
Floral decorations
Garden ornaments and furniture
Heraldry, Ornamental
Illustration of books
Lattice windows
Majolica painting
Nose ornaments
Railroad stations—Decoration
Ship decoration
Textile design

Vase painting
Wedding decorations

If all of these narrower terms were included within the scope of the general heading, then researchers who wanted only the general-level books on **Decoration and ornament** would not be able to find them without having to wade through, at the same time, all of the hundreds of cluttering records for the much narrower topics. Specific entry prevents general terms from being overloaded by the inclusion of too many related but narrower topics, and sometimes researchers *do* want to start out with very general "overview" books.

PREDICTABILITY IN SELECTION OF TERMS

Second, when there are several possible levels of relevant headings available in *LCSH*, it is the principle of specific entry alone that makes the choice of which level to use predictable. Works on blue crabs, for instance, could conceivably be cataloged under **Crabs**, **Crustacea**, or **Chesapeake Bay**, or even under **Ecology**, **Estuaries**, **Invertebrates**, **Marine biology**, **Marine invertebrates**, **Coastal fauna**, **Oceanography**, **Arthropoda**, or any of two dozen other terms—all of which appear as valid general headings in the *LCSH* list. The problem is that when you look in the direction of generality there is no logical or predictable stopping point, because all of the general headings could potentially apply. You could never tell which one would be the best to use. The solution is that when you search in the direction of specificity, there is indeed a predictable stopping point: the heading that is the tightest fit for what you want. The right term to stop at in the *LCSH* list, here, is **Blue crab**.

It is the predictability of the rule that creates the "control" of the controlled vocabulary—without the specificity convention, users could not know in advance which level of term to choose, and the problem of guesswork among variant headings would remain, in spite of the existence of the *LCSH* list. Without this rule, use of the list itself would be rendered no more efficient than having to guess which nonstandardized keywords to use, outside the list.

This, by the way, is the main problem with user-created tags: they can be, and are, assigned by different people at all levels of generality for the same book, and they are usually at very general levels. Different taggers may well assign all of the terms above to the same book. There's no "uniform heading" or "scope-match specificity" or "specific entry" among tags.

LOSS OF RELATIONSHIP NETWORKS
IN FACETED CATALOGS

A similar problem shows up when *LCSH* subject strings are broken up into their individual "facet" component terms. Such breakups sever the links between **English language** and **England** and **Dialects** and **London** and put the different elements in separate "silos." Faceted catalogs—all too prevalent among research libraries these days—can be compared to disassembled watches: it's like all of the cogs and gears have been taken apart and put separately into different bins, accompanied by the naïve advice that "now you can combine them in any way *you* want!" The problem is that the watch no longer works to show, systematically rather than haphazardly, what the library has when the defined relationships of its structural parts are disregarded.

Although there is an unfortunate tendency in library catalogs nowadays to lose the sharpness of their subject categorizations (due to the widespread acceptance of inadequately reviewed copy cataloging from the OCLC system, many of whose contributors do not abide by the three cataloging principles), there is still more than enough substance to the principle of specific entry that you should make use of it: *as a rule*, look in the direction of cross-references leading to specific headings, and stop only at the level of terminology that provides the tightest fit for your topic, rather than the general levels above it. (Look also for headings in browse menus with specific subdivisions.) Look for general levels only after you've first tried to be as specific as possible, rather than vice versa. If you match your retrieval technique to the rules the catalogers are supposed to follow, your results will usually be much more on target.

The principle of specific entry is essential not just as a rule for determining which headings are best for any particular topic but also for mapping the relationships of those headings to other, related topics off to the side. Again, the provision of an overview of the network of relationships among headings is entirely lost in faceted OPACs that cannot show either cross-references or browse displays of precoordinated subjects with subdivisions in a single list.

FIVE WAYS TO FIND THE RIGHT SUBJECT
HEADINGS

So, then, how exactly do you find the right heading(s) for your topic? There are five techniques: two involve using the *LCSH* list of subject headings, and the other three involve the use of the library's catalog directly.

There is a "good news" and "bad news" situation here right at the start. The bad news is that many academic libraries have recently adopted OPAC search systems, mirroring Google's single search box, that hide—or even entirely eliminate—most of the features (cross-references, browse menus, alphabetically adjacent displays, discussed below) that will enable you to get from the keywords you think up to the standardized LCSH category strings of terms. They have done this on the basis of a kind of mania sweeping the library profession these days proposing that word clouds and tags and algorithmic relevance ranking and faceted searching can replace the search mechanisms I am about to describe. They cannot, for reasons that will become apparent.

The good news, however, is that no matter where you are, you can still search the OPAC of the Library of Congress and then use the results of your *subject* searches there to do specific *title* searches for the same books in your local catalog. This freely accessible catalog is the best one available, and it approximates a model search system that should be copied more widely. The URL for the Library of Congress online catalog is catalog.loc.gov.

The following discussion will make more sense if you have an Internet connection. The "landing page" of catalog.loc.gov is where you want to be.

The five ways to get from the words you think of to the category terms used by library catalogs are the following:

1. Follow cross-references in the *Library of Congress Subject Headings* list, especially the NT (Narrower Term) references.

The *LCSH* list is an annual roster of the terms approved for use as subject headings in library catalogs. The list also includes words or phrases that are not used, with cross-references from them to the proper terms. Thus if you look up "Morality" you will find a note to use **Ethics**. Similarly, a search for "Surgical diagnosis," which is not used, will refer you to the acceptable form, **Diagnosis, surgical**. The URL for the online list is www.loc.gov/aba/publications/FreeLCSH/freelcsh.html. This can be typed directly in your browser; an easier link to it appears on the catalog. loc.gov "landing page." Look for the visual icon of two red books and click on "LC Subject Headings." If you are inside a library you may also have access to the slowly dating "red books" print format copy of the list.

Once you find the proper term, the *LCSH* list will also show you a roster of other subject headings that are related to it so that you can systematically search either slightly different aspects of the topic or different levels of generality. Thus "Death penalty," which is not used, refers you to **Capital punishment**, and under this term you will find a list of other headings that are preceded by different code designations. These codes are very important. They are UF, BT, RT, and NT (see Figure 2.1).

UF means Used For; thus, in Figure 2.1, **Capital punishment** in boldface type is *used for* "Death penalty" or "Death sentence." In other words, if terms are preceded by UF, do not use them. They are not the acceptable search terms; instead, use the boldface heading above them. (The same printing conventions of bold and not bold are used in both the PDF and red books versions.)

BT means Broader Term(s); these *are* valid headings that you can search under (Criminal law, Punishment). These terms are not printed in boldface here, where they appear as cross-references, but they will be in boldface where they appear as headings in their own proper alphabetical places in the *LCSH* list.

RT means Related Term(s). RT references are also valid headings (Executions and executioners).

Capital punishment   *(May Subd Geog)*
　　　[HV8694-HV8699]
　　UF　Abolition of capital punishment
　　　　Death penalty
　　　　Death sentence
　　BT　Criminal law
　　　　Punishment
　　RT　Executions and executioners
　　NT　Crucifixion
　　　　Death row
　　　　Discrimination in capital punishment
　　　　Electrocution
　　　　Garrote
　　　　Hanging
　　　　Last meal before execution
　　　　Stoning
　— **Religious aspects**
　— — **Baptists, [Catholic Church, etc.]**
　— — **Buddhism, [Christianity, etc.]**
Capital punishment (Canon law)
　　BT　Canon law
Capital punishment (Germanic law)
　　BT　Law, Germanic

Figure 2.1 **Capital punishment** subject heading from LCSH red books.

NT means Narrower Term(s); these, too, are valid headings (Death row, Discrimination in capital punishment, Electrocution, etc.).

Sometimes the designation SA (See Also) will appear; it can alert you to other appearances of the heading in still other contexts.

Frequently the cross-reference USE or *See* will appear to get you from the wrong term(s) to the right terms, as in "Death penalty USE Capital punishment" (in the PDF *LCSH* list); in the online catalog itself, "Death penalty *See:* **Capital punishment**."

There are three crucial points here, none of which is intuitively obvious. The first is that the BTs, RTs, and NTs are *not subsets or subdivisions* of the boldface term above. They are *not included* in the coverage of the boldface term; if you want any of these subjects, you must look for them directly. Thus **Death row** and **Hanging** are not included in the coverage of the term **Capital punishment**; if you want any of these topics you must search for them individually and directly.

The second point is that cross-references tell you explicitly which terms *are* "included" in the proper heading, in that all of the UF terms are effectively folded into the coverage of the boldface term under which they appear. That's why you shouldn't use them—they, unlike the other cross-references, *are* included in the uniform heading. The other cross-references (BT, RT, and NT) tell you explicitly what is *not* covered by the boldface heading. This is the kind of important information that semantic webs cannot provide; with them, you can never be sure of what linkages or inclusions among terms are being made—or not made.

The third point is that the NT cross-references are by far the most important ones to pursue. They are usually the specific entry terms that you need to start with. And they may lead to other, even more specific terms. Thus, within the *LCSH* list, **Divorce** does not provide a direct NT reference to **Children of divorced parents**, but it does start a series that leads to it. Specifically, **Divorce** provides an RT reference to **Divorced people**; this heading, in turn, provides an NT reference to **Divorced parents**; and this heading, in turn, provides NT references to both **Children of divorced parents** and **Adult children of divorced parents**. (The former term provides a further RT reference to the heading **Children of single parents**, which may be of comparative interest, once you recognize that it's there. Cross-references, like browse menus, bring to your attention what you don't know how to ask for until you see it.)

Knowledge of the narrower/broader nature of the cross-reference structure can help you to refine or expand your search, sometimes through an extended scale of headings, such as the following:

Descending order

Chordata
>   NT Vertebrates

Vertebrates
>   NT Mammals

Mammals
>   NT Primates

Primates
>   NT Monkeys

Monkeys
>   NT Baboons

Baboons
>   NT Hamadryas baboon

Ascending order

Hamadryas baboon
>   BT Baboons

Baboons
>   BT Monkeys

Monkeys
>   BT Primates

Primates
>   BT Mammals

Mammals
>   BT Vertebrates

Vertebrates
>   BT Chordata

Note that broader and narrower labels are always relative to other terms. For example, while Dreams, on the face of it, is a rather general term (certainly in relation to Children's dreams), it is nevertheless a narrower term itself in relation to Subconsciousness or Visions. BT and NT designations are thus not absolute labels. A heading that is BT or broader in relation to narrower terms below can simultaneously be an NT or narrower heading in relation to broader headings above it. No matter where you enter the hierarchical sequence, however, just remember to move in the direction of the tightest-fit headings for whatever topic you ultimately have in mind.

This, then, is the first way to find the right subject headings: look in the *LCSH* list (either PDF or "red books") and use the cross-reference codes, paying particular attention to the NT (Narrower Term) cross-references.

Figure 2.2 Initial search screen of catalog.loc.gov with arrow pointing to **"Browse."**

Beyond the *LCSH* PDF display of cross-references, you can also use the LC OPAC itself (catalog.loc.gov) to show you the necessary Narrower Term cross-reference displays. To use the *LCSH* list within the catalog you need to click on the "Browse" option that appears immediately to the right of the blank search box (see Figure 2.2).

This will produce a new screen with a drop-down arrow next to the default "Titles beginning with" line. Click on that arrow for the two options:

SUBJECTS beginning with
SUBJECTS containing

The "beginning with" option is a "left-anchored" search mode; this means that whatever terms you type in will be read in the order you type them, left to right. The advantage of this option is that you need to type in only the first word in any subject-heading string in order to see all of its subdivisions. For example, if you enter "Capital punishment" alone you will immediately be given a list of associated Narrower Terms (e.g., Death row, Hanging and all subdivisions of the heading).

The "containing" option will find all of the terms you have typed in, within any subject strings, no matter what the order in which you have typed them. I'll return to this below.

Either of these SUBJECT search options will automatically show you any Narrower Term cross-references attached to whatever terms you've asked for.

Both versions will also provide "See" cross-references from terms that are not used to the ones that are acceptable.

A significant difference between the OPAC (catalog.loc.gov) links to the cross-references and the PDF version of the *LCSH* list (www.loc.gov/aba/publications/FreeLCSH/freelcsh.html) is that the OPAC displays will not show you Broader Terms or Related Terms, whereas the PDF version will. Thus, in the OPAC you could track the descending order from **Chordata** (above) but not the ascending order from **Hamadryas baboon**. Still, in most cases the Narrower Terms are the ones most needed for effective searches.

The online catalog at the Library of Congress is a local variation of the Voyager Integrated Library System produced by ExLibris. (www.exlibrisgroup.com). The LC variation is preferable to most other online catalogs because the others have often eliminated all of the "See" cross-references that get you from the keywords you think of to the better *LCSH* headings and have also eliminated the browse displays that are needed to show both the additional NT cross-references and the menus of subdivided headings (as with **English language—Dialects**, above; or **Yugoslavia**, below). Without these cross-references and browse menus, the *LCSH* system does not work.

Two examples will illustrate their importance. (You should be online at catalog.loc.gov to follow this.) First, if you click on "Browse," select either of the SUBJECTS options, and then type in "death penalty"—which is not the approved *LCSH* heading—you will immediately get a cross-reference, "*See:* **Capital punishment**." Following that link will not only show you the many more records under the proper category term, but will also provide you with an array of cross references to even more *Narrower Terms* (**Crucifixion, Death row, Discrimination in capital punishment**, etc.) *and* an extensive browse menu of hundreds of *narrower subdivisions* of the initial topic (e.g., **Capital punishment—Biblical teaching, —Bibliography, —[scores of country subdivisions],—Encyclopedias,—History,—Moral and ethical aspects,—Religious aspects, —Public opinion**, etc.). The many country subdivisions are not recorded in the separate *LCSH* PDF list (or in the red books printed version).

Equally important, this browse menu will show you all of these subdivisions in a single list, enabling you to recognize all of the narrower options relevant to your interest in one visual roster, without endless clicking back and forth among entirely separate facet lists. (The full list will be easier to look through quickly if you change the "Records per page" box on the Browse screen from the default 25 to 100.)

In other words, in a faceted catalog display you would not be able to see the full string **Capital punishment—United States—History—20th century—Case studies** with its several terms all linked together; a faceted catalog separates the geographic, topical, chronological, and form subdivisions into separate silos, requiring multiple clicks if you wish to view each type, with still further complications if you wish to combine them. This is what I mean when I say that such catalogs "disassemble the watch mechanism": it doesn't do you any good if you can "combine the elements in any way *you* want" if they are no longer meshed and geared *with each other*. You will never be able to combine them as skillfully as the watchmaker (read: professional cataloger) assembled them, especially when facetization has destroyed the entire cross-reference network. Or again, you might consider a single-list browse menu as an overview map—you don't want to have to look at four separate maps when all the overlapping data can be displayed on one.

In summary: the *non*facetization of browse menus in LC's online catalog is one of the major features that make it so outstanding; the other is the inclusion of the cross-references themselves, including especially the crucial *See* and *Narrower Term* references. That's why you may want to start with it, even before looking at your local catalog.

A second example from the LC OPAC: if you choose the initial "LC Online Catalog Quick Search"—the default "blank search box" option—and type the name of the late Libyan dictator Moammar Gaddafi *as* "Gaddafi" (the spelling used by, among other sources, the *Washington Post*), you will get only a very few records. However, if you choose Browse and then either of the SUBJECTS options and type in the same name form, you will get a cross-reference to "*See:* Qaddafi, Muammar." The subsequent display will lead you not only to almost 200 records but also to a browse menu spelling out various narrower aspects of the books written on this individual (e.g., **Qaddafi, Muammar—Assassination attempts, —Interviews, —Political and social views, —Religion, —Views on women**, etc.) A faceted catalog will not give you the crucial cross-reference to begin with, or the browse menu—so if you have typed in the wrong term to start with, all you can do is "progressively limit" that wrong initial set, rather than be directed to the right set.

2. Look for narrower terms that are alphabetically adjacent to your starting-point term in the *LCSH* list. Not all narrower headings in the *LCSH* list receive explicit NT cross-references pointing to them. In Figure 2.3, for example, note that the NT references under the general term **African Americans** do not include any other headings that start with the phrase "African American(s)"; and yet there are

African American wood-carving
(May subd Geog)
  UF Afro-American wood-carving
      [Former heading]
      Wood-carving, African American
  BT African American decorative arts
      Wood-carving—United States
African American wrestlers
(May subd Geog)
  UF Wrestlers, African American
  BT Wrestlers—United States
African American young adults
(May subd Geog)
  UF Afro-American young adults
      [Former heading]
      Young adults, African American
  BT Young adults—United States
African American young men
(May subd Geog)
  UF Afro-American young men
      [Former heading]
      Young men, African American
  BT Young men—United States
African American young women
(May Subd Geog)
  UF Young women, African American
  BT Young women—United States
African American youth *(May Subd Geog)*
  UF Afro-American youth
      [Former heading]
      Negro youth
      [Former heading]
      Youth, African American
  BT Youth—United States
  NT Church work with African American
      youth
African American yuppies *(May Subd Geog)*
  UF Afro-American yuppies
      [Former heading]
      Buppies
      Yuppies, African American
  BT Yuppies—United States
African American yuppies in motion pictures
(Not Subd Geog)
  UF Afro-American yuppies in motion
      pictures
      [Former heading]
  BT Motion Pictures
African American *(May Subd Geog)*
  [E184.5-E185.98]
      Here are entered works on citizens of the United
  States of black African descent. Works on blacks who
  temporarily reside in the United States, such as aliens,
  students form abroad, etc., are entered under Blacks—
  United States. Works on blacks outside the United
  Sates are entered under Blacks—[places].
      UF African American—United States
          Afro-Americans
          [Former heading]
          Black Americans
          Colored people (United States)
          Negroes
          [Former heading]
      BT Africans—United States
          Ethnology—United States
      RT Blacks—United States
      SA *subdivision* African Americans *under*
          individual wars, e.g. World War,
          1939-1945—African Americans; *and*
          headings beginning with African
          American
      NT Africa—Civilization—African
          American influences
          Asia—Civilization—African American
          influences
          Associations, institution, etc.—African
          American membership
          Church work with African Americans
          Middle class African Americans

Figure 2.3 Display from *LCSH* red books of terms alphabetically adjacent to "African Americans" from "African American wood carving travelers" to NTs under African American.

more than a dozen pages of narrower terms that are alphabetically adjacent to the general heading.

Thus, preceding the general heading **African Americans** are entries such as the following:

African American actors
African American book collectors
African American capitalists and financiers
African American law teachers
African American men in popular culture
African American quiltmakers
African American teenage girls
African American whalers
African American women surgeons

Other alphabetically adjacent narrower terms follow the general heading, among them:

African Americans and mass media
African Americans in advertising
African Americans in literature
African Americans in motion pictures
African Americans in the motion picture industry
African Americans on postage stamps
African Americans with disabilities

As with the formal NT cross-references, none of these alphabetically adjacent narrower terms is "included" in the general heading **African Americans**; in the library catalog, each must be searched directly. In the current PDF edition of *Library of Congress Subject Headings* there are 13 pages of phrases starting with **African American(s)**.

Narrower term entries do not receive formal NT linkages when they are already alphabetically adjacent to the more general terms to which they would otherwise be NT-linked. As a practical matter for researchers, this means you have two places to look for the more specific terms; the cross-reference structure alone is insufficient to alert you to all of them.

It is possible to see the full list of alphabetically adjacent terms in an online OPAC browse display; but sometimes it's just easier and faster to look at the PDF *LCSH* list. On a PDF page your eye can scan laterally and diagonally, not just vertically, and can skim three columns of terms at once. Further, the displays in this list will not be cluttered with hundreds of geographic subdivisions—all of which show up in the online browse displays within the OPAC itself.

3. Within the online library catalog itself, look for "subject tracings" on relevant records that are retrieved by keyword, title, or author searches.

Sometimes a good starting point can be secured in an online catalog simply by finding one good title. To return to a previous example, a researcher looking for information on the Cockney dialect started by doing a simple keyword search for "Cockney"; this led to a list of titles that included *Cockney Dialect and Slang*, amid many other irrelevant (mainly fiction) hits (see Figure 2.4).

Cockney dialect and slang

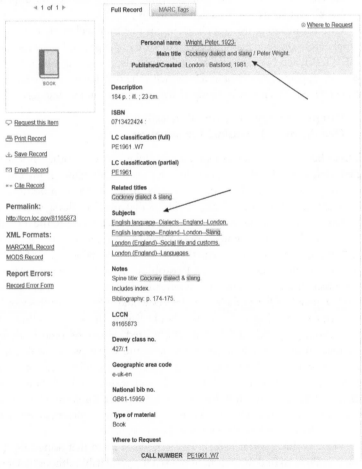

Figure 2.4 Online catalog display of record for *Cockney Dialect and Slang*, with arrows pointing to title and to its subject headings.

In looking at the display of the catalog record for the one relevant *title* he'd found, he could then discover on it the subject headings that the catalogers had added; in this case, again, the best heading was **English language—Dialects—England—London**. Clicking on in the proper category term then led him to dozens of other relevant titles, most of which lack the keyword "Cockney."

This, then, is the third way to find the right subject headings for your topic: find any good record at all, by keyword, title, or author searching, and then look at what is called the subject tracing field on the display of the catalog record. (Note that in some online catalogs you may have to deliberately click on a "Full" display of the record; if the default display is "Brief" you won't see the subject tracings.)

One advantage of using such tracings is that they will often, in effect, supply cross-references among terms that are not captured by the formal UF, BT, RT, and NT designations and which also escape alphabetical adjacency displays. For example, a book with the title *Crime and the Occult: How ESP and Parapsychology Help Detection* has two subject tracings:

> **Parapsychology in criminal investigation**
> **Occultism and criminal investigation**

These headings are not cross-reference-linked to each other, nor are they alphabetically adjacent, but their appearance together on the same catalog record effectively alerts researchers to the existence of both.

The main advantage of using tracings is that, in effect, doing so allows you to use any keywords you can think of as cross-references to the formal subject headings. For example, I once helped a grad student writing a dissertation on "the social construction of sexual perversions." The *LCSH* system uses the unheard-of term **Paraphilias** in order to avoid loading the subject heading with negative connotations of perversion or deviancy, but few people if left to their own devices would ever think of this word. Nevertheless, finding a few titles of books having the keywords "sexual perversion(s)" quickly led to this standardized subject heading in their tracings. In other words, if you know how the system works, it doesn't much matter which terms the catalogers use—"Paraphilias" was not even in the first dictionary I consulted to make sure it meant what I thought it meant—because you can still get *from* whatever you think of *to* the right headings, even when the UF, BT, RT, and NT cross-references are not adequate by themselves, through the use of tracings.

There is also a caveat here, however. Keep in mind that using subject tracings alone to find the best headings is not a good habit, although many academics fall into this rut. The problem is that the keyword searches most people start with are usually too broad. If, for example, a student interested in the effects of divorce on children simply types in the keyword "Divorce," then the tracings on all of the retrieved records will themselves be at the wrong level of generality. Similarly, if a researcher interested in blue crabs simply types in "Crabs," he will get hundreds of records whose subject tracings will themselves be at the wrong level of generality. They will all be valid *LCSH* terms—but they will also be the wrong terms, at the wrong levels of specificity, for the desired topic. It is thus bad practice to rely exclusively on subject tracings to find the right headings—if the keywords with which you start your search are not themselves accurate enough, then the tracings they lead to will also be skewed.

4. Within the online library catalog, use the left-anchored browse displays of subdivisions under a topic (via the "SUBJECTS beginning with" option in the LC OPAC using the *Browse* link) and be sure to look at the full array.

The fourth way to find the right subject term(s) for your topic is to look through the arrays of *subdivisions* that show up under appropriate headings in the catalog. This has been touched on above in the **Capital punishment** and **Qaddafi** examples, but needs more unpacking. Again, I will use the LC online catalog at catalog.loc.gov as the model of what a good catalog should do.

For example, one researcher interested in the history of Yugoslavia asked for help at the reference desk because, on his own, he'd simply done a Boolean combination of the keywords "Yugoslavia" and "history" and had been overwhelmed with way too many irrelevant records. The solution to this problem was the use of the online catalog's *browse displays*. When using the Browse option on the catalog.loc.gov search page, you can then select from its drop-down menu the line saying "SUBJECTS beginning with." If you then type in the single term **Yugoslavia**, a browse display of many screens' length will automatically appear. This list includes headings such as these:

Yugoslavia—Antiquities
Yugoslavia—Antiquities—Bibliography
Yugoslavia—Antiquities—Maps
Yugoslavia—Armed Forces—History
Yugoslavia—Bibliography
Yugoslavia—Biography
Yugoslavia—Biography—Dictionaries
Yugoslavia—Boundaries

Yugoslavia—Civilization
Yugoslavia—Civilization—Bibliography
Yugoslavia—Commerce—History
Yugoslavia—Commerce—Italy
Yugoslavia—Commercial treaties
Yugoslavia—Constitution
Yugoslavia—Cultural policy
Yugoslavia—Description and travel
Yugoslavia—Description and travel—Bibliography
Yugoslavia—Description and travel—Early works to 1800
Yugoslavia—Economic conditions
Yugoslavia—Encyclopedias
Yugoslavia—Ethnic relations
Yugoslavia—Foreign economic relations
Yugoslavia—Foreign relations—Great Britain
Yugoslavia—Foreign relations—Soviet Union
Yugoslavia—Foreign relations—United States
Yugoslavia—Geography—Bibliography
Yugoslavia—History—1992–2003
    See also: Yugoslav War, 1991–1995
Yugoslavia—History—Bibliography
Yugoslavia—History—Chronology
Yugoslavia—History—Dictionaries
Yugoslavia—History, Military
Yugoslavia—History—Sources—Bibliography
Yugoslavia—In literature
Yugoslavia—In mass media
Yugoslavia—Intellectual life
Yugoslavia—Kings and rulers—Biography
Yugoslavia—Maps
Yugoslavia—Pictorial works
Yugoslavia—Politics and government [with period subdivisions]
Yugoslavia—Relations—India
Yugoslavia—Relations—United States
Yugoslavia—Rural conditions
Yugoslavia—Social conditions
Yugoslavia—Social life and customs
Yugoslavia—Social policies
Yugoslavia—Statistics
Yugoslavia—Strategic aspects
Yugoslavia—Yearbooks

These headings provide only a sample of the full list. The researcher, in this case, was delighted: he could immediately see that, as a historian, he had many more options relevant to his interest than he had realized. He was particularly excited by many further subdivisions under **Antiquities** (not all listed above); these records were missed entirely by his keyword search using "history."

This wonderful overview mapping of options would also be missed altogether if the searcher simply types "Yugoslavia" and "history" in massive full text databases such as Google Books, hathitrust.org, or Digital Public Library of America (http://dp.la). Their Web softwares cannot display overview browse menus of subjects with subdivisions.

I cannot recommend this too strongly: use your library catalog's browse displays (or the LC catalog's if your local OPAC lacks this feature). When there are multiple screens of subdivisions, take the time to look through all of them. You will usually be able to spot important aspects of your topic that otherwise you would never have thought of—and then narrow your selection to only those aspects. This technique is almost tailor-made to solve the frequent problem of getting too much junk via keyword searches at excessively granular levels.

The bad news here, again, is that faceted catalogs that "de-couple the strings" into separate lists of topic, time, geographic, and form facets thereby destroy the principle of specific entry—e.g., having to combine the separate facets **Violence** AND **Women** produces a general retrieval that is very different from that found under the more specific *LCSH* string **Violence in women**. Similarly, finding **Afghanistan—Defenses—History—20th Century—Sources** all in one string, within a browse menu, is a lot easier than having to combine **Afghanistan** AND **History** and then having to sort through those results to find the additional topical, chronological, and form aspects that *together* hit the nail on the head. Most people won't take such extra steps.

The larger a library's holdings, the more researchers must rely on menu listings that enable them to simply recognize relevant options. There are three such menus you need to look for:

1. Cross-references, especially to *See* [or USE], NT, and RT terms
2. Alphabetically adjacent narrower or related subject headings (in either the PDF *LCSH* list or in online OPAC browse displays, as in the **African American(s)** example above)
3. Browse menus of narrowing *subdivisions* of headings that (should) appear automatically in OPAC subject searches

A great deal of intellectual time and effort by catalogers goes into the creation of these menus; without them, you simply have to guess which terms to use; and, as in this **Yugoslavia** example, no one will be able to think up beforehand even a fraction of the relevant topics that could readily be of use.

DIGRESSION: PRECOORDINATION AND POSTCOORDINATION

Inexperienced students of library science will sometimes say, "Libraries could save a lot of money if we simplify cataloging by eliminating multielement strings and simply record each element separately, because the computer software can combine the separate elements (or facets) into the same results." This is the facetization problem discussed above, but there's more to it. While it is true that the computer could indeed combine **Yugoslavia** AND **Antiquities** as separate terms, or **Yugoslavia** AND **Bibliography**, the real problem lies with the researchers themselves—the human beings who use the computers. *They* cannot combine the two elements when they are separate (rather than linked in a string of terms that shows up automatically in a browse display) unless it occurs to them in advance that **Antiquities** and **Bibliography** are indeed viable options. Real people cannot do this without the help of menu displays that show them the combinations they cannot anticipate.

When catalogers have taken the trouble to create linked strings, it is known as "precoordination" of terms; when the terms appear only as separate elements on the catalog record (or in a thesaurus) and have to be combined afterward by computer manipulations, it is known as "postcoordination." (Thus, **Philosophy—History** is a precoordinated string; **Philosophy** AND **History** would be a postcoordinate combination of individual subject facets.) The important point is that precoordinated strings of terms offer major advantages that cannot be matched in a postcoordinate system. One is that precoordinated terms provide greater clarity of meaning and avoid retrievals of irrelevancies. A postcoordinate combination of **Philosophy** AND **History** will bring up not just **Philosophy—History** but also **History—Philosophy**. **Women in advertising** is not the same as **Women** AND **Advertising**. **Women in communication** is different from **Women—Communication**, and both of these precoordinated strings avoid the many irrelevancies that would be retrieved by **Women** AND **Communication**.

Also, a precoordinate system enables you to recognize, in browse displays, multiple important aspects of a topic that you could never think up beforehand. I was once asked, "How would the ancient Greeks have transcribed animal sounds?" I found a Greek dictionary that provided the information only because I could recognize a likely heading within a browse display of subdivisions under **Greek language**:

Greek language—Noun
Greek language—Noun phrase
Greek language—Number
Greek language—Numerals
Greek language—Obscene words
Greek language—Onomatopoeic words
Greek language—Optative
Greek language—Participle
Greek language—Passive voice

It would never have occurred to me in a million years to do a (postcoordinate) combination of the separate facets **Greek language** AND **Onomatopoeic words** (or just Greek AND onomatopoeic) if left to my own guesswork, but the browse menu of precoordinated strings enabled me to spot that option when I did not know how to ask for it.

This example illustrates why it is so very important to look systematically at any and all precoordinated subdivisions that appear in the library catalog. Even if there are many screens of them, skim through them all. This insight is something that took years to crystallize for me, and I would have been a much better researcher if I'd caught on to it sooner. It is not immediately obvious that you should look at the whole roster, and so most researchers just don't do it. But I have found through experience that doing this works so well, and in such surprising ways, and in so many instances, that the technique of looking through all of the subdivision strings of a topic is a search technique that you should make use of consciously and deliberately. The provision of these browse menus in OPAC displays is one of the major advances in library science in recent decades; it solves real problems that are otherwise simply intractable in relevance-ranking keyword search systems.

Some of the many subdivisions that are possible—and that, as a reference librarian, I've found most useful to look out for—are these:

[LC Subject Heading]—Amateurs' manuals
      —Attitudes
      —Antiquities

—Bibliography
—Bio-bibliography
—Case studies
—Civilization
—Collections
—Commerce
—Comparative studies
—Correspondence
—Costume
—Criticism and interpretation
—Cross-cultural studies
—Description and travel
—Diaries
—Dictionaries
—Directories
—Early works to 1800
—Economic aspects
—Economic conditions
—Encyclopedias
—Environmental aspects
—Foreign economic relations
—Foreign public opinion
—Foreign relations
—Great Britain [or other country sub-
   divisions]
—Guidebooks
—Handbooks, manuals, etc.
—Health aspects
—History
—History—Bibliography
—History—Sources [for compilations
   of primary sources]
—Illustrations
—Influence
—Interviews
—Law and legislation
—Legal status
—Management
—Maps
—Military relations
—Moral and ethical aspects

—**Personal narratives**
—**Physiological aspects**
—**Pictorial works**
—**Problems, exercises**
—**Psychological aspects**
—**Public opinion**
—**Quotations**
—**Rating of**
—**Relations**
—**Sex differences**
—**Social aspects**
—**Social life and customs**
—**Sources** [primary sources]
—**Statistics**
—**Study and teaching**
—**United States**
—**United States—Bibliography**
—**United States—History**
—**Views on** [topic]
—**Vocational guidance**

Obviously not all of these subdivisions will appear under any one heading, but these are among the most important ones you should be on the lookout for. Few people can remember such a list, which makes a single, simple recognition menu so crucial.

If you have a basic familiarity with the more important options, you can then look for them more deliberately. You will be a better searcher if you "get the feel" of which subdivisions you can expect to find. They are frequently overlooked in library catalogs because researchers are not taught their importance and because browse lists may sometimes be lengthy. (In faceted catalogs they won't even be in one list; they will be segregated into entirely different geographic, topical, chronological, and form "silos.") In using an OPAC that does have a single list of subdivisions under a heading, however, do look through the entire list. You will be able to spot the important subdivisions, such as those above, even when you're not specifically looking for them.

Remember, too, that no matter how much we all may want simplicity in searching ("a single search box"), the reality is that the world's books on any substantive topic are themselves immensely variegated both in their own terminologies and in their relationships to other topics. This real complexity cannot be wished away, and any retrieval system that has to deal with a highly variegated literature must itself entail some complexity to map it out. A catalog for a small public library may not need complicated search features, but a research library does.

An analogy to airplane controls may be useful: the cockpit dials and switches for a small Cessna airplane will be very simple compared to those in a huge C-5 Galaxy transport. Forcing a C-5's pilot to work with only a Cessna's configuration would mean he could never fly his more sophisticated plane—he could only, at best, taxi it along the ground, which would defeat the purpose of having a heavy-lift, capacious cargo airplane to begin with. No matter how much the pilot might want a simple cockpit configuration, he would not be able to accomplish his mission with a too-simple configuration. The situation is similar with research libraries' online catalogs: if they provide only a Google-type "single search box," or a single box followed only by facet limitations, they will thereby eliminate both cross-references and browse menus and thereby *also* vitiate uniform heading, scope-match specificity, and specific entry. The entire *LCSH* system falls apart without precoordinated strings; when the watch is disassembled into its individual component parts, it no longer works. OPACs without the complexity of browse-menu–displayed precoordinated strings and cross-references can no longer do the "heavy lifting" that scholarship requires. They cannot show you in any systematic way "what the library has" in its cataloged collection—they will give you at best only fragments of the total holdings—"something quickly" rather than "the shape of the elephant." And it doesn't really matter if surveys say that students want simple Google-type search boxes—the surveys don't stick around to notice how very dissatisfied the researchers are with the results they actually get, nor do they record how grateful the students are when librarians show them the much better alternatives.

5. Use the "SUBJECTS containing" Browse option to create menus of *any* LCSH subject headings containing the words you want to search, no matter what the order of the words within the headings.

The browse displays of headings with subdivisions, just discussed in section 4, appear as a result of "left-anchored" searches—that is, if you simply type in **African Americans** or **Greek language** or **Yugoslavia** and nothing else into the "SUBJECTS beginning with" search box, the OPAC will automatically bring to your attention through a browse menu all of their subdividing aspects that you didn't know how to ask for. If you get the *first* word or words in the string correct, in other words—the left-most term(s)—then the computer display will simply show you whatever comes to the right of that word (or words) without your having to type in the full length of any of the precoordinated strings.

A second way to create browse menus is also available and, for some complex inquiries, is much more useful. In the online LC catalog (catalog. loc.gov) it is accessible through the Browse option and its drop-down menu line "SUBJECTS containing." Choosing this avenue of access allows you to type in individual words, *in any order*, appearing within any *LCSH* headings. In other words, you don't need to get the first word in the string right, which you need to do for the left-anchored searches.

For example, not all of the books on **Afghanistan** are catalogued with *LCSH* headings that place **Afghanistan** at the beginning of the string. There are hundreds of other valid headings in which the name of the country is itself a geographic subdivision of other topics, whose subject strings have entirely different and unpredictable initial terms, such as:

Abandoned children—Afghanistan
Actors—Afghanistan
Administrative law—Afghanistan

★   ★   ★

Buddhist antiquities—Afghanistan
Cabinet officers—Afghanistan—Biography

★   ★   ★

Muslim women—Afghanistan
Muslim women—Education—Afghanistan—Bibliography
Rural women—Afghanistan—Social conditions
Sex discrimination against women—Afghanistan
Single women—Legal status, laws, etc.—Afghanistan
Women—Afghanistan—Interviews
Women—Afghanistan—Social conditions
Women and war—Afghanistan
Women in development—Afghanistan—Case studies
Women in Islam—Afghanistan
Women in politics—Afghanistan
Women journalists—Afghanistan
Women—Legal status, laws, etc.—Afghanistan
Women refugees—Afghanistan—Social conditions
Women—Services for—Afghanistan—Directories
Young women—Afghanistan—Biography

If you have only a left-anchored "SUBJECTS beginning with" search capability (point 4 above), you cannot call up browse menus that will show you all of the other strings relevant to the topic **Afghanistan** that start with a different first word at the left. "SUBJECTS containing" solves this problem.

For another example, I once helped a graduate student who was doing a dissertation on "how the several Arab–Israeli conflicts over the years have been portrayed in fiction." Using the "SUBJECTS containing" option I could type in:

> Israel? AND (Arab? OR Palestin?) AND (Fiction or Literature)
> NOT Juvenile

(Capital letters are not necessary; the "?" is the symbol for truncation in the LC OPAC. Thus "Israel?" retrieves not just "Israel" but also "Israeli" or "Israelis." I added the specification "NOT Juvenile" because the students did not want to consider books written for children.) The result was an extremely useful browse display, including such headings as the following:

> **Arab-Israeli conflict—1973–1993—Fiction**
> **Arab-Israeli conflict—1993—Fiction**
> **Arab-Israeli conflict—Fiction**
> **Arab-Israeli conflict—Literature and the conflict**
> **Israel-Arab Border Conflicts—1949—Egypt—Fiction**
> **Israel-Arab Border Conflicts, 1949—Fiction**
> **Israel-Arab conflicts in literature**
> **Israel-Arab War, 1948–1949—Fiction**
> **Israel-Arab War, 1967—Fiction**
> **Israel-Arab War, 1967—Literature and the war**
> **Israel-Arab War, 1973—Fiction**
> **Israel-Arab War, 1973—Literature and the war**
> **Israeli fiction—Translations into Arabic—History and criticism**
> **Israeli literature (Arabic)**
> **Judeo-Arabic literature—Israel—History and criticism**
> **Palestinian Arabs—Israel—Fiction**

These various headings are not linked to each other by cross-references. Nor are they alphabetically adjacent to each other. Nor would any single left-anchored browse display bring them all up, unless you knew in advance the *first* word in each different string (**Arab** or **Israel** or **Israeli** or **Judeo** or **Palestinian**).

One more example: a researcher interested in "terrorism in India" was overwhelmed with hits in Google Web (over 3 million), Google Books (126,000), and Google Scholar (1,060), and he wanted to know if there was a better way to get an overview. For the book literature, the problem was solved by a "SUBJECTS containing" search for the combination:

India AND **Terroris?**

This search produced a browse menu having (among many other headings) the following:

Domestic terrorism—India—Assam
India. Prevention of Terrorism Act, 2002
International trade—Effect of terrorism on—India
Mumbai terrorist attacks. Bombay. India. 2008
Nuclear terrorism—India
September 11 Terrorist Attacks. 2001—Economic aspects—India—Congresses
State-sponsored terrorism—India
Terrorism—Economic aspects—India
Terrorism—Government policy—India, Northeastern
Terrorism—India
Terrorism—India—Bombay
Terrorism—India—Jammu and Kashmir
Terrorism—India—Prevention
Terrorism investigation—India—Bombay
Terrorism—Law and legislation—India
Terrorism—Press coverage—India
Terrorism—Prevention—India
Terrorism victims' families—India—Attitudes
Terrorists—India
Terrorists—India—Biography
Terrorists—India—Jammu and Kashmir—Case studies
Terrorists—India—Punjab—Correspondence
Trials (Terrorism)—India
Victims of state-sponsored terrorism—India
Victims of terrorism—India
Victims of terrorism—India—Punjab—Biography
Victims of terrorism—Rehabilitation—India—Jammu and Kashmir—Congresses

This "SUBJECT contains" search option is thus capable of showing you parts of "the elephant"—Indian or otherwise—of the book literature on a topic that remain concealed to the four other ways of finding the right *LCSH* subject headings. In terms of its practical utility for researchers, this too is one of the major advances in library science in recent years. (It frequently gets overlooked, however, because it requires a library's OPAC search system with capabilities different from those of any Web search engine.)

MISCELLANEOUS TIPS ON SUBJECT HEADINGS

A problem that students often have at the beginning of their projects is that of narrowing down their topic to a manageable size. It should now be apparent that are several formal mechanisms in the cataloging system that enable you to do precisely this, and in a systematic manner. They are the same five ways that lead you to the proper specific (rather than general) subject headings for your topic.

A kind of "sixth way" to find the right headings is through computer *combinations* of headings—that is, sometimes there is no single term (or string) that expresses the subject you want, but you can still hit the nail on the head, at a specific scope-match level, by combining two or more separate headings (e.g., **Mexican Americans** AND **Education, bilingual**). Such Boolean combinations will be discussed in Chapter 10.

Here are a few miscellaneous additional tips about using *Library of Congress Subject Headings*:

- The *LCSH* list usually does not list *proper names* as subject headings, but they can still appear as valid search terms within the catalog itself.
- If you are looking for foreign language books on a subject, you still have to use the *English-language subject headings* to find them. For example, I once helped a professor who wanted only Italian books on the city of Venice. He had made the mistake of searching under "Venezia." The proper heading is **Venice (Italy)**; in the Library of Congress catalog it rounds up books in all languages on that subject. The retrieved set, however, could then be limited to only those in the Italian language. It is noteworthy that a large number of the Italian books themselves do not use the word "Venezia" in their titles; for example:

  Il campiello sommerso
  Veneto: itinerari ebraici
  La chiesa del Tintoretto

Le sculture esterne di San Marco
Santi e contadini: lunario della tradizione orale veneta

- The first volume of the printed "red books" *LCSH* list includes a one-page "Table of Pattern Headings" in its Introduction; the same list shows up in the PDF version (again, at www.loc.gov/aba/publications/FreeLCSH/freelcsh.html) within its "Introduction to Library of Congress Subject Headings" section. Not all subdivisions of topics are listed under every heading, but the full range of subdivisions appropriate to certain categories of subjects is indeed listed under "type specimen" headings. Thus, for example, all of the subdivisions that could be appended to any example of "Plants or crops" are spelled out under *one* of them: **Corn**. The subdivisions listed *only* here are then useable under any other such plant or crop. There are a couple dozen such categories listed, with their corresponding headings. These pattern headings are mainly useful to catalogers, but I've had researchers, too, tell me they were useful to browse through.
- The PDF version of the *Library of Congress Subject Headings* also contains a separate list of *Supplementary Vocabularies*, which shows all of the free-floating and genre/form subdivisions available for catalogers to use (of which I provided only a small sample above). While this may be too much for most general researchers to absorb, library science students who wish to become either catalogers or reference librarians should study these lists carefully. They are important parts of the cockpit panel of the C-5 Galaxy version of the subject heading system.

The subject heading—or "controlled vocabulary"—searches discussed in this chapter are only one of several methods of gaining access to information. (Another related method of vocabulary control is provided by *descriptors*; these are like subject headings, but are used mainly in databases indexing journal articles. They will be discussed in Chapter 4.) Searches using *Library of Congress Subject Headings* will not work all the time for all subjects; they provide one way of gaining access to some relevant literature, primarily books. They will enable you to see much of "the shape" of the literature for that kind of material within a given library's collection—but not necessarily, and certainly not completely, journal articles, doctoral dissertations, manuscripts, websites, or many other nonbook formats. For the sake of providing an overview of that even larger "elephant's" parts, the ones that lie in blind spots to *LCSH* searches, let me anticipate a number of points to be discussed in subsequent chapters and mention here that eight alternative methods of searching can be used when no subject heading exists, or when you wish to turn up sources in addition to those found via controlled vocabulary searches:

- General and focused browsing (Chapter 3)
- Keyword searching (Chapter 5)
- Citation searching (Chapter 6)
- Related record searching (Chapter 7)
- Using published bibliographies (Chapter 9)
- Combining and limiting sets (Chapter 10)
- Using people sources (Chapter 12)
- Type of literature searching (Chapter 15)

Each of these approaches—like that of searching with controlled vocabulary terms—has its own advantages and disadvantages. Collectively viewed, each has strengths that compensate for weaknesses in the other search techniques. An awareness of this basic structure of options, with only these few distinct methods of searching, can have a profound effect in substantially increasing the efficiency of your research, no matter what subject area you are working in—and regardless of whether you have any prior subject expertise in that area.

CHAPTER 3

General Browsing, Focused Browsing, and Use of Classified Bookstacks

T HE FACT THAT BOOKS IN RESEARCH LIBRARIES ARE USUALLY shelved by subject, rather than by accession numbers (i.e., the order in which the books are received) or by the height of the volumes, gives researchers a major advantage in gaining subject access to their contents—one that, in many cases, cannot be matched by any computer searches, even if the same texts are available in electronic formats. This advantage, however, is nowadays in jeopardy from many library administrators who often assume that the shelving of books by subject is no longer necessary "in a digital age." Much of this view stems from the library profession's difficulty in failing to distinguish between the desirability of providing more content in digital forms, on the one hand, and, on the other, the increasing need to provide multiple avenues of access to that content—avenues beyond the mere typing of guessed-at keywords into a blank search box. Contrary to the many assertions by "single search box" advocates, real researchers have persistent problems in attempting to specify in advance all of the relevant search terms that will produce the retrievals they desire. In the real world, people need not just prior-specification search mechanisms but also avenues of access that enable them to recognize what they don't know how to ask for.

ALTERNATIVE METHODS OF SHELVING BOOK COLLECTIONS

It is indeed possible to shelve books in arrangements other than by the traditional subject categorizations of the Library of Congress or Dewey Decimal Classification systems. A library could, for example, simply arrange its volumes in the order of their acquisition. In this case, catalogers would then have only to assign sequential whole numbers to the books (1, 2, 3, …). Such a system would be capable of storing an infinite number of items, and, as long as the number that appears on the computer record corresponds to the number on the book, readers who find the catalog entry would then be able to locate its corresponding volume on the shelves. The library would save thousands of dollars every year if this scheme were used, since it would require professional catalogers only for describing the books and devising subject headings for the catalog records and not for also creating systematic call numbers with intricate subject relationships to each other. It would especially save money, too, in preventing the need for the redistribution of already-shelved books caused by unanticipated bulges of growth in particular subject classes. In a whole number or "dummy number" system, the only area that needs room for growth is the very end of the sequence. No empty spaces need be left on any shelf but the last one, because no new books would ever be interfiled with those already in place—incoming books would be shelved only at the end of the sequence, simply in the order in which they happen to arrive.

Another possibility is that the library could shelve books strictly according to their height—all 6-inch-tall books together, all 10-inch books together, and so on. If this were done, then the vertical distance between bookshelves could be adjusted precisely so that there would be no wasted space above the volumes cause by height differentials. Given that there are miles of books in any large library, this expedient would enable shelving to be much more space efficient, which would save money and create room for larger collections. Such systems are used routinely by many academic libraries in their remote storage facilities—i.e., the warehouses (usually off-campus) built to hold the overflow books for which there is no longer any space available in the main library buildings themselves. The books in these warehouses are usually placed in boxes, with all books in any one box being of exactly the same height; and the boxes themselves are stored on shelves dozens of yards higher than any that could be reached by unaided human researchers. As long as the number on the computer catalog record for the book is linked both to the barcode on the book itself and to the barcode of the box in which it rests, the actual retrieval from the box can be accomplished by cherry picker mechanisms, either human or robotic.

Either of these shelving schemes would be much less expensive to hard-pressed library budgets than the traditional practice of maintaining books in a subject-classed arrangement. So why is the latter still desirable when cheaper alternatives are available? Why shouldn't compact storage techniques be used not just in offsite warehouses but within the main library buildings themselves? Further, why couldn't massive digitization projects such as Internet Public Library (ipl.org), HathiTrust.org, or Google Books replace rather than merely supplement onsite book collections shelved in classified order? What difference does the method of shelving make to the researchers who have to *use* the books?

PROBLEMS WITH SHELVING BOOKS BY ACCESSION NUMBER OR HEIGHT

A very real problem with books shelved in these configurations is that any (and all) access to them requires skilful prior use of the online public access catalog (OPAC), and the OPAC searches only superficial records representing and "pointing to" the books (which are shelved elsewhere); it does not search the actual book texts themselves. No catalog record *of* a book can contain all of the information *in* the book—the catalog record enables you to see only the subject(s) of the book as a whole (at scope-match level), not its individual pages that contain much more extensive and specific information. Moreover, you must specify the right search terms to begin with—and at that "whole-book" level designated by only a few subject headings—when sometimes you may really need in-depth access to the individual pages of the book(s). (In some cases— not nearly all—you may also be able to search the books' tables of contents transcribed on the catalog records.) Even if the OPAC allows you to search its catalog records in class-number order, that is not at all the same thing as searching the actual books arranged in subject groupings on shelves.

When the storage of the books, by height of volumes or by sequence of acquisition, makes no attempt to shelve books on the same subjects next to each other, then there is no possibility of quickly browsing the *full texts* of related works in close physical proximity. In a height system, if one book on anthropology is 6 inches tall and another is 10 inches, they may be shelved on entirely different floors; in a sequential system, if one book came into the library a year after the other, they may be separated by hundreds of feet of cookbooks, car repair manuals, and Gothic novels.

ENHANCED RECOGNITION CAPABILITY AND FULL-TEXT DEPTH OF ACCESS

One of the major advantages of a classified arrangement of actual books in a research library is that classified shelving enables you to simply recognize relevant works whose titles, keywords, or subject headings you could not think of in advance in using the OPAC. Such shelving allows for—indeed, positively encourages and enables—discovery by serendipity or recognition, and at a full-text (not scope-match or "snippet") level. (I am assuming here that you are fortunate enough to be working in a research library that has open stacks; not all of them do.) The value of such discovery may be incalculable for any given search. One historian of prison labor, for example, found through stacks browsing the only known image of prisoners on a treadmill in the United States. "Neither the book title, nor the call number, nor the author led me to this report," he commented. "Only a hands-on shelf check did it."[1] In a similar manner, I once found an illustration of a slave coffle—a line of shackled slaves being marched under guard—very different from one that is widely reproduced, in a book I noticed next to another volume that I was actually looking for. This illustration proved to be very welcome to a historian writing a book on slavery. The presence of this particular illustration is not indicated by the book's catalog record in the computer, nor does the word "coffle" appear as a searchable keyword in the illustration's caption.

With access to books shelved by subject, you can do focused examination of contiguous, subject-related full texts—that is, you can do deep searches of not just tables of contents and back-of-the book indexes, but maps, charts, tables, illustrations, diagrams, running heads, highlighted sidebars, binding conditions, typographical or color variations for emphasis, bulleted or numbered lists, prefaces, acknowledgments, forewords, footnotes, and bibliographies. You can search individual pages and paragraphs, and even spot the particular words you want within them, all within readily recognizable conceptual contexts.

For example, I once had to answer a letter from a historian seeking information on traveling libraries that circulated among lighthouse keepers at the turn of the twentieth century. These were wooden bookcases, each with a different selection of books, that were rotated among the tenders in order to relieve the boredom and monotony of their isolated lives. I first tried searching the computer catalog of the books at the Library of Congress—with no luck. Even after searching several commercial databases covering journals and dissertations (including the largest commercial index to American history journals) I still found nothing—only, occasionally, the right words ([lighthouse★ OR lighthouse★] AND [book★ OR librar★]) in the wrong contexts.

So I decided to look directly at the books on lighthouses in the library's bookstacks. The major grouping for this topic is at VK1000-1025 ("Lighthouse service"); this area had, by a quick count, 438 volumes on 12 shelves. I rapidly scanned all of this material—literally paging through, quickly, all of the volumes.

I found 15 books that had directly relevant sections—a paragraph here, a half page there, a column elsewhere—containing descriptions of the book collections, reminiscences about them, official reports, anecdotes, and so on. I also found another 7 sources of tangential interest—on reading or studying done in lighthouses, but without mentioning the traveling libraries—and photocopied these, too, for the letter writer. The primary 15 contained a total of about 2,100 words on the traveling libraries, including a partial list of their titles.

Particularly noteworthy is the fact that, of the 15 prime sources, not one mentioned the libraries in its table of contents, and 9 of them (60 percent) did not mention the libraries in their index, either—or did not even have an index to begin with. Equally noteworthy is the fact that 13 of the sources were twentieth-century publications—9 of them published after 1970—and thus still under copyright protection.

Now it is entirely true that a Web search on lighthouse libraries will indeed retrieve much relevant material quickly—but, for the most part, it is not the same material. The bookstacks hold the copyrighted sources whose full texts are not searchable on the Internet.

FOCUSED BROWSING ACCESS VS. OPAC ACCESS: DEPTH VS. RANGE

This information on lighthouse libraries could not have been found even if the books' tables of contents and indexes had been entered into an online catalog. This level of research depth in book collections can be achieved only by focused browsing: inspecting the actual full texts in a systematic fashion, not just looking at any surrogate catalog records in an OPAC, no matter how detailed.

With the classification scheme's arrangement of books, however, the needed information could indeed be found both systematically and easily. Retrieving, via call slips or online requests, 438 books scattered in storage by random accession numbers nowhere near each other would be so time consuming and difficult as to be effectively not possible in the real world in which actual researchers must work.[2] And determining in advance which 15 had the right information from the catalog would also be impossible—the catalog records just do not contain that depth of information. And so a reader who had to guess in advance which 15 of the 438 volumes had the right information would necessarily miss most of what the library actually had to offer—information that is readily retrievable as long as we remember that focused browsing is an alternative search method for doing full text searches, other than using digitized full-text databases.

Note in this case that even searching by class numbers in the catalog is not the equivalent of searching by class area in the actual bookstacks. Even if the OPAC allowed for the construction of a list of the same 438 books, it would still not be possible to determine from that list of superficial catalog records which 15 books contained the needed information buried down at page and paragraph level. The use of subject-classified arrangements of full texts—printed books arranged in subject groupings on bookshelves in libraries with walls—thus provides a depth of subject access that cannot be matched by any computer searches of mere surrogate catalog records. "Depth" refers to the parts of the books that are searchable on the shelves but not in the OPAC: not just tables of contents and indexes, but maps, charts, tables, individual paragraphs, etc.

Note further that there was also a trade-off: in browsing only the VK1000-1025 area I was missing other classes on other aspects of lighthouses, e.g., TC375-379 (lighthouse technology), KF26-27 (multiple congressional oversight hearings), and Z6839 (subject bibliographies). The range of these aspects, however, was discoverable through use of the *LCSH* heading **Lighthouses** in the online catalog. While the classified shelving arrangement provides full-text *depth* of access to books within particular classes, it lacks the uniform headings, cross-references, and browse menus of the OPAC that show the *range* of all of the relevant classes.

FOCUSED BROWSING ACCESS VS. KEYWORD ACCESS IN FULL-TEXT WEBSITES AND DATABASES: RECOGNITION VS. PRIOR SPECIFICATION

While focused browsing of full texts in classified order on bookshelves can thus be contrasted to OPAC searching of the books' catalog records— i.e., depth vs. range—it can also be contrasted to keyword searching in those many databases or websites (e.g., Google Books, Hathi Trust, many commercial databases) that do indeed contain full texts. There is another major trade-off here, too: recognition access (in bookstacks) vs. prior-specification access (in full-text sources online).

For example, I once received a rush request from a librarian at the Supreme Court library that one of the justices needed to confirm the statement that "the United States occupation zone in Germany after World War II encompassed 5,700 square miles and a population of over 18 million people." I first tried the subscription databases *America: History and Life* and *Historical Abstracts* (two of the best sources covering history journals) in hopes that someone had written something concise on the occupation zone, but the results were much more diffuse than I wanted. So I tried our online book catalog. Just as an initial stab I did a keyword search of "occupation" and "zone" and "Germany," with a limit on the search that I wanted only records published between 1945 and 1947. Within the 145 records that came up, I spotted one pretty quickly that had a formally established corporate name on it: **Germany (Territory under Allied occupation, 1945–1955: U.S. Zone). Office of Military Government**. When I searched on this standardized term I found a very focused pool of records. There were 18 hits; one of them had the word "population" in its title.

Since this was a rush request, I immediately went back to the book-stacks to look at this one pamphlet. This initial item did indeed have population figures for the American zone in 1947, but no square mileage figure. Right next to it, however, was another report that had a 1946 population figure—17,174,367—close to the "18 million" in the original inquiry, but obviously being a very different keyword character string. And it also had an area figure for the American zone—but in square kilometers, not in square miles. That was no problem, as the figure could easily be converted. The significant point, here, is that the chart providing the area figure did not say "square kilometers" written out—it said simply "sq. km."

The equally significant point is that this particular pamphlet is indeed digitized in Google Books, but, even so, I could not find it there. If you search Google Books for the three words with which I started my own search in LC's online catalog, namely "occupation" and "zone" and "Germany," and limit to publications between 1945 and 1947, you got (at the time) 653 hits; the exact pamphlet I found in the stacks showed up as the 307th item in the Google "relevance-ranked" display. (I could find it in the list only because, at that point, I already knew the precise source I was looking for, and I simply scrolled through the whole list until I spotted it. The number and the ordinal position are those as of March 2008; Google displays, however, change not only from one day to the next but also, frequently, from one minute to the next. A search in Google Books for the same three keywords in July of 2013 produced 889,000 hits.)

I cannot emphasize the following point enough, because it is so strongly counterintuitive to theorists who do not actually have to do such searches or find such information themselves, and yet it is nonetheless true: you cannot "progressively refine" such a set of 653 items (let alone 889,000) down to the right pamphlet by simply typing in extra keywords. Why not? Because the terms "18 million" or "square miles"— the keywords contained in the justice's question—are not the words that actually appear in the table between paragraphs 2 and 3, on page 6 of that pamphlet; nor do they appear anywhere else. In order to do "progressive refinement" you have to know in advance which exact words will produce the refinement you seek, and it is precisely that knowledge that we lack when we are moving around in unfamiliar subject areas. In fact, I could not get the relevant table to show up at all, even in snippet form, even after I had discovered the right keywords (via stacks browsing), in spite of the fact that I could view other snippets from the same pamphlet. The Google software is such that it won't show you *every* snippet containing the words you type in; and the company is playing it safe, legally, in not providing full-text views of post-1922 works, such as this occupation zone pamphlet.

The point is this: even if the Google keyword search software would display every instance of every word asked for, I still would never have known in advance the precise keywords (like "sq. km.") that I needed to type in—I would have typed the phrase "square miles" written out, because it would not have occurred to me to think in terms of kilometers, let alone in terms of abbreviations. (The same point applies not just to Google Books but to any full-text database or website.)

The fact that the pamphlet is digitized therefore does not mean that it is easily accessible online—quite the contrary: it is not findable because Google's keyword search mechanism does not provide adequate access to it.

By using the classified bookstacks, however, I employed *a different search technique for for full-text searching*—a technique that enabled me to recognize what I could not specify in advance in a blank search box. I could find the source I needed because it was physically right next to the one that I started off looking for—and the one I was looking for was itself one of only 18 records, not one of 653. And I could skim both that initial full text—down to the level of its individual tables—and the one right next to it quickly, precisely because they were physically shelved right next to each other, within a limited class—I had only a very small contextual range of materials (less than one shelf) to inspect.

Classified bookstacks thus allow researchers to find through recognition within full texts what they don't know how to ask for: we can look not just at tables of contents (which can sometimes be included in OPAC records), but also maps, charts, tables, illustrations, etc., most of which cannot be digitized at all (for copyright reasons). Moreover, we can examine all these features within limited physical shelf areas—we won't have hundreds of thousands of electronic records to wade through, most of which have relevant words in irrelevant contexts. Such quick and focused browsing provides deep access via recognition in ways that digitized libraries of the very same texts do not.

Another example: an editor compiling a handbook of miscellaneous facts on library history needed to identify which book was the first one ever to be printed in French. I tried numerous full-text subscription databases and Internet sites; in the French sources I searched for "premier livre" (first book) combined with "langue française" (French language). After finding only conflicting and incorrect answers, I finally did some focused browsing in the library's bookstacks in the Z103 (Bibliography) shelves. I quickly found a 1927 *Manuel du Bibliophile Français (1470–1920)*, which identified the volume *Reçueil des Histoires de Troyes* (1466)—and this *Manuel* cleared up what had been a major point of confusion: although this was the first book printed in the French language, it was not printed within France itself; it was produced in Cologne, Germany. My point here, however, is that the relevant passage in this bibliography refers to it as "le premier livre dans notre langue" (the first book in our language). In searching full-text databases it never occurred to me to type in "notre langue" rather than "langue française." (The *Manuel* itself, as of this writing, is not digitized in Google Books.)

It is especially noteworthy that any proposed use of Google Books, Digital Public Library of America, or Hathi Trust to replace (rather than supplement) classified bookstacks would entirely segregate foreign language materials into multiple electronic "zones" that could not be searched simultaneously by the specification of English keywords. With classified bookstacks, on the other hand, books in all languages are grouped together by subject in the same physical locales; often an English-speaker (such as me) can simply notice relevant foreign books on a topic simply because they are shelved in the same classification areas as the English works. (I would not have thought of the title word *Bibliophile*, rather than *Bibliographie*, if I'd had to specify that, either, in a blank search box; but I could immediately recognize its relevance when I saw it on the shelf.) Some enthusiasts of Web e-books would thus unwittingly re-create in reality the disastrous consequences mythologized in the Tower of Babel story—scholars relying on such sources alone could not retrieve together the relevant works in multiple languages on their subjects.

SENDING BOOKS OFFSITE "BECAUSE THEY ARE IN GOOGLE BOOKS"

The distinctions discussed above should be of particular concern to Faculty Library Committees, as they may be the only ones in a position to stop library administrators from sending too many books offsite "because they are in Google Books."

Both "depth" access and "recognition" access come into play simultaneously in the need to maintain browsable book stacks. Focused browsing of subject-grouped books enables researchers to find very specific information only accessible at full-text levels that are not present in OPAC records; it enables recognition access to terms or other elements (e.g., illustrations) within those full-text books that cannot be specified in advance in Google-type searches; and it enables those full-text/recognition searches to be done within manageably *limited* ranges of books, rather than within excessively granular sets of thousands of texts retrieved by online keyword searches. It also enables full-text searching to be done (down to individual page levels) even within books—especially those still under copyright protection—that have not been digitized at all.

It is in regard to these concerns that library administrators frequently have "blind spots": since they often don't use libraries for research projects of their own, they don't grasp the need for recognition access of terms at the full-text level provided by browsing. They naïvely assume that if all of the words in a book are searchable in full-text databases, then all of the search terms needed to find those books are also specifiable in advance. They are not. In Google-type keywords searches, highly relevant works are often missed because the best search terms cannot be guessed at, and they are also missed because even specifying the right terms can produce thousands of unwanted "noise" retrievals.

The result is that too many books needed for scholarship get sent off to remote storage warehouses, thereby precluding not only all depth access to nondigitized texts, but also all recognition access to any texts—both those with digital counterparts and those that are not digitized at all.

Although historians, anthropologists, biographers, linguists, and others have frequently experienced the advantages of direct access to classified bookshelves, almost no one bothers to write down the specific examples of the successes it generates. It just takes too much time and too many words (as above!) to explain why it is crucially important when all other methods of searching fail. Most academics themselves cannot articulate the difference between recognition vs. prior specification access, and yet it is the facile dismissal by library administrators of the importance of recognition mechanisms, especially at deep (page, paragraph, sentence) levels, that is especially galling to the researchers who most need it. This dismissal is usually done with the patronizing air that prior-specification keyword retrieval in full-text databases can now "replace" classified shelving, that most physical books (even the copyrighted and nondigitized) can therefore be sent to offsite storage, and that advocacy for retaining a noncomputerized access mechanism to full texts—focused browsing of physical books—*must* be "sentimental" rather than rational. Until recently, scholars could simply assume that no research library administrator would even think of undermining the practice of shelving books by subject. Unfortunately, that assumption is no longer a safe one—the abandonment is being actively promoted by bean counters who overlook the very real trade-offs among the different search techniques for *finding* the beans.

BROWSING IN OTHER CONTEXTS

The larger principles of browsing for information have applications beyond the use of library bookstacks. Another situation, for example, is that of using primary sources in archives or manuscript collections. Primary records are those generated by a particular event, by those who participated in it, or by those who directly witnessed it; and they are usually unpublished. Thus, a researcher interested in World War II propaganda would be interested in such primary sources as copies of leaflets dropped from airplanes, typescript accounts of the flights written by those who planned or flew them, and firsthand accounts of civilians on the ground who found the leaflets. Secondary sources are the later analyses and reports written by nonparticipants, usually in published literature—although a published source can itself be primary if it is written by a participant or a witness or if it directly quotes one. Many collections of primary manuscripts exist on an incredible array of subjects and can be identified through the sources identified in Chapters 13 and 14.

However, such collections are more often than not poorly indexed or not indexed at all and are not arranged by subject. In such cases, researchers must simply browse through the material to see what's there.

Similarly, "focused browsing" might be the term applicable to direct inspection of particular sites or limited physical areas. For example, genealogists may wish to know where, exactly, a certain ancestor is buried in a cemetery, and existing maps of the area may not be detailed or complete enough to show this level of information. Similarly, private investigators looking into an automobile (or other) accident case often need to find eyewitnesses; to do so, they physically go to the site of the accident, preferably at the same time of day as the incident, and knock on doors or talk to those habitually in the area. In such cases, direct examination of the specific site is necessary. The principle is the same, however: if you don't know exactly where the needed information exists, put yourself in a situation or a physical area where it is *likely* to exist and then look around so that you can recognize valuable clues or indicators when you see them.

Some of the major themes of this book are that a variety of search techniques can be used to find information, that each of them always has both advantages and disadvantages, and that no one of them can be counted on to do the entire job of in-depth research. What is required is usually a mixture of approaches so that the various trade-offs can balance and compensate for each other. My observation, however, is that in this age of proliferating Internet resources, the research techniques of general and (especially) focused browsing of printed books on library shelves, for both depth penetration and recognition access, tends to be overlooked by researchers who do not understand the limitations of the Web—in both content and search mechanism capabilities—or of computer databases in general. While it is certainly true that browsing bookstacks is very seldom the *first* search technique to be employed in attacking any research problem, the fact remains that the vast bulk of humanity's memory contained in post-1922 books does not exist digitally in readable forms (beyond "snippet" levels) and probably never will without many decades of delay (for copyright reasons). Further, Internet search mechanisms, which require prior specification of keywords and then merely rank rather than conceptually categorize the results, cannot provide access to much material relevant to a topic in a way that allows for recognition, at full-text levels, of what cannot be specified in advance. Researchers who neglect the direct inspection of the full texts of books arranged in subject groupings on library bookshelves are missing a vast store of information that cannot be retrieved in any other way.

CHAPTER 4

Subject Headings and Descriptors in Databases for Journal Articles

A LIBRARY'S ONLINE PUBLIC ACCESS CATALOG (OPAC) WILL BE useful for identifying books relevant to your topic; it may also cover other formats (maps, photos, manuscripts, etc., or even a few selected websites), but it will not index individual journal, magazine, or newspaper articles. For the latter, there are many hundreds of commercially produced databases to which libraries can simply subscribe without having to duplicate (via their own staff's efforts) the work of indexing hundreds of thousands of individual articles in addition to the books acquired in their local collections. It is true that some libraries provide "discovery" search capabilities, whereby multiple databases (including both the local OPAC and the commercial databases to which the library subscribes) can be searched simultaneously from a single search box.[1] The idea here is, in the currently fashionable terminology, to break down barriers between different "silos" of information so that "everything" can be searched "seamlessly" through one search box.

"Discovery" or federated searching of multiple sources is occasionally quite useful, as I will show later, but it also creates as many problems as it solves. This is because many important trade-offs among the different databases are concealed when only one search approach is provided to all of them at once. The peculiar vocabularies (descriptors) and "limit" features of individual files are usually the very features that make the individual databases most useful, but these are essentially buried or lost entirely in cross-searching.

In any event, remember that when you search any library's online catalog by itself, you are not getting access to individual journal articles. The title of the journal as a whole (e.g., *Harvard Business Review, Accounting Journal, History of Religions*) will indeed be included in the OPAC, with a blanket call number applied to all of its individual volumes, but the catalog record will tell you nothing about the subject contents of any individual articles within the run of the journal. For that kind of access, you need the separate indexes to periodicals (i.e., popular magazines, scholarly journals, newspapers, etc.) produced by commercial vendors such as ProQuest, EBSCOhost, or Gale.

DESCRIPTORS AND THESAURI

Although all databases that index journals can be searched by keywords, some can also be searched by subject headings or "descriptors"—the latter being another designation for controlled vocabulary terms. Descriptors, however, are usually single words or short phrases and do not have the more elaborate phrase structures of *Library of Congress Subject Headings* with precoordinated subdivision strings (see Chapter 2). Nonetheless, the purpose of descriptors is like that of subject headings: within a given database, they serve as standardized collocation or "grouping" mechanisms. In *Historical Abstracts*, for example, the descriptor **Normandy Landing** serves to round up articles whose titles use many different keywords: "D-Day," "Overlord," "Omaha Beach," "The Longest Day," and so on. If you find the right descriptors for your topic, your results will be much better than if you simply type in the keywords that you think of yourself. Descriptors, like subject headings, solve the problem of variant synonyms for the same concept; they are an analogous method of "controlling" or standardizing the search terms within a particular database.

Many databases, especially full-text files, use no descriptors at all; in those, you do need to think up as many relevant keyword terms and phrases as you can, and you'll essentially use the same keyword guesses in all of the uncontrolled files you search. When you search files using descriptors as subject terms, however, you will usually get the best results by tailoring your searches individually within each database, because it is not a safe assumption that the descriptors are standardized across multiple databases. (In contrast, it generally *is* safe to assume that book catalogs in large libraries will use the same list of *Library of Congress Subject Headings* for their category terms.) There are some exceptions, however: *Historical Abstracts* and *America: History and Life*, the two largest indexes to history journals, generally use the same descriptors, and the different ProQuest databases covering current newspaper articles use the same indexing terms.

Some individual databases have a separately published "thesaurus" listing the approved subject descriptors for use in that file, for example:

- *Thesaurus of ERIC Descriptors* (ORYX Press, revised irregularly) is the list of terms for the largest database covering journal articles and research reports in the field of education. It also appears online as well within the subscription database version from ProQuest.
- *Thesaurus of Psychological Index Terms* (American Psychological Association, revised irregularly) is used for the *PsycINFO, PsycARTICLES,* and *PsycBOOKS* databases; it too appears in both print and online versions.
- *Art and Architecture Thesaurus Online* www.getty.edu/research/tools/ is used by the *Avery Index to Architectural Periodicals* and the *Bibliography of the History of Art.*
- *Thesaurus of Sociological Indexing Terms* is used by *Sociological Abstracts* and is findable via a clickable tab within that database.
- *MeSH (Medical Subject Headings)* is used by the various databases offered by the National Library of Medicine (*MEDLINE, NLM Catalog, PubMed, PMC [PubMed Central], TOXLINE,* and others) and by *CINAHL (Cumulative Indexing to Nursing and Allied Health Literature).* This roster of subject terms has features that allow greater scope and precision within medical literature searching than does *LCSH* within regular library catalogs, e.g., Major Concept limits, Tree Structures, and Explode commands in addition to displays of Subdivisions. For an overview see www.nlm.nih.gov/mesh/.

Descriptor fields in online records for journal articles are, then, analogous to the subject tracings that show up on catalog records for books. They show the controlled terms that the indexers have added to the merely-transcribed keywords of the article citation (or abstract) itself.

THE IMPORTANCE OF "FULL" DISPLAYS

In a standard library OPAC a book with the title *Chechnya: Tombstone of Russian Power* is cataloged with the subject tracing **Chechnia (Russia)—History—Civil War, 1994–**. In the *Historical Abstracts* database covering journal articles, however, an article with the title "Russo-Chechen Conflict, 1800–2000: A Deadly Embrace" is indexed with three different descriptors: **War**, **Russia**, and **Chechnia (Russia)**. This

Russo-Chechen **Conflict**, 1800-2000: A Deadly Embrace.

By: Seely, Robert. Russo-Chechen **Conflict**, 1800-2000: A Deadly Embrace. 2001, p1. 333p.
Historical Period: **1800** to 2000.

Subjects: RUSSIA; CHECHNIA (Russia); WAR

Database: Historical Abstracts with Full Text

Add to folder

Figure 4.1 *Historical Abstracts* brief record for article "Russo-Chechen Conflict, 1800–2000: A Deadly Embrace."

Russo-Chechen **Conflict**, 1800-2000: A Deadly Embrace.

Authors:	Seely, Robert
Source:	Russo-Chechen **Conflict**, 1800-2000: A Deadly Embrace; 2001, p1, 333p
Historical Period:	**1800** to 2000
Document Type:	Book
Subject Terms:	WAR
Geographic Terms:	RUSSIA
	CHECHNIA (Russia)
Notes:	Publication Information: London: F. Cass, 2001. 333 pp.
Accession Number:	46564932
Database:	Historical Abstracts with Full Text

Figure 4.2 *Historical Abstracts* detailed record for the same article shown in Figure 4.1, showing descriptors with arrows pointing to them.

important descriptor/subject field is most graphically emphasized in the "Detailed record" format (see Figures 4.1 and 4.2).

It is always a good idea to look at the "Full" or "Detailed" display of any good record you find, rather than the default brief display. In many databases, *only* the full record will show you the controlled (or standardized) terms that the indexers have assigned, which are the subject words you will need to use for the most systematic retrieval. (In some databases, the list of controlled terms, gleaned from the set of retrieved records, will show up automatically as a sidebar.)

In this database, some of the citations and abstracts use the keywords "Chechnya" (with a "y") or "Chechen"—but the standardized descriptor **Chechnia (Russia)**, attached to all such variants, enables them to be retrieved all together.

This brings up a point alluded to earlier on a major problem with federated searching—i.e., doing searches across multiple databases simultaneously.

Note that *Historical Abstracts* uses a descriptor with the spelling **Chechnia**. But the *PAIS* (Public Affairs Information Service) database—one of the very best for coverage of international relations—uses the descriptor **Chechnya**, while the *Russian Academy of Sciences Bibliographies* database uses the spelling **Chechenskii** (in its descriptor **Chechenskii krizis 1991–**). If you search all three files simultaneously using a term that is standardized for only one of them, you will miss most of what the other two databases have to offer without realizing you have missed the bulk of what is available. But you might still readily conclude—erroneously—that you have "covered" all three because, technically, you were searching all of them at once. I will have more to say on federated searching later, but in general remember this: unless your search terms are unusually distinctive (i.e., not subject to variant forms) you will usually be better off searching relevant databases one at a time, with their own terminologies, rather than mashing them together in a single federated or "discovery" search.

This advice runs directly counter to a fashionable belief in the library field, noted above, that information should not be segregated in different "silos" but, rather, should be merged all together into a single "seamless" search. The silo databases for individual disciplinary areas are there for a reason, however: they cover the most important journals within their subjects, undiluted by thousands of tangential periodicals, and they enable those core journals to be indexed with special standardized terms that are the most appropriate to their own fields.

Access to descriptor terms, via the technique of always looking at the "Detailed" (or "Full") display of any relevant retrieved record, will always be possible even if the record is initially found through a keyword search and even if the database does not provide direct access to a formal list of it indexing terms in a separate thesaurus. For access to the latter, keep an eye out for any clickable tab saying "Thesaurus" or "Subjects" or "Browse" or "Topics" at the top or side of your search screen. (My experience is that most researchers don't even notice these tabs, let alone use them.) These displays tend to change or even disappear in unpredictable ways, however, especially when one database vendor is bought out by another—a rather frequent occurrence. In any event, whether or not you use the tabs, always look at the Detailed or Full display of any relevant record you find to see which indexing terms are being used by that database.

LCSH VS. DESCRIPTORS

Note, too, an important difference between *LCSH* subject headings vs. descriptors, namely, that databases using descriptors as indexing terms often use very broad categories (e.g., **War**, with no specification of *which* war). The assumption is that specificity will be achieved by Boolean "AND" combinations of several terms, each serving to limit the scope of the others when all are specified simultaneously. Thus *Historical Abstracts* indexes articles on the Chechnian conflict by requiring a combination such as "**Chechnia** AND (**Russia** OR **Soviet Union**) AND (**War** OR **Violence**)," whereas *LCSH* provides a single string, **Chechnia— History—Civil War, 1994–**. (See the discussion of precoordination vs. postcoordination in Chapter 2.) Descriptors are usually one- or two-word terms, not extended strings. Combining them, or course, requires you to know in advance which descriptor terms you wish to combine— whereas *LCSH* subject strings (in browse displays) enable you to recognize many of the combinations you want. Thesauri of descriptors may be arranged differently than the *LSCH* list; cross-references may be lacking; subdivisions will be minimal (if present at all); and there will certainly be no linkages to LC classification numbers.

What is very confusing to many researchers is that the same databases that use either *descriptors* or *subject headings* can *also* be searched by keywords—that is, the "natural language" words used by the authors of the articles (or books). These are the words that appear within sources themselves, either in their full texts or just in their titles or abstracts. Descriptors, in contrast, come from formal lists of standardized terms, used by professional indexers, and descriptors, like subject headings, are *added to* records, rather than *transcribed from* them, in order to create retrievable terms held in common on records that otherwise might not have any shared keywords, even though they are talking about the same subjects. Again, however, many databases lack descriptors (or subject headings) entirely—they can be searched *only* by keywords. I'll return to this crucial distinction in the next chapter.

MAJOR SUBSCRIPTION DATABASES THAT USE DESCRIPTORS

For the time being, however, let me discuss a few commercial databases to which many research libraries subscribe and talk a bit more about their descriptor capabilities. (Note that many of the databases described below are licensed by more than one vendor, and so it is possible for the same database to show up within systems having different search softwares.) The *Gale Directory of Databases* (Gale Cengage, annual) lists over 21,000 online databases available to libraries, so the following clusters of databases provide only a sampling of some of the more important sources. They are arranged by vendor, rather than by subject, because the different search softwares provided by these vendors have different tab displays, usually at the top of any search screen, for getting you into their descriptor indexes. As mentioned above, using these tabs can alert you to cross-references, related terms, and browse menus that can often provide much more on-target results, with much less clutter from irrelevancies, than if you simply type in whatever keywords occur to you. While it is not necessary to read each of the following descriptions in detail, it will be worth your while to at least skim them, because so many of these databases cover much greater ranges of subjects than are apparent from their titles.

EBSCOhost DATABASES

EBSCO Publishing is a very large vendor offering more than 375 different databases; libraries subscribing to its service will pick and choose which individual files they want, depending on their budgets and clienteles. Be careful, then: an "EBSCO search" in one library may cover very different files from those subscribed to in a different library.

To find the descriptors being used within the individual databases, look for tabs along the top of their search screens with labels such as "Subjects," "Subject Terms," "Indexes," or "Thesaurus" (these will vary from one database to the next). Some (not all) of these links will lead you to *browse menus* that will bring to your attention many more relevant search terms than you would be able to think up on your own. (These search options will vanish entirely when multiple databases are combined for federated searching, because, again, the subject descriptors and browse menus are very different from one database to the next; and federated searching "sees" only features [primarily keywords] that are common across multiple files.)

Among the more important EBSCOhost databases[2] are the following:

Wilson databases: these venerable sources, formerly published by the H. W. Wilson Company, are now mounted on a new search platform. They cover hundreds of the most important journals (and other sources) within their respective fields:

- *Applied Science & Business Periodicals Retrospective: 1913–1983*
- *Applied Science & Technology Full Text*
- *Art Full Text*
- *Art Index Retrospective*

- *Biography Index Past and Present*
- *Biological & Agricultural Index Plus*
- *Book Review Digest*
- *Book Review Digest Retrospective: 1908–1982*
- *Business Abstracts with Full Text*
- *Education Full Text*
- *Essay and General Literature Index*
- *Essay and General Literature Index Retrospective: 1900–1984*
- *Fiction Core Collection*
- *General Science Full Text*
- *Humanities & Social Sciences Index Retrospective: 1907–1984*
- *Humanities Full Text*
- *Index to Legal Periodicals & Books Full Text*
- *Index to Legal Periodicals Retrospective: 1908–1981*
- *Library Literature & Information Science Full Text*
- *Library Literature & Information Science Retrospective: 1905–1983*
- *OmniFile Full Text Mega*
- *Play Index*
- *Readers' Guide Full Text Mega*
- *Readers' Guide Retrospective: 1890–1982*
- *Short Story Index*
- *Short Story Index Retrospective: 1915–1983*
- *Social Sciences Full Text*

These databases can be searched singly or in a group, and several of them have also now been merged with other EBSCO databases within their respective subject areas. Descriptions of the more important non-merged Wilson databases are given individually below; those that have been merged into larger EBSCO files are treated in the description of these merged "*Source*" titles.

Academic Search Complete is one of the largest full-text databases; it indexes over 13,600 journals and provides text searching for nearly 9,100 (7,900 of which are peer-reviewed). More titles are being added continually. Subjects covered include animal science, anthropology, area studies, astronomy, biology, chemistry, civil engineering, electrical engineering, ethnic and multicultural studies, food science and technology, general science, geography, geology, law, materials science, mathematics, mechanical engineering, music, pharmaceutical sciences, physics, psychology, religion and theology, veterinary science, women's studies, and zoology. For the vast majority of titles, coverage extends only from the 1990s or 2000s forward; however, this database, like *JSTOR* (see Chapter 5), is digitizing many of its journals, full text, back to their first issues—in some cases as far back as 1887. In addition to searches by keywords and descriptors, *Academic Search Complete* also offers citation searching (see Chapter 6) within over 1,450 of its titles. A smaller edition of this database called *Academic Search Premier* indexes the same 13,600+ journals but provides fewer full texts (about 4,700).

AGRICOLA is the largest database for agricultural subjects, including over 4 million citations (but not full texts) of journal articles, book chapters, monographs, dissertations, patents, software, audiovisual material, and technical reports. It covers agriculture, animal and veterinary sciences, entomology, plant sciences, forestry, aquaculture and fisheries, farming and farming systems, agricultural economics, extension and education, food and human nutrition, agricultural engineering and technology, and earth and environmental sciences.

America: History & Life and *Historical Abstracts*: the former is the largest single database for U.S. and Canadian history, covering subjects from prehistoric times to the present; it indexes about 1,800 journals back to 1955. The corresponding database for all other regions of the world is *Historical Abstracts*, covering the period from 1450 to the present; it indexes 3,100 journals back to 1955. Both sources index journals in over 40 languages, providing English language abstracts, and both provide extensive coverage of book reviews. (There are also new full-text versions with the titles *America: History & Life with Full Text* and *Historical Abstracts with Full Text*.) They are also surprisingly good for current affairs as well as for history; and "history" in these databases is interpreted in a very broad sense—not just geopolitical events, but also history of art, literature, music, education, business, philosophy, photography, science, and so on. (I once helped a researcher who needed to know "how science was taught in France from the 1880s until World War I"—*Historical Abstracts* could nail that exactly.) It's worth trying these databases for *any* subjects having historical aspects.

Applied Science & Business Periodicals Retrospective: 1913–1983 is a combination of three of the old Wilson printed indexes: *Industrial Arts Index* and its two successors *Applied Science & Technology Index* and *Business Periodicals Index* for the years up to 1983. The retrospective (i.e., back to 1913) *Industrial Arts/Applied Science* component is also included in *Applied Science & Technology Source* (below), but the retrospective *Business* and *Industrial Arts* years (prior to 1982) are found only here—they are not in the other EBSCO *Business* databases described below.

Applied Science & Technology Source is a merger of the former EBSCO *Computers & Applied Sciences Complete* database and the Wilson

Applied Science & Technology Index/Abstracts/Full Text databases. It covers over 2,200 journals will full texts of about 1,400. The former Wilson *Applied Science & Technology Index Retrospective: 1913–1983*, which indexes 850 periodicals for this earlier span, is also included, without abstracts or full texts for those years. This combined database covers acoustics, aeronautics and space science, applied mathematics, artificial intelligence and machine learning, atmospheric sciences, automatic control, automotive engineering, chemical engineering, chemistry, civil engineering, communication and information technology, computer databases and software, computer technology and applications, computer theory and systems, construction, electrical and electronic engineering, engineering and biomedical materials, energy resources and research, engineering (civil, electrical, environmental, industrial, mechanical), engineering materials, environmental sciences and waste management, fire and fire prevention, food and food industry, geology, industrial and mechanical arts, machinery, marine technology and oceanography, mathematics, metallurgy, metallurgy, meteorology, mineralogy, neural networks, optical and neural computing, petroleum and gas, physics, plastics, product reviews, robotics, solid state technology, space science, social and professional issues relevant to engineering, telecommunications, textile industry and fabrics, and transportation.

Art Source is a merger of the EBSCO database *Art & Architecture Complete* and various Wilson databases (*Art Index/Abstracts/Full Text*); over 700 journals are indexed, with full texts of more than 600, with 220 full texts of books. The former *Art Index Retrospective: 1929–1983* is also included, but it does not provide abstracts or full texts for those years. (The Wilson database *Art Museum Image Gallery*, which provided a digital library of 100,000 images and multimedia sources, has not been included, but over 63,000 images are provided by other sources.) This combined *Art* database covers general art, advertising art, antiques, archaeology, architecture and architectural history, art history, city planning, computer graphics, computers in art and architecture, contemporary art, costume, crafts, decorative arts, fine arts, folk art, glassware, graphic arts, industrial design, interior design, graphic arts, interior design, jewelry, landscape architecture, motion pictures, museology, non-Western art, painting, photography, pottery, printmaking, sculpture, television, textiles, video, and woodwork.

ATLA Catholic Periodical Literature and Index Online indexes 200 periodicals back to 1981.

ATLA Religion Database with ATLA Serials is the best starting point for journal articles and essays from book anthologies in the fields of religion and theology. The database, produced by the American Theological Libraries Association, indexes 546 current journals plus another 1,138 retrospectively back to 1949 (and in some cases back to the nineteenth century), and also more than 260,000 essays from 16,700 multi-authored books. Full texts of over 230 journals are included.

Avery Index to Architectural Periodicals is the largest index in its field, covering over 2,500 U.S. and foreign journals from the 1930s (with selective coverage back to the 1860s, and even to 1741 in one instance [*Saggi di dissertazioni accademiche*]). Subjects include architecture, archaeology, design, historic preservation, interior design, landscape architecture, urban design, and urban planning history.

Biography Reference Bank covers over 600,000 individuals, with links to 300,000 full-text articles. This combined source covers articles from over 3,500 magazines, thousands of academic journals, and over 9,000 books. Popular full-text Wilson reference series such as *Current Biography, World Authors,* and *Junior Authors & Illustrators* are included. The database indexes autobiographies, bibliographies, biographies, book reviews, collections of letters, critical studies, diaries, drama, exhibition reviews, fiction (biographical novels), interviews, journals, juvenile literature, memoirs, obituaries, photos and pictorial works, poetry, and videos. You can search not just by names of individuals but by occupations and subject and genre categories (e.g., actors, architects, economists, explorers, handicapped, murder victims).

Biological Abstracts indexes more than 4,300 journals internationally back to 1969. *Biological Abstracts Archive 1926–1968* provides full retrospective coverage of the old volumes of the printed index.

Biological & Agricultural Index Plus covers over 380 journals from 1983 to the present, with full texts of over 100 starting in 1997. The print version of *Biological & Agricultural Index* covers back to 1964. Coverage includes agricultural chemicals, agricultural economics, agricultural engineering, agronomy, animal husbandry, animal sciences, bacteriology, biochemistry, biology, biotechnology, botany, conservation, cytology, dairying, ecology, entomology, environmental science, fishery science, food science, forestry, genetics, horticulture, immunology, limnology, livestock, marine biology, microbiology, mycology, nutrition, paleontology, pesticides, physiology, plant pathology, poultry, soil science, veterinary medicine, virology, weed sciences, wildlife management, and zoology.

Book Review Digest provides generous abstracts of reviews, or full texts in some cases, since 1983; it also includes citations for any book reviews appearing in any of over 5,000 journals. *Book Review Digest Retrospective: 1905–1982* provides 1.5 million evaluative passages from reviews of 300,000 older books. Access is provided not just by authors' names and titles of their books but also through controlled subject headings. You can therefore search for reviews—and read many excerpts of them—simply by subject, without knowing in advance any specific authors or titles. This enables you to identify books by subject—either fiction or nonfiction (primarily in humanities and social sciences areas)—and at the same time to get substantive evaluations of them. (Doing subject searches for books in you library's OPAC will identify relevant books but will not usually link you immediately to reviews or evaluations of them.) This is sometimes a good alternative to Amazon for quickly finding reviews of a book; these reviews all come from journals having editorial oversight. There is one major qualification to be aware of, however: the reviews indexed in these sources are almost all contemporary with the initial appearance of the reviewed book. For the scholarly literary criticism that may come much later you will need to check additional sources. (See the section on "Literary Criticism" in Chapter 14.)

Business Abstracts with Full Text is a continuation of the Wilson database as a separate file, not merged with *Business Source Complete* (below). It provides full texts of articles from more than 460 publications back to 1982, with indexing of 880 publications back to 1981. (The former Wilson *Business Periodicals Retrospective 1913–1982* continues as a part of the separate database *Applied Science & Business Periodicals Retrospective: 1913–1983*). Coverage includes accounting, acquisitions and mergers, advertising, banking, building and construction, chemicals and pharmaceuticals, communications, computers, cosmetics industry, economics, electronics, engineering, entertainment industry, finance, financial data, government regulations, health care, hospitality and tourism, human resources, industrial relations, industry reports, insurance, international business, investment research reports, labor, management, market research reports, mass media, occupational safety and health, oil and gas, paper and pulp industries, personnel, public relations, public utilities, publishing, purchasing, real estate, retail trade, small business, specific business, specific industries, specific trades, SWOT analyses, taxation, technology, and transportation.

Business Source Complete is one of the very largest business databases; it indexes over 4,500 journals back to 1886, with full texts of about 2,400 of them (for recent decades). It also covers nonjournal full-text sources such as case studies, company profiles, conference proceedings, country reports, faculty seminar videos, financial data, industry reports, investment research reports, market research reports, monographs, SWOT (strengths, weaknesses, opportunities, and threats) analyses, and trade publications. Additionally, the database provides biographical profiles of its 40,000 most cited authors. Citation searching (see Chapter 6) is possible within 1,300 of the journals covered. Smaller versions of the database are also available: *Business Source Premier* provides full texts of 2,200 journals, and *Business Source Elite* provides full texts of 1,000.

Canadian Reference Center offers full texts of leading Canadian magazines and newspapers, as well as biographical write-ups, maps, photos, and other images from Canadian Press.

Communication and Mass Media Complete indexes 800 titles as far back as 1915 (although primarily from the 1990s forward), with full texts of over 500 of them.

EconLit is the premier index to economic journals as well as books, essays in collective volumes, dissertations, working papers, and book reviews; its coverage extends back to 1969. *EconLit with Full Text*, also available, provides full texts of more than 560 of the journals.

Education Source indexes more than 2,300 journals, with full texts of over 1,700 of them and texts of over 550 books. It contains the former Wilson *Education Index* (and *Abstract/Full Text*) databases, and *Education Index Retrospective: 1929–1983*. Coverage includes administration and supervision, adult education, athletics, arts, classroom management, comparative and international education, competency-based education, computers in education, continuing education, counseling, distance education, education specialties, educational technology, elementary education, government funding, health and physical education, higher education, instructional media, language arts and linguistics, laptops in the classroom, library and information science, literacy standards, multicultural/ethnic education, multilingual education, parent–teacher relations, personnel service, physical education, policy, prayer in public schools, preschool education, psychology and mental health, religious education, science and mathematics, secondary education, social studies, special education, student counseling, teacher education and evaluation, teaching methods and curriculum, teacher's unions, testing, and vocational education.

Energy & Power Source indexes nearly 1,500 publications dealing with coal, electric power, gas, nuclear reactors, petroleum, and renewable energy sources; aspects of these industries including exploration, extraction, clean-up, marketing, and sales are covered. Full texts of many of the sources are available.

Environment Complete indexes more than 2,400 journals internationally back to 1888, with current coverage of over 1,250 titles. Full texts of approximately 1,000 are searchable; 200 monographs are included. Coverage of the subject area is very broad: agriculture, renewable energy sources, marine sciences, geography, pollution and waste management, environmental technology, environmental law, public policy, social impacts, and urban planning.

Essay and General Literature Index picks out essays appearing in book anthologies; it annually indexes more than 300 essay collections and 20 annual or serial publications. It covers back to 1985, indexing a total of over 86,000 essays in 7,000 anthologies or edited volumes. *Essay and General Literature Index Retrospective: 1900–1984* covers an additional 249,000 essays back to the turn of the last century. Subjects covered include archaeology, architecture, art, children's literature, classical studies, drama, economics, fiction, film, folklore, history, linguistics, music, poetry, political science, religion, and women's studies.

Film & Television Literature Index provides indexing and abstracting coverage of 380 publications cover-to-cover, with another 250 indexed selectively. *Film & Television Literature Index with Full Text* offers the same coverage plus full texts of 120 journals and tens of thousands of photographs from the MPTV Image Archive.

FRANCIS is a huge index to more than 2,300 social sciences and humanities journals worldwide, in multiple languages (although with a French emphasis), back to 1972. Journals, books, dissertations, conference proceedings, and reports are covered. Subject headings are provided in both English and French.

FSTA—Food Science & Technology Abstracts covers over 4,600 publications back to 1969.

Hospitality & Tourism Complete is a full-text database covering 830 current periodicals with indexing coverage back to 1930.

Garden, Landscape & Horticulture Index provides abstract-level coverage of over 500 titles, mostly in English, mainly from the 1990s forward.

General Science Full Text covers 300 American and British journals and popular magazines from 1984 to the present with abstracts from 1993 forward with full texts of about 100 of the journals, starting in 1995. (The printed version of *General Science Index* covers back to 1978.) Subjects covered include anthropology, astronomy, atmospheric sciences, biological sciences, botany, chemistry, computers, earth sciences, environment and conservation, food and nutrition, genetics, mathematics, medicine and health, microbiology, oceanography, physics, physiology, psychology, pollution biology, and zoology.

GeoRef covers the world's geosciences literature, indexing 3,500 journals back to 1669 for North America, and to 1933 from the rest of the world.

Humanities Source is a merger of the EBSCO *Humanities International Complete* database with the Wilson *Humanities Index/Abstracts/Full*

Text/Retrospective. It indexes over 2,300 journals with full texts of more than 1,400 (and 700+ books). It includes full back files of the Wilson paper sets *Humanities Index* (1974–1984), *Social Sciences and Humanities Index* (1965–1974), *and International Index* (1907–1965). Subject coverage includes archaeology, area studies, art, classical studies, communications, dance, drama, film, folklore, gender studies, history, journalism, language and linguistics, literary and political/social criticism, music, performing arts, philosophy, religion, and theology.

Index to Jewish Periodicals covers more than 200 periodicals back to 1988.

Legal Source is a merger of the former EBSCO database *Legal Collection* with the Wilson files *Index to Legal Periodicals and Books/Full Text/Retrospective: 1908–1981.* Coverage includes full texts of more than 1,100 journals (including 300 law reviews) and 1,400 monographs per year from 1982 to the present, from the U.S., Puerto Rico, Canada, Great Britain, Ireland, Australia, and New Zealand. Subject coverage includes administrative law, antitrust law, banking and business law, constitutional law, corporate law, court decisions, criminal law, domestic relations, energy and natural resources, environmental protection, estate planning, ethics, family law, federal law, food/drug/cosmetic law, insurance law, international law, Internet and information science law, intellectual property law, international law, Internet law, labor and human resource law, landlord/tenant law, legal librarianship, malpractice suits, maritime law, medicine and health care law, minorities, multinational corporations, negligence, nonprofit corporations, occupational health and safety, organized crime, patent and trademark law, probate, public law and politics, probate, product liability, real estate law, securities and antitrust legislation, sports and entertainment law, tax law and estate planning, and trade regulation.

LGBT Life indexes and abstracts more than 200 periodicals (130 full-text) and 330 reference works, with 170 full-text monographs and selective coverage of thousands of other sources.

Library & Information Science Source merges the EBSCO database *LISTA with Full Text* with the Wilson *Library Literature & Information Science Index/Full Text/Retrospective: 1905–1983.* Over 500 journals are indexed with full texts of more than 430 (and 30 books). Coverage includes automation, care and restoration of books, cataloging, censorship, circulation, classification, copyright, education for librarianship, employment, government aid, indexing, information brokers, Internet software, library associations and conferences, library equipment and supplies, library schools, literature for children and young adults, personnel administration, preservation of materials, public relations, publishing, online searching, public relations, publishing, rare books, reference services, and websites.

MEDLINE Complete is the largest full-text database for biomedical research. While there is a free version of *MEDLINE* on the open Internet (a Google or Bing search of its title will bring it up immediately), the free version does not have the 2,100 full-text journals provided in this subscription database. Some of the text coverage extends back to 1865.

Middle Eastern & Central Asian Studies covers academic and policy-related publications on the Middle East, Central Asia, and North Africa from 1900 to the present.

Military and Government Collection indexes over 400 journals, with over 300 full text, since 1962. It also includes full texts of the U.S. Government Printing Office's *Background Notes on Countries of the World.*

MLA International Bibliography, from the Modern Language Association, is the largest database for literary studies; it also provides the best coverage of research in linguistics and folklore. It indexes 4,400 journals internationally back to the 1920s.

The Music Index Online is one of the best databases in its field, covering more than 480 periodicals internationally from 1970, with selective coverage of another 200. (The printed *Music Index* covers back to 1949.)

Philosopher's Index provides abstracts of articles from more than 600 journals from 85 countries, back to 1940; it also indexes books, anthologies, and book reviews.

Political Science Complete indexes and abstracts 2,900 journals and offers full text of 550 of them. It also provides full texts of 340 reference books and 38,000 conference papers. Coverage is primarily from the 1990s forward, with some titles indexed in earlier decades.

PsycINFO, from the American Psychological Association (APA), is the largest database in its field. It indexes nearly 2,500 periodicals in 30 languages going back to the 1800s. It also covers books, anthologies, and dissertations. A related database, *PsycARTICLES*, provides full texts of 80 journals back to 1894; another, *PsycBOOKS*, provides full texts of 55,000 chapters from 3,500 books from current publishers and 2,600 "classic" books in the field dating from the 1600s. Thousands of signed articles from the 8-volume *Encyclopedia of Psychology* (APA and Oxford University Press, 2000) are also provided, full text. *PsycCRITIQUES* is a full-text database of over 40,000 book reviews dating back to 1956. *PsycEXTRA* provides full texts of "grey literature" not indexed in the other APA databases: technical, annual, and government reports, as well as newsletters, conference papers, and brochures. *PsycTESTS* provides full texts of many psychological tests.

Readers' Guide to Periodical Literature is an index to over 450 general newsstand type magazines and many scholarly journals, published in the United States (with a few Canadian titles) from 1983 forward. *Readers' Guide Full Text Mega* adds abstracts since 1984 and full texts of 250 of the magazines since 1994; *Readers' Guide Full Text Select* covers only those 250 journals, so it is a 100 percent full-text source. *Readers' Guide Retrospective: 1890–1982* indexes 550 U.S. magazines including everything in the old print volumes of both *Readers' Guide* and *Nineteenth Century Readers' Guide*. Subjects covered include aeronautics, African-Americans, aging, antiques, archaeology, arts, astronomy, automobiles, biography, business, Canada, children, computers, crafts, consumer education, current events and news, dance, drama, education, entertainment, environment, fashion, fiction, film and television, fine arts, food recipes and cooking, gardening, health and medicine, history, hobbies, home improvement, journalism, leisure activities, literature, medicine, music, nutrition, photography, politics, popular culture, religion, science, sports and fitness, television, transportation, and travel.

RILM Abstracts of Music Literature indexes 11,000 journals internationally back to 1967, including selective coverage of music articles from thousands of nonmusic journals. Conference proceedings are covered back to 1835. *RILM Retrospective Abstracts of Music Literature* covers pre-1967 decades. *RIPM Music Periodicals provides indexing and full texts of periodicals back to 1766.*

Social Sciences Full Text indexes over 750 scholarly journals, with full texts of 330 of the as far back as 1972. *Social Sciences Index Retrospective: 1907–1983* covers the print volumes of *Social Sciences Index* (1974–1983), *Social Sciences and Humanities Index* (1965–1974), and *International Index* (1907–1965). These databases cover addiction studies, anthropology, area studies, community health and medical care, communications, consumer affairs, corrections, criminal justice, criminology, economics, environmental studies, ethics, family studies, gender studies, geography, gerontology, human ecology, international relations, law, mass media, minority studies, nursing, pharmacology, planning and public administration, policy sciences, political science, psychiatry, psychology and psychological tests, public administration, public health and welfare, social work, sociology, and urban studies.

SocINDEX is a huge sociology database; it provides abstracts of articles from more than 1,300 core journals back to 1895, and selective indexing of approximately 3,000 others insofar as they have articles of sociological interest. Books, conference papers, and other sources are also covered. *SocINDEX with Full Text* adds full text of more than 890 of the journals back to 1908, and texts of more than 850 books and over 16,800 conference papers.

Textile Technology Complete indexes and abstracts more than 470 periodicals, with full texts of 50 of them. Books, conference papers, theses, and technical reports are also indexed, with full texts of 50 of the books. Coverage is primarily from the 1990s forward, but some titles are indexed from earlier decades.

Women's Studies International is the largest general database in its field, covering over 800 sources primarily from 1972 forward (with some earlier years), It indexes journals, books, book chapters, newsletters, newspapers, proceedings, reports, grey literature, and websites.

PROQUEST DATABASES

ProQuest, based in Ann Arbor, Michigan, is another of the major database vendors in the information field. It provides hundreds of databases (both indexing/abstracting and full text) available through its own search software and files from companies that it has bought or merged with (e.g., CSA Illumina, Dialog, DataStar, Chadwyck-Healey, HeritageQuest, UMI Microfilm, UPA Microforms), which may have search pages that look very different. From the wide range of ProQuest databases available, libraries must tailor their own subscriptions to fit their local budgets and the needs of their own clienteles. An important implication for students is that it doesn't mean much to say simply "I searched ProQuest for my topic"—a comment heard frequently by reference librarians—because the set of ProQuest databases available in one library may be very different from the set subscribed to in another.

Some of the ProQuest databases have controlled descriptors; some are strictly keyword files. Among the many files[3] offered by this company are the following:

ABI/INFORM Complete is one of the very best databases for business researchers. It indexes over 6,800 journals as far back as 1923 to the present and provides full texts of over 5,400 (including full text of *The Wall Street Journal* back to 1984), as well as full texts of thousands of annual reports, country reports, working papers, business cases and dissertations, and market/industry research reports (including Petrosil reports on the energy industry). New sources are being added continually. Smaller segmented editions of the database are also available: *ABI/INFORM Global*, *ABI/INFORM Research*, *ABI/INFORM Trade & Industry*, and *ABI/INFORM Dateline*.

Design and Applied Arts Index (DAAI) selectively indexes and abstracts more than 500 design and applied arts periodicals back to 1973. Coverage includes advertising, architecture, book design, ceramics, computer aided design, design history, education, glass, garden design, graphic design, fashion and clothing, furniture, illustration, interior design, jewelry, landscape architecture, metalsmithing, packaging, produce design, textiles, theater, urban design, Web design, and wood.

GeoRef is the best index for geology, covering sources for North America back to 1669 and for the rest of the world back to 1933. Currently more than 3,500 journals in 40 languages are indexed and abstracted; books, conference papers, theses, dissertations, and maps are also covered.

Index Islamicus covers over 3,000 journals, some extending back to 1906. It covers Islam, the Middle East, Muslim areas of Asian and Africa, and Muslim minorities elsewhere. Subject coverage is not just religious and geopolitical; also included are accounting, archaeology, arts bibliography, economics, education, geography, history, law, literature, natural and applied science, philosophy, social sciences, theology, travel, and zoology.

International Index to Music Periodicals indexes and abstracts about 450 music periodicals from 20 countries, primarily from 1996 forward but with some coverage extending back as far as 1874. It covers both scholarly and popular sources.

International Index to Performing Arts provides coverage of about 250 periodicals, primarily from 1998 forward but with retrospective coverage of some journals going back to their first issue. It covers the fields of "dance, film, television, drama, theater, stagecraft, musical theater, circus performance, opera, pantomime, puppetry, magic, performance art and more."

LISA: Library and Information Science Abstracts covers over 440 periodicals in more than 20 languages back to 1969.

PAIS International (1972–) and *PAIS Archive* (1915–1976). The Public Affairs Information Service is the largest index to public policy and international relations journals, worldwide, from over 120 countries back to 1915. Over 4,100 journals are indexed. In addition to journal articles, the combined databases include books, government publications, grey literature, reports, conference papers, and websites. Note that newspapers and newsletters are *not* indexed here, but statistical sources are very well covered. Subjects include agriculture and forestry, banking and finance, culture and religion, economics, education, energy resources and policy, environment, government, health, human rights, labor issues, law and ethics, manufacturing, media and communications, military and defense policy, politics, population and demographics, science and technology, social conditions, trade, and transportation.

PolicyFile is an index primarily to think tank publications; it also covers studies done by nongovernmental organizations, research institutes, universities, and advocacy groups. More than 500 source groups are covered in over 75 public policy topic areas. While this is not a full-text database itself, in most cases it will link you to the full texts of the documents mounted on the sources' own servers.

ProQuest Biological Science Collection indexes more than 1,500 periodicals back to 1982, with 750 of them full-text.

ProQuest Central is one of the very largest aggregations of full-text sources, indexing over 10,000 periodicals with most in full text. Beyond periodicals, over 1,000 U.S., Canadian, and international newspapers, 50,000 dissertations, and thousands of market reports covering 43 industries in 40 countries are provided. This one database is a combination of more than two dozen of the other ProQuest databases.

ProQuest Computer Science Collection provides more than 750 full-text journals back to 1981.

ProQuest Congressional is the best overall index to U.S. congressional hearings, reports, documents, prints, bills, laws, regulations, and some legislative histories; it is produced by CIS (Congressional Information Service), now a ProQuest subsidiary. Coverage of historical materials extends back to 1789 (full text *U.S. Serial Set, Hearings, Bills and Resolutions* as optional modules) or the early 1800s. Many libraries that subscribe to *ProQuest Congressional* without its full-text modules will nonetheless have microfiche sets of the texts of all of the hearings, reports, prints, documents, and legislative histories. (For more details on this database and its relatives see Chapter 13.)

ProQuest Criminal Justice abstracts and indexes 450 titles back to 1969, with about a hundred in full text.

ProQuest Environmental Science Collection provides full texts of 1,100 journals as far back as 1967, covering environmental science, pollution, water management, sustainability, and ecology.

Ethnic NewsWatch and *Ethnic NewsWatch: A History* (combined) provide full texts of over 340 publications (newspapers, magazines, and journals) from African American, Asian American, Jewish, Native American, Arab American, Eastern European, and other ethnic communities. Dozens of Latino publications are presented in Spanish. Coverage is from 1959 forward.

ProQuest Health and Medical Complete indexes over 1,950 publications from 1986 forward, with full texts of 1,660 of them.

ProQuest Military Collection indexes over 600 periodicals, with more than 400 full text. A few of the periodicals have extensive backfiles: *Marine Corps Gazette* back to 1916; *Foreign Affairs* to 1923; and *Leatherneck* to 1921.

ProQuest Newsstand indexes 1,370 U.S. and foreign newspapers, over 1,270 of which are full text; it is updated daily with some coverage far back as 1977. Major titles such as *The New York Times, The Washington Post, The Wall Street Journal,* and *USA Today* are included. Controlled indexing descriptors cover subjects, individual companies or organizations, people, products (indexed by NAICS/SIC codes), geographic areas, and, generally, the *who, what, why, where,* and *when* topics of each article. The indexing standardization here is thus better than just the keyword search capabilities of many other newspaper sources. Regional "bundles" are available separately: **Canadian, Latin American, U.S. Hispanic, Middle East,** and **Australia & New Zealand Newsstand**, among many others. **ProQuest International Newsstand** provides full texts of about 660 papers since 1977 from around the world, also with controlled indexing descriptors. (The separate database **ProQuest Historical Newspapers and Periodicals**, which is only keyword-searchable, without any of these descriptors, will be discussed in Chapter 5.)

ProQuest Public Health indexes over 750 journals and provides full texts of over 520; coverage extends back to 1972. Newspapers, trade sources, reports, and dissertations are also covered in the subject areas of allergies and immunology, behavioral sciences, biology and genetics, biostatistics, communicable diseases, disaster preparedness, drug abuse and alcoholism, environmental health, epidemiology, nursing, nutrition, obesity, pediatrics, physical fitness, population studies, social services, special education and rehabilitation, and statistics.

ProQuest Religion provides full-text coverage of over 260 religion and theology journals, most in full text, from 1986 forward.

ProQuest Research Library is a kind of small "one-stop" database indexing over 5,000 titles in all subject areas, with over 3,600 in full text, from 1971 forward. It provides a good sampling of the core scholarly journals, newspapers, trade magazines, and general periodicals from the larger ProQuest family. Coverage is very broad. This is a good source for short term papers or general research that doesn't require the depth of the other databases.

ProQuest Science Journals indexes over 1,600 journals, with full texts of more than 1,200 since 1986. All major fields—biology, chemistry, physics, astronomy, earth sciences, engineering—are covered.

ProQuest Statistical Insight is the best starting point database for just about any kind of statistics. It indexes publications from hundreds of U.S. government agencies from 1973 (with full texts from 2004 forward); from 50 state governments and hundreds of private, commercial, and academic sources from 1980 (with full texts from 2008 forward); and from about a hundred international intergovernmental organizations from 1983 (with full texts from 2007). Many libraries have additional microfiche sets of *all* of the indexed documents. Over a million individually indexed tables can be searched in its Tables Collection. Data can be searched by any number of categorical breakdowns: *geographic* (by city, census division, county, foreign country, outlying area, region, SMSA, state, urban-rural and metro-nonmetro area); *economic* (by commodity, employment status, income, individual company or institution, industry, occupation); or *demographic* (by age, disease, educational attainment, marital status, race or ethnic group, sex).

Social Services Abstracts indexes and abstracts over 1,300 journals since 1979 in all areas of social work, including human services, social welfare, social policy, and community development.

Sociological Abstracts covers nearly 2,000 journals extending back to 1952. Books, chapters of anthologies, conference papers, and dissertations are also covered. Starting in 2002, many entries include not just abstracts of articles, but the full bibliographies that appear at the ends of the articles, with links to other CSA databases whose own entries cite these same footnoted articles.

Worldwide Political Science Abstracts covers approximately 1,500 journals since 1975 in subject areas of international relations, law, and public policy. Two-thirds of the sources covered are published outside the United States. Like *Sociological Abstracts*, it provides "cited reference linking" of sources listed in the footnotes of the articles it indexes, from 2004 forward—i.e., it will bring to your attention articles in other CSA databases that make use of the same footnote sources.

The 600+ *Dialog* and *DataStar* databases that are now under the ProQuest corporate umbrella are especially thorough in covering current information, worldwide, in areas of aerospace, biomedical research, biotechnology, business and finance, chemicals, energy and development, food and agriculture, government regulations, intellectual property, medicine, news and media, pharmaceuticals, social sciences, and science and technology.[4] Special libraries serving corporate, law, or scientific organizations that are particularly dependent on the most up-to-date and most specialized information are heavy users of these files. (*ProQuest Dialog* will remain as a collective designation; the name *DataStar* will disappear.)

GALE CENGAGE DATABASES

Some of the databases in this family offer a clickable "Browse Subjects" or "Subject Guide Search" option at the tops of their search screens; use of this entry point will provide you with cross-references and browse menus of subdivisions that can be very useful in alerting you to the best terms to use for your search. In other words, as with the EBSCO and ProQuest databases don't just start typing in keywords as soon as you see the first search screen. You can often get much better results if you take a moment to familiarize yourself with the extra options available, especially on the "Advanced" search screens.

The Gale databases share what they call an "InfoTrac" platform and are sometimes referred to by this term, but remember that "InfoTrac" is not one big database—the designation covers a wide variety of individual titles, discussed below, and different libraries will have subscriptions to various databases within the family, depending on their clienteles.

Several of the more important Gale Cengage databases are listed here;[5] others from the same company strictly keyword indexes (without indexing by descriptors) and will be discussed in Chapter 5.

Academic OneFile is a huge general database geared toward college and university users, covering all subject areas across humanities, social sciences, and science/technology fields. It indexes nearly 14,000 journals (more than 10,000 peer-reviewed) and provides full texts of more than 6,500 (3,200+ refereed) from roughly 1980 forward. It includes full-text coverage of *The New York Times* and the *Times (London)* back to 1985 and also provides transcripts of thousands of NPR, CNN, and CBC broadcasts.

General OneFile is another huge database, this one directed more towards a public library audience; it indexes over 13,000 journals, with full texts of more than 8,100. Hundreds of newspapers from about 1980 forward are also included. Seventy percent of the titles indexed are unique to this database, and there is only about a 30 percent overlap with the coverage of ***Academic OneFile***. Transcripts of National Public Radio broadcasts from 1990 forward are searchable. An especially valuable feature is that it provides full texts of 3,000 (out of 6,000) of the journals recommended in Bowker's *Magazines for Libraries*, a standard source used by libraries to identify the most important magazines and journals in all subject areas, that they may want to subscribe to.

Business Insights: Essentials (formerly *Business and Company Resource Center*) is a huge database of full-text sources (since 1980) including company profiles (with corporate parent/sibling relationships), industry rankings, product and brand information, company performance ratings, investment reports, market research reports, business rankings, corporate chronologies, industry statistics, current investment ratings, comprehensive financial overviews, financial ratios, pricing momentum and key ratio measures, industry newsletter news and analysis, and coverage of business events and trends. It also provides SWOT (strengths, weaknesses, opportunities, and threats) analyses on the most popular companies in the world.

Various *Collection* databases in particular subject areas include:

Agriculture Collection
Communications and Mass Media Collection
Criminal Justice Collection
Culinary Arts Collection
Environmental Studies and Policy Collection
Fine Arts and Music Collection
Gardening, Landscape and Horticulture Collection
Home Improvement Collection
Nursing and Allied Health Collection
Psychology Collection
Hospitality, Tourism and Leisure Collection

Each of these provides full-text access to journals within its field from 1980 to date. Coverage ranges from only a hundred or so titles (e.g., *Gardening*) to over a thousand (*Nursing*).

CPI.Q, or *Canadian Periodicals Index Quarterly*, indexes 1,200 Canadian periodicals (English and French) from 1980, with full texts of 550 including the *Globe and Mail* and *Maclean's* from 1983 forward.

LegalTrac indexes more than 1,500 periodicals, 200 of them full text, back to 1980. It covers law reviews, law journals, specialty law and bar association journals, legal newspapers, Federal and State Cases, and British Commonwealth and European Union Cases.

Literature Resource Center provides full-text access to thousands of literary biographies and interviews, including online versions of such major printed sources as *Dictionary of Literary Biography* and *Contemporary Authors*. It includes hundreds of thousands of full-text critical articles on particular literary works from various Gale reference sets and 360 journals. It also provides 30,000 full texts of contemporary poems, plays, and short stories.

FIRSTSEARCH DATABASES

The FirstSearch system is an aggregation of subscription databases[6] made available by the Online Computer Library Center (OCLC) in Dublin, Ohio.

WorldCat is a huge database that essentially combines the individual library catalogs of about 70,000 libraries in 170 countries and territories, including the records of three dozen national libraries. It lists not just books (in 479 languages), but also manuscripts, maps, photographs, sound recordings, motion pictures, posters, cuneiform clay tablets—just about any format imaginable, if it has been collected by a member institution. Library locations are given for almost all items. Although the records tend to use *Library of Congress Subject Headings*, there is great inconsistency in their application, since there are so many contributing catalogers of various skill levels. Usually keywords have to be used in addition to *LCSH* terms. (A free version is available at www.worldcat.org, but it is does not have the more sophisticated search capabilities of the subscription database.)

ArticleFirst is an index to 16,000 journals since 1990 in the areas of business, humanities, medicine, popular culture, science, social science, and technology.

Ebooks is a catalog of all of the electronic books cataloged by OCLC member libraries; it includes over 665,000 records.

OAIster is an index, with links to full texts, of open archive collections mounted by over 1,100 contributors worldwide. It indexes millions of digital journals, books, images, films, sound recordings, technical reports, and theses.

PapersFirst is an index to millions of individual papers from published conferences, symposia, expositions, and professional meetings, since 1993, insofar as they are collected by the British Library Document Supply Centre.

Scipio is an index to auction and sales catalogs covering art objects (furniture, jewelry, paintings, rugs, sculpture, textiles, etc.) and rare books; coverage extends back to the sixteenth century.

MISCELLANEOUS DATABASES WITH CONTROLLED DESCRIPTORS

Not all subscription databases are aggregated within services such as EBSCOhost, ProQuest, or Gale; your library may have many individual subscriptions to other files that are not included under these umbrellas. (Some of the titles listed above may also be available in your own library from different aggregators, which would change the search pages providing access to them.) Let me mention just a few more indexes to journals articles here because of their particular usefulness.

L'Annee Philologique (EBSCO) is the best database for Classical Studies (Greek and Roman antiquity); it covers 1,500 periodicals back to 1924. Although this database lacks controlled descriptor terms, it does allow searches to be limited by broad "Subjects and Disciplines" before you type in your keywords. And in any event, this file should be mentioned in conjunction with the medieval and modern history databases discussed next.

Iter: Gateway to the Middle Ages & Renaissance (University of Toronto) covers literature dealing with the period from A.D. 400 to 1700, indexing over 1,700 scholarly journals published since 1784, as well as books, encyclopedia articles, essays in collections (since 1874), conference proceedings, and dissertations. Iter can be searched not only by keywords, but also by *Library of Congress Subject* Headings and Dewey Decimal class numbers. Another good source covering much of this historical period is *Brepolis Medieval Bibliographies* (Brepolis Publishers), which includes two cross-searchable files, *International Medieval Bibliography (IMB)* and *Bibliographie de Civilisation Médiévale*. These cover the centuries from A.D. 300 to 1500 and index over 4,500 journals as well as tens of thousands of book reviews, essays in anthologies, festschriften, catalogs, conference papers, and monographs. (*IMB* covers only journals, essays within anthologies, and conference proceedings; it is the *Bibliographie* component that extends coverage to whole books.) The cross-file searching of these two databases enables you to limit subject searches to particular geographic areas and to particular centuries of interest. (Note the crucial distinctions: the "geographic" here refers to the subject coverage of the articles, not to their places of publication; similarly the "centuries" refers to the subject time-periods of the articles, not to their dates of publication.) Be sure to look for the "Advanced search" tab near the top of the screen to see these important options; the default "Simple search" screen does not bring them to your attention. And once you get the "Advanced search" screen, be sure to look for the *additional* line that says "More search possibilities: Click here"—this will bring up still more search boxes enabling you to use the databases' controlled vocabulary much more efficiently, through "Browse" menus of subject headings with subdivisions.

(To step back for a moment, in surveying "history" literature in general, remember *L'Annee Philologique* for the ancient world, *Iter* and the *Brepolis* files for medieval and Renaissance periods, and a combination of *America: History and Life* [for United States and Canada] and *Historical Abstracts* [all other countries], the latter for periods from ca. 1450 to the present.)

Bibliography of Asian Studies, published by the Association for Asian Studies, is the best index to Western-language journals on this area of the world; it indexes over a half-million articles from 1971 forward primarily in humanities and social sciences areas and very selectively in sciences. (The print version extends back to 1941). Chapters in edited volumes and anthologies/festschriften are also indexed, as are conference papers. Coverage of dissertations and master's theses is not good.

Bibliography of the History of Art is the largest database covering scholarly writings on the history of Western art, indexing over 1,200 journals up to the end of 2009. (This file, unlike most of the other discussed in this chapter, is freely available on the open Internet at http://library.getty.edu/bha.)

ERIC, from the Educational Resources Information Center, is a huge index to journal articles and research reports in the field of education; a corresponding microfiche set of the reports is available in many academic libraries. (This database, too, is now freely available on the Internet at www.eric.ed.gov; and the free site now includes many full texts of the reports.)

IBZ Online: International Bibliography of Periodical Literature. This is the online version of the printed index *Internationale Bibliographie der Zeitschriftenliteratur;* the database is available from K. G. Saur Verlag. While the print version began in 1886, the online version (as of this writing) starts in 1983. It indexes about 11,500 journals internationally (40 countries, 40 languages), although with a German emphasis (much as the **FRANCIS** database in the EBSCO system has a French emphasis). It focuses mainly on subjects in the humanities and social sciences. Subject headings are in both German and English.

HOW TO IDENTIFY DATABASES IN ALL SUBJECT AREAS

The best source for identifying which subscription databases exist in all subject areas is the annual printed directory *Gale Directory of Databases* (Gale Cengage); it lists both online sources and CD-ROMs (and other formats). An online version of this title is available through *Gale Directory Library*, which is itself a subscription database. Since the sources listed in this *Directory* are not freely available on the Web, however, your best bet is to check with the reference librarians of your own library to find out which subscriptions you have access to locally. When you talk to the librarians, however, do not just ask for particular databases; be sure to tell them the subject you are working on, or the information that you are ultimately trying to find, and ask them for recommendations on which files to search.

CROSS-DISCIPLINARY SEARCHING
AND FEDERATED SEARCHING

One of most important concepts to remember in doing any kind of subject searching is that any database covers not just the subject indicated in its title but also *other subjects from the perspective of that discipline* (e.g., subjects such as Art, African Americans, communications, computers, developing countries, management, religion, shipwrecks, tea, women, et al.). (The same point applies to specialized encyclopedias, discussed in Chapter 1.) Virtually no subject is limited to a single index; rather, all the indexes may cover any subject, but from differing viewpoints.

Sometimes the cross-disciplinary potential of the various indexes (both online and printed) is surprising, as is shown in the following examples.

- *Business Source Complete* picks up an article titled "Case Study of a Decision Analysis: Hamlet's Soliloquy" from the journal *Interfaces*.
- *Legal Source* cites a law review article "Hamlet and the Law of Homicide," and others such as "Shakespeare and the Law," "The Lady Doth Protest Too Much Methinks: The Use of Figurative Language from Shakespeare's Hamlet in American Case Law," and "Examples Gross as Earth: Hamlet's Inaction and the Problem of Stare Decisis."
- *General Science Full Text* indexes an article "Was Shakespeare a Playwright?" in *Science Digest*.
- *Art Source* picks up such things as an article in an architectural journal on the reconstruction of the Globe Theatre in London, and an *Art News* report on the discovery of a long-lost portrait of the Bard.
- *Biological and Agricultural Index*, too, indexes articles such as "On the Nature of Shakespeare's Cursed Hebona" and "Shakespeare, Kittredge, and Galen" (on the use of a medicinal term in one of the plays).
- *Applied Science and Technology Source* covers topics such as **Art, Aesthetics, Airplanes in art, Ancient art, Lasers/art use, Mural painting and decoration**, and **Renaissance art**; one of the articles indexed in this database is "Robots Take the Lead in Ballet."
- *General Science Full Texts* covers not just **Art** but dozen of narrower topics such as:

Alchemy in art
Anghiari (Italy), Battle of, 1440 in art
Animals in art
Biological illustrations
Birds in art
Chemistry and art
Computers/Art uses
Fish in art
Forgeries of works of art
Geology and art
Mathematics and art
Organic matter/Art uses
Plants in art
Science and art
Weather in art
Women in art

Articles under the descriptor **Native Americans** appear not just in *Humanities Index* and *Social Sciences Index*. The same topic is covered—confining ourselves just to the former Wilson indexes that are now (one way or another) EBSCO files—in *all* of the following:

Applied Science and Technology Index
Art Index
Biological and Agricultural Index
Book Review Digest
Business Periodicals Index
Education Index
General Science Index
Index to Legal Periodicals
Readers' Guide

An important qualification is in order, however: as of this writing, at least two other EBSCO/Wilson databases, *Book Review Digest* and *Essay and General Literature Index*, use the controlled heading **Indians of North America** rather than **Native Americans**.

PROBLEMS WITH VARIANT SEARCH TERMS

When more files are added the problem becomes much greater. To press the same inquiry into other databases (both controlled and keyword), you could also find material on the same subject in:

- *America: History and Life* (**Indians**)
- *Anthropology Plus* (**North American Indians, Mexican Indians**)
- *ATLA Religion Database* (**Indians of North America, Indians of Central America, Indians of Mexico**)
- *Avery Index to Architectural Periodicals* (**Indians of North America** as a subject heading: **Native American** as a subdivision of other headings, e.g., **Culture—Native American**)
- *Dissertation Abstracts* (author keywords)
- *Environment Complete* (**Indians of North America, Indians of Central America, Indians of Mexico**)
- *Environmental Sciences and Pollution Management* (author keywords)
- *Garden, Landscape & Horticulture Index* (**Indians of North America, Indians of Central America, Indians of Mexico**)
- *GPO [Government Printing Office]* (**Indians of North America**)
- *Index to Jewish Periodicals* (**Native Americans** and some others)
- *International Index to Music Periodicals* (**Native Americans**)
- *MLA International Bibliography* (**Native Americans**)
- *ProQuest Historical Newspapers* (author keywords)
- *Nineteenth Century Masterfile* (a variety of descriptors and keywords)
- *PAIS* (**Indians of North America, Indians of Canada, Indians of Mexico**)
- *Periodicals Contents Index* (author keywords)
- *PsycINFO* (**American Indians**)
- *Short Story Index* (**Indians of North America**)
- *Sociological Abstracts* (**American Indians**), and
- *Subject Collections*, a printed guide to libraries with special holdings in various subject areas (**Indians of North America and Mexico**).

If you did a federated search of all of these files together using only **Native Americans** as your search term, you would miss most of what is covered by these latter databases—and you wouldn't know that you've missed anything, since "all" of the databases were included in the federated search.

Of course, in most cases a researcher will not need to use the full range of perspectives on a topic such as American Indians and may be quite satisfied with what she finds in only *Social Sciences Full Text, Humanities Source,* or *America: History and Life.* Indeed, in most instances—particularly at the start of an inquiry—it is advisable to begin with the particular databases that provide the greatest disciplinary focus on the core literature of one's subject area (e.g., *Historical Abstracts, PsycINFO,*

Sociological Abstracts, etc.) rather than to do a federated or "discovery" search of as many files as possible, all at once.

Federated searching "across silos" is *sometimes* the best way to cover the same topic in multiple databases, but primarily if your topic has unusually distinctive keywords that do not admit of alternative phrasings and that are also unlikely to appear in unwanted contexts. I've had questions on the "Chimborazo" (a volcano in Ecuador), on "memsahibs" (wives of British colonial officials in India), on "nadaismo" (an artistic/cultural movement in Colombia in the 1950s and 1960s that spilled over into political protests), on "asbestos cleavage planes," and on "batrachotoxin" (a kind of poison derived from South American frogs)—none of which were connected to controlled vocabulary terms, and all of which lent themselves to searches within multiple databases, with minimal appearances of the right word(s) in undesired contexts.

It is easy to misjudge how distinctive a particular keyword is, however. To return to an example from Chapter 2: if you search multiple databases at the same time for the name of the late Libyan dictator Muammar **G**addafi (with a "G") you will miss all of the records having the name spelled **Q**addafi (with a "Q"). All of the elaborate mechanisms for "drilling down" within a federated set created by specifying only one of these spellings will not solve the basic problem of the lack of a cross-reference alerting you to the other form you didn't think of. The bottom line: be very wary of "one-stop" or "seamless" searches. While they hold out the promise of showing you "the whole elephant" they may in fact still leave you in the situation of the Six Blind Men.

In pursuing cross-disciplinary inquiries I would emphasize in particular the complementary nature of literary, historical, and social sciences databases. For example, if you want information on French writers at the turn of the last century, don't use just the *MLA International Bibliography*—try *Historical Abstracts, FRANCIS, Dissertation Abstracts, Periodicals Index Online* (covering 1665 to 1995), *IBZ*, and the *Web of Science* (covering 13,500+ journals in all subject areas, not just science). If you are searching in anthropology, don't use just *Anthropology Plus*—try the *MLA International Bibliography, Historical Abstracts, Social Sciences Index, Humanities Index, ATLA Religion Index*, and the others just mentioned. The first rule is this: *don't confine yourself to only those databases that have your subject words in the title of the database.* The second rule is this: it is usually better to search the disparate databases separately and individually, tailoring your terms to the peculiarities of each one, rather than to cover them simultaneously in a federated search. The third rule is this: talk to the reference librarians about which databases provide the best coverage for you topic; they may also be helpful in showing you how to find the best search terms.

FINDING WHICH JOURNALS EXIST, WHICH ARE ELECTRONICALLY AVAILABLE, AND WHERE THEY ARE INDEXED

Sometimes researchers just want to get an overview of which journals exist within a particular subject area. Sometimes they want to know where a particular journal can be found online. Sometimes they want to know where a particular journal indexed, especially if it is not available full text online. A number of sources, both electronic and printed, are useful in supplying this information:

- At least four subscription databases will tell you which journals are available in electronic form (and keyword searchable) from your home library's terminals. (Undoubtedly there will be further competition in this area.) The problem here is that many vendors of individual databases (e.g., ProQuest, EBSCO, JSTOR) now provide overlapping full-text electronic access to many of the same journals, but often the different services offer the same titles with different years of coverage. If you want to know which electronic serials are accessible from your library's terminals, check the subscription databases *Serials Solutions, TDNet, Article Finder,* or *EZB: Electronic Journals Library.* Each of them identifies which electronic journals are available through all of your library's *other* database subscriptions, with notes on which years of coverage are available for each journal from each provider. Live links to the online journals are provided. Each of these subscription files will always be locally tailored to list only the electronic holdings of your own library.
- *Directory of Open Access Journals* www.doaj.org is a listing of over 9.500 free, full-text journals, of which over 4,800 are searchable at the article level. All subjects and languages are within scope— but keep in mind that the vast majority of copyrighted journals do not appear here.
- *Fulltext Sources Online* (Information Today, semiannual) is available as either a subscription database or a printed directory; it lists over 52,000 periodicals, newspapers, newsletters, newswires, and TV/radio transcripts that are commercially available online; it also tell which aggregator services provide which years of

coverage. It has indexes by Subjects, Geographic areas covered, and Languages.

- *Ulrich's Periodicals Directory* (ProQuest, annual) is another printed directory (an online subscription version is available); it is the largest roster of which journals and periodicals are currently being published worldwide, listing over 300,000 titles. For each one it will tell you if there is an electronic version (over 80,000 are covered) and which indexes or databases, if any, cover that periodical. The same listings provide bibliographic information, publishers' contact information (address, website, phone number), circulation figures, and subscription costs. The titles are categorized in broad subject groupings.

- *The Standard Periodical Directory* (Oxbridge Communications, annual) is a comprehensive printed list of over 60,000 U.S. and Canadian magazines, journals, newsletters, newspapers, directories, and yearbooks. It arranges entries in broad subject areas and provides information on electronic availability, circulation, and contacts, but it does not tell you where its journals are indexed.

- *Gale Directory of Publications and Broadcast Media* (Gale Cengage, annual) lists over 55,000 newspapers, journals, and magazines worldwide, as well as radio and television stations. It is particularly good in listing local newspapers and magazines, arranged by State/City or Province for U.S. and Canadian publications, by Country for other areas. Another very useful feature is its listings of ethnic publications (Black, Foreign Language, Hispanic, Jewish) in the United States and Canada.

- *Magazines for Libraries*, edited by Cheryl LaGuardia (ProQuest, revised irregularly), is a selective, annotated guide to the most important journals in all subject areas. Full paragraph descriptions are given for each title. This volume is a major resource for libraries in making decisions about which magazines and journals to subscribe to. Writers, too, frequently look here when they wish to determine which journals might be interested in their articles. Over 6,000 serials (arranged by broad subject areas) are described; contact information, electronic availability, and indexing information are included.

- *Indexed Periodicals: A Guide to 170 Years of Coverage in 33 Indexing Services* by Joseph Marconi (Pierian Press, 1976) is useful for finding index coverage of old periodicals.

- *Chicorel Index to Abstracting and Indexing Services* (Chicorel Index Series, vols. 11 and 11A; 2nd ed., 1978) also provides information on where older periodicals are indexed.

If you're going to be a good researcher, you have to remember that many journals are not available electronically, and many thousands are not indexed anywhere. Nevertheless, you may wish to be aware of the existence of the nonelectronic, and unindexed, serials in your field of interest, since the information in them may be of great value. To identify all of the journals being published in any subject area, use *Ulrich's* in combination with *The Standard Periodical Directory*.

IDENTIFYING THE BEST JOURNALS

To find out which periodicals are considered the best or the most important in their subject fields, use *Magazines for Libraries* (above). If your library subscribes to it, the *Journal Citation Reports* database from the Institute for Scientific Information, a subsidiary of Thomson Reuters, provides ranked listings of which journals in the sciences and social sciences are most heavily cited by other journals—a good indication of their importance. (As of this writing, however, humanities journals are not covered in this database.)

Thomson Reuter's *Science Citation Index, Social Sciences Citation Index*, and *Arts and Humanities Citation Index* also provide lists of which journals are indexed by each source, in broad subject categories. The titles within these subject areas are listed alphabetically, rather than in ranked order; but the mere fact that a journal is listed here to begin with means that it is very important in its area and is being frequently cited by other journals. These subject-category journal lists are available online at http://ip-science.thomsonreuters.com/mjl/. Click on the title of the database you want, then select the "View Subject Category" link to bring up the list of journal titles within each category.

Google Scholar has now introduced a ranking algorithm to identify its most important journals; a search on the phrase "Google Scholar metrics" will bring up the list.

PROBLEMS WITH ABBREVIATIONS OF JOURNAL TITLES

One frustrating problem that researchers sometimes have with older serials is one that can usually be prevented with a bit of foresight; it concerns abbreviations of journal titles. Online indexes, as a rule, provide citations with full journal title information rather than abbreviations; but footnotes or bibliographies sometimes abbreviate the titles of the journals they cite. If all you have is an abbreviation, you may have considerable trouble in trying to look up the title in your library's catalog or elsewhere (e.g., "Educ" can stand for "Education" or "Educational"; "Ann" can be "Annual" or "Annals"; "Com" can be "Community" or "Commerce"; "Res" can be "Resources" or "Research"; "Soc" can be "Society" or "Social"; and so on).[7] The articles or prepositions that are left out can also cause problems. One researcher looking for *Bull. Hist. Med.* assumed that it meant *Bulletin of Historical Medicine*. It doesn't—it's *Bulletin of the History of Medicine*. Minor variations like these greatly complicate keyword searches.

A wise researcher, then, in copying or creating a journal citation, will *never abbreviate the title of a journal*. **Never.** The few extra seconds it takes to record the full title may save you hours of frustration at a later date—especially if you are looking for an article in a library other than the one in which you wrote down the citation.

There are, however, reference sources that will provide full titles of most journal abbreviations, and while they can solve many such problems, they won't solve all of them, so it's better to avoid creating the problem in the first place. The best sources for expanding abbreviated or incomplete journal title references are these:

- *Periodical Title Abbreviations* (Thomson Gale, revised irregularly) lists over 230,000 abbreviations and their spelled-out forms.
- *Acronyms, Initialisms and Abbreviations Dictionary* (Gale Cengage, annual) is a multivolume set not limited to journal abbreviations, but it does have some that are not in *Periodical Title Abbreviations*.
- *World List of Scientific Periodicals* (Butterworth, 1963 and supplements). This venerable set is still very useful for spelling out the full titles of old scientific journals, worldwide, published from 1900 to the 1970s.

THE 1981 CHANGE IN CATALOGING RULES FOR SERIALS

Another problem with serials is that there was a change in library cataloging rules as of 1981, and it still causes confusion today. In current practice, a journal such as *Journal of the American Medical Association* would be entered in a library catalog under just this title. Under the old rules, however, it would appear as *American Medical Association. Journal*. The old rule was that *if the name of the society or organization appears in the title*, then catalog the journal under the first word of the *society name* and not under the first word (e.g., *Journal, Annals, Bulletin, Proceedings,* etc.) of the title. Note the important distinction, however: the old rule applied only if the name of an *organization* appeared in the title; thus a form such as *Journal of Medicine* would file "as is," but a form such as *Journal of the Medicine Society* would file as *Medicine Society. Journal.*

This distinction continues to cause much confusion in the search for old periodical titles, especially those that both began and ceased publication during the period before 1981, for it leads many researchers who look under the wrong entry form to conclude that a library does not own a particular serial when it actually is available. Compounding the problem is the fact that many journals that began publication prior to 1981 are still being published today—but if they were cataloged at the time of their initial appearance, the library's record for that title may still be under the old form. This means that you may have to look under the old form of entry (under the organization's name rather than under *Journal* or *Proceedings*) in order to find the call number for *current* years of the journal. The important point is that you need to be aware of the potential problem with this kind of journal title.

Let me take this opportunity to emphasize a more general rule: *if you fail to find any title that you are looking for, under **any** circumstances, be sure to talk to the reference librarians.* There are many tricks and exceptions to cataloging rules that are not obvious to nonlibrarians, so always talk to the reference staff whenever you have *any* problem in locating any item you have identified.

CHAPTER 5

Keyword Searches

THE VARIOUS DATABASES DISCUSSED SO FAR ARE OF THE CON-
trolled vocabulary type. The advantages of databases using standardized search terms (subject headings or descriptors) is that they solve the
problems of synonym variations (e.g., "death penalty," "capital punishment"), of foreign-language terms (*"peine de mort," "pena capitale"*), and
of relationship connections to other topics (through BT, RT, and NT
cross-references, alphabetical menus of search terms, online browse displays of subdivisions, subject tracing fields within full record displays, and
linkages of headings to classification numbers). The conceptual grouping
function of controlled vocabularies saves researchers the considerable
trouble of having to search using a wide variety of terms for material on
one subject, and the associative function (referring to cross-references
and browse menus) maps out formal paths not only to preferable search
terms but also to multiple related topics and to unanticipated aspects "off
to the side" of the same topic.

DISADVANTAGES OF CONTROLLED
VOCABULARY SEARCHES

There are, however, corresponding disadvantages to any controlled vocabulary system. First, the grouping function is sometimes achieved at
the expense of blurring fine distinctions between subjects. Several years
ago, for example, a reader was interested in the idea of "patients actively
participating in the therapeutic process"; at the time, this was a new field
of interest in the medical profession. The only subject heading available was **Patient compliance**, which is not the same thing as active

participation; nonetheless, this term was used to include the latter idea until enough of a literature grew up that a new heading, **Patient participation**, was created to deal with it. Similarly, I once helped a reader who wanted books on "subfractional horsepower electric motors." I showed her the *LCSH* heading **Electric motors, Fractional horsepower**, but she insisted that she wanted only *sub*fractional and not fractional. When we looked at the entries under the **Fractional** heading, however, we saw that it included works on subfractional motors. Evidently the cataloger, seeing no separate heading in the list for "Subfractional," simply chose the closest heading that did exist. This often happens—especially if the cataloger is not in a position to notice new works being written on the narrower topic.[1] Distinctions that are important to subject specialists may not be perceived as important by library catalogers, especially at their first appearance, so if you wish to retrieve library materials within the subject heading system you must use the terms chosen by the catalogers. *LCSH* headings thus often include subject areas that are not precisely indicated by the terminology of the heading. (If there is any doubt about what a heading means or includes, simply call up the list of records cataloged under it; the retrieved titles and note fields will clarify its scope of coverage.)

Second, a controlled vocabulary system cannot get too specific within one subject without losing its categorization function. This is particularly true of a book catalog, which seeks to summarize the contents of works as a whole (rather than indexing individual parts, sections, chapters, or paragraphs). Thus the researcher who was looking for material on the dental identification of Hitler's deputy Martin Bormann could find a general heading on **Bormann, Martin, 1900–1945** but not a precise one on "Bormann, Martin, 1900–1945—Dental identification." Similarly a researcher looking for "effects of wing design on reducing heat stress at supersonic speeds in military aircraft" will not find a controlled vocabulary term that is nearly as precise as he would wish.

Note, however, that many headings sometimes referred to as "orphans"— those that are applied to only one book—are in fact parts of larger categories, in spite of apparently retrieving only one item. For example, the headings **Church work with cowgirls** and **Church work with employed women** (as of this writing) both point to only one book apiece in the catalog of the Library of Congress. And yet these headings themselves are parts of a larger group, created by the appearance of both headings within an OPAC browse display of alphabetically adjacent related terms:

Church work with abused women
Church work with alcoholics
Church work with cowgirls
Church work with disaster victims
Church work with divorced people
Church work with employed women
Church work with families
Church work with immigrants
Church work with people with disabilities
Church work with tourists
Church work with women
Church work with youth

The full menu of related terms extends to hundreds of such phrases, many with further subdivisions. *LCSH* terms that are orphans in terms of their conceptual grouping function are seldom orphans in terms of their associative or relationship-mapping function.

A third difficulty with controlled vocabularies is that, by nature, they are relatively slow to change. The reason is that a cataloger cannot simply insert a new term into the *LCSH* list without integrating it with the existing terms through a web of cross-references that must extend *from* the new word to others, and *to* the new word from the others. These cross-references have to include broader (BT), related (RT), and narrower (NT) relationships defined in both directions. In other words these links have to be created not just "out" from the new term alone. The other existing terms have to be modified too, to show their own links back to their new neighbor. Any new term may also have to be linked to particular classification numbers. This intellectual work—again, it's sort of like creating, or extending, a huge crossword puzzle that has been expanding for more than a century—takes considerable time and effort, so catalogers are cautious about acting too quickly. (This is one major difference between subject cataloging and tagging—tag terms can be applied by anyone at all with no thought for either their standardization or their relationships or formal linkages to other terms.) They find it is often advisable to wait until a new subject has achieved a recognizable critical mass in determining its own vocabulary. If your topic is in a new field, then, or is of recent development—or if it was a kind of "flash-in-the-pan" academic fad—its terms may not appear in the system. For example, you will find an established heading for **Behaviorism (Psychology)** but not for "neobehavorism."

Fourth, the formal cross-references of a controlled vocabulary system may not, by themselves, be adequate to get you from the terms you know to the heading that is acceptable. In *Psychological Abstracts*, for instance, articles on the psychological problems of hostages were indexed for many years under the term **Crime victims**. A cross-reference from "Hostages" to this heading was introduced only in 1982, but **Hostages** did not become a descriptor in its own right until 1988. (Note, however, that in the *LCSH* system cross-references are only one of five mechanisms that enable you to get from whatever term you think up to the controlled term[s]; see Chapter 2). Many of those who disparage controlled vocabularies seem to be unaware that the networks relating terms to each other include many more linkages than just cross-references.)

In spite of such disadvantages, however, researchers must also keep clearly in mind the fundamental advantages of controlled vocabulary sources, specifically those of the *Library of Congress Subject Headings* system: uniform heading, scope-match specificity, and specific entry (see Chapter 2). The combination of these principles produces the characteristic of plenitude in a controlled catalog: an ability to show users, in a systematic manner, many more relevant options for researching their topics than they are capable of articulating beforehand. Conceptual categorization of materials allows researchers to simply recognize, within the conceptual groupings, works whose individual titles (or other keywords) they could never think up beforehand. Further, linkages, subdivisions, and adjacency mappings extend the fields of recognition possibilities in a systematic manner that minimizes guesswork while at the same time eliminating excessively granular retrievals of thousands of irrelevant records.

"RESEARCHERS ACCUSTOMED TO GOOGLE DON'T USE SUBJECT HEADINGS"

It is sometimes maintained today that subject headings (or descriptors) are no longer necessary because most researchers are accustomed to Google keyword searching and don't use subject headings. I fully agree with the latter part of the statement, that most researchers don't use them, but it is incorrect to conclude that therefore they are no longer necessary. The fact is—and I see this on a daily basis—they continue to solve too many very real, and very serious, research problems for those who know of their existence. Students who are shown the right subject headings for their topics—and how to find them—are immensely grateful. They do indeed appreciate the advantages of searching by controlled terms once those advantages are pointed out to them—and once they are shown what keyword searching is not doing for them. But no one learns what controlled vocabularies can do without some prior (or point-of-use) instruction on what they are and how they work. Instruction classes that focus entirely on how to do critical thinking usually don't notice, themselves, the crucial distinctions between controlled vocabulary vs. keyword searches. The philosophy of the late Apple chairman Steve Jobs, that consumers don't know what they want until it's put in front of them, is very relevant here. (The library field, unfortunately, has a habit of simply following Google rather than focusing on alternatives to it that work much better in the niche areas libraries must fill.)

PROBLEMS WITH KEYWORD SEARCHES

While is it indeed true that most researchers don't know how to use subject headings or descriptors, it is equally true that most researchers don't know how to do effective keyword searches either. This may sound strange or counterintuitive, but it is nonetheless quite true, for several reasons.

First, most researchers do not realize that the keywords they type in are not categories. I've already provided multiple examples in Chapter 2, but let me add another here: a senior researcher who was working on "technological innovation in the low countries" showed me the print-outs he had made on his own. It was evident that he had typed in the keyword term "low countries" in the assumption that doing so would also include everything relevant on Belgium, the Netherlands, and Luxembourg without any further specification. He didn't realize that the databases he used were simply looking for the character string "l-o-w [space] c-o-u-n-t-r-i-e-s." They were not picking up the names of the particular countries since those are formed by different character strings. Nor did he realize that he was getting only English-language sources, because the English character string misses the French and German character strings "Pays-Bas" and "Niederlande"—as well as "Belgique" and "Belgien" (among other language forms for the individual countries). In effect, he assumed that his keyword search term was an inclusive conceptual category, rather than a precise letter string—because, in his own mind, it *was* an inclusive conceptual category. This is a very common mistaken assumption among all researchers who do only keyword searches. They think their search terms include much more than they actually do.

What is particularly harmful to good research here, beyond the basic confusion of categories vs. character strings, is that the "categories" people ask for—or think they are asking for—are usually much too broad to begin with. Researchers routinely ask for what they think they can get rather than for what they really want, and so they (mistakenly) phrase their keyword inquiries in very general terms. Actually, however, specific searches work better than general searches. The result is that the sets of records they retrieve, right from the start, do not contain the "on-target" records they really want, and progressively limiting such bad initial sets (via additional keywords, "facets," or any other mechanism) will do nothing to steer them to *other* sets that would be preferable— i.e, you can't narrow down to the best sources if you're looking within the wrong sets to begin with. You need cross-references to better search terms that will produce better initial sets rather than limiting mechanisms applied to the wrong sets.

A further problem is the most people who are accustomed to Google keyword searches do not know about use of quotation marks, word truncation, proximity searching, use of parentheses, or differences between Boolean AND, OR, and NOT operators—all of which can greatly modify the results of keyword inquiries (see Chapter 10).

Most researchers frame their questions within what might be called a "horizon of expectations"—i.e., a set of assumptions of what, or how much, information they are likely to find. If, then, they subsequently find any information at all that falls within this circumscribed set of expectations, they will go away satisfied—even though they may well have searched the wrong databases (or not enough of the right ones), typed in the wrong search terms, and assumed that "relevance ranked" results show all of the best material that is available. This is what I mean in saying that most students are in the situation of the Six Blind Men of India in researching the elephant. (This is also my major criticism of automated systems that steer students toward a single search box, with the snake oil come-on that "under-the-hood programming" will automatically provide them with the best results, no matter what terms they type in.)

While it is true, then, that most people don't understand subject headings, it is equally true that that very same people also don't understand keyword searching—and that they are also not given any instruction on the major differences of the two search techniques. I've emphasized the point so much because, in my decades of working with tens of thousands of researchers, I've found this distinction to be absolutely crucial do doing effective research—and yet it is seldom taught to anyone other than librarians. And too many librarians themselves, these days, seem to be losing sight of it, particularly in teaching classes on how to do research. I don't mean to minimize the importance of the focus of many such classes on critical thinking, but I do mean to emphasize that it doesn't much matter how well you can do critical thinking in evaluating websites (or other sites) if you've typed in the wrong search terms to begin with. Right from the start you will be radically skewing the range of resources that you perceive, as did each of the Six Blind Men. (To anticipate upcoming chapters, there are still other "blind spots" overlooked by both keyword *and* controlled vocabulary searches; they show up when compared to the results achieved by citation searches and related record searches, use of published bibliographies, talking to people, and so on. All of the latter, alternative search techniques will be explained in due course.)

When all is said and done, then, keyword searching necessarily entails the problem of the unpredictability of the many variant ways the same subject can be expressed, both within a single language (Huron Indians, Wyandot Indians) and across multiple languages (Venice, Venizia, Venidig). And no software algorithm will solve this problem when it is confined to dealing with only the words retrievable from the given documents (or citations or abstracts) themselves, which contain only the various authors' own wordings.

A second problem with keyword searching, no matter how skillfully it is done, is its likelihood to retrieve the right words in the wrong conceptual contexts. This point needs no further elaboration—anyone who has done Internet searches runs into this problem. And it cannot be solved by computer algorithms; indeed, it is their operation that is *causing* the problem.

A third problem with keyword searching, especially in full-text databases or websites, is that of excessively granular retrievals—i.e., such searches often, if not usually, produce results numbering in the tens of thousands of hits, including pages that simply mention the desired keywords in references that are tangential or superficial. Keyword searching in full-text databases misses the scope-match level of specificity (providing whole books on a topic)—it frequently "overshoots the mark" in a way that buries many useful hits within way too much unwanted chaff.

MAJOR ADVANTAGES OF KEYWORD SEARCHING

Nonetheless, just as with controlled headings, there are major advantages to keyword searching as well as drawbacks. The advantages show up precisely in the area where subject headings don't work well. The fact is, there will always be many topics that simply fall between the cracks of any subject heading or descriptor system. No thesaurus has a term for "managing sociotechnical change," for example; but a keyword search of the exact word "sociotechnical" combined with "manage★" or "plan★" (the asterisk being a truncation or word-stemming symbol) will turn up multiple hits, in several databases, that are directly relevant. Similarly, there's no adequate subject heading for "Elfreth's Alley" in Philadelphia, or for the "Edenton Tea Party" in colonial North Carolina, or for "nadaismo" (a literary and political movement in Colombia), or for "water meadows" in Great Britain, or for "memsahibs" (wives of British colonial officials in India)—and yet in each case the research problem could be solved by keyword searching for these exact terms. The nature of these subjects is such that there aren't multiple different vocabulary terms for them.

The basic trade-off between keyword vs. controlled vocabulary searching is that of precision, on the one hand, and predictability, conceptual categorization, relationship mapping, and plenitude, on the other. The latter considerations come into play especially when the subject cannot be specified cleanly in precise keywords.

Although the databases discussed in Chapters 2 and 4 are controlled vocabulary types that employ subject headings or descriptors, all of them can also be searched by keywords appearing anywhere within their titles or abstracts (or, in some cases, full texts). And most can also be searched by combinations of both controlled terms and uncontrolled keywords in Boolean combinations (see Chapter 10).

The databases discussed below, unlike those in Chapter 4, are primarily searchable by keywords alone. This point applies especially to the many full-text databases. When searching such resources, you are essentially combing them for the words used by the authors of the individual works, who were writing their texts with little or no regard as to whether their peculiar terminologies or turns of phrase would be similar to those of any other writers on the same topics.

MAJOR KEYWORD DATABASES

The following databases are available through a variety of different vendors. Some search title keywords within citations; others search at the level of abstracts; still others provide full-text depth. The list is by no means exhaustive, but these are some of the most important keyword-searchable resources that most scholars need to know about.

Web of Science, a subscription service from Thomson Reuters, is a combination of several separate indexes, *Science Citation Index Expanded* (1900–), *Social Sciences Citation Index* (1900–), *Arts & Humanities Citation Index* (1975–), *Book Citation Index* (2005–), *Conference Proceedings Citation Index* (1990–), and *Data Citation Index*. They will be described more fully in Chapter 6. Libraries that subscribe can limit their access to any individual component—they don't have to take all of them. They may further choose the years of coverage they want to pay for—say, for journal coverage, only back to 1990 or 1980. The roughly 13,500 journals selected for indexing are chosen in large part (although not exclusively) on the basis of how frequently they are cited by articles appearing in other journals. What this means is that Web of Science covers the cream of the crop of academic journals in all fields remarkably well. The indexing extends to citations and abstracts, not full texts. A particularly useful feature is that the titles of journal articles written in foreign languages are translated into English for keyword searching (although the original language of the article will always be clearly specified). In other words, you can do your searches only with English-language terms, although your results may then include citations to articles in languages other than English.

Note an important limitation: *Web of Science* focuses only on journals that have footnotes to begin with—it does not "see" important news or commentary magazines and journals whose articles lack this scholarly apparatus. Many of the more popular and influential newsstand-type publications are of this nonfootnote type, and so are not indexed here. Web of Science is a particularly good source, however, for cross-disciplinary searching since it covers so many subject areas simultaneously.

Scopus from Elsevier is a similar but even larger database, covering about 22,000 journals in all academic subject areas (see Chaper 6).

Periodicals Index Online, from ProQuest, indexes citations to articles in more than 6,000 journals in 60 languages going back to 1665, up to 2005 You can search for keywords appearing in the titles of articles (as well as in their authors' names and journal titles), but not abstracts or full texts. Coverage is international, in English, French, German, Spanish, Italian, and most other Western languages. Unlike the Web of Science, this database does not translate foreign language article titles; as a practical matter, this means that you have to think up keyword synonyms and phrase variations in all of the languages in which you want retrieval. Boolean combinations, proximity searching, use of parentheses, and word truncation are allowed. Searches can be limited by language, by years of publication, and by any of 37 broad subject categories:

Agriculture, Ancient Civilizations, Anthropology/Ethnology, Applied Arts, Archaeology, Architecture, Area Studies (Africa), Area Studies (Asia), Area Studies (Australasia), Area Studies (Europe), Area Studies (Middle East), Black Studies, Business/Management, Economics, Education, Fine Arts, Folklore, Geography, History (General), History (The Americas), Humanities (General), Jewish Studies, Law, Library/Information Science, Linguistics/Philology, Literature, Music, Performing Arts, Philosophy, Political Science, Psychology, Public Administration, Religion/Theology, Social Affairs, Social Sciences (General), Sociology, and Women's Studies.

Although coverage is quite strong in social sciences and humanities, it is comparatively weak in the sciences. It is, however, another source that is particularly good for cross-disciplinary searching, through all of the 37 areas listed. One historian of slavery, for example, found here an article with specific data on the cost of transporting a slave from Baltimore to New Orleans; she hadn't found such information elsewhere because the article appeared in an obscure economics journal rather than in a history journal. This database covers both fields simultaneously. Most indexes cover only recent decades of publication; the fact that *Periodicals Index Online* covers so many journals internationally over a span of more than three centuries makes it an extremely valuable resource.

Periodicals Archive Online is a companion database to Periodicals Index Online; the difference is that this one provides keyword-searchable full texts of articles back to 1802, but only from about 600 of the journals, of which about 140 are in languages other than English. (Approximately 50 new journals are added every year.)

19th Century Masterfile, from Paratext, includes a complete computerized version of a venerable printed source, Poole's Index to Periodical Literature (1802–1906), which covers nearly 500 American and English periodicals. In addition to the Index itself, Paratext has augmented Poole's with dates for all citations—not in the originals—and corrected all title abbreviations. The database, however, goes way beyond this, with some coverage back to the 1200s and forward to about 1930. The goal of the company is to include all relevant indexes to material published in English before 1930, with links to any full text of the source documents, wherever available. So far, links to more than 13 million full texts within other library subscriptions (e.g., *JSTOR, American Periodicals Series, Hein Online, Accessible Archives,* Google Books) or in freely available websites. (You won't see the full-text links to subscription services if your local library doesn't pay for them.) The database, up to now, has digitized and edited more than 70 indexes to nineteenth-century magazines, newspapers, books, U.S. patents, and government publications (both American and British). Among these are the following:

- *A.L.A. Index to General Literature* (an index to book contents, 1893–1910)
- *A.L.A. Portrait* Index (listing citations to 40,000 portraits of individuals before 1906)
- *Accessible Archives* index of nineteenth-century American newspapers (1728–1922)
- American Association of Law Libraries, *Index to Legal Periodicals* (1908–1935)
- *American State Papers* (1789–1838)
- Ames, *Comprehensive Index to the Publications of U.S. Government 1881–1893*
- *Annals of Congress* (1789–1824), *Register of Debates* (1824–1837), and *Congressional Globe* (1833–1873)
- *ARTstor Digital Library* (This is a subscription database containing more than a million digital art images from museums and photo archives. *19th Century MasterFile* indexes the images and provides links to them if your library subscribes to *ARTstor*.)
- *Burlington Free Press* (1848–1870)
- *Catalogue of the Public Documents of the 53rd to the 76th Congress* (1893–1940)
- *Checklist of the United States Public Documents* (1789–1909)
- Cobbett, *Parliamentary History of England, 1066–1803*
- Cotgreave, *Contents-Subject Index to General and Periodical Literature* (1850–1899)
- *Cumulative Subject Index to the Monthly Catalog of United States Government Publications* (1895–1976)
- *Cumulative Title Index to United States Public Documents, 1789–1900*
- ERIC documents [education]
- *Farmer's Bulletin* index, 1889–1939
- Galloupe, *General Index to Engineering Periodicals* (1883–1893)
- *Granite Monthly* (1877–1930)
- Greeley, *Public Documents of the First Fourteen Congresses* (1789–1817)
- *Hansard's British Parliamentary Debates: House of Commons, First and Second Series 1803–1830*
- *Hansard's British Parliamentary Debates: House of Lords, First and Second Series 1803–1830* [further coverage of *Hansard's* is planned]
- *Harper's Magazine Index* (1850–1892)

- *Harvard University Library Catalog* (pre-1931)
- Hickcox, *Monthly Catalog of U.S. Government Publications* (1885–1894)
- *Index of Patents Issued from the U.S. Patent Office* (1790–1873)
- *Index to the Journals of the Continental Congress 1774–1789*
- *Index to the Oregon Spectator* (1846–1854)
- Johnson, *Descriptive Index to Engineering Literature* (1884–1891) continued by *Engineering Index* to 1900
- Jones and Chipman, *Index to Legal Periodical Literature* (1786–1922)
- *Library Journal Index* (1876–1897)
- Maclay, *Sketches of Debate in the First Senate of the United States 1789–1791*
- *Making of America* journals (Cornell/Michigan; 36 titles indexed)
- *Messages and Papers of the Presidents* (1789–1897)
- *New York Daily Tribune Index* (1875–1906)
- *New York Times Index* (1863–1905)
- *Palmer's Index to the Times (London)* (1880–1890)
- Poore, *Descriptive Catalogue of the Government Publications of the United States 1774–1881*
- *Psychological Index* (1894–1905)
- *Records of U. S. Congressional Serial Set* (1818–1930)
- Richardson, *Index to Periodical Articles on Religion* (1890–1899)
- Royal Society, *Catalogue of Scientific Papers* (1800–1900) and *Subject Indexes*
- *St. Nicholas* (1873–1928)
- Smithsonian Institution, *Annual Reports* (1849–1961)
- *Southern Historical Society Papers* (1876–1910)
- Swem, *Virginia Historical Index* (1619–1930)
- Wright, *American Fiction* (1851–1875)

The publisher of the database keeps looking to add other sources, in all subject areas, for the pre-1930 time period, so coverage will be increasing.

PERSI (Periodicals Source Index), from HeritageQuest, is an index to more than 6,500 U.S. and Canadian local history and genealogy periodicals going back to the early 1800s. Although most are in English, some French Canadian periodicals are covered. This is a particularly good source for really obscure topics in American history, and it serves as an excellent supplement to the major index in the field, *America: History & Life*, which does not notice most of these smaller-circulation journals. The researcher, for example, who was interested in the "Edenton Tea Party" in North Carolina in 1774 found nothing on it in *AH&L* but turned up 15 articles in *PERSI*. Biographical articles on individuals who participated in the Revolutionary wars often show up here, as do articles on the history of particular local buildings (e.g., taverns and inns), obscure sites ("Elfreth's Alley" in Pennsylvania), or whole towns. My experience is that anyone who uses *AH&L* should also search *PERSI* (and vice versa).

Several databases are particularly good in providing full-texts of old periodicals and newspapers:

American Periodicals (ProQuest) is a collection of full texts of more than 1,800 American periodicals published between 1740 and the early twentieth century. It includes what used to be *American Periodicals from the Center for Research Libraries*, which provides more than 300 full texts with full-color scans documenting the emergence of color printing.

American Antiquarian Society Historical Periodicals Collection (EBSCO) is a full-text database of more than 7,600 American periodicals published between 1691 and 1877. Series 1 contains 500 titles between 1691 and 1820; Series 2 has over 1,000 titles from 1821 to 1837; Series 3 has over 1,800 titles from 1838 to 1852; Series 4 has over 1,200 titles from 1853 to 1865; and Series 5 has over 1,500 titles from 1866 to 1877. (Libraries can subscribe to the individual components without getting the full set.)

ProQuest Historical Newspapers (ProQuest) provides text-level searching of dozens of American newspapers, digitized all the way back to their first issues. Major titles such as the *New York Times, Washington Post, Wall Street Journal,* and *Christian Science Monitor* are found here, along with other papers from Boston, Chicago, Atlanta, Los Angeles, St. Louis, Detroit, Cincinnati, and Baltimore. The *Times of India* (1838–2002) and the *Irish Times* (1851–2010) are also covered (if libraries choose), along with four historical Jewish newspapers, and a ***Historical Black American*** newspapers component is also available.

America's Historical Newspapers (Readex) provides full texts of more than a thousand newspapers from all 50 states and the District of Columbia, from 1690 to 1922. A companion database, ***African American Newspapers 1827–1998*** provides 270 additional titles from 35 States. Readex also offers several full-text databases of foreign papers: ***African Newspapers,*** 1800–1922; ***Latin American Newspapers,*** 1805–1922; and ***South Asian Newspapers,*** 1864–1922. Libraries can also subscribe to a cross-searching combination database, ***World Newspaper Archive.***

Accessible Archives (from Accessible Archives) provides full texts of dozens of American newspapers and periodicals, primarily from the period of the Revolution through the Civil War; it includes several major African American titles, as well as scores of county histories, written mainly between 1870 and 1900, for more than 30 states. Full texts of dozens of military unit histories are also searchable.

Chronicling America at http://chroniclingamerica.loc.gov/is a free website created by the Library of Congress; as of this writing it provides full texts of more than 1,000 newspapers from, at present, about two dozen states from 1836 to 1922. Many of the titles are represented by only one or two issues, however. This is an ongoing project. Bibliographical information about hundreds of other U.S. newspapers back to 1690 is also searchable. Other free websites having full texts of some nineteenth-century American periodicals are the two *Making of America* sites, from Cornell (http://digital.library.cornell.edu/m/moa/; offering only about three dozen periodicals), and from the University of Michigan (http://quod.lib.umich.edu/m/moagrp/; 13 periodicals). The latter sites include digitized books as well, although not nearly on the scale of Google Books. Google has yet another free site with texts of old newspapers, *Google News Archive* at http://news.google.com/archivesearch; and although the site has "millions" of articles it is not possible, as of this writing, to get an overview listing of which newspapers and which dates of coverage are included.

17th–18th Century Burney Collection Newspapers (Gale Cengage) includes full texts of over 1,270 titles, primarily from London, but also from English provinces, Ireland, Scotland, and the American colonies from 1603 to the early 1800s. It also covers broadsides, pamphlets, proclamations, Acts of Parliament, and even some books. *19th Century British Newspapers* provides about 50 major titles from England, Scotland, Ireland, and Wales. The two databases are available in a merged file called *British Newspapers 1600–1900*.

Nineteenth Century US Newspapers Digital Archive (Gale Cengage) includes about 250 full-text titles from the 1800s.

19th Century UK Periodicals (Gale Cengage), a work in progress, will eventually offer full runs of 600 titles from 1800 to 1900.

British Periodicals (ProQuest), parts I and II, together provide full texts of nearly 500 titles from the seventeenth through the early twentieth centuries.

The Times Digital Archive 1785–1985 (Gale Cengage) provides every issue of this major London paper from 1785 to 1985. The same publisher also offer separate databases for other London papers, the *Illustrated London News Historical Archive 1842–2003*, the *Financial Times Historical Archive 1886–2006*, the *Times Literary Supplement Historical Archive, 1902–2005*, and *The Sunday Times Digital Archive 1822–2006*.

The several titles above from Gale Cengage, from the **Burney Collection** through the **Sunday Times Digital Archive**, can all be cross-searched simultaneously through the company's **Gale NewsVault** search interface. The latter searches all of their more than 2,000 titles and 10 million digitized pages.

British Newspaper Archive (British Library) is an ongoing project to digitize 40 million pages of its newspapers, chosen from 52,000 titles covering 350 years. Searching is free, but downloading requires payment, at www.britishnewspaperarchive.co.uk.

NewspaperArchive (NewspaperArchive) is a huge full-text database of more than 5,800 newspapers from eleven countries: the United States, United Kingdom, Canada, China, Denmark, France, Germany, Ireland, Jamaica, Japan, and South Africa. Some coverage extends back to the 1600s.

Eureka.CC (CEDROM SNI) is another large database of about 3,000 newspapers and periodicals internationally, going back to 1980. It is particularly good for Canadian and French language news coverage. It has content from every state in the United States and every province in Canada.

Early American Imprints, Series I: Evans, 1639–1800 (Readex) provides full texts of almost every nonserial publication in the American colonies within this span of years, including advertisements, ballads, broadsides, captivity narratives, cookbooks, devotional literature and sermons, diaries, emblem books, grammars, hymns, maps, memoirs, nonfiction books, novels, plays and playbills, textbooks, trade catalogs, and travel literature. Coverage is extended by **Series II: Shaw-Shoemaker, 1801–1819**; the two can be searched simultaneously in libraries that subscribe to them. More than 36,000 items are keyword searchable.

Early English Books Online (EEBO) (Chadwyck-Healey) provides virtually every book—over 100,000 titles—published from 1473 to 1700 in England, Scotland, Ireland, Wales, and British North America, as well as books in English published anywhere else in the world. (**EEBO** includes some American texts not in the **Early American Imprints** databases.)

Eighteenth Century Collections Online (ECCO) (Gale Cengage) offers more than 180,000 full texts of books, pamphlets, and broadsides published in the United Kingdom from 1701 to 1800 (both English and foreign language) as well as some North American imprints.

Early European Books (ProQuest) is a full-text database, with annual additions, seeking to include all works printed in Europe prior to 1701 in all languages, as well as pre-1701 works in European languages printed outside Europe. It currently includes about 18,000 titles. The texts are presented in full color, complete with images of bindings, edges, endpapers, blank pages, and loose inserts. It is essentially a supplement to the *EEBO* database (above) in that it concentrates on digitizing the contents of predominately non-Anglophone libraries, but it also includes material duplicated in *EEBO* if the English works form integral parts of those libraries.

C19: The Nineteenth Century Index (ProQuest/Chadwyck-Healey) enables you to cross-search more than a dozen different databases covering books, newspapers, periodicals, and other formats from the nineteenth century. It includes the *Nineteenth Century Short Title* Catalogue, which is a list of virtually every book in the English language published anywhere in that century, keyed to a microfiche set of the books. (Your own library may or may not own this separate microfiche collection; as of this writing the texts of these microfiche book have not been digitized, but *C19* provides links to many of the same titles in Google Books.) The database, as of this writing, searches these files:

- *American Periodicals from the Center for Research Libraries*
- *American Periodicals Series*
- *Archive Finder*
- *British Periodicals*
- *Dictionary of Nineteenth Century Journalism*
- *House of Commons Parliamentary Papers*
- *Niles' Register, 1811–1849*
- *The Nineteenth Century*
- *Nineteenth Century Short Title Catalogue*
- *Palmer's Index to the Times*
- *Periodicals Index Online/Periodicals Archive Online*
- *Poole's Index to Periodical Literature*
- *Proceedings of the Old Bailey*
- *The Wellesley Index to Victorian Periodicals*
- *U.S. Congressional Serial Set*

Other sources will be added in the future.

Dissertations and Theses: Full Text (ProQuest) provides the best access to doctoral dissertations. Although coverage is worldwide, the emphasis is on U.S. and Canadian sources. More than 2.7 million titles are searchable from 1861 to the present. (More than 2.1 million can be ordered from ProQuest in paper or microfiche formats; more than 1.2 million can be downloaded as PDFs.) From July 1980 forward, abstracts can be searched; prior to that, only titles are searchable for subject content. Master's theses are abstracted from 1988 forward. From 1997 forward, full texts are online for most dissertations and masters' theses.

Dissertations are a true gold mine of scholarship in all subject areas, but (contrary to a widespread assumption) the vast majority of them do not wind up as published books. As with *Web of Science* and *Periodicals Index Online*, give this database a try no matter what topic you are researching. It has controlled headings at very broad levels (e.g., Law; History; United States; Education, Higher; Sociology, General; Literature, Modern; Literature, American; Women's Studies; and so on), but these are useful only in combination with uncontrolled keywords. Remember that you must play around with synonyms in this database, without the help of any cross-references (e.g., "cattle industry" in addition to "beef industry"). In helping a priest interested in "the theology of humor" I found this database to be very useful—but the keyword "theology" had to be combined not just with "humor" but also with terms such as "laughter," "comic," and "comedy"—each of which produced a different set of results.

The Library of Congress, alone of all libraries in the world, owns a virtually complete set of American doctoral dissertations (but not master's theses) on microfilm and microfiche. Doctoral dissertations from countries other than the U.S. and Canada are systematically collected and made available via interlibrary loan by the Center for Research Libraries in Chicago at www.crl.edu/collections/topics/dissertations. Many Canadian theses are available full text online at www.collectionscanada.ca/thesescanada/. Dissertations from MIT (usually not in ProQuest) are available at http://dspace.mit.edu/handle/1721.1/7582, or type "MIT theses" in Google, Bing, or Yahoo!. A general websites for dissertations and theses are provided by OpenThesis at www.openthesis.org/and the Networked Digital Library of Theses and Dissertations at www.ndltd.org/.

Here's a tip for academics whose own dissertations were written prior to 1997: if you order an unbound photocopy (the cheapest option) of your dissertation from ProQuest, at that point the company will also digitize the work and make it full-text readable (and downloadable) through its *Dissertations and Theses: Full Text* subscription service. Pre-1997 texts are being added to the database individually only on as "as ordered" basis. Making your dissertation widely available in full text format in this database can have the spin-off benefit of inducing more people to look at it who would otherwise not bother to order an individual copy. One qualification: these pre-'97 texts can be found only through author, title, or name-of-institution searches. Their abstracts are not present, and their full texts, even though digitized, are not keyword searchable (unlike the texts from 1997 forward).

JSTOR (pronounced Jay-Store) is an online collection of full back-files of about 2,000 academic journals; hundreds more titles will be added in the future. In each case, the vendor goes back to Volume 1, Number 1 of each title and digitizes the entire run of the journal, up to nearly the present. In other words, the virtue of this database is its retrospective coverage: some of the full-text journals here go back hundreds of years (in one case, *Philosophical Transactions* of the Royal Society, to 1665). But there are no subject headings or descriptors here—only keywords are searchable. Libraries can subscribe to a number of separate component collections, including Arts & Sciences, Life Sciences, Biological Sciences, Business, Ecology & Botany, Health & General Sciences, Language & Literature, Mathematics & Statistics, and Music. Check with your local reference librarians to see what is included in your own library's sub-scription, because *JSTOR* access may be very different in coverage from one library to another. The company has recently expanded its service to provide full texts of more than 15,000 books from several major univer-sity presses; this *Books at JSTOR* component will continue to grow along with the expansion of serials coverage. A very tiny portion—only 6 per-cent—of the *JSTOR* articles (pre-1923 U.S. and pre-1870 non-U.S.)[2] has now been made freely searchable at www.jstor.org; but the vast bulk of the database's content is still available only via subscription.

Project Muse is a full-text database of about 600 current high-qual-ity academic journals, from more than a hundred publishers, generally from the mid- or late 1990s or early 2000s forward. (More titles will be added.) Over 12,300 academic books are also included. Articles here are searchable via controlled subject headings as well as by keywords, but it's easiest to remember this database in conjunction with *JSTOR* as it pro-vides the more recent years of some (not all) of the journals found there.

LexisNexis is a huge conglomeration of over 45,000 sources world-wide; as with many other online services, subscribing libraries can pick and choose which component parts they wish to pay for. Corporate or professional library subscriptions entail selections from an extensive menu of hundreds individual component databases and are likely to be quite different from academic library offerings such as **LexisNexis Aca-demic** or **LexisNexis Library Express** (below), which are standardized in their coverage. One major difference is that corporate subscriptions may include real estate records, vehicle registration records, personal data on over 450 million individuals (telephone and cell phone numbers, drivers licenses, professional licenses, voter registrations, death records, selected marriage and divorce records, criminal histories, employment locators), and asset records (real estate and county assessor records, foreclosures, bankruptcies, tax liens). Academic library subscriptions will not include this public record data.

Several separate databases[3] within the conglomeration are available, among them the following:

- **LexisNexis Library Express** is the version most likely to be found in public or state libraries. It provides full texts of more than 9,500 sources, including 2,500 newspapers worldwide, 1,000 magazines and journals, more than 1,000 newsletters, broadcast transcripts (NBC, ABC, CBS, BBC, CNN, NPR, Fox, etc., including foreign sources worldwide), business and trade publications, market research reports, 300+ legal periodicals, 500 law reviews, U.S. court decisions, country and state profiles, patents (from 1971 forward), SEC filings, medical and biographical sources, and a Company Dossier service with detailed data on 53 million U.S. and foreign firms.
- **LexisNexis Academic** is geared to college and university libraries; it is very similar in content to **Library Express**, but has a different pricing structure for this clientele. It also includes nearly 300 college and university newspapers and the *Sheperd's Citations* service, which are not available in *Library Express*.
- **LexisNexis Scholastic** provides very similar content to *Library Express*, with federal and state legislative and bill-tracking information. It is geared toward high school libraries.

Factiva (from Factiva) is another very large full-text database, covering about 36,000 publications worldwide in 28 languages. It provides global coverage of more than 4,500 newspapers. Hundreds of newswire services are also included, and 25,000 websites and blogs are indexed. Coverage extends primarily from the 1990s forward, with some titles back to the late 1970s. *Factiva* is particularly strong in its business coverage: tens of thousands of SEC company reports and investment analyses are available in full text, with directory information for 17 million public companies worldwide. The database also tracks business and general news websites.

HeinOnline (Hein) is a huge compilation of full-text material in the field of law; it contains dozens of component indexes and full-text libraries,[4] among them the following:

- Law Journal Library (more than 1,800 U.S. and international titles)
- American Indian Law Collection (more than 900 titles)
- Code of Federal Regulations (both current and retrospective to 1938)

- English Reports, Full Reprint (1220–1867)—more than 100,000 cases
- Federal Register Library (back to 1936; also United States Government Manual back to 1935, and Weekly Compilation of Presidential Documents to 1965)
- Foreign & International Law Resources Database (including International Yearbooks and Serials; U.S. Law Digests; International Tribunals/Judicial Decisions; and more)
- Foreign Relations of the United States (the full set of 500+ volumes providing primary source documents in U.S. diplomatic history)
- History of Bankruptcy (books, legislative histories, documents, treatises)
- Kluwer Law International Journal Library (20+ major European law journals)
- Legal Classics (more than 3,000 works)
- Sessions Laws Library (all 50 states, Washington, DC, and U.S. territories)
- Subject Compilations of State Laws (1960 to date; thousand of sources for comparing laws on hundreds of subjects)
- Taxation & Economic Reform in America, 1781– (federal level tax regulations, laws, and hundreds of legislative histories)
- Treaties and Agreements Library (all U.S. treaties and agreements: in force, expired, or not yet officially published)
- United Nations Law Collection (a huge compilation of all relevant U.N. publications, including [among much else] texts of all treaties registered with the U.N. since 1946, and with the League of Nations from 1920 to 1946)
- United States Code (all versions from 1925–1926 to current edition)
- U.S. Attorney General Opinions
- U.S. Congressional Documents (including complete Congressional Record and its predecessors Annals of Congress, Register of Debates, and Congressional Globe; also Cannon's, Hind's, and Deschler's Precedents)
- U.S. Federal Agency Documents, Decisions, and Appeals (complete case/decision law opinions of federal regulatory agencies)
- U.S. Federal Legislative History Library (hundreds of legislative histories for major U.S. legislation since 1789, with full texts of 250+)
- U.S. Presidential Library (including Messages and Papers of the Presidents, Public Papers of the Presidents, CFR Title 13 [proclamations,

executive orders], Economic Report of the President, Weekly Compilation of Presidential Documents, Daily Compilation of Presidential Documents)

- U.S. Supreme Court Library (including official U.S. Reports [1754-], Preliminary Reports, and Slip Opinions; also dozens of books on the Court, and major Periodicals: Supreme Court Economic Review, Supreme Court Review, and United States Supreme Court Bulletin)
- U.S. Statutes at Large (1789–)
- World Constitutions Illustrated (an ongoing project attempting to provide the complete constitutional history of every country, with complete editions, translations, and commentaries)
- World Trials Library (trial transcripts, court documents, and monographs on famous and not-so-famous trials worldwide; includes full Nuremberg Trial transcripts)

A fuller listing of sources covered in this subscription database can be found at www.heinonline.org/.

Columbia International Affairs Online (CIAO) (Columbia University Press) is another very good keyword index to full texts of public policy studies since 1991.

OpinionArchives (OpinionArchives) is a full-text database of major "commentary" magazines, digitizing the full run of each. Among them are *American Spectator, Commentary, Commonweal, Dissent, Harper's, The Nation, National Review, The New Leader, The New Republic, The New York Review of Books, The New Yorker, The Progressive, Washington Monthly*, and *The Weekly Standard*.

The *Gale Directory of Databases* (31st ed., 2000), already mentioned in Chapter 4, is the best index to all of the 21,000+ subscription databases available through libraries.

PRINTED SOURCES FOR KEYWORD ACCESS TO OLDER JOURNALS

Three printed keyword indexes for which there are no online equivalents are occasionally useful for searching older journals; all were published by the now-defunct Carollton Press, Inc. They are:

- *Combined Retrospective Index to Journals in History 1838–1974* (11 vols.)
- *Combined Retrospective Index to Journals in Political Science 1866– 1874* (8 vols.)

- *Combined Retrospective Index to Journals in Sociology 1895–1978* (6 vols.)

Three good sources for identifying printed indexes to older journals, for which there are no database equivalents, are these:

- Bonnie R. Nelson's *A Guide to Published Library Catalogs* (Scarecrow Press, 1982). Many research libraries over the years have specialized in collecting resources in particular subject areas; often these libraries published printed catalogs of their holdings, and sometimes these old catalogs included entries not just for books, but for individual journal articles within the subject areas of the catalog. For example, before the appearance of the H. W. Wilson Company's *Art Index* (covering articles from 1929 forward), the Metropolitan Museum of Art in New York did extensive indexing of art periodicals, which can be found in its published *Library Catalog of the Metropolitan Museum of Art* (48 vols.; G. K. Hall, 1980, 2nd ed.). Nelson's book identifies dozens of such printed catalogs in all subject areas.
- Robert Balay's *Early Periodical Indexes: Bibliographies and Indexes of Literature Published in Periodicals before 1900* (Scarecrow, 2000). This is an annotated list of about 400 indexes to old journal articles, categorized by broad subject areas with a more detailed index by specific topics.
- Norma Oland Ireland's *An Index to Indexes* (F. W. Faxon Company, 1942; reprinted by Gregg Press, 1972) is a subject bibliography of over 1,000 printed indexes in over 280 subject areas. (The Paratext database *19th Century Masterfile* is attempting to eventually cover all such publications online; but that is a very long-term goal.)

These guides to old indexes are sometimes useful when sources like *Readers' Guide Retrospective, Periodicals Index Online, Web of Science, JSTOR,* or *19th Century Masterfile* don't turn up the older information you need.

KEYWORD SEARCHING ON THE INTERNET

Although the focus of this book is on sources that are not accessible on the open Internet, it remains true that an amazing and wonderful variety of material is indeed accessible there. The crucial point, however, is that the mere presence of good material on the Web does not automatically assure efficient access to it—the latter is a function of the search techniques that the Web allows (or eliminates) for finding its content.

Virtually all Web searching is done via uncontrolled keywords, because the various search engines do not have software that enables controlled vocabularies to be exploited—i.e., they lack mechanisms for displaying cross-references or browse menus; indeed, most websites are not indexed with controlled subject headings or descriptors to begin with. This is eminently understandable because the Web includes billions of sites, and the cataloging elements added to records in OPACs (standardized subject headings and displays of their networks of linkages to each other) must be created by human beings rather than by computer algorithms. Cataloging must therefore be confined to a comparatively small niche area, the subset of information resources deemed important for library collections; it cannot provide access to the entire Internet.

When billions of sites require indexing, automated means (bypassing direct human inspection) *must* be employed; there is literally no alternative. Algorithms, however, must work directly—and in most cases only—with the unstandardized keywords available to them within the various websites. They can rank the display of requested keywords in marvelously ingenious and useful ways, according to various weighting criteria: for instance, a site **A**, to which other sites (**B, C, D**) link, will rank higher in importance than those sites without such links; if the linking sites (**B, C, D**) are themselves extensively connected to still other sites (**E, F, G**, etc.), then these additional attachments will provide a cumulative additional weight to the relevance ranking of **A**.

Nevertheless, as anyone who had done any Web searching already knows, these relevance ranking mechanisms do not solve the problems discussed above (e.g., getting the right words in the wrong contexts, excessively granular retrievals). They especially do not solve—and in fact greatly exacerbate—the problem of getting an overall perspective on relevant literature. (The growing proliferation of echo chambers and filter bubbles—i.e., producing search results weighted and skewed by individuals' own idiosyncratic past search histories—further diminishes the Web's capacity to provide inclusive overview perspectives.) In general, scholarly research—as opposed to quick information seeking (see Appendix B)—seeks to gain exactly that overall view. Scholars wish to be reasonably assured that they are not overlooking especially important sources and that they are also not wasting time re-inventing the wheel in duplicating research that has already been done. Searching the open Internet (i.e., the sites freely available), as valuable and as necessary as it is, cannot solve these problems.

FULL-TEXT BOOK AND JOURNAL SITES ON THE OPEN INTERNET

A number of free sites on the Internet now provide access to texts of many books and journal articles. The most prominent are Google Books, Google Scholar, Hathi Trust www.hathitrust.org, and the Digital Public Library of America (DPLA) http://dp.la.

Google Books is an ongoing attempt to digitize every book in the world; it currently includes tens of millions of volumes from dozens of major libraries internationally. Google Scholar is a comparable attempt to bring all open-source journal articles into a single database. Hathi Trust and DPLA are other sites for digital books and other resources from many contributing libraries.

The good intentions of all such sites are greatly hamstrung by the unavoidable reality of copyright restrictions. If copyright laws worldwide were all repealed, then such websites could indeed cover "everything" within their domains, but copyright is a reality that will simply not go away. The millions of people who create information and whose livelihoods depend on their creations do not agree that "information wants to be free." Unlike some academic authors who may be satisfied by payments in the form of enhanced résumés that lead to increased chances for tenure and promotion, most other writers require more direct monetary compensation for their labors. It is highly likely that a system of trade-offs among *what, who,* and *where* restrictions on access to copyrighted information will continue to obtain. The alternative of, in effect, government-enforced socialism in the publishing world would entail greatly increased tax burdens on all citizens to pay for their immediate online access to "all" publications without restrictive passwords or site restrictions. It would also require outright coercion of any individuals who wish to opt out of any such government-controlled system and who wish to charge prices for their work determined by supply and demand considerations rather than by imposed price controls. Further, the prospect that every nonacademic author will voluntarily and selflessly contribute his or her own work product freely to the open Internet, for the good of all people everywhere, without government intervention—that prospect entails nothing short of a radical transformation of human nature itself. (Even academics wish to receive royalty payments for their books, if not for their journal articles.) Changes in technology do not produce changes in human nature or in the need to make a living.

The alternative of government-regulated control of information has been shown by history, notably by the failure of the communist system, to be unworkable in the long run. The market system of supply and demand, which requires restrictions entailing who can pay for access to what resources, seems more likely to prevail for most of the world's information economy. Nor are copyright restrictions the only legal barriers to the provision of free digital access to "everything"—the realities of antitrust laws against monopolistic suppression of competition also play a role in the world of online information. (My own crystal ball is too cloudy to foresee what specific court decisions will be made in these areas, other than to predict that neither copyright nor anti-monopoly laws will simply vanish; nor, I suspect, will the U.S. Supreme Court [or any other tribunal elsewhere] give unqualified assent to the notion that the world's information "wants to be free.")

That said, these free sites are still capable of providing amazing results within the niche fields that remain legally open to them. Even if it continues to provide only provide snippet-level access to most books published after 1922, Google Books is still wonderfully useful on questions the call for very specific information and for simply distributing so many out-of-print books so widely. For example:

- I once helped a researcher whose family was interested in a particular ancestor, a John DeHart. DeHart was a member of the Continental Congress, but the family knew he had resigned from that body and wanted to know why. Google Books turned up pages from two relevant books very quickly, because the words "John DeHart" and "Continental Congress" and "resigned" were, in combination, very distinctive and did not provide a mountain of irrelevant retrievals. It turns out that DeHart did not want to support the now-famous resolution of Richard Henry Lee that the states should be free from Britain. (When I provided printouts of the relevant pages, the young woman who asked the question told me "this is probably not what my grandmother wants to hear," but that, since the information did solve the family mystery, she was still glad to get it.)
- A historian interested in the office of the Judge Advocate General in the Civil War period wanted to know if there is a published list of the staffers in that office at the time. (He was aware that unpublished records of the office might exist at the National Archives, but he wanted to save himself the trip over there.) Various bibliographies of old government manuals identified the *Official Register of the United States*, which does list federal personnel from the period, although sometimes only at

the "director" level. I went back into the stacks and brought out all of our volumes from 1859 to 1867. The interesting thing was that the 1867 volume does list the individual staff members in the office, not just the Judge Advocate himself, whereas the volumes from 1859 to 1865 gave only the Judge Advocate's name, with no staffers. Unfortunately, the Library of Congress's set is missing the 1866 volume, which would have been important if it did list all of the individual staffers, as it was so close to the Civil War. I could find the missing 1866 volume, however, in Google Books. It turns out that this volume lists only the Judge Advocate's name (like the preceding volumes, unlike the succeeding 1867 volume)—but establishing that fact, through Google Books, saved the historian a great deal of time in having to track down the 1866 volume in another library.

- Another researcher wanted to find a particular article with the title "Philip Lee Phillips, Cartobibliographer" written by Walt Ristow—but she did not have any information on when or where the article was published. Google Books provided enough snippet information to establish that the paper first appeared in a German journal, *Kartensammlung und Kartendokumentation*, in 1971, as well as in a German festschrift, *Karten in Bibliotheken* (also in 1971), and that it was reprinted in the American journal *Surveying and Mapping* in 1972. Neither Google Books nor Google Scholar (for open source journals) provided the text of the article itself, but with the adequate citations provided by the snippet references, paper copies could be quickly located.

- Another historian wanted to find a copy of a National Security Agency memorandum, and the only reference to it he had was its report number, NSAM 182. This very distinctive number showed up in the snippet display of a footnote from a book in Google Books; the citation there indicated that the text of the memo had been reprinted in the "Gravel" edition of the *Pentagon Papers*, vol. 2, page 69. This Gravel edition of the *Pentagon Papers* had not itself been fully digitized, but with the citation information provided by the Google snippet, a paper copy of the volume could be quickly retrieved.

In each case, very specific—not "overview"—information was needed, and Google is a godsend in such situations. When scholars are trying to achieve overviews of extensive bodies of literature on their topics, the Internet search engines are not nearly as good as the several other mechanisms discussed in this book. These are the kinds of inquiries that they cannot handle well:

- "What is available on film versions of *Othello*?"
- "I'm doing a dissertation on *Japonisme*—what has already been written on this?"
- "What has been done on 'Terrorism in India'?"
- "I have to write a paper on the information-seeking habits of tourists."
- "How do people behave when they visit zoos?"
- "What are the justifications for the wars in Iraq and Afghanistan?"
- "Why do people who have been told repeatedly about the dangers of HIV/AIDS continue to act irresponsibly?"
- "What do you have on racial discrimination in France in the 1920s?"
- "I have to write something on German perceptions of American Indians."
- "I want to compare the treatment of POWs and MIAs in the Vietnam and Yom Kippur wars."
- "I have to write on paper on sexuality in late Roman times."

It isn't difficult to find *some* information on many of these topics on the open Internet, or via Wikipedia, but if you are doing any kind of scholarly research on these topics you will certainly need sources *in addition to* those on the Net. Google, Google Scholar, Hathi Trust, and DPLA are wonderful sources for many inquiries; but they do not cover nearly "everything," nor does their keyword search software enable you to find all of the relevant sources that they do include. The whole family of resources on the open Internet can best be described as "necessary but not sufficient" for scholarly research. It is the other sources that are also necessary—resources available only through real libraries—that are the focus of the present book.

OTHER APPROACHES TO THE INTERNET

The term "invisible Web" is slippery; I use it to refer to those portions of the open, freely available Internet that are not indexed by the spiders and crawlers of the major search engines. I do not include within it the hundreds—indeed thousands—of subscription databases available through libraries; these, as I use the term, are not on the "free" or "open"

Internet to begin with. There is room for legitimate disagreement here; some would say that any password-protected commercial database that is both electronic and remotely accessible is part of the "invisible" Web. I would restrict the "invisible" designation to sources that are electronic, remotely accessible, and also freely accessible from anywhere, at any time, by anybody—but at the same time lying beyond the reach of the conventional spiders. For example, as of the present writing, the online catalog of the Library of Congress is freely available at catalog.loc.gov (see Chapter 2), but the individual book (and other) records within it are not crawled by the various search engines. You can use the Internet to get *to* the catalog, and once you're there you can then search within it, but a Google or Bing or Yahoo! search will not "see" or retrieve the individual OPAC records directly. (This limitation will soon be overcome. Direct Internet access to the catalog records themselves, however, will not provide any access to cross-references or browse displays; for that reason use of the the Library's separate OPAC [catalog.loc.gov] will continue to provide superior search capabilities.)

There are whole books written on how to access the "invisible" or "the deep" Web—i.e., the free and yet hidden sites within it. Although, again, the free Internet—whether spidered/crawled or invisible—is outside the scope of this book (which is detailed enough already), there are nevertheless some avenues of Internet access beyond what is provided by the search engines that reference librarians find to be particularly noteworthy:

- *Internet Public Library* at www.ipl.org is a link to authoritative sources, categorized by subject. It provides, through its "Resources by Subject" groupings, a conceptual categorization of highly recommended Internet sources that might otherwise be buried by the relevance-ranked keyword access of the search engines.
- *Refdesk.com* also provides useful categorizations. Its home page, while overwhelming detailed, repays some study. Particularly useful for academic purposes is its list of "Refdesk subject categories" near the bottom of the screen.
- *Libraryspot.com* is somewhat similar index to multiple online reference sources and is also worth checking.
- *Directory of Open Access Journals* at www.doaj.org allows article-level searching of more than 10,000 free journals on the Internet.

While looking at these sources, however, don't overlook the reference librarians themselves in your local library.

To sum up, keyword searching is the means of subject searching used by most students, most of the time. It is a powerful search tool especially in those situations when you can clearly specify what you wish to see, in precise terms. It is best understood, however, in relation to controlled vocabulary searching: each of the two approaches has strengths and weaknesses that complement the other. The main point to remember is that keyword searching is *not* conceptual category searching: it will give you exactly the words you specify, and if there are other ways to express the same subject you will not be retrieving those other expressions. While very powerful in turning up precise information, keyword searching is notoriously unreliable in providing overview perspectives that give you reasonable confidence you have not overlooked something important. It is a necessary component of the scholar's search toolkit; but it is only one of several tools.

CHAPTER 6

Citation Searches

W E HAVE SEEN SO FAR THAT THE TECHNIQUES OF CONTROLLED vocabulary searching, general browsing and focused browsing in classified bookstacks, and keyword searching each has distinct advantages and disadvantages. Each approach works very well in some situations, but very poorly in others. Still other means of gaining subject access to written records exist; one of the most important is *citation searching*. This approach, like the others, is potentially applicable in any subject area, and it, too, has both strengths and limitations.

THE NATURE OF CITATION SEARCHING: CIRCUMVENTING VOCABULARY PROBLEMS

In citation searching you must start with a known source—one that you've already identified—relevant to your topic. It may be a book, a journal article, a conference paper, a dissertation, a website, a technical report, or an unpublished manuscript—it can be any kind of knowledge record. Further, the date of the starting-point source is irrelevant: it can be something written last year or centuries ago. What a citation search will give you is a list of subsequent publications that cite the source in a footnote. The assumption is that a later work that cites an earlier one is probably talking about the same subject, or at least playing in the same intellectual ballpark. This is sometimes not true—a work can be cited in a context irrelevant to your interests—but such connections work often enough that you need to be aware of this search technique. The advantage here is that, unlike the situations with controlled vocabulary or keyword searches, you do not have to worry of about finding correct subject headings or cross-references or narrower terms, nor do you have to think up all of the keyword synonyms or variant phrases for expressing your topic. Citation searching allows you to do subject searches in a way that circumvents vocabulary problems entirely. All you need, in most searches of this kind, is the author's name, which you've already identified, and the source's title (or the title and date of the journal in which it appears).

THE MIRROR IMAGE OF FOOTNOTE CHASING

It is useful to think of citation searching as a kind of mirror image of footnote chasing. If you've already found a good source on your topic, you will certainly look at its footnotes and bibliography for further references to extend your search to other relevant materials; that is just common sense. Remember, however, that in doing so you are essentially looking backward in time—that is, at *previous* sources published before your starting-point source. Citation searching, in contrast, takes you forward in time, to *subsequent* sources published after your source—and yet still conceptually connected to it. And so it is just as useful as footnote chasing, but comparatively few people do it because most do not know it is possible to pursue this kind of inquiry. You should make it a rule, however: whenever you find a good source, check to see if some other author has referred to that work by citing it in a subsequent article, book, or website.

Citation searching can now be done via several subscription databases; in such cases your result will usually be a list of academic journal articles—not books or Web pages—that reference your source. Considerable citation searching can now also be done on the open Internet; the results here will be lists of websites or digitized books and journal articles citing your starting point. We will first consider the subscription databases, available only through libraries, that enable you to do this kind of searching, since their results will always entail some kind of editorial vetting for quality.

WEB OF SCIENCE AND ITS COMPONENT DATABASES

The *Web of Science* database is published by Thomson Reuters. It is a combination of three main component parts: the *Science Citation Index Expanded (SCI-EXPANDED,* or just *SCI), the Social Sciences Citation Index (SSCI),* and the *Arts & Humanities Citation Index (A&HCI).* Collectively they cover about 13,500 journals in 45 languages, about two-thirds of which (8,600+ titles) are in the *Science* component. The *SSCI*, however, covers about 3,100 titles and the *A&HCI* about 1,700. (Three additional components, *Book Citation Index, Conference Proceedings Citation Index*, and *Data Citation Index*, will be discussed below.)

What is especially important to begin with is that the 13,500 journals that are covered represent the cream of the crop of academic journals in all subject areas. Thomson Reuters has some very sophisticated computer algorithms that enable them to identify which journals are being most frequently cited in the footnotes of other journals—and those are the titles they go after to index. Other databases (e.g., *AnthopologyPlus, PsycINFO, MEDLINE*) will provide more extensive coverage of many more journals in their respective fields, but *Web of Science* provides excellent selective coverage of the best journals in each area—and merges them in a way that allows cross-disciplinary searching of all at the same time. (It is possible, however, to limit one's searches to only the *SCI, SSCI,* or *A&HCI* sections individually.)

These *Web of Science* databases were touched on in Chapter 5 because they also allow keyword searching (as well as related record searching, to be discussed in chapter 7). But it is worth looking at them in more detail.[1]

Science Citation Index Expanded currently provides abstract-level indexing of more than 8,600 journals; retrospective coverage extends back to 1900. (For the early decades, however, hundreds [rather than thousands] of titles are covered.) Major journals in all of these fields are indexed:

> Acoustics, Agricultural Economics & Policy, Agricultural Engineering, Agriculture (Dairy & Animal Science), Agriculture (Multidisciplinary), Agriculture (Soil Science), Agronomy, Allergy, Anatomy & Morphology, Andrology, Anesthesiology, Astronomy & Astrophysics, Automation & Control Systems, Behavioral Sciences, Biochemical Research Methods, Biochemistry & Molecular Biology, Biodiversity Conservation, Biology, Biology (Miscellaneous), Biophysics, Biotechnology & Applied Microbiology, Cardiac & Cardiovascular Systems, Cell Biology, Chemistry (Analytical), Chemistry (Applied), Chemistry (Inorganic & Nuclear), Chemistry (Medicinal), Chemistry (Multidisciplinary), Chemistry (Organic), Chemistry (Physical), Clinical Neurology, Computer Science (Artificial Intelligence), Computer Science (Hardware & Architecture), Computer Science (Information Systems), Computer Science (Interdisciplinary Applications), Computer Science (Software Engineering), Computer Science (Theory & Methods), Construction & Building

Technology, Critical Care Medicine, Crystallography, Dentistry (Oral Surgery & Medicine), Dermatology & Venereal Diseases, Developmental Biology, Ecology, Education (Scientific Disciplines), Electrochemistry, Emergency Medicine, Endocrinology & Metabolism, Energy & Fuels, Engineering (Aerospace), Engineering (Biomedical), Engineering (Chemical), Engineering (Civil), Engineering (Electrical & Electronic), Engineering (Environmental), Engineering (Geological), Engineering (Industrial), Engineering (Manufacturing), Engineering (Marine), Engineering (Mechanical), Engineering (Multidisciplinary), Engineering (Ocean), Engineering (Petroleum), Entomology, Environmental Sciences, Evolutionary Biology, Fisheries, Food Science & Technology, Forestry, Gastroenterology & Hepatology, Genetics & Heredity, Geochemistry & Geophysics, Geography (Physical), Geology, Geosciences (Multidisciplinary), Geriatrics & Gerontology, Health Care Sciences & Services, Hematology, History & Philosophy of Science, Horticulture, Imaging Science & Photographic Technology, Immunology, Infectious Diseases, Information Science & Library Science, Instruments & Instrumentation, Integrative & Complementary Medicine, Limnology, Marine & Freshwater Biology, Materials Science (Biomaterials), Materials Science (Ceramics), Materials Science (Characterization & Testing), Materials Science (Coatings & Films), Materials Science (Composites), Materials Science (Multidisciplinary), Materials Science (Paper & Wood), Materials Science (Textiles), Mathematics, Mathematics (Applied), Mathematics (Interdisciplinary Applications), Mechanics, Medical Ethics, Medical Informatics, Medical Laboratory Technology, Medicine (General & Internal), Medicine (Legal), Medicine (Research & Experimental), Metallurgy & Metallurgical Engineering, Meteorology & Atmospheric Sciences, Microbiology, Microscopy, Mineralogy, Mining & Mineral Processing, Multidisciplinary Sciences, Mycology, Neuroimaging, Neurosciences, Nuclear Science & Technology, Nursing, Nutrition & Dietetics, Obstetrics & Gynecology, Oceanography, Oncology, Operations Research & Management Science, Ophthalmology, Optics, Ornithology, Orthopedics, Otorhinolaryngology, Paleontology, Parasitology, Pathology, Pediatrics, Peripheral Vascular Disease, Pharmacology & Pharmacy, Physics (Applied), Physics (Atomic, Molecular & Chemical), Physics (Condensed Matter), Physics (Fluids & Plasmas), Physics (Mathematical), Physics (Multidisciplinary), Physics (Nuclear), Physics (Particles & Fields), Physiology, Plant Sciences, Polymer Science, Psychiatry, Psychology, Public & Environmental & Occupational Health, Radiology & Nuclear Medicine & Medical Imaging, Rehabilitation, Remote Sensing, Reproductive Biology, Respiratory System, Rheumatism, Robotics, Spectroscopy, Sport Sciences, Statistics & Probability, Substance Abuse, Surgery, Telecommunications, Thermodynamics, Toxicology, Transplantation, Transportation Science & Technology, Tropical

Medicine, Urology & Nephrology, Veterinary Sciences, Virology, Water Resources, Zoology.

Social Sciences Citation Index covers more than 3,100 scholarly journals published worldwide, with coverage back to 1900. (Fewer titles are covered in the early decades.) It also picks up, selectively, social science articles appearing within approximately 3,500 science and technology journals. Major journals are indexed in all of these disciplines:

> Anthropology, Area Studies, Business, Business (Finance), Communication, Criminology & Penology, Demography, Economics, Education & Educational Research, Education (Special), Environmental Studies, Ergonomics, Ethics, Ethnic Studies, Family Studies, Geography, Gerontology, Health Policy & Services, History, History & Philosophy of Science, History of Social Sciences, Hospitality (Leisure, Sport & Tourism), Industrial Relations & Labor, Information Science & Library Science, International Relations, Law, Linguistics, Management, Nursing, Planning & Development, Political Science, Psychiatry, Psychology, Psychology (Applied), Psychology (Biological), Psychology (Clinical), Psychology (Developmental), Psychology (Educational), Psychology (Experimental), Psychology (Mathematical), Psychology (Multidisciplinary), Psychology (Psychoanalysis), Psychology (Social), Public Administration, Public & Environmental & Occupational Health, Rehabilitation, Social Issues, Social Sciences (Biomedical), Social Sciences (Interdisciplinary), Social Sciences (Mathematical Methods), Social Work, Sociology, Substance Abuse, Transportation, Urban Studies, Women's Studies.

Arts & Humanities Citation Index covers over 1,700 journals internationally back to 1975. It also picks up, selectively, humanities-related articles appearing in the science and social sciences fields. (For example, articles on foot and ankle injuries in ballet dancers, appearing in medical journals, are indexed here.) All of the following disciplines are covered:

> Archaeology, Architecture, Art, Asian Studies, Classics, Dance, Film & Radio & Television, Folklore, History, History & Philosophy of Science, Humanities (Multidisciplinary), Language & Linguistics, Literary Reviews, Literary Theory & Criticism, Literature, Literature (African, Australian, Canadian), Literature (American), Literature (British Isles), Literature (German, Dutch, Scandinavian), Literature (Romance), Literature (Slavic), Medieval & Renaissance Studies, Music, Philosophy, Poetry, Religion, Theater.

Other components have recently been added to the family:

Book Citation Index (BCI): whereas the *SCI, SCCI,* and *A&HCI* cover scholarly journals, the *BCI* covers over 30,000 scholarly books, with 10,000 new titles to be added every year. Both "series" and "nonseries" books are covered provided that they include full footnote information. Two separate components are available: a *Science* edition covering Physics/ Chemistry, Engineering/Computing/Technology, Clinical Medicine, Life Sciences, and Agriculture/Biology; and a *Social Sciences & Humanities* edition. The *Science* component extends back to 2005 and comprises 42 percent of the coverage; the *Social Sciences & Humanities* (also back to 2005) comprises 58 percent of the coverage. (Books, as opposed to journal articles, tend to be more important in the latter fields.) The company also offers a *Conference Proceedings Citation Index (CPCI)*; it, too, comes in two components, *Science* and *Social Sciences & Humanities*. Together they cover over 110,000 proceedings in 256 categories since 1990, with about 12,000 new conferences added yearly. A new *Data Citation Index* identifies manipulable data sets in repositories around the world, and works making use of them.

The ideal subscription to the *Web of Science* database would combines all of these indexes, with coverage of the *SCI* back to 1900, the *SSCI* to 1900, and the *A&HCI* to 1975. Individual libraries, however, may opt for subscriptions to only one or two of the files rather than all, and they may select fewer years of retrospective coverage within any of them. In any event, the important point is this: *Do not be misled by the word* **Science** *in the title; your library's subscription may well include full coverage of the social sciences and humanities journals (and books/proceedings/datasets) as well.* Indeed, your local library may list its subscriptions under the titles of the individual component databases rather than under the collective *Web of Science* designation. In any event, remember that if the collective *Web* title is used, the most important academic journals (and many recent books) in all fields are covered.

The overall value of these indexes is that they provide three different ways of doing subject searches in any subject area: by keywords, by footnote citations, and by related records (see Chapter 7 for the latter). Each of these search methods compensates for weaknesses in controlled vocabulary indexes; two of them (citation and related record) compensate for weaknesses in keyword searching, too—that is, they enable you find articles that lie in blind spots to the alternative indexing methods.

The citation search method is particularly valuable because, again, it circumvents vocabulary problems entirely.

An example is provided by the reader who was interested in the Norse colonization of America before Columbus. He had already found one good scholarly article discussing the evidence, but on running it through the *SSCI* he found a subsequent article by another scholar who disagreed with the conclusions of the first. And this was followed by a rebuttal by the original writer. The combination of perspectives developed by this dialogue brought up considerable information that did not appear in the first article.

Another example is provided by the researcher who wanted articles on "the economics of antiquities looting." He found, in the *SSCI* component, one article from 1995 with those exact words in the title; he then discovered that this starting point had been cited by 17 subsequent articles from 1996 through 2008, and the citing articles have titles such as these:

- "Protecting newly discovered antiquities"
- "Cultural security: the evolving role of art in international security"
- "Heritage for sale? A case study from Israel"
- "Intellectual property crimes"
- "Occupiers' title to cultural property: Nineteenth-century removal of Egyptian artifacts"
- "Spoil of war? A solution to the Hermitage trove debate"

These articles, while all playing in the same intellectual ballpark, nonetheless express the subject in a wide variety of keywords that could never have been thought up in advance. And although the keywords are apparently all over the map, they are nonetheless conceptually anchored by being linked to that initial relevant source: as disparate as they may be, they generally will not appear in irrelevant contexts. A citation search thus enables you to recognize directly relevant sources whose terminology you would not be able to think up on your own and which would also be missed by any relevance ranking algorithm working only with the words you've actually typed.

TWO DIFFERENT WAYS TO DO CITATION SEARCHING

Within the *Web of Science* there are two different ways to do citation searching. First, you can start by doing a regular keyword search to find articles indexed within any of the 13,500 journals (and other sources) covered by the database; any retrieved item will contain a note telling you if it has been cited by subsequent sources and will provide a live link that will bring up a list of all of them.

Second, you can use the "Cited Reference Search" tab on the *Web of Science* search screen. In order to find this link, however, you must first click on the downward arrow next to the default "Basis Search" option. "Cited Reference Search" will then appear in the drop-down menu. If you begin here, you can look for any source at all—even if it is not an article that is keyword indexed within the 13,500 journals or the books or proceedings. It could be an article appearing in any of the tens of thousand of other journals *outside* the *Web of Science*'s range of keyword indexing, or it could be something other than a journal article to begin with: a book or a doctoral dissertation or any other source published anywhere, at any time. "Cited Reference Search" will then tell you if that source—wherever it comes from and whenever published—has been cited by any article within any of the 13,500 journals, books, or conference proceedings indexed in *Web of Science*.

There are, of course, limitations to the technique of citation searching: you must already have a good source to start with; further, there is no guarantee that all of the subsequent relevant literature, or all of the best sources, will cite your starting point source. It is quite possible that good works exist that are not linked by footnote connections. Sometimes, too, a good source will be cited by another in a context that is not conceptually relevant to your interest. Again, there are always trade-offs you need to keep in mind. Citation searching solves many research problems that are otherwise intractable, but it cannot solve all of them (any more than controlled vocabulary or keyword searching can solve all problems). In many situations, however, it does produce results that are strikingly better than the alternative techniques provide.

DIGRESSION: THE CROSS-DISCIPLINARY COVERAGE OF *WEB OF SCIENCE*

The importance of cross-disciplinary searching has already been discussed in Chapter 4 but is worth returning to in the present context because of the remarkable range of disciplines covered simultaneously by the *Web of Science* databases. The extent of that coverage is indicated in the descriptions, above, of its *SCI, SSCI, A&HCI, BCI,* and *CPCI* components.

Even within the *Science Citation Index* itself, apart from the others, the range of cross-disciplinary coverage is amazing. Eugene Garfield, the creator of these *Citation* databases, mentions a spectacular example in his book *Citation Indexing: Its Theory and Application in Science Technology, and Humanities* (John Wiley & Sons, 1979, p. 4):

From 1961 to 1969 a citation for one of the classic papers published by Albert Einstein in *Annallen der Physik* in 1906 is linked [by the *SCI*] to papers in the *Journal of Dairy Sciences, Journal of the Chemical Society, Journal of Polymer Science, Journal of Pharmacy and Pharmacology, Comparative Biochemistry and Physiology, Journal of General Physiology, International Journal of Engineering Science, Journal of Materials, Journal of the Water Pollution Control Federation, American Ceramic Society Bulletin, Journal of the Acoustical Society of America, Chemical Engineering Science, Industrial and Engineering Chemistry Process Design and Development, Journal of Colloid and Interface Science, Journal of Fluid Mechanics, Journal of Lubrication Technology, Journal of Molecular Biology, Journal of Food Science, Journal of Biological Chemistry, Journal of Sedimentary Petrology, Review of Scientific Instruments,* and the *Journal of the Electrochemical Society.*

Students of literature or classics, particularly, should keep the *Arts & Humanities Citation Index* in mind as something to be used routinely as a supplement to the *MLA International Bibliography,* the *Annual Bibliography of English Language and Literature,* and *L'Année Philologique.* For example, I once helped a professor who was interested in the ancient explorer Pytheas. A *Web of Science* search on this topic produces articles from the journals *Arctic, Mariner's Mirror, Prairie Schooner, Library Journal,* and the book series *History of Mechanism and Marine Science*—none of which are covered in the standard index for classical studies, *L'Année Philologique.*

Similarly, a musicologist compiling a massive bibliography on the Russian composer Alexander Scriabin found, via *Web of Science,* an article on "The Evolution of One-Handed Piano Compositions" that references him in the *Journal of Hand Surgery.* Obviously this publication is not indexed in any of the conventional music or performing arts databases. Likewise, a philosopher interested in "Aristotle's conception of time" found an article on "Changes in Concepts of Time from Aristotle to Einstein" in *Astrophysics and Space Science,* a journal not indexed by the major philosophy database, *The Philosopher's Index.*

CYCLING SOURCES AND "REVIEWS" OF JOURNAL ARTICLES

A particularly useful extension of citation searching is to "cycle" sources— that is, once you have found a first set of articles citing your original source, you can then look to see who cited *them.* This will give you a second set; you can then see who cited this group, which will provide a third set, and so on. By pursuing this process as far as is productive, you can sometimes generate a great deal of information on even very obscure topics.

While the *Web of Science* is useful in enabling you to follow the development of a debate or the progress of a scholarly discussion, it is also very useful when the various book review databases fail, for there is still a chance that the book you're interested in may have been commented on, or referred to critically or favorably, in a journal article even if it has not been formally reviewed. The *Web of Science* also provides the best way to find a "review" (or a critical response to) a journal article, as these are not covered by book review indexes. It is especially good for giving a new lease on life to the material you locate through old bibliographies—if the latter refer you to somewhat dated articles, you can find out if someone has used them as background sources for a new look at the subject. It is particularly worthwhile to see if anyone has cited old state-of-the-art review articles (see Chapter 8).

These databases often plays a part, too, in academic circles on questions of tenure or promotion, for departments wish to know not only whether a candidate has published, but also if he or she has been cited by other scholars in the field, especially in the most important journals. (Academics who wish to document how frequently their own works have been cited, however, should not confine their searches to *Web of Science* alone because now there are many other databases that provide citation searching.)

OTHER FEATURES OF *WEB OF SCIENCE*

Several other features of the *Web of Science* are worth noting:

1. Journal article citations in this database, especially within the last 15 years, routinely provide the e-mail address of the first-listed author of each article. And even if this information is lacking, the citations will always provide the first author's institutional address. Once you have that information it is usually easy to find the organization's website, which will in turn lead to either the e-mail address or a phone number. (In more recent years the e-mail and institutional addresses have been provided for all authors.)

2. You can search, to begin with, through the organizational affiliation of authors—that is, you can search under the name of any institution (such as a university department) and find out who within it has published a paper in any given year or range of years. For example, if you want to search for articles whose authors are in the English department of Loyola University

of Chicago, you would scroll down to "Address" in the drop-down menu of search options (next to the search box) and type "Loyola and Chicago and English."

3. Similarly, you can search for papers written under grants from particular funding agencies. You would choose "Funding Agency" from the drop-down menu and then search under, say, "Homeland Security."

4. The *Arts & Humanities* component, unlike the *SCI* and *SSCI*, follows an editorial practice of "implicit citation," which takes effect when you do a citation (not keyword) search. What this means is that if a written work, a music score, a play, a painting, a statue, an architectural drawing, etc., *is even mentioned in the text of the journal article* and not formally cited as a footnote, it is still treated as a footnote reference for citation indexing purposes. Plato's *Republic*, for example, is often mentioned in journal articles without being cited formally in a footnote; but the *A&HCI* treats any such passing reference as the equivalent of a footnote.

5. The same *A&HCI*, unlike the other two, adds "enhancement" terms, for keyword searching, to the titles of journal articles that are not fully informative. For example, in the article title "Doing Justice to Bartleby (Melville)," the editors have added "Melville" to make the citation more findable. (These extra words give you a search advantage not found in the *MLA International Bibliography*, which indexes many of the same journals.)

6. All of the journal indexes have an additional keyword enhancement feature, brought about by a computer algorithm rather than by human editorial intervention. It is called KeyWords Plus. It works like this: suppose you have an article **A** that includes citations to articles **B, C, D**, and so on, in its footnotes. The algorithm scans the titles of the footnoted articles **B, C, D**, et al. and extracts from them words or phrases that it finds repeated. These "Plus" keywords are then added as searchable terms on the indexing record for article **A** itself, even though the author of **A** did not use them in his own title or abstract.

7. The one academic subject that is not well covered at all by *Web of Science* is the area of military and naval science. Apparently the major journals in this field are not cited frequently enough by other journals to be noticed by the *Web* algorithms.

8. As mentioned in Chapter 4, you can get an online list of all of the journal titles that are indexed, by subject category, in

the *SCI, SSCI,* or the *A&HCI* by going to http://ip-science. thomsonreuters.com/mjl/ and selecting the title of the database. (This is particularly useful to authors who want to get a quick list of the most important journals in any field.)

Thomson Reuters also offers a separate subscription to a related database called *Journal Citation Reports (JCR).* This provides statistical information showing the relative importance and ranking of individual journals within their disciplinary fields. Data are also given regarding a journal's "Impact Factor" (measuring how frequently an average article in the journal is cited in a given year) and its "Immediacy Index" (measuring how quickly an average article is cited). Unfortunately, *JCR* covers only the *Science* and *Social Sciences* journals within the overall *Web of Science* universe; it does not provide any data for the *Arts & Humanities* titles. (Institutions may also subscribe to the publisher's *InCites* service, which provides reports on departmental [and other] rankings and comparisons to peer institutions; *InCites* uses the *JCR* data, but the company does all the analytical work for you.)

Although the editors do a very good job of indexing the most important journals in all subject areas, no single index can be relied on to cover all relevant individual articles. Quality papers have a way of showing up rather far afield from where they might be expected to appear—which means that you will always have to use multiple databases or bibliographies for thorough searching. Remember, too, that none of these *Citation* databases provide access through controlled subject headings or descriptors. If you search the same journals through other databases that index them using controlled terms (e.g., *Historical Abstracts, PsycINFO, Academic Search Complete,* etc.), you will be able to see different results within them.

Thomson Reuters also publishes a more specialized citation database: *Biosis Citation Index* covers 6,000 titles in biomedical fields back to 1926; it offers enhanced search features (e.g., indexing by Enzyme Commission numbers) not found in the regular *SCI* database.

SCOPUS AND OTHER CITATION SEARCH DATABASES

Citation search capabilities are now appearing in many databases beyond those in the Thomson Reuters family. Some of the more prominent databases offering this search method are listed here.

Scopus

Scopus (from Elsevier) is another subscription database; a full description of it is freely available at www.info.sciverse.com/scopus/scopus-in-detail/facts/. Essentially, it is the largest citation index available, covering about 22,000 scholarly journals worldwide in "scientific, technical, medical, and social sciences fields and arts and humanities," as well as more than 370 book series. Its criterion of selection is whether a source is peer-reviewed, not whether the source is frequently cited by others. About 60 percent of its coverage comes after 1995; the 40 percent of earlier sources date back as far as 1823. Although the bulk of its indexing lies in scientific fields, it indexes many more social sciences and humanities journals that does *Web of Science*. It, too, allows keyword searching, citation searching, and related record searching; it also enables researchers to zero in immediately on literature review articles (see Chapter 8).

EBSCOHOST DATABASES

In each of these databases look for the search tab "Cited References" along the top bar of the search page. (You won't notice it at all if you're not deliberately looking for it.)

- *Academic Search Complete* (or *Premiere*)
- *America: History & Life*
- *Business Source Complete*
- *CINAHL with Full Text* (*Cumulative Index to Nursing and Allied Health Literature*
- *Communication & Mass Media Complete*
- *EconLit*
- *Environment Complete*
- *Food Science Source*
- *GreenFILE*
- *Historical Abstracts*
- *Information Science & Technology Abstracts*
- *Jewish Studies Source*
- *LGBT with Full Text*
- *Library, Information Science & Technology Abstracts*
- *Literary Reference Center Plus*
- *Music Index*
- *PsycINFO*

Other databases will undoubtedly be added to this list in the future. Note that if you do a federated search of several EBSCO databases simultaneously, the "Cited References" search option will disappear. That is one reason it is usually best to search each of the databases you want *separately*, rather than in a merged pool.

The EBSCO databases that offer citation indexing—and it's not all of them—also provide another way to get at articles that cite your starting-point source: if you initially do a keyword or subject search and find any relevant articles, the records for any of them may also provide a link indicating "Time Cited in This Database"—clicking on this will provide you with subsequent articles that cite these initial sources. In other words, you can start the process via a keyword (or descriptor) search, and then extend your results via citation searching.

ProQuest Databases

The citation-search feature in these databases is, unfortunately, extremely well hidden. You must first select an individual database (not the default merged pool of all of them), then select "Advanced" search, then use the drop-down menu next to any of the search boxes, to find the search option for "References – REF" in order to do citation searching. As of this writing, these databases offer this search feature:

- *ABI/INFORM Global*
- *ProQuest Accounting & Tax*
- *ProQuest Asian & Business Journals*
- *ProQuest Banking Information Sources*
- *ProQuest Computing*
- *ProQuest Dissertations & Theses*
- *ProQuest Education Journals*
- *ProQuest Health & Medical Complete*
- *ProQuest Medical Library*
- *ProQuest Military Collection*
- *ProQuest Nursing & Allied Health Source*
- *ProQuest Psychology Journals*
- *ProQuest Religion*
- *ProQuest Science Journals*
- *ProQuest Social Science Journals*
- *ProQuest Telecommunication*
- *Sociological Abstracts*
- *Worldwide Political Science Abstracts*

Again, the "References – REF" search option (in the drop-down menus) will not appear at all if you do a federated search of multiple databases simultaneously.

Sage Journals (Sage) offers nearly 700 journals, with "References" as a search option in the drop-down menus of its "Advanced" search screen.

Academics, take note: if you are looking to see how often your have been cited yourself for promotion or tenure review purposes, using the citation search features of these other databases can turn up many additional hits that are not recorded in *Web of Science*.

Still other databases from other vendors are likely to offer citation searching in the future; the important point is to be aware of the possibility of doing this kind of search, and to actively look for it on any "Advanced" search screen you happen to be working with. (Always choose the database's "Advanced" search screen to begin with, and take a minute to familiarize yourself with its search tabs at the top of the screen and its drop-down menus next to the search boxes. Very few researchers do this, but it can make an enormous improvement in the quality of retrievals.)

Note, further, that many databases offering full texts of academic journals essentially allow a form of citation searching simply by the fact that they make the keywords of the footnotes just as searchable as words within the articles; so, even if the files do not formally index the footnotes as a separate document type (indicated in a drop-down menu), you can still search for the titles of articles or books as keyword phrases (i.e., within quotation marks), and you may well get "hits" of these titles appearing within the full-text digitized footnotes or bibliographies.

CITATION SEARCHING ON THE INTERNET

Google Scholar, which includes texts of academic and other journals, is essentially a keyword searchable file, with the usual term weighting (or relevance ranking) found elsewhere in Google, but Scholar provides and additional "wrinkle" in that, like *Web of Science* and several EBSCO databases, it will tell you if any given hit that comes up has been "Cited by" any other articles within the database. The only problem here is that you never know what you're getting in Scholar—or, just as important, what you are not getting. The company will not reveal which journals are indexed, nor which issues are being searched, or how much of a backfile is included.

Most of the databases discussed so far in this chapter will tell you if any given source has been cited in the footnotes of a subsequent journal article. Many researchers, of course, wish to know in addition if their given source has been cited by any books. The best way to look for this kind of linkage (apart from *Book Citation Index*) as of this writing is through either Google Books, Amazon's Look Inside the Book feature, the Hathi Trust Digital Library (www.hathitrust.org), or the Internet Archive (https://archive.org). These services make full texts of books keyword-searchable; again, that makes their footnotes searchable as well. In using Google Books or Hathi Trust, be sure to use quotation marks around any title (or other) phrases that you wish to look for.

The overall point of this chapter is that citation searching provides a useful way around the persistent problem of determining the best search terms for your topic. Given the weaknesses of keyword searching, you want to be aware of the other methods of getting at your topic that will bring to your attention relevant works whose keywords you cannot specify in advance. The traditional ways of circumventing this difficulty lie in controlled vocabulary searching and in browsing classified book-stacks (both of which enable you to recognize relevant terms within carefully defined conceptual categories). Citation searching provides yet another way around the problem. Still other ways will be discussed in the next chapters.

CHAPTER 7

Related Record Searches

Y ET ANOTHER MECHANISM EXISTS THAT, IN MANY CASES, circumvents the major problem of keyword searching by enabling you to recognize highly relevant sources whose terminology you cannot think of in advance. This mechanism is related record searching. *Web of Science* and *Scopus* provide the best starting points for this kind of inquiry, although the search technique is starting to show up in other databases as well.

FINDING ARTICLES WITH SHARED FOOTNOTE REFERENCES

In order to do a related record search you must first do a keyword search. In the *Web of Science*, for instance, if you find any good record that way, click on it to bring up the "Full" display of the citation (showing its abstract). The same display will present you with a column to right of the screen, usually providing you with a clickable option saying "View Related Records." Pursuing this link will provide you with a list of all other articles in the database that have footnotes in common with your starting-point article.

These are not articles that cite each other—rather, they are articles written independently that nonetheless cite several of the same sources in their footnotes. Articles having shared footnotes are usually covering the same subject area; the important point, however, is that they may be referring to their common topic with entirely different keywords. The list of related records, generated from the starting-point article, will be displayed in ranked order—those articles having the most footnotes in common with it at the top, down through those having only a single shared reference.

CIRCUMVENTING VOCABULARY PROBLEMS

In the previous chapter I mentioned the researcher looking for articles on "the economics of antiquities looting." He found one good article having those exact words in the title, through a keyword search; then, through a citation search, he found many subsequent articles because they referenced that first article. In the same instance, however, he could find still other relevant articles through a related record search because they had multiple footnotes in common with that same initial source. Among these articles having shared footnotes were such titles as the following:

- "Protecting newly discovered antiquities: Thinking outside the 'fee simple' box"
- "Evaluating the effectiveness of foreign laws on national ownership of cultural property in United States courts"
- "Reaffirming McClain: The National Stolen Property Act and the abiding trade in looted cultural objects"
- "Who owns the past in US museums? An economic analysis of cultural patrimony ownership"
- "A Tale of 2 innocents—Creating equitable balance between the rights of former owners and good faith purchasers of stolen art"

Related record searching is thus another mechanism that brings to your attention in a systematic manner relevant sources whose keywords you could never think up in advance. Further, since your search is tied to an already-discovered relevant article, that linkage provides a kind of contextual anchor that precludes widespread retrieval of thousands of articles having keywords wandering off into contexts that are irrelevant.

Another example is provided by a criminologist who was looking for articles on "statement analysis." I had never heard of this topic before she came to the reference desk, but she explained that it has to do with detecting signs of deception in either written or oral communications. A keyword search in *Web of Science* will turn up a few good hits within a welter of retrievals on "financial statement analysis" (which is something very different), with additional articles that cite the few relevant ones. But a related record search, starting from those few good keyword articles, produces scores of articles having such titles as these:

- "Reality monitoring and the judgment of the truthfulness of accounts—an experimental study"
- "Assessing credibility in cases of alleged sexual abuse of children"
- "Empirical support for statement validity assessment"
- "The less travelled road to truth: verbal cues in deception detection in accounts of fabricated and self-experienced events"
- "The detection of deception with the reality monitoring approach: a review of the empirical evidence"
- "Ways to a linguistic 'truth-detection test'?"
- "The language of deceit: an investigation of the verbal cues to deception in the interrogation context"
- "The usefulness of the criteria-based content analysis technique in distinguishing between truthful and fabricated allegations—a critical review"
- "Paraverbal indicators of deception: a meta-analytic synthesis"
- "Why professionals fail to catch liars and how they can improve"

What is especially useful about this search technique is that it can produce relevant hits no matter what their temporal relationship to the starting-point article—that is, the related record articles may be not just subsequent articles (as with citation search results), but also previous articles (as with footnote chasing), or even articles written in the same year. This search technique thus offers advantages over both of these other techniques for exploiting footnote references.

Further, you can "cycle" related record articles: if you find any good hits through this approach, you can then see if *they* lead to still other related records, because the same "View-Related Records" option is likely to show up on their own "Full" displays.

One limitation of *Web of Science* and *Scopus* coverage is that both databases "see" only scholarly journals—those having footnotes—to begin with. They do not cover the many other newsstand or commentary journals, which may well be of high quality, whose articles do not have these scholarly appendages.

I mentioned above that these two databases are no longer unique in offering related-record search capabilities. As of this writing several others (e.g., ProQuest's *Dissertations and Theses* and *ABI/INFORM Complete*) offer this search option. Undoubtedly others will follow. Some—not all—of the initial bibliographic citations you find in these databases will provide a link that says "Documents with shared references." Clicking there will produce a display of related citations in ranked order—i.e., those with the most shared footnotes at the top, down through those with only a single shared reference—with explicit listings of how many "references in common" there are for each. The qualification is that, at least in ProQuest databases, not every record has such a link. In *Dissertations*, for instance, none of the pre-1997 records have it.

DIFFERENT WAYS TO PROGRESS FROM AN INITIAL STARTING-POINT ARTICLE

Remember that whenever you find a good article on your topic, you can do several things with it to find additional conceptually related sources that may be using keywords you could not think of on your own:

1. When you look at the actual full text of the article in your library (i.e., not just a citation to it), either online or in print, you can look at its footnotes. This is simply a matter of common sense. Remember, however, that footnote chasing always leads you backwards in time, to previous sources.

2. You can do a citation search, in *Web of Science, Scopus,* or various other databases and websites. Citation searching is the mirror image of footnote chasing: it will always take you forward in time, to subsequent sources that are nonetheless linked to your initial source.

3. If the article appears in one of the 13,500+ journals (and some books and conference proceedings) indexed in *Web of Science,* or in the 22,000 journals indexed in *Scopus,* you can do a related record search. Articles having shared footnotes can lead you to previous or subsequent sources or to those written within the same year. The latter is sort of like searching "sideways" in time. More databases will provide this search capability in the future.

4. If you can find a citation to the article in a database that uses controlled vocabulary terms, display the record in its "Full" form to see which descriptors that database uses to index the article (see Chapter 4). Use those terms to search for similar articles.

All four of these search mechanisms are capable of producing results that cannot be matched by searching keywords. The advantage they offer, each in a different way, is that of laying out menus of works relevant to your topic in ways that enable you to simply recognize good sources whose terminology you would not otherwise think of. These are some of the best solutions to the problem of "what words do I type

in to get the best results?"—the most serious difficulty routinely encountered in Internet searching. They show you directly relevant records
whose search terms you don't know how to ask for, and they do it in
ways that assure conceptually anchored retrievals that do not have tens
of thousands of hits having the right words in the wrong contexts. (Yet
another search technique having comparable capabilities is that of using
published subject bibliographies, to be discussed in Chapter 9.)

A repeated theme of this book is that no one way of searching does
everything. And here I would re-emphasize that Internet keyword
searching alone—no matter how the terms are relevance-ranked—is
particularly problematic if your goal is to get an overview of the full
range of literature on your topic. The same applies to "discovery" and
federated searches of multiple subscription databases merged into a
single pool. You simply have to be aware of the unavoidable trade-offs
among search techniques so that your overall strategy can balance their
respective strengths and weaknesses against each other. Each will show
you different parts of "the elephant." What you cannot see with one way
of searching, you can see with the others.

CHAPTER 8

Higher-Level Overview Sources: Literature Review Articles

W E HAVE ALREADY CONSIDERED USING SPECIALIZED ENCY-clopedia articles to provide initial overviews of unfamiliar subjects, but there are still other ways to gain overview information in systematic ways. Discovering these alternatives, however, requires a bit more sophistication in searching. All researchers, no matter what their subject areas, are especially well advised to look for a particular type or subset of journal articles called *review articles*. These should not be confused with book reviews.

THE NATURE OF REVIEW ARTICLES

Review articles are a type of literature unto themselves; in these, an author tries systematically to read all the relevant literature on a subject, sometimes also to interview experts in the field, and then to organize, synthesize, and critically evaluate the range of information. His or her goal is to provide a state-of-the-art assessment of knowledge in the particular field, and sometimes to indicate areas that need further research. A literature review article is somewhat like an encyclopedia article in trying to present a concise overview of a subject, but there are two important differences: (1) a review article is usually written for specialists rather than laypeople and so may assume familiarity with technical jargon; and (2) its bibliography will usually be extensive rather than selective or merely introductory.

In other words, if you are doing serious research and can find a literature review article on your subject in the early stages of your investigation, you are in great shape. The important point is that you have to look specifically for this type of literature. If you don't deliberately limit your search by this document type, you may well lose sight of any review articles that come up within a simple keyword retrieval, as they can easily be lost or buried within much larger sets of citations. You want to make the review articles come up *first*. There are several ways to achieve this focus.

SPECIFIC DATABASES AND OTHER SOURCES FOR FINDING REVIEW ARTICLES

Web of Science Database.

The coverage of this file has been discussed in the two previous chapters; briefly, it indexes more than 13,500+ high-quality journals (and some thousands of books and conference proceedings) in almost all subject areas. Again, don't be misled by the word *Science* in its title—it also covers social sciences and humanities sources. What is particularly relevant in the present context is that allows you to limit your results, via a drop-down menu of options, to any of three dozen specific types of literature, among them:

Article
Art Exhibit Review
Bibliography
Book Review
Chronology
Database Review
Editorial Material
Film Review
Hardware Review
Item About an Individual
Letter
Music Performance Review
Poetry
Record Review
Review
Software Review
TV Review, Radio Review, Video
Theater Review

The crucial element to select here is simply "Review"; this is the designation in this database for "literature review" or "state-of-the-art" overview articles. (Note that other, and very different, "review" types are given separate designations of their own.)

Unfortunately, this option, as of this writing, is rather well hidden. To find it you must first get past the single search box of the initial default page by clicking on "Add Another Field"; you need to have at least two search boxes on the screen for this to work. With the second box, use its drop-down menu to get past the initial "Topic" option and scroll down until you find "Document Type." Click on that. The new search box on its left will then present a default line saying "All Document Types." Use its drop-down menu to locate the "Review" option and click there. This change in the second box will now limit your keywords in the first "Topic" box to search for only literature reviews.

Since this database is so marvelously cross-disciplinary, covering almost all subject areas, it can find review articles on just about anything (assuming they exist to begin with, of course). I am always astonished at how frequently they turn up, no matter what people are working on; in my own experience in helping readers I've found literature review articles with titles such as these:

- "Visitor behavior in zoos: A review" (2006; 82 footnotes)
- "The Biology of [asbestos] cleavage fragments: A brief synthesis and analysis of current knowledge" (2004; 136 footnotes)
- "The physics and chemistry behind the bubbling properties of Champagne and sparkling wines: A state-of-the-art review" (2005; 64 footnotes)
- "Athenian finance, 545-404 BC" [the abstract of which says it presents "an overview of the achievement of 20th-century scholarship"] (2001; 105 footnotes)
- "Understanding attitudes toward affirmative action programs in employment: Summary and meta-analysis of 35 years of research" (2006; 190 footnotes)
- "Through the back door: Evading the Chinese Exclusion Act along the Niagara Frontier, 1900 to 1924" (2008; 245 footnotes)
- "Risk factors in school shootings" (2000; 159 footnotes)
- "A literature review of the sponge-dwelling gobiid fishes of the genus Elacatinus from the western Atlantic, with description of two new Caribbean species" (2009; 23 footnotes)
- "Examining information behavior through social networks: An interdisciplinary review" (2009; 89 footnotes)

- "Women directors on corporate boards: a review and research agenda" (2009; 126 footnotes)

Using the "Review" feature of this database is an excellent way to find such articles quickly, across the whole range of scholarly disciplines.

I have noticed, however, that the coding for the "Review" document type is not always applied where it should be, and that additional review articles can sometimes be squeezed out of the same database by doing a regular keyword search in the "Advanced Search" box. To find the "Advanced" box to begin with, you must click on the drop-down arrow next to the default "Basic Search" option. Once there, ignore the lower box that allows limits by document types. Instead, simply type in your topical keywords but add a particular string of additional terms, as in this example that seeks additional review articles about "visitors' behavior in zoos":

> TS=zoo* AND (TS=visitor* OR TS=touris*) AND (TS="meta-analysis" OR TS=metaanalysis OR TS=survey OR TS=synthesis OR TS=overview OR TS="systematic analysis" OR TI=review).

Among the results provided by this string is the article "Visitors' effects on the welfare of animals in the zoo: A review" (2007; 63 footnotes), which is a good complement to the first of the sample articles listed above; but this 2007 article itself is mistakenly *coded* within the Document Type drop-down menu as a regular "Article" rather than as a "Review," and so it would not show up to begin with if you had limited your search to "Review."

(In the string of terms given above, "TS" refers to the word[s] following the "=" sign as findable in any of the Topical Subject fields of the record [i.e., titles, abstracts, or "KeyWords Plus" terms]; but "TI" limits the subsequent word's appearance only to the Title field. In these situations it is best to limit the keyword "review" only to appearances within the *titles* of articles; if allowed to appear with abstracts, the term too often appears in the wrong context. The asterisk [*] is a truncation symbol; its use will retrieve all instances of words having the same stem, such as "zoo," "zoos," "zoological," etc. In this instance, one *could* simply search for "meta*" rather than type the full terms "meta-analysis" OR "metaanalysis"; but doing that will open up the door to the appearance of too many undesirable words having the same stem, such as "metaphor," "metaphorical," "metabolism," "metallic," or "metastasis." [See Chapter 10 for more on truncation.])

Scopus Database

As discussed previously, this source covers 22,000 peer-reviewed jounals in all subject areas. It too has a clickable limit feature that allows you to narrow your search exclusively to literature "Review" articles. Its coverage extends well past that of *Web of Science*, particularly in Humanities and Social Sciences fields.

Annual Review of ... (Series)

Various publishers (especially Annual Reviews, Inc.) produce different series of review articles in many fields. They have titles such as *Annual Review of Anthropology; of Astronomy and Astrophysics; of Biochemistry; of Environment and Resources; of Information Science and Technology; of Law and Social Science; of Materials Research; of Physical Chemistry; of Political Science; of Psychology; of Sociology.*

Library & Information Science Source (EBSCO)

This database covers more than 500 journals in the fields of library and information science, with more than 440 of them full text. It is useful in finding review-type articles because reference librarians often publish for each other annotated bibliographies or bibliographic essays that discuss all the best sources (including websites) or finding aids on particular subjects (e.g., on women in religion, on novels set in academia, on the human–companion animal bond, on AfricanAmerican health issues). Unfortunately, nobody *except* reference librarians uses this source for this purpose, but it deserves a wider audience because the articles and annotated bibliographies to which it points are often first-rate starting points for research.

The *Syntopicon* Index

This comprises volumes 1 and 2 of the set *Great Books of the Western World*, 2nd ed., 60 vols. (Encyclopaedia Britannica, 1990). It provides 102 review articles on philosophical subjects, with indexing of relevant passages from all of the 517 works included in the set. A kind of shortcut to many of the indexed passages is provided by Mortimer Adler and Charles Van Doren's *Great Treasury of Western Thought* (1,771 pages; Bowker, 1977), which provides in one volume long quotations of the actual texts of many of the philosophical and literary works that are referred to in the *Syntopicon*'s review articles. *Great Treasury* also includes quotations from many classic works beyond those that are included in the *Great Books* set.

Institute for Philosophical Research Monographs

This organization, founded by Mortimer Adler to expand on the reviews done in the *Syntopicon*, produced several articles and full-length books that summarize the history of thought on various important ideas. Among these publications are:

- *The Idea of Freedom* by Mortimer Adler, 2 vols. (Doubleday, 1958–1961).This massive 1,443-page study is skillfully digested by Charles Van Doren in "The Idea of Freedom," Parts One and Two, in *The Great Ideas Today* (1972), pp. 300–392, and (1973), pp. 232–300.
- *The Idea of Justice* by Otto Bird (Frederick A. Praeger, 1968).This book-length study is summarized in Bird's "The Idea of Justice," *The Great Ideas Today* (1974), pp. 166–209.
- *The Idea of Happiness* by V. J. McGill (Praeger, 1967); summarized by McGill in "The Idea of Happiness," *The Great Ideas Today* (1967), pp. 272–308, and updated by Deal W. Hudson=s "Contemporary Views of Happiness," *The Great Ideas Today* (1992), pp. 170–216.
- *The Idea of Love* by Robert G. Hazo (Praeger, 1967).
- *The Idea of Progress* by Charles Van Doren (Praeger, 1967).
- "The Idea of Religion," Parts One and Two, by Jonathan Edward Sullivan, O.P., in *The Great Ideas Today* (1977), pp. 204–276, and (1978), pp. 218–312. (An even better overview of religious frameworks, both theistic and secular, is provided by Roy Clouser's *The Myth of Religious Neutrality* [rev. ed.; University of Notre Dame Press, 2005]).
- "The Idea of Equality" by Mortimer Adler in *The Great Ideas Today* (1968), pp. 302–350.
- "On the Idea of Beauty" by Donald Merriell in *The Great Ideas Today* (1979), pp. 184–222.

Each of these studies spells out very articulately what might be called "the range of options" of thought that has been covered on these most important topics over a span of more than two millenia. Since many of the books that are discussed "talk past each other" by using the same terms with different meanings, these volumes (and essays) serve a very useful purpose in regridding the various discussions in a way that standardizes their terminologies and allows better comparisons of the ideas. Especially recommended are the extraordinarily insightful overviews of *Freedom* by Van Doren (following Adler), *Justice* by Bird, and "Religion" by Sullivan and Clouser.

CONGRESSIONAL HEARINGS

These are frequently overlooked by academic researchers, but they can be real gold mines of information. Congressional investigations and oversight reviews extend into an amazing range of subject areas in the social sciences and sciences. (One estimate is that 20 hearings are held every day.) When the U.S. Congress wishes to find the best information on the current state of any situation, it generally gets it, for it can readily summon the best experts to testify. (See the further discussion of hearings, with examples, in Chapter 13.)

CONGRESSIONAL COMMITTEE PRINTS AND CRS REPORTS

In addition to drawing on hearings for information, Congress can use the Congressional Research Service (CRS) of the Library of Congress, which often produces book-length "state of the situation" reports on public policy issues. The virtue of these studies is that they are strictly objective, factual, and nonpartisan; CRS analysts are not allowed to advocate particular positions—they can only present the range of facts and issues that need to be considered by lawmakers. *ProQuest Congressional Publications* provides full-text level access. This database includes Legislative Reference Service (the predecessor of CRS) and CRS reports back to 1916, and all other committee prints back to 1817.

Additional online sources for CRS reports include:

- Open CRS at http://opencrs.com/
- Penny Hill Press at www.pennyhill.com/. Colleagues who work in CRS tell me, however, that these open sources on the Internet are never as up to date as CRS's own internal database, which is not publicly searchable. Another good source of older CRS reports is a printed index called *Major Studies and Issue Briefs of the Congressional Research Service* (UPA subdivision of LexisNexis Academic & Library Solutions), which has a 1916–1989 cumulative index and which is linked to a microfiche set of the actual reports.

As of the present writing, the Congressional Research Service is not allowed to mount either its own reports online or its own database listing the reports; CRS can provide its research studies *only* to members of Congress and their staffs. Congressional offices, however, are usually happy to obtain copies for constituents who request them, but the requests must be made to the members' offices, not to CRS itself.

DOCTORAL DISSERTATIONS

These are sometimes useful for review-type surveys of the literature of particular subject areas, especially in areas of the humanities and social sciences—although sciences are covered, too—that don't get picked up by the *Annual Review*–type series. Frequently writers will begin their dissertations with a survey of the literature of a field to present a background and context for their own contribution to it. The best index is the database *Dissertations & Theses: Full-Text* from ProQuest; it includes full texts of American and Canadian dissertations and master's theses since 1997. (Full texts are offered selectively prior to that year). Many libraries, however, will subscribe to the *Dissertations* database only at the indexing level of abstracts, without the full texts themselves. The company will sell copies of individual dissertations or master's theses from all years, however, in either microfiche or paper formats, but master's theses are not covered as extensively as dissertations. (For additional sources of dissertations, see Chapter 5.)

Review articles or overviews located through any of the above sources can often be updated by running them through the citation indexes (Chapter 6) to see if there has been any subsequent discussion of them.

The overall point to remember is that literature review sources, like encyclopedia articles, are often excellent starting points for research projects. Encyclopedias provide quick overviews of new or unfamiliar subjects, while reviews provide overviews not only of the content of the subject, but of *the range of literature* on the subject as well. Finding such articles early in your research can give you reasonable confidence that your are not completely overlooking sources that are very important—and whose existence might be brought to your attention later on, rather painfully, if you *do* overlook them. (This is a perennial concern for graduate students who are writing dissertations.) Finding these overviews can also give you a reasonable sense that you're not laboriously reinventing the wheel in duplicating research that has already been done by prior investigators. But you do have to look for both specialized encyclopedia articles and literature reviews specifically—otherwise they can easily be overlooked or buried within huge jumbles of results from larger, unfocused computer searches that fail both to notice and to zero in on these literature formats.

CHAPTER 9

Published Subject Bibliographies

ANOTHER VERY GOOD WAY TO GET AN OVERVIEW OF WORK that has already been done on your topic is through subject bibliographies. Those that are compiled by scholars and published either in book form or online are especially important because they usually cover citations to important studies that are not picked up by any computer indexes or websites.

ADVANTAGES OF SUBJECT BIBLIOGRAPHIES

Bibliographies compiled by scholars offer several advantages over computer-generated printouts: the scholars often provide evaluative rather than merely descriptive annotations, and they choose the entries to begin with according to a deep knowledge of the subject rather than according to algorithmic term-weighting criteria applied only to a few keywords. They often include nuggets that can be found only by serendipity, focused browsing, and persistent research over many years in obscure sources that may not be digitally accessible. And they may include types of materials, foreign language sources, and dates of coverage that lie in blind spots to the databases and websites. In some cases they approach the goal of offering "everything" available (up to a certain year) much more closely than do the databases, and in others they may provide a selective distillation of only the very best sources not simply chosen but also *arranged* in light of an expert compiler's deep appreciation of a subject.

A bibliography can give you much more extensive and specific information than a library catalog; it can save you a great deal of browsing time by rounding up in one place citations to works that are widely scattered in bookstacks; and it can list journal articles on a subject all in one place, so you won't have to repeat the same searches in dozens of relevant databases—or worry about having to tailor your searches to the individual vocabularies of each of them when doing federated searches. It may also pick up "fugitive" material such as dissertations, theses, pamphlets, manuscripts, corporate reports, conference papers, or government documents that are not covered by most online sources. Further, it can alert you to the existence of relevant works not held by your local library and not digitized in any database or website, but still available to you through interlibrary loan.

For example:

- A doctoral student who was about to do a dissertation on "Japonisme" (a term in art history referring to a certain vogue in art circles a century ago for all things Japanese—scroll paintings, rock gardens, calligraphy, etc.) was delighted to find Gabriel P. Weisberg and Yvonne M. L. Weisberg's *Japonisme: An Annotated Bibliography* (Garland, 1990), which is a 445-page listing of relevant sources, most of which do not have the keyword "Japonisme" in their titles.
- Another student who was about to write a paper on the Italian film director Vittorio De Sica was most appreciative in having John Daretta's *Vittoria De Sica: A Guide to References and Resources* (G. K. Hall, 1983) pointed out to him; it is 340 pages long.
- A grad student writing on the Soviet dictator Joseph Stalin, and who did not read Russian, found much of what he needed in David R. Egan's *Joseph Stalin: An Annotated Bibliography of English-Language Periodical Literature to 2005* (487 pages; Scarecrow Press, 2007) and in Marty Bloomberg's *Stalin: An Annotated Guide to Books in English* (128 pages; Borgo Press, 1993).
- A reader who wanted to know "what are the best books in military studies?" was immediately well served by Robert H. Berlin's *Military Classics* (U.S. Army Command and General Staff College, Combat Studies Institute, 1988), a concise 71-page annotated list.
- A historian who asked about sources on "spying in the ancient world" was delighted to have R. M. Sheldon's 232-page *Espionage in the Ancient World: An Annotated Bibliography of Books and*

Articles in Western Languages (McFarland, 2003) brought quickly to his attention.

- Another dissertation writer working on "art in the New Deal" was equally happy to be shown Martin L. Kalfatovic's 504-page *The New Deal Fine Arts Projects: A Bibliography, 1933–1992* (Scarecrow Press, 1994).
- A researcher interested in writing about silent films in India found an excellent starting point in R. K. Verma's *Filmography: Silent Cinema, 1913–1934* (M. Verma, 2000), a 416-page listing every silent film ever made in that country.

BOOLEAN COMBINATIONS

One of the most useful features of a published bibliography is that it will often enable you to do a simple Boolean combination in records that are not covered by computer databases. This type of inquiry involves looking for the overlapping of two subjects at the same time, and with databases such overlaps are very easy to produce. For example, I once helped a student who wanted to find comparisons of the educational philosophies of Aristotle and John Dewey. A search of a few databases combining "Aristotle AND Dewey" turned up a list of recent works discussing both thinkers. However, through a published bibliography we could do a similar search for older material not in the online files. We simply consulted Milton Thomas's *John Dewey: A Centennial Bibliography* (University of Chicago Press, 1962; 370 pages), which is an exhaustive list of studies about Dewey. In looking in its index, under "Aristotle," we were immediately led to a number of works that discussed the two, some of which had not appeared on the printouts.

Similarly, a researcher interested in comparisons of the Chinese political leader Sun Yat-Sen to George Washington or Abraham Lincoln found several relevant articles listed in Sydney H. Chang's *Bibliography of Sun Yat-Sen in China's Republican Revolution, 1885–1925* (2nd ed., University Press of America, 1998). This source is 549 pages long, but the relevant articles in it could be located immediately by simply looking it its index under "Washington" and "Lincoln."

Another reader once asked for information about an anti-Semitic speech allegedly given by Benjamin Franklin at the Continental Congress in Philadelphia. A keyword search of the largest database on American history, *America: History & Life*, using the combination "Benjamin Franklin" AND (anti-semit★ OR antisemit★ OR jew★ OR Hebrew★)

turns up several articles, but five of them are on a Benjamin Franklin Peixotto (a U.S. consul to Romania, who concerned himself with the affairs of Romanian Jews); one is on a Benjamin Franklin Davega (a Sephardic Jew in California in the nineteenth century); one is concerned with the Benjamin Franklin public library in a Jewish neighborhood in Los Angeles; and of the four on the "right" Benjamin Franklin, only one talks about the speech. A perusal of the massive two-volume bibliography *Benjamin Franklin: A Reference Guide* (1,130 pages; G. K. Hall, 1983–1888), under its index term "Franklin, Benjamin—alleged anti-Semitism," however, leads to *seventeen* citations about the speech—and just from the annotations of the entries one can tell that it is known to be a forgery.

Remember, then, that published bibliographies enable you to find "overview" listings of relevant literature that are often much better than those provided by computer databases—and that published sources *also* enable you to do Boolean combinations. You simply look for a bibliography on the first subject (Dewey, Sun Yat-Sen, Franklin) and then look for the second topic (Aristotle, Washington/Lincoln, anti-Semitism) in its index.

SOLVING VOCABULARY PROBLEMS

Two problems keep coming up in almost any research. The first is that the range of terms applicable to one's topic of interest is too extensive and unpredictable to assure systematic retrieval of the best relevant sources through keyword searches alone—relevance-ranking algorithms simply do not provide a solution here. As mentioned before, one traditional method of dealing with this difficulty is the assignment of controlled vocabulary subject headings or descriptors to records, but this brings up the second problem: not all relevant literature is indexed to begin with in online catalogs or databases having controlled vocabularies. And even those that do have controlled terms may not have subject headings or descriptors corresponding closely enough to the subject(s) you may have in mind.

In the precomputer age, another major solution to the problem of widely varying keywords was created—a solution that also compensates for any lack of adequate controlled headings in the the library's catalog (whether card format or online). This is the practice of classified shelving of relevant books together, so that limited subject-defined groups of full-text books right next to each other could be quickly skimmed down to the page and paragraph level. Such focused browsing enabled relevant passages to be recognized, within manageably bordered ranges of books, no matter what terms their authors may have employed.

Beyond classified shelving, however, scholars in the precomputer age could also appeal to another solution to problems of both unpredictable keywords and inadequate controlled vocabularies: they could look for subject bibliographies (or printed indexes to journal articles). If a good bibliography could be found, the literature relevant to a topic—specifically, lists of annotated citations to the literature—could be quickly scanned all in one place, no matter what terms (or what languages) were used by the authors of that literature. Such bibliographies are still there, and they have not been superseded by databases.

STRUCTURED ARRANGEMENTS OF THE LITERATURE ON A TOPIC

The best bibliographies also provide additional features for organizing their materials and reducing the need to skim too much material of only tangential interest: they provide *structured arrangements* of the citations according to the compiler's deep understanding of the component aspects of the topic. The grouping of citations by categorizations within a broad subject allows for additional focus and cuts down on wasted effort—that is, one need not skim all of the entries in an entire bibliography, hundreds of pages long, if one's interest is only in certain aspects of the topic. For example, Robert V. Remini and Robert O. Rupp's 314-page *Andrew Jackson: A Bibliography* (Meckler, 1991) arranges its annotated citations according to these breakdowns:

1. Manuscript and Archival Resources
2. Writings of Andrew Jackson
3. Biographical Publications
4. Childhood and Early Development
5. Early Career—Tennessee Years
6. Military Career
7. The Presidential Election of 1824
8. The Presidential Election of 1828
9. Campaign Literature
10. The Jackson Administration, 1829–1837
11. Labor
12. Economics and Class
13. Public Lands

14. The Presidential Election of 1832
15. Political Antimasonry
16. The Rise of the Whig Opposition
17. Assault and the Assassination Attempt
18. The Press
19. General Works on Politics
20. Administration Personalities
21. Post-Presidential Years
22. Personal Life of Andrew Jackson
23. Other Views of Jackson and His Times
24. Historiographical Method
25. Iconography

Many of these sections are themselves much more finely subdivided. This kind of conceptual arrangement and presentation simply could not be matched by relevance ranking of the same material by computer algorithms. The latter would produce an unsystematic jumble of the 2,231 citations in the bibliography, such that it would not be possible to discern the above "shape" of the literature.

THE IMPORTANCE OF INDEXES WITHIN BIBLIOGRAPHIES

Bibliographies usually provide an additional mechanism enabling searches to be finely focused: they provide indexes that enable researchers to zero in immediately on the few citations dealing only with very narrow aspects of the broad topics (as in the Dewey–Aristotle, Sun Yat-Sen–Washington/Lincoln, and Franklin–anti-semitism examples above). In the *Andrew Jackson* bibliography, its compilers have provided two different indexes at the back of the book: "Index to Authors" and "Index to Subjects." Such aids, once again, allow quick *recognition* of *groups* of relevant sources whose individual keywords could never be specified in advance.

TRADE-OFFS

The main advantage offered by scholarly bibliographies is that they can save you the trouble of reinventing the wheel—of doing the laborious spadework of identifying relevant sources. Further, such compilations usually provide you with assurance that you have not overlooked any particularly important sources in doing a literature review.

One disadvantage, or perhaps limitation, of bibliographies lies in the fact that their compilers will almost never tell you in detail how the list was assembled or which sources were consulted—you won't know what they themselves have overlooked, in other words. Nonetheless, it is usually safe to assume that a certain expertise is embedded in any bibliography good enough to achieve publication by a reputable publisher and that this human-added quality cannot be duplicated by algorithm-generated printouts.

The other limitation lies in the inevitable fact that published sources become dated. Remember, however, that *"dated" does not mean "outdated"*: especially in humanities and social sciences areas, the best literature is often—and in literary studies I am tempted to say usually—not the most recent. Since so much current scholarship, unfortunately, relies exclusively on freely available Internet resources, it is certainly not a safe assumption that it will have taken account of, and digested, the best of the earlier material that lies beyond the reach of the open Internet.

PROBLEMS CAUSING BIBLIOGRAPHIES TO BE OVERLOOKED

How, then, do you find out if there is a good subject bibliography on your topic? There are three big problems facing researchers in this area. The first is that, far too often, students simply assume that "everything is online" to begin with, and so they don't even consider the possibility of looking for a published bibliography.

The second problem is that most researchers, in formulating their inquiries for websites, online catalogs, or subscription databases, routinely type in only *subject* keywords—not *format* designations such as "bibliography." The result is that even if bibliographies are included in the retrievals, they are often buried under so many other hits that their existence goes unnoticed. The best place to start a search is in the library's online catalog. You can find bibliographies by looking for the subdivision **Bibliography** attached to the LC Subject Headings for your topic. (You can also add the term within a Boolean combination with other terms; see Chapter 10.) The further problem here, as indicated in Chapter 2, is that most people fail to find the right *LCSH* term(s) to begin with. The most common mistake is to search under broad rather than specific headings. The result is that you won't find the subdivision **Bibliography** if you're not looking at the right *heading* that it's a subdivision *of*.

A third stumbling block for most researchers is that they are not aware of the peculiar shelving of subject bibliographies in their libraries' bookstacks. In either the Library of Congress or Dewey Decimal Classification schemes, *bibliographies on a particular subject are usually not shelved with the regular books on that subject.* In the LC scheme, for example, books on **Indians of North America** tend to get call numbers within the range of E51-99 ("Pre-Columbian America and Indians of North America"). Works with the subject heading **Indians of North America—Bibliography**, however, get classed in Z1209-10, a designation that probably puts them on an entirely different floor in the library—and there will be no dummy cards *in the bookstacks* to tell you that relevant bibliographies do exist, but in a different place. (The subject heading system *in the catalog*, however, will alert you to the different shelving areas.)

The reason for this is that rounding up all subject bibliographies in one place (at the very end of the class scheme, in Z call numbers) gives them an aggregate power that would be dissipated if they were scattered throughout the regular B through V classes. Having all—or most, anyway—of the bibliographies on American history right next to each other in Z1201 through Z1363 enables researchers to recognize many other search options that would never occur to them if the bibliographies were dispersed (e.g., bibliographies on American county histories are in this area, too; and many of them provide good avenues of access for researching Native American topics). Shelving all of the published bibliographies, on all subjects, next to each other in Z1201 through Z8999 thus gives them a cumulative capacity to serve as a kind of index to the rest of the classification scheme, much like the index volume at the end of an encyclopedia.

The Dewey Decimal Classification system provides an analogous situation; in it, however, bibliographies on all subjects are usually grouped together at the *front* of the scheme, in class 016, rather than at the end. Thus, while a regular book on civil engineering would be classed in 624, a published bibliography would be shelved at 016.624—and, once again, such numbering probably puts the bibliographies on an entirely different floor in the library. (Note that individual libraries do not *have* to shelve their bibliographies in either the Z or 016 areas; they can choose to class them directly into the various subject areas. To do this costs more money, however, since most of the copy cataloging that is available for them to use from the shared OCLC network will offer records with Z and 016 numbers already established and immediately downloadable. [OCLC is the name of the company that creates a database combining the catalogs of over 70,000 libraries worldwide; the catalog records from any one library can be used by all of the others.] Having to create their own, different numbers in all of the various classes is more expensive than simply accepting what is already available, so most libraries will indeed separate the bibliographies from the monographs. You simply have to be aware of the separation when you are browsing in the bookstacks.)

The sad fact, then, is that most researcher overlook the existence of published bibliographies repeatedly—they don't type in format designations in entering their search terms; they don't find bibliographies in the online catalog because they don't find the right LC subject headings to which the **Bibliography** subdivision is attached, and they miss them in the bookstacks because they don't realize they're shelved in a separate area. (Curiously, bibliographic instruction classes taught by librarians almost routinely fail to alert researchers to these difficulties.)

The primary solution here is to find the right LC subject headings to begin with, and then to keep an eye out for a **Bibliography** subdivision. Catalog records with this format designation will then steer researchers to books having the correct Z (or 016) class numbers in the stacks.

FINDING BIBLIOGRAPHIES

There are variations on this solution, however; other mechanisms, too, are available for finding bibliographies. The more important options are as follows.

THE LIBRARY'S ONLINE PUBLIC ACCESS CATALOG (OPAC)

Three forms of heading in the Library of Congress system are relevant. After you have determined the proper *LCSH* word or phrase for your topic (or the one that comes closest) through the various methods discussed in Chapter 2, plug it into the following forms:

> **[Subject heading]—Bibliography**
> > (for example, **Terrorism—Bibliography**)
>
> **[Subject heading]—[Geographic and/or Topical subdivision]—Bibliography**
> > (for example, **Terrorism—United States—History—Bibliography**)

Remember that by using *browse display menus* of the subdivisions of headings, you can simply recognize the **Bibliography** subdivision wherever it may appear. You can also do a Boolean combination right from the start, e.g., "**Terrorism** AND **Bibliography**" if you keep in mind that format designations are important (see Chapters 10 and 15).

Additionally, if a book has a bibliography several pages long at its end, the catalog record for the book will usually provide a Note field pointing out its existence and its length. So even if you don't find the form **Subject heading—Bibliography** in the *LCSH* system, you may still be able to pick out bibliographies on records that appear under *any LCSH* heading, if you look for this Note information. (A caveat here: The Note field itself may appear only in the "Full" display of the catalog record, not in the default "Brief" record [see Figure 9.1].)

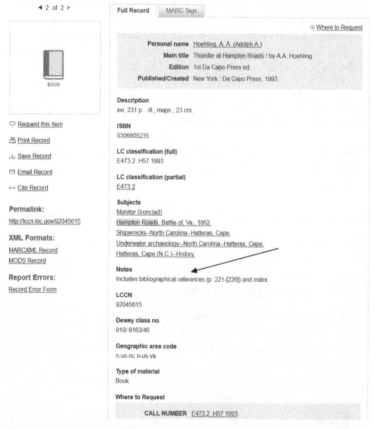

Figure 9.1 Screenshot of full catalog record for *Thunder at Hampton Roads* by Heohling, with arrow pointing to Bibliography note.

THE Z1201-Z8999 (OR 016 IN DEWEY) BOOKSTACKS AREAS

It is a good idea to just browse around in these areas to get a sense of what's there. In the LC classification system there is a further structure to the arrangement of Z-class subject bibliographies:

Z120-Z4890	Geographically localized subject bibliographies (arranged by continent in the order of North America, South America, Europe, Asian, Africa, Australia and Oceania), with narrower local subdivisions (country, state, county, etc.) within each.
Z5000-Z7999	Subject bibliographies (usually lacking geographic limitations or focus, arranged alphabetically by subject).
Z8000-Z8999	Personal bibliographies (on individual people, usually literary authors or historical figures), arranged alphabetically by the surname of the subject.

The personal bibliographies on individual authors are often excellent sources to start with when you are looking for literary criticisms of particular stories, plays, or poems. A published bibliography on an author—there are thousands of them—will usually give you a much better overview of the range of criticism available on any particular work than a database search (such as the *MLA International Bibliography*) can provide.

Note that the tripartite structuring of this arrangement will cause some scattering. Thus, bibliographies on American drama will be classed in Z1231.D7 (within the North American continent grouping), whereas those on English drama will appear in Z2014.D7 (within the European section), and those on Drama in general (without a particular geographic focus) will appear in Z5781-85, which lies within the "D" alphabetical subject range in the middle group. And bibliographies on individual dramatists will appear in the Z8000s, as Ibsen in Z8431 and Shakespeare in Z8811-13.

Similarly, bibliographies on Philosophy in general will appear in the "P" section of the alphabetical sequence (Z7125-30), but a bibliography on a particular philosopher such as Socrates will appear in Z88824.34. It's very hard to see this scattering when you're simply looking directly at the bookshelves, but if you understand the structure of the arrangement before you plunge in, you can use the collections more efficiently. Remember in particular that all bibliographies on individual people are segregated in the Z8000s, subarranged by the subject's surname. A complete listing of the various Z-class categorizations can be found in printed form in the *Super LCCS* volume *Class Z: Bibliography and Library*

Science [Gale Cengage, revised irregularly]; it is likely to be available in any library that uses the LC Classification scheme. The full list of LC Classes and their subdivisions is also now online at a free website: http://www.loc.gov/aba/publications/FreeLCC/freelcc.html.

BIBLIOGRAPHIC INDEX (H.W. WILSON CO., 1937–2011)

Bibliographic Index in its printed form was an annual subject index to published subject bibliographies. Although it is no longer published, it still provides very good access to tens of thousands of bibliographies within its extensive span of coverage. (A corresponding database no longer exists, having been discontinued during the merger of its publisher, the H.W. Wilson Company, with EBSCO.) This source lists not only bibliographies published as separate books, but also those that appear at the ends of books and journal articles. Those that are indexed usually contain at least 50 citations, in English or any of a dozen other languages. The editors examined 2,800 periodicals and 5,000 books each year and used LC subject headings for its category terms.

ENCYCLOPEDIA ARTICLES

The bibliographies at the ends of these are often very good for providing concise lists of the most highly recommended works on a subject, rather than overwhelming printouts of "everything." As mentioned in Chapter 1, a good trick for identifying a short list of "best" books is to compare the bibliographies from two or more different encyclopedia articles. I recommend using the *Encyclopaedia Britannica* as one of the sources, since its bibliographies are usually evaluative—that is, the *Britannica* writers don't just list sources; they give a running commentary on their quality in short bibliographical essays at the ends of the subject articles. To find another encyclopedia article to use in comparison, consult the sources listed in Chapter 1, especially the subscription database *Reference Universe*, which indexes the individual articles in tens of thousands of specialized encyclopedias (and provides links to many full texts). If the bibliography from the specialized source mentions the same titles recommended by the *Britannica*, you can be confident you've found some good starting points. (For example, I once wanted to read a book about Confucius, but I wanted only *one*, and I didn't know which of the many available titles to choose. I compared the bibliography from the "Confucius" article in the *Encyclopedia of Philosophy* to that in the *Britannica*; both recommended H. G. Creel's *Confucius: The Man and the Myth* [reprinted as *Confucius and the Chinese Way*], so that's the one I read.)

Even if the *Britannica* does not have an article on your topic, you can still usually find articles with bibliographies, from multiple other encyclopedias, by using *Reference Universe*.

REVIEW ARTICLES

These have excellent and lengthy bibliographies and can be located by the approaches discussed in Chapter 8.

OXFORD BIBLIOGRAPHIES ONLINE

This subscription database from Oxford Univesity Press is made up of scores of separate lengthy, annotated bibliographies on subjects in the social sciences and humanities; its purpose is to provide what I've been calling "the shape of the elephant" of the literature within each subject area. Each bibliography identifies the "essential literature" of its topic, providing introductory overviews, identifying standard works (if they exist), and providing evaluative and comparative annotations of relevant books, articles, primary sources, online resources, and other formats of material deemed essential to an overview of the subject. The bibliographies are compiled by teams of established scholars in their fields and are revised and expanded to keep abreast of new developments. Current modules cover the following:

- African Studies
- American Literature
- Anthropology
- Atlantic History
- Biblical Studies
- British and Irish Literature
- Buddhism
- Childhood Studies
- Chinese Studies
- Cinema and Media Studies
- Classics
- Communication
- Criminology
- Ecology
- Education
- Geography
- Hinduism
- International Law

- International Relations
- Islamic Studies
- Jewish Studies
- Latin American Studies
- Latino Studies
- Linguistics
- Management
- Medieval Studies
- Military History
- Music
- Philosophy
- Political Science
- Psychology
- Public Health
- Renaissance and Reformation
- Social Work
- Sociology
- Victorian Literature

Additional bibliographies are planned. A continually updated list is provided at www.oxfordbibliographiesonline.com. Each broad subject may have scores of subdivisions, each section beginning with its own introductory overview essay before providing a structured bibliography identifying and evaluating the most important literature in its area. The Islamic Studies module, for example, has more than a hundred component sections, a sampling of which is as follows:

Africa, Islam in
Ahmad Khan, Sayyid
Apostasy
Arabic Language and Islam
Azhar, al-
Balkans, Islam in the
Banna, Hasan al-
Caliph and Caliphate

★   ★   ★

Democracy and Islam
Education
Ethics
Europe, Islam in

★   ★   ★

Human Rights
Indonesia, Islam in
Jihad

★ ★ ★

Qaeda, al-
Qur'an

Each such subtopic has its own further development; the "Qaeda, al-" section, for instance, has these components, created to give a perceptible "shape" to the literature covered:

Introduction
General Overviews
English Translations
Historical Development
    Events
    Ideological Studies
Structure
    Organization
    Branches
    Leadership
    Strategies
    Suicide Attacks
    Ideology
    Development

Every segment of the entire database will be continuously updated. Its individual subject sections can be also be ordered as e-books; a listing may be found by typing "Oxford Bibliographies Online Research Guides" in the Amazon.com search box.

Book Review Digest Plus and Book Review Digest Retrospective: 1905–1982

These subscription databases from EBSCO can be searched simultaneously for coverage of 850,000 current and older books. You can search not just for known book titles but also—and this is their strength—via controlled subject headings; they will then provide, immediately, a string of evaluative reviews of any of the books under the chosen heading(s). It is of course possible, and quite convenient, to get immediate reviews of individual book titles via either Amazon.com or LibraryThing.com, but subject searches in the latter two are done via uncontrolled keywords or user-supplied tags rather than standardized subject headings (with all the advantages and disadvantages discussed in Chapters 2 and 5), so these EBSCO databases allow a kind of systematic searching for evaluated sources, extending back more than a century, that are not available through the Internet sites. (The reviews on Amazon don't usually cover books that are decades old.)

LIBRARY & INFORMATION SCIENCE SOURCE

This is another EBCSO subscription database, covering 500 journals; as mentioned in Chapters 4 and 8 it is primarily used by librarians. What makes it useful for general researchers is that reference librarians often publish annotated bibliographies of sources either for hot topics that readers are currently asking about or for collection development. Among the bibliographies published in recent years are "Recommended Core Bibliography of Textile and Clothing Resources for Academic and Public Libraries," "Unitarian Universalism: A Research Guide," "Afro-Latinos: An Annotated Guide for Collection Building," "Penning Hollywood: Resources for Would-Be Screenwriters," "Finding United States Historical Images in Print and Online," and "Meditation and Health: An Annotated Bibliography."

WEB OF SCIENCE

This database, discussed previously, has a new feature: when you find any good article citation within it, clicking on the number following the designation "Cited References" (the number of footnotes in the article) will bring up a full bibliography of the footnotes themselves. Generating such a bibliography from review articles is particularly useful. This works, however, only for articles entered from 2012 and after; the "Cited References" link attached to pre-2012 records in the database will not provide full bibliographic information for their footnotes—i.e., in the "Cited References" footnotes for that period you will get the titles of the journals in which the articles appeared but not the titles of the articles themselves.

READERS' ADVISORY SOURCES

Bibliographies are also frequently more useful than databases when questions of a "readers' advisory" nature arise—that is, when people just want recommendations of good books to read, in any subject area. There are many specialized publications in these areas, for mysteries, historical fiction, love stories, science fiction, horror stories, war stories, and so on. Usually they can be found through a combination search of:

[*LCSH* heading] AND **Bibliography** AND (**Fiction** OR **Stories** OR **Literature**)

There is also a subscription database, *FictionConnection* (R.R. Bowker), for readers' advisory information; it enables you to search for novels by Genre, Topic, Location (e.g., New England, Europe, New York City), Setting (e.g., College/University, Small Town, Island), Time Frame, Character, Character Traits (e.g., Married, Mother, Serial Killer, Ex-convict), Reading Level, and other criteria. On the open Internet both Amazon and LibraryThing also provide readers' recommendations. For advice on what to read, however, it's often best to talk to your local librarians—they frequently deal with questions of this kind and may know immediately of many good sources.

For general lists of what to read for self-education, a number of "great books" lists are available. In addition to the sets of the *Harvard Classics* (various printings) and the *Great Books of the Western World*, 2nd ed., 60 vols. (Encyclopaedia Britannica, 1990), analogous rosters may be found in Charles Van Doren's *The Joy of Reading* (Harmony Books, 1985), Clifton Fadiman and John S. Major's *New Lifetime Reading Plan* (HarperCollins, 1997), Mortimer Adler's *Reforming Education* (Macmillan, 1998, pp. 318–350), Harold Bloom's *The Western Canon* (Harcourt Brace, 1994; pp. 531–567), and Michael Dirda's *Classics for Pleasure* (Harcourt, 2007). An interesting older great books list is Asa Don Dickinson's *The World's Best Books, Homer to Hemingway: 3000 Books of 3000 Years, 1050 B.C. to 1950 A.D., Selected on the Basis of a Consensus of Expert Opinion* (H. W. Wilson Company, 1953). Dickinson assembled it by collating scores of previous lists of classics. A good list of "The Great Books of the East," compiled by William Theodore de Bary, appears in the 1987 annual volume of *The Great Ideas Today* (Encyclopaedia Britannica, Inc., pp. 222–244). Online collections of copyright-free full texts of great books can be found at www.grtbooks.com, and www.thegreatideas.org/greatbooks.html.

To sum up: for any kind of scholarly or in-depth research, it is important to look for published subject bibliographies compiled by scholars in addition to lists generated by typing keywords into databases. The former can not only turn up valuable resources—recent as well as old—that are missed by the databases, they can also often provide systematic overviews of "the shape" of the literature relevant to a topic (which most of the databases do not do at all). Moreover, they allow you to recognize sources within their coverage whose keywords you could never think up in advance. It is important to actively search for such bibliographies, especially since they are so frequently overlooked for the reasons given above. Almost every researcher has had the experience of using a bibliography that appears at the end of a book or article, but it is comparatively rare—at least from this reference librarian's perspective—for researchers to start out by looking for a separate subject bibliography, as opposed to simply using one that happens to come their way as a by-product of something else they've done. A hallmark of the experts is that they actively look for such lists, especially in the early stages of their investigations. The best researchers regard the aggregate of subject bibliographies as collectively forming an avenue of access to sources that is quite different from, and not superseded by, the alternative avenue of searching provided by the aggregate of all of the databases now available.

CHAPTER 10

Truncations, Combinations, and Limitations

FINDING THE BEST SEARCH TERMS FOR YOUR TOPIC, WHETHER keywords or controlled vocabulary headings, is obviously very important to the success of your research. Equally important, however, are considerations of what to do with those terms once you've decided what they should be—that is, how you type them can make a radical difference in determining what records they retrieve. By "how you type them" I am referring to the many combinations, truncations, word proximity specifications, and field limitations that are possible. For example, the combination of the search terms

Motion pictures AND women

will produce results that are very different from typing in the same string in quotation marks: "motion pictures and women"—which in turn will produce very different results from the strings "motion pictures for women" or "motion pictures about women." (Eliminating the quotation marks would, in most databases, leave the conjunction AND operative, but would make the prepositions "for" and "about" invisible to the search software.)

Similarly, within the *LCSH* system **Philosophy** AND **Research** will produce results much different from either **Research—Philosophy** or **Philosophy—Research**. (In most databases the connector could by typed in either upper or lowercase—"AND" or "and"—without making a difference.)

A researcher trying to find articles on the "information-seeking behavior of tourists" could type in that string of terms—but (in databases providing abstracts of articles) she would get better results with

touris* AND "information se*"

This phrasing would include any of the variant forms *tourist* [singular], *tourists* [plural] and even *tourism*, as well as *information seeking, information seeker* [singular], *information seekers* [plural], *information search, information searching, information searcher* [singular], or *information searchers* [plural]. The same inquirer would get better results by *omitting* the word "behavior" entirely—it isn't necessary for the concept, and the specification that that particular keyword *must* be present would unwittingly eliminate any relevant records that use "activities" or "practices" or other such terms rather than "behavior."

Similarly, to return to an example mentioned in Chapter 2, a search for portrayals of the Arab–Israeli conflicts in fiction, the phrasing

Israelis AND Arabs OR Palestinians AND literature OR fiction

will produce a huge jumble of results that bear no resemblance to those produced by a more carefully crafted string using parenthetical groupings, such as

Israel* AND (Arab* OR Palestin*) AND (literature OR fiction)

Moreover, while the above string would work in most commercial databases, the same terms would have to be typed in differently in many library OPACs that use the question mark rather than the asterisk as the truncation symbol:

Israel? AND (Arab? OR Palestin?) AND (literature OR fiction)

Again, it's not just a matter of simply finding the right words to begin with—how you type them in changes what they will find.

The major considerations governing "how you type them in" are those of word truncation, wildcards, Boolean combinations of terms, word proximity specifications, and limitations of searches by various criteria (language, date, geographic area code, document type, etc.).

WORD TRUNCATION AND WILDCARD SYMBOLS

Most subscription databases use the asterisk (*) for word truncation, also known as word stemming. This feature saves you the trouble of having to key in, individually, multiple words having the same stem. Thus, typing *child** will find not just the singular form of the word, but also *child's*, *children*, or *children's*—any words having the same stem. Similarly, *Athen** will retrieve not just *Athens* but also *Athenian* or *Athenians*, and *comput** will bring up *computer, computers, computerization*, or *computing.*

You have to be careful, however: *child** will also retrieve *childbearing, childbed, childbirth, childhood, childish*, or *childlike* if those terms are present in the database you are searching, and their presence can greatly increase the number of "noise" records that only get in the way of what you want. Similarly, *Athen** will also bring up *Athena, Athenia, Athenaeum, Athenagoras, Athènes, Atheniensium*, and *athenischen*. And *comput** can retrieve *computable, computative, computation*, or *computational.*

As in the example of Arab–Israeli fiction, some OPACs such as the online catalog of the Library of Congress (which uses the Voyager system from Ex Libris—also used by about 1,300 other libraries) use the question mark (?) rather than the asterisk for word truncation. Still other databases use the exclamation point (!).

The term "wildcard" usually refers to retrieval of variant characters within individual words, rather than to the word stemming that takes place at the end of the terms. For example, in the *Historical Abstracts* database, there are two wildcard symbols: the question mark (?) can be used inside a word to replace any one character; thus *ne?t* will retrieve *neat, next*, or *nest.* The pound sign (#), however, when used internally, can replace more than a single internal character; thus *colo#r* will retrieve either *color* or the British spelling *colour.*

All of this, of course, can be very confusing and difficult to remember since different databases have different conventions. The one *very* important point to remember is that most of them will have a Help icon that you can click on, which will spell out the information you need regarding which symbol(s) to use within whichever database you're searching. Look for that icon and skim whatever information it brings up. You really need to know *how to type in* the words you want.

BOOLEAN COMBINATIONS

"Boolean" combinations derive their name from the nineteenth-century British mathematician and logician George Boole; the term refers to the capacities of most databases to combine multiple search elements within one inquiry. For example, a researcher interested in the topic "computer-assisted instructional techniques in the field of geography" was initially referred to the *ERIC* database, a large index to journal articles and research reports in the field of education. This index has a list of controlled descriptor terms. The *Thesaurus of ERIC Descriptors* listed several different relevant terms for each of the two elements he wished to combine:

Programmed Instruction	**Geographic Concepts**
Learning Laboratories	**Geography**
Programmed Instruction Materials	**Geography Instruction**
Computer Assisted Instruction	**Human Geography**
	Physical Geography
	World Geography

The *ERIC* database can search all of the first-column terms at once, and all of the second column, then cross the two sets against each other to present only those citations that retrieve at least one descriptor from each column simultaneously. Had he so desired, the searcher could have introduced a third set of terms, specifying the output to only those citations having any of the additional descriptors **Secondary Schools**, **Secondary Education**, **Secondary School Curriculum**, and so on. A further specification could have limited the results to only articles or reports published within the last five years.

The computer accomplishes this operation of combining and screening terms via Boolean combinations, which are illustrated in Figure 10.1. If Circle A represents the set of citations retrieved by expressing one subject (either controlled descriptors or keywords or both), and Circle B represents another subject, then the area of overlap in Figure 10.1a represents those citations that deal with both subjects simultaneously. Other circles or limiting factors can be introduced for further specification. And other types of combinations are possible, as shown in Figures 10.1b and 10.1c.

In the above example, the way that the search terms are entered can also be simplified. If the terms are first specified as having come from descriptor (rather than keyword) fields, an expression such as the following would work:

(**Programmed** OR **Learning Laboratories** OR **Computer Assisted Instruction**) AND **Geograph***

The word **Programmed** by itself, being common to two of the descriptors, need not be typed in twice. The asterisk (*) after **Geograph*** is the truncation symbol that tells the computer to retrieve any terms having the same stem, equivalent here to (**Geography** OR **Geographic**).

The use of parentheses, as in the above example, enables you to use multiple Boolean combinations of different kinds within the same search

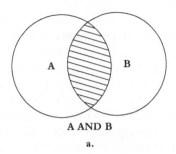

A AND B

a.

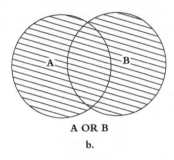

A OR B

b.

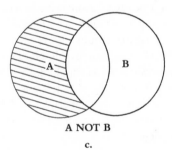

A NOT B

c.

Figure 10.1 Venn diagrams (a, b, c) showing Boolean AND, OR, and NOT intersecting circles, respectively.

specification. Another of the examples given above could be further extended as in Chapter 2, thus:

> Israel? AND (Arab? OR Palestin?) AND (literature OR fiction)
> NOT (juvenile OR children's)

This OPAC search would turn up books on the portrayal of the various Arab–Israeli conflicts in fiction, but would eliminate the many propagandistic story books written for children.

Similarly, the reader who vaguely remembered a book about someone who bicycled through France, but couldn't recall the exact title or author, found what he needed in *Book Review Digest Plus* by doing a combined search of "bicycl*" (to include "bicycler" or "bicycling" as well) and "France" as subject words, but NOT-ing out the phrase "tour de France" (in quotation marks), which would provide multiple unwanted hits. (In this database, the terms are entered in separate search boxes, with the AND, OR, and NOT operators given in drop-down menus for each box.)

Be particularly wary of how you use the NOT operator. For example, suppose you want articles on "dog food AND cat food"; in this case, if Circle A represents "dog food" and Circle B represents "cat food," then the AND combination of the two will give you the shaded area of Figure 10.1a. Now suppose you want either "dog food OR cat food." The OR operator between the terms will give you the shaded area in Figure 10.1b. But now suppose you specify "dog food NOT cat food." The NOT operator here will give you only the shaded area of Circle A—not the entire Circle A—represented in Figure 10.1c. The area where the circles overlap contains citations that talk about both dog food AND cat food (as in Figure 10.1a)—but by saying you wish to eliminate the articles that include cat food (all of Circle B), you have unwittingly eliminated some entries in Circle A *that also* talk about dog food. Be careful about using NOT as a connecting term, in other words—you may be eliminating more than you wish.

Note that some databases require the capitalization of connecting terms (AND, OR, NOT, or sometimes OR NOT), whereas others allow either capital or lowercase entry. Again, look for the Help icon within whichever database you are using to determine its conventions. Don't just start typing keywords into the first blank search box you see—take a (very brief) moment to familiarize yourself with *how to type in* the terms you want. *This is important.*

COMBINATIONS USING COMPONENT WORDS *WITHIN* CONTROLLED SUBJECT STRINGS

The ability to search and combine component words that are shared by multiple controlled vocabulary strings is very useful in many situations. For example, in the *Library of Congress Subject Headings* list (see Chapter 2), there are more than 17 pages of headings that start with the terms **African American(s)**; these include such terms as the following:

African American actors
African American architecture
African American baseball umpires

African American cooking
African American diplomats
African American families
African American History Month
African American leadership
African American painting
African American parents
African American preaching
African American quilts
African American radio stations
African American students
African American veterans
African American wit and humor
African American women
African American women composers
African American women surgeons
African Americans—Biography
African Americans—Civil rights
African Americans—Folklore
African Americans—History
African Americans—Legal status, laws, etc.
African Americans—Relations with Korean Americans
African Americans—Religion
African Americans and mass media
African Americans in art
African Americans in the motion picture industry
African Americans with disabilities

Similarly, there are 10 pages of headings that start with the word **Television**; among them are the following:

Television
    NT **Animals on Television**
Businessmen on television
Detective teams on television
Medical personnel on television
Sex on television
Violence on television
Television—Art direction
Television—Censorship
Television—State-setting and scenery
Television—Vocational guidance
Television actors and actresses

Television addiction
Television and literature
Television broadcasting of news
Television crime shows
Television in adult education
Television in politics
Television news anchors
Television personalities
Television plays, Hindi
Television programs
    NT **Action and adventure television programs**
        Live television programs
        Lost television programs
        Medical television programs
        Television comedies
        Television reruns
        Women's television programs
Television talk shows
Television weathercasting

While there are thus hundreds of separate headings with either **African American(s)** or **Television** in them, there are also precoordinated headings that combine the two concepts, such as:

African American television journalists
African American television viewers
African American women on television
African Americans on television

The point here is that the component word search capability of online catalogs can easily cross *all* of the many **African American(s)** headings against *all* of the **Television** headings without your having to type them all in individually:

You will need to be connected to the Internet to follow this: from the catalog.loc.gov search page select "Advanced Search" and then change the drop-down menus for each of the first two search boxes from "Keyword Anywhere (GKEY)" to "Subject ALL (KSUB)." Type "African American?" in the first box and "television?" in the second box. This method of searching takes you directly to the catalog records having the subject terms you've entered—unlike the Browse search screen, it entirely bypasses the intervening display of browse menus that would alert you to other headings or cross-references (see Figure 10.2).

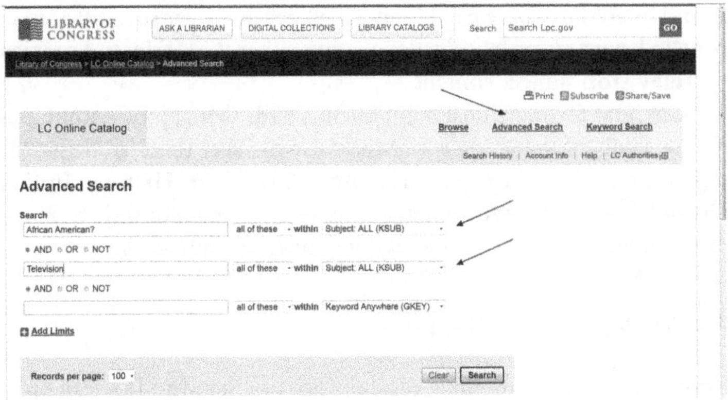

Figure 10.2 LC catalog Advanced Search screenshot with two drop-down menus changed to "Subject ALL: KSUB" for the two boxes: African American? AND television.

This combination of *LCSH* elements produces more than 400 records. Particularly interesting is that among the retrieved hits are Geraldine Woods's *The Oprah Winfrey Story* (1991) and Paul Mooney's *Black is the New White: A Memoir* (2010). The subject headings (or tracings) attached to the former book show that it has the separate headings:

Television personalities
African Americans—Biography

The tracings on the latter also show separate headings:

Television comedy writers—United States—Biography
African American comedians—Biography

What is significant here is that a researcher found works having the desired words (among the 400+ hits) not only *within* precoordinated strings such as **African American television personalities** but also, as in these instances, *across* entirely *different* strings attached to the same record. In a sense, then, the capacity to do Boolean combinations of individual words within different subject heading strings is a kind of sixth way to find the right *LCSH* headings for your topic, in addition to the five discussed in Chapter 2. Note, however, that this is not a conventional keyword search of words transcribed from titles of the books themselves. Rather, it is a keyword search of terms within the artificially created phrases—LC subject headings—that were *added to* the catalog records by librarians. If these controlled vocabulary terms had not been added, these records would not have been found at all because their own titles do not contain keywords specifically designating either the **African American** or **Television** subject content.

Searching for individual component words that appear within many different subject headings is very useful whenever there are large clusters of related headings. (**Art**, **Business**, **Civil War**, **History**, **Indians**, **United States**, and **Women** are other component words that each appears within a large multitude of different *LCSH* phrases.)

PROXIMITY SEARCHES

Beyond the word-combining capabilities of the standard Boolean operators AND, OR, and NOT, many databases allow more nuanced retrieval through word proximity searching. In these instances you can tell the computer not just to find two terms anywhere at all, but within specified distances of nearness, or in a specified order.

For example, in the *Periodicals Index Online* database (indexing more than 6,000 journals in 60 languages back to 1665) you can use either NEAR or FBY (Followed By) operators. Though you can always type in the term "life insurance" in quotation marks, which would assure retrieval of those two words immediately next to each other, in that order, you could also type:

life NEAR.5 insurance [This would give you both words, in either order, with up to five intervening words]

life FBY.3 insurance [This would give you both words, in the order specified, with up to three intervening words, as in the phrases "life casualty insurance," "life and health insurance," or "life and employers' liability insurance"]

Other databases have similar functions but use different operators, such as

Life N5 insurance   [Either order, up to 5 words apart]

Life W3 insurance   [Same order, up to 3 words apart]

Life PRE/3 insurance   [Same order, up to 3 words apart]

Again: take the very brief moment required to click on the Help icon in whatever database you're searching to see which conventions it is using. The use of these proximity operators can *greatly* cut down the number of junk hits that have the right words in contexts you don't want.

Proximity searching is also very useful when you are trying to pin down a phrase or quotation when you have only incomplete information about it. For instance, the researcher trying to identify which Supreme Court justice said that he couldn't define pornography, but that "I know it when I see it" used a proximity search within *Academic Search Complete*:

Justice N15 pornography N15 "when I see it"

This quickly turned up references to the remark made by Justice Potter Stewart.

LIMITATIONS OF SETS

Many databases allow limitations of search results by language, by date of publication, or by other features. The Help screens can provide this information; in many cases, the limit options will show up in columns along the margins of search screens or be presented below the search boxes in Advanced Search screens. Although the default setting for search screens, in most databases, will be for a "simple" single box, always look for and change your setting to the Advanced search mode. This will bring to your attention many possibilities for limiting your searches in ways that will greatly reduce the clutter of unwanted hits having the right terms in the wrong contexts. Many of these limit features are extremely important and should be actively sought out.

LIMITING BY TIME PERIODS

While many databases allow you to limit your results to dates *of publication* of articles, it is rare to find files that enable you to limit to the dates *of subject coverage* you want. Thus, if you are looking for articles on the situation of the Copts in Egypt between 1900 and 1930, it would not be adequate to find only articles published between those dates, because there could be (and are) articles written *about* the Copts in that period that were themselves published much later. In this connection, two of the best databases for coverage of history journals, *America: History & Life (AH&L)* and *Historical Abstracts (HA)*—both from EBSCO, have exactly the desired capability. Not only can you fill in search boxes asking for month/year ranges of "Published Date," you can also search by "Historical Period"—the latter enabling you to specify which years of *subject* coverage of the articles you wish to find. These databases were described in Chapter 4; to repeat that information briefly here, *AH&L* is the largest single database covering U.S. and Canadian history (from prehistoric times to the present); *HA* is the largest covering all other areas (from ca. 1450 forward, with some minimal coverage of earlier eras). Both files interpret "history" in a very broad sense, covering the history of art, education, literature, philosophy, religion, and so on—not just politics and rulers and international relations.

This limiting-by-dates-of-subject-coverage feature is extremely useful in historical inquiries, but my experience is that very few users of these databases—even among professional historians—are aware of it or notice this option on the search screens. You have to change the screen display from the default Basic Search to the Advanced Search for this search option to appear; further, you have to scroll down to the bottom half of the search page to see it.

An example of the utility of this feature is provided by the researcher who wanted information on "education in the Philippines between 1898 and 1916." Within *Historical* Abstracts, use of the Historical Period limit boxes (coupled with **education** and **Philippine*** as subject-descriptor terms) produced 36 hits right on the button—as opposed to 76 that appear when the Historical Period limitation is not used. Similar precision is obtainable with questions on "racial discrimination in France in the 1920s" or "student movements in Uruguay in the 1960s and '70s" or "Russian foreign policy in the 1700s" or (in *America: History & Life*) "Jewish identity in Atlanta the 1930s."

The *Brepolis Medieval Bibliographies* database has a somewhat similar feature, although not as sophisticated—its Thematic Search option (on the Advanced search screen) allows you to limit your subject searches to whatever *centuries* you are interested in.

In the *ProQuest Statistical Insight* database, if you first do a subject search you will then see a clickable limit option "Date Covered" that allows you to select whatever range of years of subject coverage you wish the statistics to reflect. (This is different from the distinct "Date Published" option.)

LIMITING BY GEOGRAPHIC AREA CODES

A particularly useful, but generally neglected, limit feature within online book catalogs is the capacity to specify geographic area codes. This capability is present with OPACs using the Voyager search software but, tragically, has been eliminated entirely by several other catalog systems (including *WorldCat*)—that is, even though the data are present on the catalog records themselves, some current OPAC systems have been dumbed down to the point that they cannot "see" or make use of them. (The unfortunate assumption in the library world is that OPACs should be "more like Google"—and the search software of Google Books cannot make use of area codes.)

The utility of limiting by area codes in online book catalogs is best illustrated by examples. One researcher, for instance, wanted to retrieve a set of any books on the folklore of Indians of North America. This inquiry is complicated by several factors; one is that the notion of "folk" cultural practices is divided among many different *LCSH* terms, among them:

Folk art
Folk artists
Folk dance
Folk dancing
Folk drama
Folk festivals
Folk literature
Folk music
Folk poetry
Folk singers
Folk songs
Folklore

Another complication is that there are many different terms within *LCSH* for North American Indian groups. While there is a general heading for **Indians of North America**, there are also numerous narrower terms linked to it, such as:

Algonquian Indians
Athapascan Indians
Caddoan Indians
Off-reservation Indians
Ojibwa Indians
Piegan Indians
Reservation Indians
Sewee Indians
Shoshoni Indians
Tinne Indians

Yet another complication is that several of these narrower terms themselves lead to *further* narrower headings; thus, under **Algonquian Indians** one finds a list of *over 50* additional groups, such as:

Abenaki Indians
Cheyenne Indians
Fox Indians

> **Narragansett Indians**
> **Ojibwa Indians**
> **Potawatomi Indians**
> **Wampanoag Indians**

The important point here, as Chapter 2 explained, is that the many narrower terms are *not included* by the more general terms such as **Indians of North America** or even **Algonquian Indians**, and so must be searched separately. Obviously it would be very difficult to round up all of the many specific cross-referenced terms to begin with, and combining all of them with a lengthy series of Boolean OR operators would inevitably overload the search system.

This is a situation in which component word searching can combine with geographic area codes to solve a difficult problem very efficiently. Again, I'll use the OPAC of the Library of Congress (catalog.loc.gov) as the exemplar here, both because it is freely available on the Internet and because many universities' local catalogs have jettisoned the necessary capability in their own search software. Let me first note a useful trick mentioned above, but not elaborated. Searchers in this catalog need first to select the "Keyword Search" option on the initial page, and then select from its drop-down menu the option "EXPERT (use index codes and operators)."

Within this EXPERT search box you can then specify in which field, on the catalog records, you wish their desired terms to be found.

The major field delimiters are these:

KSUB (or lowercase ksub) for the subject headings field

KTIL (or ktil) for the title field

KPNC (or kpnc) for the author names field.

Other codes are listed in the drop-down menus of the Advanced Search mode.

In the present example, one could type this string into the EXPERT search box:

KSUB folk? AND KSUB Indians AND K043 n

This search tells the OPAC to look for any appearance of the words **folk** or **folklore** as parts of any subject headings, combined with the appearance of the term **Indians** within any subject headings, combined further with the geographic area code (whose field is specified by K043) for any records whose subject content concerns North America (designated by the **n**). (Note that a different field called KPUB—irrelevant here—exists for designating the geographic *place of publication* of a work;

what we want in most cases is the area code indicating the geographic *subject* of the work.)

The use of the geographic area code for North America neatly solves the problem of including *all* of the North American tribes while, at the same time, excluding all of the records having to do with Indians in South American locales or those from India itself (designated **East Indian[s]** in *LCSH*). You could not achieve this comprehensiveness, and this precision, with a keyword search; a good library OPAC search mechanism, however, enables you to see "the whole elephant" clearly, in ways that Internet mechanisms cannot match.

A similar example is provided by the reader who wanted books on "child trafficking in Asia." **Child trafficking** is an *LCSH* heading, so the search could be phased as:

KSUB "child trafficking" and K043 a

The code "a" takes in all of Asia, and so this search turns up works not only on Asia in general but also those specifically on Afghanistan, Bangladesh, Burma, Cambodia, China, India, Indonesia, Nepal, Pakistan, Philippines, Sri Lanka, and Thailand.

A very important distinction to note is that, in the area code system (unlike the *LCSH* subject heading system), the broader codes *do include the narrower geographic codes within them*. Thus the code **n** will retrieve not just works about North America as a whole but also its further subdivisions such as **n-cn** (Canada), **n-us** (the United States as a whole), **n-us-ut** (Utah), **n-us-wy** (Wyoming), and **n-mx** (Mexico). And note that these narrower codes are automatically included simply by specifying "**n**"—that is, you do not have to make use of truncation or word-stemming symbols (e.g., **n**?) to retrieve all of the narrower areas together.

The major geographic area codes are these:

n	=	North America
s	=	South America
cl	=	Central (or Latin) America
e	=	Europe
a	=	Asia
f	=	Africa
u-at	=	Australia
po	=	Pacific Oceania
b	=	Commonwealth countries
d	=	Developing countries
xd	=	Western hemisphere

The full list of codes is available online at www.loc.gov/marc/geoar-eas/gacs_code.html; it is also findable by typing "MARC Code list for Geographic Areas" in Google, Bing, or Yahoo!. Within the large conti-nental categories, individual countries or regions can be further speci-fied, for example:

a–af	=	Afghanistan
a–cc	=	China
a–cc–hk	=	Hong Kong
a–iq	=	Iran
a–ja	=	Japan
e–fr	=	France
e–gx	=	Germany
e–ge	=	the former East Germany
e–gw	=	the former West Germany
e–it	=	Italy
e–ru	=	Russia (Federation)
e–ur	=	the former Soviet Union
n–cn	=	Canada
n–cn–ab	=	Alberta
n–us–al	=	Alabama
n–us–il	=	Illinois
n–usc	=	Middle West
n–usn	=	New England
n–usp	=	western States
n–usu	=	southern States

You can also bring up this information in a way similar to finding the *LCSH* subject tracings for a particular book: find any relevant record through a keyword, author, or title search, and then display the record in its Full Record format. For example, in Figure 10.3, W. R. Smyser's book *Germany and America: New Identities, Fateful Rift?* (Westview, 1993) shows two codes, **n–us** and **e–gx**. Remember, then, that displays of records in the full format will bring to your attention *not just subject headings but also geographic area codes*. (The geographic area code is also shown in Figure 2.4.) The Full Record format is the default display in catalog.loc.gov, but it may not be in other libraries' OPACs.

Germany and America : new identities, fateful rift?

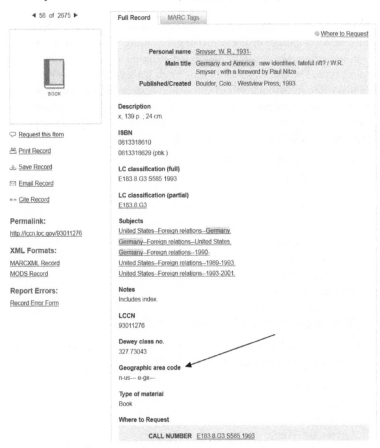

◄ 58 of 2675 ►

| Full Record | MARC Tags |

⊕ Where to Request

Personal name Smyser, W. R., 1931-
Main title Germany and America : new identities, fateful rift? / W.R.
Smyser ; with a foreword by Paul Nitze.
Published/Created Boulder, Colo. : Westview Press, 1993.

BOOK

⊊ Request this Item

🖷 Print Record

⬇ Save Record

✉ Email Record

❝❞ Cite Record

Permalink:
http://lccn.loc.gov/93011276

XML Formats:
MARCXML Record
MODS Record

Report Errors:
Record Error Form

Description
x, 139 p. ; 24 cm.

ISBN
0813318610
0813318629 (pbk.)

LC classification (full)
E183.8.G3 S585 1993

LC classification (partial)
E183.8.G3

Subjects
United States--Foreign relations--Germany.
Germany--Foreign relations--United States.
Germany--Foreign relations--1990-
United States--Foreign relations--1989-1993.
United States--Foreign relations--1993-2001.

Notes
Includes index.

LCCN
93011276

Dewey class no.
327.73043

Geographic area code
n-us--- e-gx---

Type of material
Book

Where to Request

CALL NUMBER E183.8.G3 S585 1993

Figure 10.3 Full display of catalog record for Smyser's *Germany and America* with arrow pointing to geographic area codes.

Unfortunately, since many individual libraries have chosen OPAC systems that are incapable of using these codes, their catalogers no longer add them to the records they create locally, and these deficient records are then picked up for use by all the other libraries in the system. The OPAC of the Library of Congress, at least (as of this writing), is still the best source for doing searches with geographic area codes. (Even here, however, the system is not perfect because LC itself accepts copy catalog records from other libraries to speed up its own operations.)

LIMITING BY DOCUMENT TYPES

Many commercial databases allow for limitations by other considerations, such as "by language" or "by year(s) of publication." A particularly useful—but, unfortunately, generally neglected—option is limitation by document type. The best researchers can often achieve amazingly on-target results through exploitation of this search feature. Within the ProQuest *ERIC* database for resources in the field of education, for example, you can limit your retrieval to any of more than fifty very specific types of material, of which the following is only a sample:

Collected Works: Proceedings
Creative Works
Dissertations/theses
Guides: Classroom
Book/Product Reviews
Journal Articles
Non-Print Media
Reference Materials: Bibliographies
Reports: Research
Tests/Questionnaires
Multilingual/Bilingual Materials

Similarly, within EBSCO's *PsycINFO* database (see Chapter 4) you can limit by several document types, among them:

Bibliography
Chapter
Column/Opinion
Comment/Reply
Dissertation
Editorial
Encyclopedia Entry
Journal Article
Obituary
Review-Book

In Chapter 8 there is a similar list of the document types that can be "limited" to in the *Web of Science* database (e.g., Article, Bibliography, Book Review, Editorial Material, Letter, Software Review, and Review).

With options such as these, teachers searching *ERIC* can zero in on curriculum guides ("Guides: Classroom") or tests; psychology grad students using *PsycINFO* can look immediately to see if doctoral dissertations have already been done on their topics; and general researchers in

Web of Science can quickly locate literature review articles in any academic field. (In the above example of the researcher who wanted information on "education in the Philippines from 1898 and 1916," a limitation to literature review articles in the *Web* database produced just such an article, with 94 footnotes, on "textbook wars" in public education in the Philippines from 1904 to 1907.)

Without the document type limiting features, the best material could easily be lost within large jumbles of mostly irrelevant hits—especially since the *format* of any document will usually not be revealed by its title or abstract keywords. Moreover, as I've mentioned before, it is very rare for any researchers (other than librarians) to specify format designations in their searches; most people simply type in *subject* keywords without any thought for the different *document types* in which they might appear. But if you limit, right from the start, the field in which your search terms apply (obituaries, literature reviews, curriculum guides, etc.), then you will immediately be zeroing in on only the most relevant literature while simultaneously excluding vast ranges of material that would otherwise bury the best sources within mountains of unwanted chaff. Crossing that line—i.e., adding format designations to your subject searches—goes a long way toward moving you from the amateur level to that of professional researcher.

In a sense, then, *where* you type the words (within which format fields) is just as important as *how* you type them. The same point applies to other "nonformat" parts of the records: sometimes, especially in keyword databases not having controlled subject descriptors, you will get the best results by restricting some your search terms to appearances specifically within titles of articles in combination with other terms appearing in broader sections of the same records, in either abstracts or full texts. In the ProQuest *Dissertations and Theses Full Text* database, for example, you will usually get a better set of on-target results by limiting your searches to the title and abstract fields *rather than* searching full texts right off the bat. The title/abstract combination is indicated by the drop-down menu option "Anywhere except full text—ALL."

In most subscription databases you cannot rely on relevance-ranking computer algorithms to make these distinctions among searchable fields for you.

COMBINING KEYWORDS WITH CITATION OR RELATED RECORD SEARCHES

A couple peculiar but very useful options in doing Boolean combinations show up in the *Web of Science* database (described in Chapter 6).

These are the capabilities of combining keyword results with citation search results as well as results of related record searches with further keyword specifications. Let me give some examples.

A search for articles on the topic "changing paradigms in the concept of property" can be done in very interesting ways in the *Web* database. One approach, of course, is simply to look for a simple combination of the keywords "property" and "paradigm*"; this does produce relevant hits such as articles entitled "Protecting Intellectual Property—New Technologies, New Paradigms," "Information, Incentives, and Property Rights— The Emergence of an Alternative Paradigm," and "Symposium—Toward a 3rd Intellectual Property Paradigm."

There are other ways to come at this topic, however. Anyone who writes about paradigms in a scholarly journal probably has a footnote citing the book that put this term into prominence: Thomas Kuhn's *The Structure of Scientific Revolutions*. Similarly, a scholarly discussion of private property is likely to cite the classic work on the subject, John Locke's *Second Treatise on Civil Government*. When footnotes are introduced as search elements, a researcher then has a large variety of relevant elements that can be brought into a Boolean combination:

#1 the word "property" itself appearing in the title of an article
#2 a footnote referring to John Locke's work on property
#3 the word "paradigm*" appearing in the title of an article
#4 a footnote referring to Kuhn's book on paradigms

In the *Web's* Advanced Search box one can then combine the results of several these separate searches:

(#1 OR #2) AND (#3 OR #4)

The results will include a number of relevant articles that do not have both keywords in their titles. The article entitled "The Concept of Private Property in Constitutional Law—The Ideology of the Scientific Turn in Legal Analysis," for instance, has the work "Property" in its title, but not the word "Paradigm." The latter concept is included however, because this article cites Kuhn's work in a footnote.

Similarly, the article "Paradigms as Ideologies—Liberal vs. Marxian Economics" does not have the word "Property" in its title, but it does have a footnote citing Locke's *Second Treatise*. And the articles "A Consent Theory of Contract" and "The Constitution and Nature of Law" have neither relevant keyword in their titles, but each article cites both Kuhn and Locke in its footnotes. The ability to search footnote citations, and to combine them with either keywords or other footnote references, is an option that few researchers think of, but it can provide extraordinary results.

Another researcher interested in assessing models for comparing the operations of the U.S. and German Supreme Courts found useful results by first assembling a set of articles *citing* important authors who had already done relevant work on the two courts and then combining those sets with the keyword "model*"—thereby finding some hits that were quite good, even though they did not contain the keywords "Supreme Court" or "Bundesverfassungsgericht" (the German federal constitutional court) in their titles or abstracts.

If you want to be an expert searcher you should watch for opportunities to employ this search technique, especially if there are standard works (or authors) in your field of interest that are likely to be cited frequently.

Another wrinkle on combining search elements comes from the capability of the *Web of Science* database to cross *related record* search results (see Chapter 7) with keywords. For example, I once helped a young woman who wanted information on the linguistic remnants of African slaves' speech in Venezuela and its influence or survival in the local Spanish. This involved three steps:

1. An initial keyword search: Venezuela* and (Africa* or slave*) and (language* or linguistic* or lexic* or speech). This immediately turned up one good article on "Some Lexical Linkages between Africa and Venezuela."

2. A related record search starting from this one article led to a listing of 399 other articles in the database that have footnotes in common with it. The important consideration here is that none of these necessarily has any *keywords* in common with the starting-point article—only articles having *footnotes* in common with it define the set. Thus, right at the top of the list was an article with the title "Studies in *Afro-Hispano*american Linguistics"—a literature review article with 146 footnotes—which is in the ballpark, but without using any of the (Venezuela* and [Africa* or slave*]) keywords I had specified.

3. Since articles within the list of 399 could have any words at all, I then used the "Refine Results" box to specify that I wanted only those (within the set of 399) that did have the exact keyword "Venezuela*" somewhere in their titles or abstracts—but not necessarily any of the *other* terms I had originally specified. This refinement produced an article entitled "Black Rural

Speech in Venezuela." I had initially missed this highly relevant source because I hadn't thought to use the keyword "Black" in my search. But the related record search *plus* the keyword refinement of it brought it to my attention even when I couldn't specify all of the relevant terms.

REFRESHER: COMBINATIONS WITHOUT COMPUTERS

Combining terms, or sets of terms, via computer searches is an extremely useful capability, especially if you employ refinements such as word truncation, proximity searching, field specification, and set limitation. But it is also important to remember that you have additional, and very powerful, mechanisms that enable you to effectively combine two or more search elements in ways that lie "outside the box" of postcoordinating computer systems. These other mechanisms have already been touched on separately but should be brought together for emphasis as they are so often overlooked:

- Precoordinated subject heading strings in *Library of Congress Subject Headings*, particularly in online catalog browse displays (Chapter 2)
- Index pages or tables of contents in published bibliographies (Chapter 9)
- Subject-classified bookstacks enabling you to do focused browsing (Chapter 3)

Precoordinated *LCSH* terms, discussed in Chapter 2, effectively combine two or more search elements into a single subject heading, such as the following:

Women in aeronautics
Sports for children
Theater in propaganda
Minorities in medicine—United States—Statistics
Education and heredity
Doping in sports
Architecture and energy conservation—Canada
Erotic proverbs, Yiddish
Church work with criminals
Hallucinogenic drugs and religious experience in art—Mexico
Odors in the Bible

Smallpox in animals
Miniature pigs as laboratory animals
Television and children—South Africa—Longitudinal studies

Many of the strings within the *LCSH* system, again, are created by the use of standardized subdivisions, and these linkages often show up in online browse displays without being recorded in the *LCSH* list of subject headings:

United States—History—Civil War, 1861-1865—Regimental histories—Illinois infantry—51st—Company E
World War, 1939-1945—Underground movements—France—Chronology
Juvenile delinquency—Great Britain—History—Sources
Corporations—Charitable contributions—Japan—Directories
Hospitals—Job descriptions
Potatoes—Social aspects—Ireland—History
Mexican American agricultural laborers—Bibliography
Cancer—Psychological aspects—Case studies
Bird droppings—Pictorial works
Toilet training—Germany—Folklore
Flatulence—Dictionaries—French

There are hundreds of thousands of actual and potential precoordinated headings in any OPAC that uses the *LCSH* system. Reference librarians are trained literally to *think in these terms*. To the extent that you anticipate the probabilities that there may be precoordinated headings for your subjects, you can exploit whole arrays of them via cross-reference links and, especially, browse displays in online catalogs (at least in the OPACs that are structured well enough to display them). The ability to exploit browse displays will frequently enable you to surpass any results obtainable from combining separate terms in a blank search box, because browse menus enable you to recognize combinations that you could never think of in advance.

Another mechanism for combining two subjects without using a computer is that of published bibliographies, as discussed in Chapter 9. The trick here is simply to find a bibliography on the first topic of interest and then to look for the second topic within its index (or table of contents). This search technique is especially useful when looking for a particular topic in connection with a literary or historical figure, as there are thousands of excellent book-length bibliographies available on such individuals. For example, a scholar looking for material comparing the philosophy of Sartre with that of Christianity could turn to François Lapointe's *Jean-Paul Sartre and His Critics: An Annotated Bibliography 1938–1980)*, 2nd ed. (Philosophy Documentation Center, 1981). He could then simply turn to its index to see which of the studies is listed under "Christianity." (There are 11.) Similarly, a researcher looking for material discussing both Samuel Beckett and Alberto Giacometti turned to Cathleen Andonian's 754-page *Samuel Beckett: A Reference Guide* (G. K. Hall, 1989) and simply looked under "Giacometti" in its Subject Index to find four articles (including two that do not show up in an online search of the *MLA International Bibliography*.)

Yet another mechanism exists, "outside the box" of computerized retrievals, for effectively combining two subjects: focused shelf-browsing, as discussed in Chapter 3. There, the example of "traveling libraries in lighthouses" is relevant. In that case, after first exhausting all of the computer databases I could think of, I went directly to the bookstacks having the group of texts on "Lighthouse Service" (VK1000-VK1025) and quickly flipped through all the volumes on those several shelves, looking for "libraries" as either an index entry or a text work within the books. I found 15 directly relevant sources. The trick here, then, is similar to that with published bibliographies: start by finding the classification area for the first subject, then look for the second subject within the books shelved in that limited class area. This focused browsing technique enables you to cross subjects that cannot be brought together by Boolean searches in computers.

The moral of the last several paragraphs can be summarized briefly: do not rely exclusively on Internet searches for in-depth or scholarly research, as they are too limited both in the content covered and in the search techniques they provide for *access* to the contents. The same can be said even for the many thousands of commercial databases that are not freely accessible on the open Internet. Don't allow yourself to be boxed in exclusively by computerized resources; even within them, don't think that you always have to rely solely on postcoordinate combinations (see Chapter 2) of only the terms you can guess at on your own. If you want to be a good researcher, you need to be aware of *all* of the options available.

CHAPTER 11

Locating Material in Other Libraries

I F NEITHER THE INTERNET NOR YOUR OWN LIBRARY HAS THE full texts of the sources you've identified through subject heading searches, keyword searches, citation or related record searches, or those done through published bibliographies, several mechanisms are available that will usually enable you locate copies.

WORLDCAT AND THE *PRE-1956 NATIONAL UNION CATALOG*

The first place to look is the *WorldCat* database. A free version exists on the Internet at www.worldcat.org. Essentially, it is a merger of the individual catalogs of more than 70,000 libraries in 170 countries; it contains records for more than 2 billion items (albeit with much duplication). In addition to books, it lists maps, magazines and journals, prints, photographs, sound recordings, photographic slides, newspapers, motion pictures, manuscripts, and many other formats. Whatever gets cataloged by any of the participating libraries winds up in the pot for everyone to search. Library locations are provided for most (but not all) of the items.

There is also a subscription version of *WorldCat* available through most public and academic libraries; it has better search software than the free version, enabling you to make more complex inquiries. (If you are using the free version, however, be sure to select the Advanced Search screen, which is not its default page.) This database forms the backbone of the interlibrary loan network within which most libraries operate.

Another source for identifying library locations of older resources is also useful. It is the *National Union Catalog: Pre-1956 Imprints* (London: Mansell, 1968–1981). This is a 754-volume printed set listing more than 12 million entries (both catalog records and cross-references), with library locations, for works published worldwide before 1956 as reported by about 1,100 libraries in North America. Although many cyberlibrarians now look upon the set with open contempt as a bibliographic dinosaur and assume that "it's all been digitized," they are unfortunately mistaken. Two major studies have recently confirmed that about 25 to 27.8 percent of the *NUC*'s entries do not appear at all in *WorldCat*.[1] Moreover, these figures are conservative because they do not count additional features of the *NUC*—cross-references, additional library locations, and bibliographic notes—that are also missing in *WorldCat*. Large libraries that must deal with difficult or exceptional questions are well advised to retain their sets. (In my own experience at the Library of Congress, I still refer to the *NUC* two or three times a month.) This printed set has not been digitized by anyone.

The *Pre-'56 NUC* (or *NUC*) is arranged alphabetically by authors' names (including corporate authors), with entries by titles when no names are apparent. (It cannot be searched by subject.) Like *WorldCat* it lists not just books but many other formats as well: pamphlets, maps, music (scores and print material but not sound recordings), government documents (local, state, and federal), microforms, serials, conference proceedings, annuals, and even some manuscripts. Most of the listed works are in the Roman, Greek, or Gaelic alphabets, but there are also many entries in Arabic, Cyrillic, Chinese, Japanese, Hebrew, Korean, the various Indic alphabets, and other non-Latin characters.

One very important point about the *National Union Catalog: Pre-1956 Imprints* is that it is made up of two different alphabetical sequences, and both must be consulted when you are looking for a record that fails to appear in *WorldCat*. The first extends from A to Z in volumes 1 through 685; but volumes 686 through 754 provide an entirely separate A–Z sequence with about 900,000 entries, cross-references, and additional library locations not found in the first alphabet. (The reason is that the first sequence took decades to publish, and in the meantime the project continued to receive reports of new entries and locations that fell within letters of the alphabet that had already been printed. These additional reports form the second sequence.) The lists of additional library locations (for works reported in the first 685 volumes) appear in tabular form at the end of each volume in the second (686–754) sequence. The most common library location symbols are listed on the endpapers of each volume; the full list is printed in volumes 200, 560, and 754.[2]

Regrettably, whenever an *NUC* set is sent to remote storage, the volumes of this second alphabetical sequence are never requested because no one knows they are there or how much they contain. Indeed, *NUC* sets in remote storage tend not to be consulted at all, since the people who have set them offsite tend to be the same people who are also misinforming patrons that "it's all in the computer."

A few samples of questions that could not be answered by *WorldCat*:

- Entries in the *Pre-'56 NUC* that are not in *WorldCat* are *Anais et d'Orberville* (3 vols., 1808), T. 1 (i.e., volume 1), and the 1900 printing of Daniel Jeremiah Bell's *The Primitive Baptist Church Discipline and Guide.*
- A crucial cross-reference from the *International Conference on Light* (1928) to the subsequent *International Congress on Light* (1932) appears in the *NUC* but not in *WorldCat.*
- Additional library locations not in *WorldCat* can be found in the *NUC*, as for the titles *Paix et Droit: Organe de l'Alliance Israélite Universelle;* Charles D. Sawin's *Criminals* (1890); *Report of the Royal Commission Appointed to Consider the Law Relating to Indictable Offenses* (1879); or *Report of the Proceedings of the Second General Peace Congress* (Paris, 1849).
- Note fields in the *NUC* catalog records are sometimes more complete and informative than those for the same records in *WorldCat*. One reader needed "some authoritative source to confirm the publication dates" of an early twentieth-century periodical, *The Esoterist.* The *NUC* entry gives the beginning and ending dates of the journal's run—as does *WorldCat*—but explicitly adds "No more published." It also specifies the range of missing issues in the one set that is identified.

In short, the *Pre-'56 NUC* continues to show—occasionally—entries, cross-references, library locations, and note field information that is not found in any online source. The underlying reason is that many large libraries did not do a good job of retrospective conversion when they switched from their old card catalogs to the new online versions. A lot of their older records were incorrectly or only partially digitized or not digitized at all. That's why the old printed union catalogs still retain their value in turning up older records that slipped through the cracks of the digital conversions.

EUROPEAN MULTI-CATALOG SITES

An online catalog that merges the holdings of more than 70 major university, special, and national libraries in the United Kingdom and Ireland may be freely searched at http://copac.ac.uk. COPAC turns up many items not in *WorldCat*. The German site mounted by the Karlsruhe Institute of Technology at www.bibliothek.kit.edu/cms/website-durchsuchen. php also covers libraries not in *WorldCat*, as does *The European Library* at www.theeuropeanlibrary.org, which searches 48 national and research libraries in Europe.

FULL-TEXT WEBSITES CREATED FROM MULTIPLE LIBRARY HOLDINGS

Google Books provides full texts of millions of volumes digitized from a score of major research libraries at http://books.google.com/advanced_book_search. In general, however, volumes published after 1922 appear only in snippets because of copyright restrictions. HathiTrust.org is another free website for full texts of books that are in the public domain; it, too, scans its texts from participating libraries. The Internet Archive (archive.org) is also useful. Hundreds of additional full-text databases, covering both pre- and post-1922 texts, are available through the research libraries that subscribe to them (see Chapters 4 and 5).

OTHER DATABASES AND UNION LISTS

Catalogs that merge the files or holdings of several libraries are called "union lists." Although *WorldCat* and the *Pre-'56 NUC* both list some unpublished manuscripts, there are additional union lists specifically for these materials. They will tell you which archives or manuscript repositories hold whose papers (either individuals' papers or those of corporate bodies). The first is the *National Union Catalog of Manuscript Collections* (*NUCMC*, pronounced "nuckmuck" by librarians); it is freely available on the open Internet at www.loc.gov/coll/nucmc. It covers 116,000 collections held in 1,800 repositories in the United States; its listings are included in *WorldCat*; and there is also a printed version of it. The free online version, however, is preferable because it covers not only the *NUCMC* catalog records but also those in the OCLC Archival and Mixed Collections file.

The second is *Archive Finder*, a ProQuest subscription database covering more than 220,000 manuscript collections in the United States, United Kingdom, and Ireland. It includes everything in *NUCMC* from 1959 to 2006, with additional material (but not the extra OCLC listings). Another subscription source is *ArchiveGrid* from OCLC, which lists manuscript collections in the United States, often with the full texts of their accompanying finding guides.

For locating copies of journals, especially older titles, two printed sources are noteworthy for their capacity to turn up entries (with library locations) that are not in *WorldCat*. They are the *Union List of Serials* (*ULS*) and *New Serial Titles*. The former is a 5-volume set published by the H. W. Wilson Company (3rd ed., 1965) listing about 227,000 titles and cross-references for journals that began publication before 1950, as reported by 956 U.S. and Canadian libraries. The latter is a series of multivolume cumulative supplements to it (1950–1970, 1971–1975, 1976–1980, etc.); after 1980 it can be considered superseded by *WorldCat*. If you are looking for old periodical titles, be sure to check the *Pre-'56 NUC* too, which lists many titles not in the *ULS*.

Any number of specialized union lists exist, recording library holdings in particular regions (e.g., *California Union List of Periodicals, Journal Holdings in the Washington-Baltimore Area*) or for particular subjects (e.g., *Union List of Military Periodicals*; *Education Journals: A Union List*). There are also union lists from other countries (e.g., *British Union-Catalogue of Periodicals*, France's *Catalogue Collectif des Périodiques*) and combinations of subject and area holdings (e.g., *Union List of Statistical Serials in British Libraries*; *Art Serials: Union List of Art Periodicals and Serials in Research Libraries in the Washington DC Metropolitan Area*).

Such publications are usually given the form subdivision—**Union lists** within the *Library of Congress Subject Headings* system. As of this writing, in LC's own online catalog there are more than 2,900 entries that have this designation. These specialized lists sometimes provide titles and library locations that do not show up in *WorldCat* or printed catalogs. For example, the old periodical *Filmplay Journal* (1921–) is not recorded in *WorldCat*, the *Pre-'56 NUC*, or *Union List of Serials*; it is listed, with a library location, in *Union List of Film Periodicals: Holdings of Selected American Collections* (Greenwood Press, 1984).

SEARCHING VARIANT SPELLINGS

One trick to be aware of in using any union catalog, whether online or printed, is to try slightly variant spellings of names or titles if the one you start with does not work. This is important because the different libraries contributing to the union catalogs may have used different cataloging practices in listing the same items; also, researchers themselves may not have accurate citations to begin with for the items they wish to find. In my own experience, for example, I've found works by "Lessem" that were initially asked for under the name "Lessen"; "Bullettino di Pisano" when "Bolletino" was cited; "Schmidt" when "Smith" was cited; "Abernethy" when the original footnote read "Abernathy"; and a crucial cross-reference (in the second alphabet of the *NUC*) from "Maurus, Hartmannus" to "Mohr, Hartmann" when the researcher's original citation said "Hartman, Mauri." This approach works *with surprising frequency*. If you don't find what you want in using any citation as originally recorded, don't trust its accuracy. Play around with variant forms. Many footnotes are simply inaccurate to begin with.

FINDING COPIES OF BOOKS FOR SALE

If you are looking for a copy of any particular out-of-print publication, you are no longer limited to searching the holdings of libraries. Various Internet sites can now systematically find books (or other publications) for sale from secondhand book dealers worldwide. Four sites in particular should be searched:

- www.bookfinder.com
- http://used.addall.com
- www.abebooks.com
- www.eBay.com

The first two are "meta" engines that combine the results of multiple book-search engines. Abebooks, while ostensibly covered by the other two engines, will still sometimes show additional titles if you search it directly. I have often found books and magazines in these sites that do not appear in *WorldCat* or the various printed union catalogs, and usually the researchers looking for an older book—especially a beloved title remembered from childhood—are delighted to find copies that they can actually purchase. The same sites are useful if you wish to determine the market value of an old book: the listings you get will tell you what prices are currently being asked for it. (One tip: if you are searching for an old book and do not find it listed under its title, try searching its author's name without specifying the title: sometimes old books are reprinted under different titles.)

DETERMINING WHICH LIBRARIES HAVE
SPECIAL COLLECTIONS ON YOUR SUBJECT

No matter how good the coverage of *WorldCat*, the other online sources, and all of the printed union catalogs, research libraries will always have many items that are recorded only on their own premises. It is foolish to think that "everything is online." If, then, you cannot find a desired item in full-text format online, pinpoint the location of it through a union list or database, or find a copy for sale, then the next best thing is to identify a collection that is *likely* to have it. Several good sources for determining the existence and location of specialized subject collections exist, for the United States and internationally:

1. *Subject Collections*, compiled by Lee Ash and William G. Miller (New York: Bowker, 1993, 7th ed.). This venerable source is still useful for identifying well over 65,000 special collections in more than 5,800 university, college, public, and special libraries and museums in the United States and Canada. Entries are arranged alphabetically according to *Library of Congress Subject Headings* (with additional subject terms as needed); each provides the address of the library, an estimate of the number of items in the collections, and, frequently, descriptive notes.

2. *Repositories of Primary Sources*. This is a free website maintained by the University of Idaho at www.uiweb.uidaho.edu/special-collections/Other.Repositories.html. It lists "over 5000 websites describing holdings of manuscripts, archives, rare books, historical photographs and other primary sources for the research scholar."

3. *Directory of Special Libraries and Information Centers* (Gale Cengage, revised irregularly). The subtitle of this multivolume set is "A Guide to More Than 36,000 Special Libraries, Research Libraries, Information Centers, Archives, and Data Centers Maintained by Government Agencies, Business, Industry, Newspapers, Educational Institutions, Nonprofit Organizations, and Societies in the Fields of Science and Engineering, Medicine, Law, Art, Religion, the Social Sciences, and Humanities." Although the emphasis is on U.S. resources, more than 2,800 Canadian and 16,000 international collections are included as well. The alphabetical listing of all of the libraries is followed by a geographic listing (Country/State or Province/City), a Personnel Index, and a detailed subject index of more than 4,300

terms and cross-references. Seven appendixes provide further information:

- Networks and Consortia
- Regional and Subregional Libraries for the Blind and Physically Handicapped
- Patent and Trademark Depository Libraries
- Regional Government Depository Libraries
- United Nations Depository Libraries
- World Bank Depository Libraries
- European Community Depository Libraries (in the United States)

An online version of this *Directory* is included in the subscription database *Gale Directory Library*.

4. *Subject Directory of Special Libraries and Information Centers* (Gale Cengage, revised irregularly). This printed set rearranges the information from the *Directory of Special Libraries and Information Centers* in a subject classified list. Volume 1 lists "Business, Government, and Law Libraries"; volume 2, "Computers, Engineering, and Science Libraries"; and volume 3, "Health Sciences Libraries." Each volume has its own subject index.

5. *World Guide to Special Libraries* (K. G. Saur, revised irregularly). This two-volume printed set lists more than 32,000 libraries in 160 countries. "General" libraries and those for "Humanities, Social Sciences, Medicine and Life Sciences, and Science and Technology" are covered, with detailed subject indexing.

6. *Directory of Special Collections in Western Europe*, edited by Alison Gallico (Bowker-Saur, 1993). This is a list of approximately 700 special collections in 11 countries, in the arts, humanities, sciences, and social sciences. Details are given as to time periods covered, languages, formats, and contact information (which will probably have to be updated by checking the libraries' current websites). Entries are arranged by country, then alphabetically by institution. Indexes are by subject and geographic location; the subject indexes are in English, French, German, and Spanish.

7. *Directory of Museums, Galleries, and Buildings of Interest in the United Kingdom* (Routledge, 2008, 4th ed.). This volume covers more than its title indicates; it indexes special collections in museums, galleries, and local exhibits under 3,000 subjects, and provides "a breakdown of the collections held by each organization" with "details of special collections [including] the period covered as well as the number of items held."

8. *The Aslib Directory of Literary and Historical Collections in the United Kingdom* (Aslib, 1993). Although now out of print, this one-volume listing of 1,030 institutional libraries in the United Kingdom is still useful for its detailed subject index. Contact information must be updated by checking the collections' current websites.

9. *Historical Research in Europe: A Guide to Archives and Libraries* is a website maintained by the University of Wisconsin–Madison at http://digicoll.library.wisc.edu/HistResEur/.

10. *The European Library* website at www.theeuropeanlibrary.org provides direct links to the catalogs, dissertation lists, and digital collections of about 50 of the individual national libraries of Europe.

As with union lists, there are also many specialized guides to libraries in particular regions within the United States and to those in other countries (e.g., *Special Collections at Georgetown; Special Collections and Subject Area Strengths in Maine Libraries; Special Collections in German Libraries*). Other library directories exist for particular subject areas (e.g., *Directory of Music Research Libraries; International Directory of Art Libraries; Tribal Libraries in the United States* [American Indian collections]). The librarians in your area can tell you which ones exist locally. A good shortcut is to search for two forms of heading in the *LCSH* system:

Library resources—[Place]
[Subject heading]—Library resources

(See also the sections on Special Collections, Online and Microform, in Chapter 13—these sources may contain individual items that you are looking for and that do not show up anywhere else.)

INTERLIBRARY LOAN AND DOCUMENT DELIVERY

The United States, Canada, and Great Britain are particularly blessed with having good interlibrary loan (ILL) networks. If you cannot find a copy of the article or book you've identified, ask your local librarian (either academic or public) about the possibility of borrowing from another library. (It would be best to first consult with the reference librarians, however, especially if you need a journal article—not all of the journals held by your library will show up in its online catalog listings. When libraries have subscriptions to databases from Gale, EBSCOhost, ProQuest, *LexisNexis*, and other vendors, they may effectively have full-text access to thousands of electronic journals not recorded in their own local catalog. The reference librarians will know how to check if any journal shows up in electronic form, from any of these various vendors. They offer tens of thousands of online journals not in *JSTOR*.) Remember, too, that many obscure and out-of-print books that don't show up in your library's OPAC may still be available in Google Books or Hathi Trust (www.hathitrust.org) or may be purchasable via the websites listed above.

You can sometimes have copies made at a remote library by contacting it and asking if it maintains a list of local freelance researchers for hire.

The overall point to keep in mind is that if you have identified a good source that is not online, not purchasable, and not available in your local library, don't give up. The same local library is likely to have additional sources beyond those available on the open Web for identifying which other libraries either have the desired item or are likely to have it.

CHAPTER 12

People Sources

S O FAR WE HAVE EXAMINED SEVEN MAJOR AVENUES OF SUBJECT access to information: controlled vocabulary searches, systematic and focused browsing of full texts shelved in subject-classified order, keyword searches, citation searches, related record searches, searches through published subject bibliographies, and Boolean combination/limitation searches. The eighth major avenue—talking to people—is the one most favored by journalists, but it is also valuable for other researchers.

INHIBITING ASSUMPTIONS

It is particularly important for academics not to overlook this method, as most academics (especially grad students) have a tendency to develop an overly strong bias toward either Internet sources or—less so today—the printed sources in libraries or archives. A kind of mental "wall" often develops that blocks the perception of information simply because it hasn't been written down somewhere. The assumption is that "if the information I want is not findable on the Internet or in a library, then it just doesn't exist." This usually unconscious belief has the undesirable result of inducing people to change their research questions to fit whatever information they *can* find online or in print—even if it's not what they really want—and to diminish the scope of their papers accordingly.

This assumption can be very detrimental to quality research. Even the subscription databases providing full-text access to journals are constrained by the fact that the articles themselves may be several months old, due to the time lag involved in submission, review, acceptance, editing, publication, and embargoes, before they appear online, and many

Internet sites, in spite of their impressive immediacy, are often superficial, untrustworthy in authority, and ephemeral in duration (making them undesirable as sources that can be footnoted). Even if these drawbacks did not exist in the alternative sources of information, however, the use of people sources would still be valuable because finding someone who has firsthand experience with a subject can usually provide you not just with information that has never existed in print or online, but also with insight into how you might better frame your questions to begin with.

It may seem obvious to state this, and, indeed, I have found few people who would say they disagree with these observations. Still—and this is the problem—many people who intellectually know that doing good research must take them outside the box of the Internet and outside the walls of libraries will not act as though they know it. When it finally comes to doing research, they are very shy about going beyond online and print sources to find what they want. They will often use friends as sources, because friends won't make them feel shy about asking what (they think) strangers might regard as "stupid" questions, but that unwarranted shyness can stand in the way of real breakthroughs in research. After 35 years as a reference librarian, helping tens of thousands of students, I think the only element that sometimes approaches "stupidity"— "imprudence" would be a better word—in the equation comes from that very shyness in not speaking up because of an assumption that other people will not respond helpfully.

Part of the difficulty lies in the way that "research methods" or "information literacy" classes are taught in colleges. Very often they are confined exclusively to presentations on "how to do critical thinking about websites"—with the unspoken implication that any of the myriad sources not online aren't worth talking about, or don't even exist. (The same classes are also noticeably deficient in another way: they fail to explain the crucial differences between controlled subject terms and keywords—i.e., *what words should you type in*? Group discussions cannot solve this problem when no one in the group, including the instructor, is aware of the distinction.) Alternatively, the classes are confined to the presentation of a relatively few sources, usually within a particular subject area, from a prescribed bibliography; and correlative assignments are sometimes made with the stipulation that "you should use the sources on this list" coupled with "don't bother the reference librarians—you should do your research on your own."

Unfortunately, students tend unwittingly to learn more than they should from such experiences: they learn that doing research equals "playing library games" within only the boundaries of the prescribed list of sources or that it means using the Internet alone, as long as they "think critically" about whatever Google (or Bing or ProQuest or *JSTOR*) serves up on its first three screens. Coupled with such learning is the message that talking to people is "bothering" them and may even have a faint odor of "cheating" to it because it's not doing "your own" work. Professors seem unaware of the long-term damage this does, not only to their students' subsequent academic careers but also to the future satisfaction of their curiosity about topics of personal interest. Being told not to talk to people for purposes of a particular class assignment often produces the kind of result Mark Twain referred to in an anecdote about a cat: "We should be careful to get out of an experience only the wisdom that is in it—and stop there, lest we be like the cat that sits down on a hot stove-lid. She will never sit down on a hot stove-lid again—and that is well; but she will also never sit down on a cold one anymore."[1] Reference librarians notice the limiting effect of such "learning" all the time, in the reluctance that students—and their professors, too—display in asking for much-needed reference help in all other situations. The only "bad" question is the one that you stifle and don't ask to begin with.

Genuine learning should obviously be a broadening rather than a limiting experience; and in doing research the most important lesson to learn is that *any* source is fair game. (I'll qualify that by specifying any legally available source.) One should always go to wherever the information needed is most likely to be, and often this will be in someone's head rather than on a computer screen or in a book. Remember too, however, that you can travel back from talking to an expert into the printed literature, for often the expert will know the best written sources or can offer shortcuts that will make subsequent library or Internet searches more efficient.

THE VALUE OF CONTACTING PEOPLE DIRECTLY

Talking to people can provide unanticipated insights into your area of research, feedback on problem points, and a structure or "shape" of perception that written or online sources often cannot match. Conversations can quickly reveal which areas of inquiry are valuable and worth pursuing and which are likely to waste time. People sources can also often identify quickly what are the "crackpot" positions, with concealed propositions and entailed ideologies, which may be very hard to discern otherwise if the subject field you're exploring is new to you.

Experts, enthusiasts, and buffs are available without direct personal contact—i.e., in ways that circumvent the shyness factor—through social network sites and special interest groups available on the Internet (including Facebook). These links to organizations—some of which will require membership fees—enable you to throw out a question to a wide variety of people interested in a particular subject area. Sometimes you will receive direct replies from anyone interested enough to respond; sometimes your question may initiate a response chain online. As with other people sources, such contacts can provide you with either direct answers or possible leads.

As convenient as Internet sites can be, it is best not to be naïve in using them. One student, for example, sent a request to a Shakespeare discussion group, asking for the sources of such quotes as "Alas, Poor Yorick" and "Double, double, toil and trouble"—and he even gave the group a deadline for responding! Needless to say, such an inquiry evoked several replies that can only be deemed less than charitable. Keep in mind that, while the enthusiasts who populate the various discussion groups are generally very helpful, they are often not kindly disposed toward questions creating the appearance that a student is simply trying to circumvent the work of real engagement with the subject of their interest.

What is even more important to remember is that, right from the start, not every expert is reachable via Internet groups—millions of knowledgeable people in different subject areas simply do not participate at all in such online venues. (This may seem to be a common-sense observation, but the view from a reference desk is that too many researchers are oblivious to it.) Even those who do participate will not choose to respond to every inquiry that gets tossed into their pool. (Most of these people have actual lives outside their online connections.) In other words, there is still a vast ocean of experts who can still be reached only by phone, letter, or direct e-mail—or, sometimes, by just showing up at their office.

I do not mean to minimize the importance of Internet connections, however. For example, I once had to find out if the U.S. Army had ever used the phrase "Certified Disability Discharge" in reference to veterans' status. At the time I could not find this exact phrase in either online or print sources, but I found a veterans' information homepage on the Web, and I sent my question to the group's e-mail address. The experts on the other end found some knowledgeable "old-timers" to talk to who clarified the use of the term.

Talking to people can provide you with a quick overview of a whole field; it can also give you not only the answer to a particular question but also the larger context in which the question should be asked. For example, someone who was once looking for information on the U.S. market for padlocks imported from India first did considerable library research on his own, but only in talking to knowledgeable people in the field did he really get oriented. He was told that there are several different grades of padlocks, which have different markets; that it's better to concentrate of small areas, as data on large areas are unreliable; that there were forthcoming national standards for padlocks, which imported items might have to meet in another year or two; that he should first have the locks tested for quality (using current military specifications as interim standards, if applicable to the grade of item being imported) and to have a written contract that all other locks will be comparable before paying for any; that he must consider not only the price of the items but also the shipping charges and import duties; and that the big chain stores would certainly be able to buy much more cheaply than he, so his best bet would be to market through independent "Mom and Pop"–type hardware stores.

The experts that this researcher talked to not only provided him with answers, but also alerted him to *whole new areas of questions* he had to consider, none of which he had thought of on his own. It's impossible to get this kind of corrective feedback from websites or printed sources that do not allow interaction with their readers and that cannot be modified on the spot to accommodate slightly different inquiries. For this kind of thing you just have to talk to someone who has experience. (Note, too, that an array of concerns such as those listed in this example would not readily be elicited by e-mail correspondence—for the simple reason that few contacts would want to do that much typing! The same information flows much more easily over the phone. That is an important distinction: phone calls work better than e-mails, especially if they have been preceded by e-mails providing a general notion of the problem—and, further, in-person interviews are usually much more productive than phone calls.)

Another example: I once had to identify, quickly, the company that built a particular bank vault that allegedly survived the collapse of the World Trade Center. The Library of Congress had just been given a special appropriation in the wake of the September 11 attacks—to acquire a super-secure vault for its own treasures—and needed to know what kind of vault to purchase. One of the LC administrators remembered reading a newspaper article about some gold bullion being removed from a vault that had survived the collapse of the Twin Towers and wanted to know the manufacturer of that particular vault. From the *ProQuest* database of full-text newspapers I could quickly find the article (*Wall Street Journal*, November 1, 2001) reporting the recovery of the gold; the article identifies the owner of the vault as the trading arm of the Bank of Nova Scotia, specifically its "ScotiaMacotta unit." Unfortunately, the reporter consistently misspelled the firm's name, which is actually ScotiaMocatta, and this threw off my keyword searching for the next 20 minutes. In any event I soon found the correct spelling through a printed business directory, which also provided the company's New York telephone number—which proved to be nonworking. However, since I also had the parent company's name, Bank of Nova Scotia, I could come at the problem through its office; doing so resulted in several telephone referrals until I finally found a man who knew that the head of all of the company's security operations, with oversight of all its bank vaults, was situated in Toronto.

When I called this Director of Protective Services, he proved to be very helpful and immediately gave me the name of the bank vault manufacturer and offered to provide further contacts. But he also gave me some other very important information that I hadn't asked for: the media reports of the vault's survival were misleading. The vault in question, he told me, was not within the Twin Towers; it was actually located on two levels of 4 World Trade Center, a nine-story building off to the side. This smaller building itself only partially collapsed, and none of the events of that terrible day threatened the structural integrity of the vault. (It was surrounded by an underground parking area at levels 3 and 4 below ground, and the many cars in the area were not damaged either, other than to be covered by layers of dust.) This fact was not at all apparent from the original newspaper article, which did leave the impression that the vault had directly withstood the collapse of the Twin Towers themselves.

The point here, for researchers, is simple but important: even when I had the full resources of the largest library in the world at my disposal, with hundreds of full-text subscription databases freely accessible inside, as well as the entire open Internet (which I also searched), the information that I really needed turned out to be only in the head of someone sitting in a Toronto business office. And not only could he provide the information I specifically asked for, he could also point out an unsuspected problem in the assumptions with which I was working. This kind of thing happens all the time for researchers who go "outside the boxes" of both libraries and the Internet and talk directly to knowledgeable people.

Note also, however, that the library resources were extremely helpful in providing the starting point for the string of telephone calls, especially since the initial *Wall Street Journal* article was not freely accessible on the open Internet.

No matter what your channel of contacting people, a word of caution is in order: a judicious mixture of personal, print, and online sources is often the ideal in doing good research. Just as academics often overemphasize print or online sources, so journalists sometimes tend to overemphasize people contacts to the outright neglect of relevant print sources. The aims of academics and journalists are not usually the same, of course, but there is enough overlap that each group can learn from the search techniques of the other. And both groups, these days, need to wary of relying too much on blog statements as documentation; these occupy a kind of middle ground between print and people sources.

TIPS ON USING PEOPLE SOURCES

Contrary to widespread assumptions, you don't have to have special training or credentials to jump into research by telephone or interview. (This is not to say that the training journalists go through is unnecessary; as with any other research skill, the more experience you get in locating and interviewing people, the better you'll be at it.) The most important initial factor is your attitude going into the search: don't be shy! It's okay to just jump in and do it. All you really have to do is find a good starting-point contact and then be persistent in developing referrals until you find someone who knows what he or she is talking about.

The main stumbling block most researchers have is their own inhibiting belief that other people will not respond. But most interviewees are flattered that you would consider them knowledgeable in some area and will usually respond helpfully. Experience will show that the odds are in your favor—telephone or e-mail or (better) in-person contacts will usually be friendly and will often volunteer much more information than you originally request.

One tip to be aware of initially: if you are referred to a particular person regarding some subject and that person immediately refers you to a "better" expert—as in, "I'm not the best person to talk to on that—you really need to talk to X"—don't just drop the first contact immediately. He or she may very well still be a good source.[2] You might say something like, "Fine, thanks for that referral and I'll certainly follow up on it, but let me ask: What is your own take on this? Does it affect you? Do you see anything, or can you recommend anything that you think needs to be [changed, developed, looked at, brought up, etc.]?"; and after that,

"Do you have any thoughts about what I questions I should ask X when I'm trying to get better oriented on this? Are there people you know of who would disagree with X?"

If you run into people who have important information but are reluctant to help, there's a kind of journalists' trick to get them to be more forthcoming; it's sometimes called "baiting the hook." It works as a second stage in the interview process: after your initial interview, write up your account of what was discussed and then ask the person to review your wording for accuracy and completeness. At this point the interviewee will sometimes add a great deal of important information, or clarify important distinctions, that did not surface in the initial contact. I am not, of course, saying that you should allow the contact person to rewrite your paper; its final version remains a matter of your own judgment. But getting feedback at this second stage will often elicit additional information or qualifications, and asking for "a check of my write-up for accuracy" is a good way to get a follow-up interview.

A related problem in some inquiries is that of "shrinkage of testimony." Private investigators and journalists frequently run into this. Sometimes a source will be very garrulous and free with statements when you first talk to him, but if he is later subject to cross-examination by an unsympathetic interrogator, or if he comes to realize he will somehow be held accountable for his opinions, he may quickly clam up. (The technique of baiting the hook is useful here: ask the person to review your write-up of his comments for accuracy. He may not be able to retreat very far if you are indeed accurate in what you've recorded from the prior contact.) This situation points up the advantage of a printed source: it will be the same no matter how often you refer to it. The corresponding disadvantage to a print source is that the situation may have changed substantially since the words, charts, or statistics were printed.

Talking to people, or getting a chain of referrals, also sometimes entails the "jerk problem"—occasionally you may indeed run into someone who is uncooperative, discouraging, or even rude. The solution is two-fold: don't take whatever they say personally, and try to get the names of other people to talk to, even from the jerks. If you encounter rudeness or abruptness, your attitude should be "So what?"—you can usually solve informational problems by getting a chain of enough referrals to work around whoever is the obstacle. You may even find that these same people become more informative once you've talked to other sources who do not accept their views or their perspectival "frame"; you may be able to draw out even the jerks if you "bait the hook" by asking them to review or comment on your written account of what the other people have said. Emphasize that you're trying to be balanced and fair in getting an overview of the situation.

Journalists require multiple sources to verify their information; that same standard may not apply to private researchers who have only personal (not public) uses in mind for the information they seek. Still, depending on the complexity and extent of your area of interest, it is a wise rule not to stop your inquiries with the first person who tells you what you want to hear, especially if you know that alternative viewpoints do exist. Remember the Blind Men of India. Just as you cannot get an overview of a large subject from a single print source or website, you need to be equally careful about relying on any single "people source."

I've known researchers who use fictional heroes for inspiration. When confronted with a puzzle, they would ask themselves questions along the line of "What would [Sherlock Holmes, Hercule Poirot, Nancy Drew, Emma Peel, Miss Marple] do in this situation?" The detectives we admire so much in novels or on television are not limited by laptops or printed sources in solving their mysteries; neither should we be in solving ours! And, further, going down the "people source" trail sometimes results in adventures that will make your own life more interesting to others when you recount the stories. It's always worth a try.

Some recalcitrant souls will undoubtedly still be intimidated by their lack of "credentials," even though lack of training is truly irrelevant to their success. For academics, it is hoped that the obvious will allay their fears: they already have credentials precisely because of their university affiliation. The best way to start a telephone conversation with a potential source is to mention this right up front:

> I'm a student/grad student at _____ University, and I'm not sure who to talk to—maybe you could help or direct me to the right person. I'm trying to find information on _____.

Nonacademics can say something similar:

> My name is _____ and I'm with _____, although I'm not calling in that connection. I'm trying to find information on _____; you may not know much about this yourself, but can you point me to someone there who might be able to get me started on this?

In obtaining information from people, the "secret" that is so hard for so many people to believe is precisely this: there is no secret. Just make the call anyway and be honest about your reasons. It's okay to ask for help. The odds are that you will succeed if you are simply persistent in developing a chain of referrals.

When interviewing someone you should keep several specific things in mind. First, if the nature of your inquiry is particularly complex, do some prior homework. At least talk to the reference librarians of your local library to see if they can suggest some overview or orientation sources. An expert will be more helpful if you convey the impression that you've already done some work on your own and are willing to do more—and that you're not simply dumping the whole problem (especially a class assignment) into his or her lap to solve for you. (This applies to Internet inquiries and e-mails as well as to direct interviews or phone calls.)

Second, it usually works better if you are talking with the person face to face, maybe over a cup of coffee. Remember, you will also have the opportunity for follow-up contact.

Third, explain the purpose of your research—that is, what you're ultimately trying to do and what you'll use the information for (e.g., personal curiosity, term paper, dissertation, publication, broadcast). Be open and honest. It will help here if you can say which sources you have already tried and why you thought the present contact was necessary to get beyond their inadequacies.

Fourth, tell them if you have a publication deadline; but do not make your own procrastination their problem. Don't wait until the last minute to tell an expert you need an answer immediately.

Fifth, try to be as specific as you can—if, of course, the nature of your inquiry allows for specificity. Basically, if you ask specific questions then you're likely to get on-target answers, but if you ask only vague, general questions, you're likely to get only vague, general answers.

Sixth, respect the expert's intellectual property rights. Don't simply "milk" a person for information and then pass it off as your own—be careful not to infringe on your source's own potential use of the information. People who burn their sources in this way not only ruin their chances for productive follow-up contacts, they also make the sources hesitant about helping other researchers. Anyone who uses "the network" should leave it in as good, or better, shape for the next person.

Seventh, when you talk to people about a subject that you're not familiar with, it is *very* important to ask for more contacts. Just as few researchers will rely exclusively on any one printed source if the topic at hand is of any importance, it is similarly unwise to rely on only one spoken (or social networked/e-mailed) viewpoint. People's memories of events, and their opinions, tend to be self-serving; it is therefore advisable to seek a balance of perspectives if the topic is such that it can be framed or "shaped" differently by different people.

Eighth, after you have talked to someone who has been helpful—especially if the person has gone out of his or her way for you—it is very important to write a thank-you note or email. There are several reasons for this:

- A written record of your interest in a subject will enable your source to remember you and to contact you again if additional information turns up; the same record will enable your source to use *you* as a contact for information in your shared area of interest. This is how mutually beneficial contact networks are built up.
- You will frequently find that later on, when you are finally writing your report or paper, new questions will occur to you that you did not think of the first time. When you contact your source again for further clarification, he will be more responsive if he has already received a good thank-you in writing, for such notes are useful to him in concrete ways. They provide proofs of good job performance he can readily use in justifying raises, programs extensions, and so on.
- The lack of a thank-you note can positively hurt you when you want to use a source again. This writer is aware of more than one instance in which contacts who had no obligation to help researchers nevertheless went out of their way to provide difficult-to-come-by information (sometimes a great deal of it)—and never received a word of thanks for their efforts. The result was that, in each case, the contacts "dried up" when the same researchers sought them again for more information.

When you are paying someone to help you, you can call that person at any time. But when you are getting information for free, you must at all costs avoid the impression of being thankless or pushy. It is therefore advisable to consider the sending of timely thank-you notes not simply as a nice thing to do, but rather as an integral part of the research process. If you haven't put words of thanks in writing, you have not finished your contact with that source.

The problem remains, then, that even if you do want to talk to someone who knows about your subject, how do you find that person? Where do you start? If your own circle of acquaintances (including Facebook or LinkedIn) doesn't get you far enough, you can try several sources available through libraries that may work better.

SOURCES OUTSIDE THE OPEN INTERNET FOR IDENTIFYING KNOWLEDGEABLE PEOPLE

ENCYCLOPEDIA OF ASSOCIATIONS (GALE CENGAGE, ANNUAL)

The printed version of this set will likely be found in any public library; a subscription online version is also available. The subtitle of the print copy is noteworthy: "A Guide to More Than 23,000 National and International Organizations, Including: Trade, Business, and Commercial; Environmental and Agricultural; Legal, Governmental, Public Administration, and Military; Engineering, Technological, and Natural and Social Sciences; Educational; Cultural; Social Welfare: Health and Medical; Public Affairs; Fraternal, Nationality, and Ethnic; Religious; Veterans', Hereditary, and Patriotic; Hobby and Avocational; Athletic and Sports; Labor Unions, Associations, and Federations; Chambers of Commerce and Trade and Tourism; Greek Letter and Related Organizations; and Fan Clubs."

Associations, professional societies, amateur hobby groups, and non-profit organizations are excellent switchboards for connecting researchers with highly qualified sources. They are used by journalists all the time. The very purpose of most societies is to disseminate information on their subjects and to provide a means for people with common interests to interact with each other. They usually welcome inquiries that enable them to tell you more about their field of interest. This annual *Encyclopedia* from Gale Cengage, whether print or online, is the single best listing of such groups. Each entry provides the name of the organization, its address, telephone numbers (including toll-free ones) and e-mail addresses, the name of a contact person, the number of members, and a description of the organization's purposes, activities, publications, and conventions or meetings. The organization's website will always be specified, too. The printed volumes have detailed indexes by keywords, by geographical areas, and by executives' names. Finding organizations through this directory eliminates, right from the start, a lot of misdirection to questionable or unvetted sites; the fact that an organization is listed within is a very good indication that it is not "crackpot."

There is a society for everything under the sun. The following brief list gives only the slightest hint of the range and diversity of such groups:

American Accordionists' Association
American Association for the Accreditation of Ambulatory Plastic
    Surgery Facilities
American Lumberjack Association

Baker Street Irregulars [Sherlock Holmes buffs]
Federation of Historical Bottle Collectors
Chinese Snuff Bottle Society of America
Norwegian Forest Cat Breed Council
Dance [more than 200 organizations]
Dogs [more than 300]
Domestic Violence [more than 40]
Estonian Educational Society
National Flute Association
International Franchise Association
Frog Pond—Frog Collectors Club
American Frozen Food Institute
Gemological Institute of America
Association for Gravestone Studies
Great Books Foundation
Society for Austrian and Habsburg History
Insurance [many hundreds]
North American Kant Society
American Kitefliers Association
Coin Laundry Association
Manuscript Society
Mobile Home Owners Federation
Ornithology/Birds [scores of societies]
Contemporary Quilt Art Association
American Radiological Nurses Association
Restless Legs Syndrome Foundation
Stuntwomen's Association of Motion Pictures (SWAMP)
Tall Clubs International
American Institute of Ultrasound in Medicine
Veterinary medicine [hundreds]
Window Covering Manufacturers Association
Wine [scores]
Women's groups [thousands]
Association of Zoos and Aquariums

The *Encyclopedia of Associations* is a publication everyone should browse through; it's of interest not only for research but also for finding people who have the same hobby as you. Two other complementary sets (and subscription databases) are also published by Gale Cengage: *Encyclopedia of Associations: International Organizations*, listing 32,000 groups, and *Encyclopedia of Associations: State, Regional, and Local Organizations*, listing more than 100,000. An additional useful source from CDB Research Ltd. is the *Directory of British Associations & Associations in Ireland.*

AUTHORS OF ARTICLES OR BOOKS YOU'VE READ

Writers who have published something on a particular subject often keep up to date on new developments in the field. It is usually not difficult these days to reach authors via Web connections. One particularly useful source is the *Web of Science* database (see Chapter 6), which indexes more than 13,500 high-quality academic journals in all subject areas (including social sciences and humanities). What is significant is that the database's citation to each article provides not just the institutional address of its author(s) but usually their direct e-mail address as well. If the e-mail information is lacking, it is usually a simple matter to find it via the institution's website. Many authors also have their own websites, which can be found either through a Google search or often by links from their publisher's website.

COS SCHOLAR UNIVERSE (PROQUEST)

This is a subscription database providing information on more than a million scholars at four-year universities all over the world. It's a kind of international faculty directory. You can search by individuals' names, by subjects, and by institutions and their departments. Each entry provides contact information and a description of the scholar's research interests; usually there will also be a verified list of the person's publications and co-authors (where appropriate) and departmental colleagues. The range of disciplines is covered: Agriculture, Applied Health, Applied Science, Architecture, Arts, Business, Education, Engineering, Environmental Science, Humanities, Law, Natural Science, Social Sciences, and Theology. (I once had an e-mail from a professional translator in Amsterdam who was having trouble rendering Samuel Butler's *The Way of All Flesh* into Dutch. Through this *COS Scholar* database I identified two academic specialists in Butler studies and forwarded their contact information to her. She wrote back that they turned out to be "tremendously helpful.")

DIRECTORIES IN PRINT (GALE CENGAGE, IRREGULAR)

This source has the subtitle "A Descriptive Guide to Print and Non-Print Directories, Buyer's Guides, Rosters and Other Address Lists of All Kinds." It covers more than 16,000 publications worldwide. It provides a description of the coverage of each directory and phone, e-mail, and website contacts for their publishers; it also provides separate "Subject" and "Title and Keyword" indexes. Just as there is often an association for everything, so there is frequently a published directory of contacts for every area of interest. While it is certainly true that most directory-type questions for information on specific organizations are now best handled by going directly to the organizations' websites, the problem remains of how to get overview information on the range of organizations that may be relevant to your inquiry. *Directories in Print* is a good source; the following is just a brief sampling of available published directories:

> *Academic Year, Semester and Summer Programs Abroad*
> *National Directory of Adult Day Care Centers*
> *Auto Museums Directory*
> *Celebrities in Los Angeles Cemeteries*
> *Earthworm Buyer's Guide*
> *Directory of Professional Genealogists*
> *America's Top Golf Courses*
> *Grants, Fellowships, and Prizes of Interest to Historians*
> *Directory of Historical Organizations in the United States and Canada*
> *Louisiana Legal Directory*
> *Directory of Mail Order Catalogs*
> *Official Museum Directory*
> *National Catalog of Occult Bookstores*
> *British Performing Arts Yearbook*
> *Directory of the North American Electronics Recycling Industry*
> *Specialty Travel Index*
> *Directory of German Wine Festivals*

Directories in Print also lists local directories for specific areas under names of countries, regions, states, and cities in its Subject Index.

Faculty of Local Universities

The professors at institutions of higher learning are experts in an astonishing variety of topics, and most maintain regular office hours in which they are available for consultation or simply "chewing the fat." An advantage to researchers here is that there is no problem getting past secretaries during these office hours—the scholars are there to be available to all comers.

Gale Directory Library (Gale Cengage)

This is a subscription database with the full texts of sixteen directories, including *Encyclopedia of Associations* and *Directories in Print. It also includes*

Consultants and Consulting Directory, Directory of Special Libraries and Information Centers, Encyclopedia of Business Information Sources, Encyclopedia of Government Advisory Organizations, Gale Directory of Databases, Gale Directory of Publications and Broadcast Media, Government Research Directory, International Research Centers Directory, National Directory of Nonprofit Organizations, Publishers Directory, Research Centers Directory, and *Ward's Business Directory of U.S. Private and Public Companies.*

THE LEADERSHIP LIBRARY (DATABASE) AND YELLOW BOOKS (PRINT DIRECTORIES) FROM LEADERSHIP DIRECTORIES, INC.

Their 14 print directories are all available as online subscriptions, individually or cumulatively; they include *Federal Yellow Book, Federal Regional Yellow Book, Congressional Yellow Book, State Yellow Book, Municipal Yellow Book, Government Affairs Yellow Book, Corporate Yellow Book, Financial Yellow Book, News Media Yellow Book, Foreign Representatives in the U.S. Yellow Book, Judicial Yellow Book, Law Firms Yellow Book, Associations Yellow Book,* and *Nonprofit Sector Yellow Book.* These sources are much more detailed than the *Washington Information Directory*—they provide contact information down to the level of individual bureaucrats, editors, administrators, local officials, and scholars. 700,000 individuals in thousands of organizations can be pinpointed. (A good overview of coverage can be found online at www.leadershipdirectories.com/About/CriteriaforInclusion-OnlineDirectories.aspx. The database version, under its "Explore People" link leading to "Explore the Experts Network," provides hundreds of categorizations of experts from "Administration" and "Advertising" through "Mathematics" and "Medical Professional Training" to "Western States," "White House," and "Women's Issues"—each category having scores of further topical subdivisions down to the level of individuals. Searches "by Alma Mater" are also possible.)

CARROLL PUBLISHING COMPANY DIRECTORIES AND DATABASES

These are like those from Leadership Library; they include *Carroll's Federal Directory, Carroll's Federal Regional Directory, Carroll's State Directory, Carroll's Municipal Directory,* and *Carroll's County Directory.* The company also provides separate *Organizations Charts* publications and database: *Federal, Defense* and *Defense Industry.*

WASHINGTON INFORMATION DIRECTORY (CQ PRESS, ANNUAL)

This is a subject guide to U.S. government agencies in the executive branch, to Congress and its committees and subcommittees, and to private and nongovernmental organizations—e.g., embassies think tanks, associations—in the Washington, DC, area. It describes each organization, gives a summary of its area of interest, and provides specific phone numbers, addresses, and websites. Chapters include sources in 19 broad categories:

Agriculture, Food, and Nutrition
Business and Economics
Communications and the Media
Culture and Religion
Education
Employment and Labor
Energy
Environment and Natural Resources
Government Operations
Health
Housing and Development
International Affairs
Law and Justice
Military Personnel and Veterans
National and Homeland Security
Science and Technology
Social Services and Disabilities
Transportation
U.S. Congress and Politics

Appendices provide detailed information on the current U.S. Congress, its members and committees, and ready reference information on government websites, governors and state officials, foreign embassies and ambassadors, and on the Freedom of Information Act. Detailed indexes are by Name, Organization, and Subject.

The value of having this information network at your call (and it is available to anyone) in incalculable. The U.S. federal government is an especially good place to begin looking for subject experts, as it employs thousands of them in mid-level positions. These people spend their careers keeping abreast of information in narrow areas, and all of these subject specialists can be reached by phone or e-mail. (A tip: you should first seek the specialists themselves in the department or agency, rather than the librarians in the agency library [although they may be useful, too].) They are quite helpful—and, in fact, *you* are helpful to *them*, since in answering questions from the public they justify their jobs, programs, and salaries. These are important considerations in an era of downsizing. They can also refer you to excellent private and nongovernmental contacts. The researcher mentioned above who was working on padlocks started out with the *Washington Information Directory* and then just followed a chain of referrals from the Commerce Department to various private sources.

YELLOW PAGES

This subject directory of the resources in your own area is often overlooked by those who think everything is on **craigslist** (www.craigslist. org), which is indeed another great source for local contacts of all kinds. In using Yellow Pages, especially in a thick edition—there are still a few left—be sure to consult the index section at the back, as it will lead you to the best search terms used in the subject-heading system. A website covering both white and yellow pages, both domestic and international, is *Infobel*, at www.infobel.com (although many of its links are to sites requiring fees). A subscription database providing comprehensive access to both yellow and white pages is *ReferenceUSAGov* from InfoGroup; another is *Mergent Intellect* (Mergent). Both allow "criss-cross" searches: if you have a landline telephone number or a street mailing address they will tell you who is connected to them.

These resources that are not on the open Internet—over and above the social media websites that are much more widely known—should be adequate for leading you to knowledgeable people in any field. Two additional sources with "how-to" tips that don't go out of date are John Brady's classic *The Craft of Interviewing* (Vintage Books, 1977) and Risa Sacks's *Super Searchers Go to the Source: The Interviewing and Hands-On Information Strategies of Top Primary Researchers—Online, On the Phone, and In Person* (CyberAge Books, 2001).

TALKING TO REFERENCE LIBRARIANS

A further word of advice has to do specifically with talking to reference librarians. Just as it is useful to match your book-retrieval techniques to the library's cataloging and storage techniques, so it is often advisable to match the way you ask questions to the way librarians think (and any group that can put books on "moonshining" under **Distilling, Illicit** obviously does not think like most people).

Actually, it is the librarian's responsibility to find out what you're ultimately looking for—which may not be what you request initially—through a reference interview, so if you wind up being directed to inappropriate sources, it may be more the librarian's fault than your own. Still, whatever the reason for any misdirection, you will nevertheless want to avoid it, and if you can make the librarian's job a little easier by knowing the sort of information he or she is listening for, then you will be the one to benefit. Going with the grain is more efficient than going against it.

Here are three examples of what to be aware of:

- A woman asked a librarian, "Where are your books on nineteenth-century English history?" The reference interview, however, elicited the fact that what she really wanted was, specifically, biographical information on her ancestor Samuel Earnshaw. Once this had been determined, the librarian could refer her directly to the multivolume set *Modern English Biography*, which contained the necessary information. Note that the call number for the latter set, CT773.B6, puts it in a shelving area for "National Biography, By region or country, Great Britain. England" that is far removed from the stacks area for nineteenth-century British history, DA539–DA562. (It is astonishing that so much "instruction" on how to use libraries concentrates on the arrangements of the Library of Congress or Dewey Decimal Classifications at their broadest—and least helpful—levels, instead of on how to find the right subject headings in the library's catalog, which will lead to *specific* stacks locations in a *variety* of relevant areas [see Chapter 3].) *Biography and Genealogy Master Index* and *World Biographical Information System* provide other sources. Had the librarian simply directed her to the library's bookstacks on nineteenth-century English history, the woman would have wasted much time, probably all in vain.
- A grad student who asked me, "Where are your books on Greek history?" turned out to be specifically interested in the system of tribute payments among the Greek city-states during the Peloponnesian War. With that specific target in mind I could immediately show him a concise overview article from *The Oxford Classical Dictionary*, which also identified "the standard work" on the subject; a literature review article on it from *Web of Science*;

and multiple other print and online sources, exactly on target, that gave him a much better overview of the full range of relevant literature.[3]

- A professor once asked me for information on "U.S. relations with St. Domingue" (an old name for the island of Haiti/Santo Domingo); it turned out she specifically wanted information on the migration of people from that island to Baltimore during the period of 1790–1810. I found out that she had been searching various databases with only the name form "St. Domingue," since that's what the island was called during the period of her interest, but she didn't realize that books and articles about the island at that time are usually indexed under the current name forms. I showed her four published subject bibliographies on Haiti right in the reference collection, which she said were very useful because they brought to her attention good sources that didn't use the old name form. But I could also show her (by making sample printouts) the relevance of several databases she was not familiar with: *Historical Abstracts, America: History and Life, Handbook of Latin American Studies,* and *Digital Dissertations.* In searching the latter I found an 80-page full-text master's thesis with the title "In Search of Baltimore's Black Dominguan Immigrant Community, 1793–1844" (2006); this thesis provided a bibliography of further sources. She could download the whole thing, for free, onto a memory stick. If I hadn't found out specifically what she was after—which is not at all what she asked for—neither one of us would have found this.

In each of these cases—librarians could cite tens of thousands more—the inquirers asked *not for what they really wanted but for what they thought the library could provide.* The problem is that most people have grossly inadequate assumptions about what can and cannot be found in a library and phrase their questions only in the most general terms because they don't *expect* to find much. Others tend to think that the few resources or databases they've used in the past—*LexisNexis, JSTOR, ProQuest* (not realizing how very different libraries' subscriptions to *ProQuest* can be)—are essentially all there is, beyond whatever turns up in Google and Wikipedia. As I hope this book has made clear by now, such assumptions are very badly mistaken.

Frequently professors and graduate students are more inefficient than anyone else. This hearkens back to a point made earlier, that a large number of them have never done any critical thinking about the dictum passed on to generation after generation of graduates students all over the country: "You shouldn't have to ask a librarian for help; if you can't find it on your own, you're no scholar." Researchers who have less "learning" and more common sense will not thus cut themselves off from a major source of help. Even apart from the complexities of finding the right subject headings to use in OPACs—which is almost never taught—there are hundreds of subscription databases available in academic libraries that few academics have ever heard of; and many more are produced every year. Moreover, it is frequently the case that excellent sources turn up in searches of databases that are not at all discipline-specific. For the "Peloponnesian Tribute" question (above) some of the best sources came out of *Web of Science, Bibliographic Index, Periodicals Index Online, Dissertations,* and *WilsonWeb* (now merged into EBSCO, but at the time including *Humanities Full Text, Humanities & Social Sciences Retrospective, Readers' Guide to Periodical Literature,* and *Readers' Guide Retrospective*). Often *Academic Search Complete, IBZ, ArticleFirst, General OneFile,* or *Academic One-File* are relevant, no matter the subject area.

The "find it on your own" dictum is bad advice. Phrased positively, however—and understood positively—it is good advice: "The more you learn, yourself, about library sources and retrieval systems, the better your research will be." To the extent that you learn something of the range and depth of what you can expect from a library that you cannot expect from the Internet, you will allow yourself to ask more questions—and especially specific questions—that you would otherwise think could not be answered efficiently, or at all. You will then find yourself asking, "Where can I find biographical information on my ancestor Samuel Earnshaw, who lived in nineteenth-century England?" rather than "Where are your books on nineteenth-century English history?" You will ask "What can I find about tribute payments in the Peloponnesian War?" rather than "Where are your book on Greek history?" And you'll ask for "the immigration of blacks from St. Domingue to Baltimore from 1790 to 1810" instead of "U.S. relations with St. Domingue."

What is always most useful to a reference librarian is to know what you are *ultimately* trying to find. A good way to clarify your thoughts is to ask yourself, "If there were an absolutely perfect article already written on my subject, what would the title of that article be?" (And ask yourself the same question before using any online source. Most people type the same very general phrasings into search boxes that they use when talking to reference librarians—and, again, they then miss all of the best material.)

In going outside the library to talk to people, however, you will often find that directories—either subscription databases or printed formats—available within libraries are often the best starting points in that they are capable of connecting you to whole ranges of people whom you would not find through Internet sources.

The rule to remember in all of this is that somewhere along the line in your research you should ask yourself, "*Who* would be likely to know about this subject? Whose *business* is it to know? In whose *interest* would it be?" These questions, plus a browsing familiarity with the resources listed above, can get you started on some very valuable pathways and lead you to important information not recorded in any print or online source.

CHAPTER 13

Hidden Treasures

A FEW SPECIAL TYPES OF RESOURCES CONTAIN AN INCREDIBLE wealth of information in all subject areas, but they are often overlooked because their content is not indexed by most conventional databases or catalogs. Discovering any of them, however, can provide you with the reader's equivalent of tapping into Alaska's north shore oil reserves. These resources are:

- Special collections
  - Online
  - Microform
- Government documents
- Archives, manuscripts, and public records

RESOURCES NOT COVERED BY CONVENTIONAL DATABASES OR CATALOGS AND NOT SHELVED WITH REGULAR BOOKS

Materials in these collections have certain features in common:

- They are often not covered by a library's regular online catalog and are usually discoverable only through separate databases—or printed indexes or guides—that have peculiar indexing features unlike those in an OPAC. These peculiarities always get lost when the separate databases are combined with OPACs into federated or "discovery" searches; the latter merge multiple databases into a single search and are frequently misrepresented as covering "all" of a library's holdings. In such situations the records from the special collections get jumbled into massive keyword retrievals whose display buries them rather than highlights their existence. (See the discussion of "silos" in Chapter 4 and the examples below.)

- Physical-format special collections, such as microforms, government documents, and archives/manuscripts, are stored or shelved in ways that separate them from a library's classified bookstacks. They either cannot be found through general or focused browsing (Chapter 3), or their shelving or storage configurations do not allow browsing to begin with.

It takes extra steps to get into these materials, in other words, and few people take them because to those lacking prior experience in these areas the paths are obscure and the destinations are not foreseeable. Most people tend to settle for whatever they can find quickly and easily; it's not that they are "lazy" so much as that they don't perceive the range of options available to them outside the horizon of their previous experience. In seeking special collections, government documents, or manuscript materials, it is especially important to ask for help from people who have more experience with them because frequently the best initial access comes through a custodian's or librarian's greater knowledge of what is *likely* to be found in them and of which particular databases (or other finding guides) provide the best access.

The ways to identify special collections that are not online or in microform have been discussed in Chapter 11.

SPECIAL COLLECTIONS ONLINE: SUBSCRIPTION DATABASES

Thousands of large, prepackaged research collections exist in a bewildering variety of subject areas; they are in subscription databases available only through research libraries. Of the many that are available let me provide a sample of three, and a listing of some of the others.

The Making of the Modern World (Gale Cengage): This is a huge full-text database of more than 60,000 books published between 1460 and 1850 in the range of European languages; it also includes serial literature (466 titles) whose publication began prior to 1850. (Entire runs of serials are covered even when they extend after 1850.) It is the digitized version of a prepackaged microfilm library (which may still be available in that format in many research libraries), the *Goldsmiths'-Kress Library of Economic Literature*. The collection is a treasure trove for any research on the history of business or economics—but "economics" is interpreted very broadly, and so the database provides much material on the more general social and political history of these centuries. Among the topics covered are mercantilism, agriculture and agricultural innovation, European colonial expansion (with early histories of the various geographical areas), accounting practices, slavery, demography in eighteenth-century England, the textile industry, socialism prior to Marx, trade unionism, Indians of North and South America, debtor/creditor relations, piracy, smuggling, dietary habits in various European countries, early business and technical education, commerce in Italy, penology, trade manuals, numismatics, the economy of eighteenth-century Scandinavia, Irish–English relations, social conditions, population, transport and transport technology, and even theology (with digitized works by Thomas Aquinas and Cotton Mather, among others). More than just books and serials are included: pamphlets, broadsides, proclamations, and government documents are also well represented. All are cataloged using *Library of Congress Subject Headings*. There is also a second database, *The Making of the Modern World Part II, 1851–1914*, that includes another 5,000 titles.

North American Women's Letters and Diaries, Colonial to 1950 (Alexander Street Press): This subscription database provides full texts of diaries, journals, and letters written by more than 1,300 women who either lived in or visited North America. Biographies are provided where available, and annotated bibliographies of sources are given. Searches can be done via all of the following categorizations:

Author
Age when writing
Marital status (when writing)
Maternal status (when writing)
Age at marriage
Number of marriages
Age at first childbirth
Number of children
Nationality
Race
Religion
Occupation
Year written
Month written
Document type (letter, diary, editorial, memoir)

Where written (Setting)—e.g., Battlefields, Company towns, Hospitals, Indian camps, Military bases, Shipboard, Suburbs

Where written (Geographical)—e.g., particular cities, countries, or regions

Historical events—e.g., American Revolution, Civil War battles, California Gold Rush, Reconstruction, Prohibition

Personal events—e.g., Adoption of child, Death of parent or loved one, Emigration, Household moves, Illness, Religious experience, Wedding

Subject headings

It is the capacity to limit by these specific criteria that gets lost in almost all federated or "discovery" searches of multiple databases at the same time. A partial exception is the separate database *Social and Cultural History: Letter and Diaries Online* (also from Alexander Street Press) that serves as a cumulative index not just to this collection but to several others as well: *British and Irish Women's Letters and Diaries; North American Immigrant Letters, Diaries, and Oral Histories; The American Civil War: Letters and Diaries; Black Thought and Culture; Oral History Online;* and *Manuscript Women's Letters and Diaries from the American Antiquarian Society.* Each collection is expanded as new material is found, and still other separate collections are planned. Currently the *Social and Cultural History* cumulative index covers more than 650,000 pages of letters, diaries, and journals written by 8,000 individuals since 1675; full texts of the indexed items are available only to those libraries subscribing to the individual databases. It also indexes another 4,000 English-language collections that are freely available on the Web. This latter material contains 700,000 pages from the 1550s to the present; pointers are also given to 4,300 audio and visual files on the open Web. The freely accessible websites are indexed at the same level of detail as the material that is available only to subscribers. (Note that the several proprietary databases have indexing tailored to their own individual fields; the categories listed above for the *North American Women's Diaries* database overlap, but are not identical to, the categories created for the other files—in other words, even here there is some loss of indexing specificity when all of the databases are simultaneously cross-searched via the *Social and Cultural History* index.)

eHRAF World Cultures (Human Relations Area Files): This database is an ongoing compilation of hundreds of thousands of pages of primary and secondary sources on about 280 cultural groups worldwide. The database is useful to students of anthropology, sociology, psychology, politics, literature, linguistics, history, comparative religion, art, and agricultural development—and for anyone else who wishes to compare the perceptions, customs, social institutions, values, beliefs, and daily life of all peoples of the world, past and present. The documentation for each culture is indexed, at the paragraph level, in about 750 subject categorizations provide by the database's "Outline of Cultural Materials." These categories include such topics as mortality, recorded history, food production, architecture for various functions, humor, entertainment, trial procedures, recruitment of armed forces, old-age dependency, sexual practices and norms, views on abortion, drug use, division of labor by sex, sanitary facilities, power development, interpersonal relations, art, religion, political organization, etc. Within each category is found the full-text documentation from books, articles, unpublished manuscripts, and field reports. Foreign language material is not always translated into English. Keyword searching is also possible.

The standardization of topical categories under each culture allows for ready comparisons of information, which in many cases can be statistically significant. (Not every category is filled in for every culture, however—the creation of the system is an ongoing process.) This database is an extension of an older microfiche set of documents, the *Human Relations Area Files*, containing comparable data on 350 cultures analyzed into about 600 topical categories (not all of which correspond to the 750 in the database). Although some of the texts on the 280 cultures in the database version come from this microfiche set, much of this earlier material has not been incorporated into the online version, but the latter has additional material not in the microfiche. About 400 cultures are covered if both the online and the microfiche sets are searched. (There is also another, similar database called *eHRAF Archaeology*, which enables cross-cultural comparisons of archaeological studies worldwide. It uses the same lists of cultures and topical categories, but also allows keyword searching.)

The above three online collections represent but the tip of a very large iceberg of full-text collections. Additional, comparable subscription databases include the following; this list is only a sampling of what is available:

Alexander Street Press Collections: Full Text, Audio, and Video

Academic Video Online
African American Music Reference
Alexander Street Drama [combined index to six separate drama collections]
Alexander Street Literature [combined index to eight separate literature collections]

The American Civil War: Letters and Diaries
The American Civil War Online [cross-index to three separate collections]
The American Civil War Research Database
American Film Scripts
American History in Video
American Song
Asian American Drama
Audio Drama: The L.A. Theatre Works Collection
Black Drama
Black Short Fiction and Folklore
Black Thought and Culture
Black Women Writers
British and American Women's Letters and Diaries
Caribbean Literature
Classical Music Library
Classical Music Reference Library
Classical Scores Library
Contemporary World Music
Counseling and Psychotherapy Transcripts, Client Narratives, and Reference Works
Counseling and Therapy in Video
Counseling and Therapy in Video: Volume II
Dance in Video
The Digital Karl Barth Library
The Digital Library of Classic Protestant Texts
The Digital Library of the Catholic Reformation
Early Encounters in North America
Education in Video
Ethnographic Video Online
Filmakers Library Online
The Gilded Age
Illustrated Civil War Newspapers and Magazines
Images of America: A History of American Life in Images and Texts
Images of the American Civil War
Irish Women Poets of the Romantic Period
Jazz Music Library
Latin American Women Writers
Latino Literature
Manuscript Women's Letters and Diaries from the American Antiquarian Society

Music Online [a cumulative package of eleven music databases]
North American Immigrant Letters, Diaries, and Oral Histories
North American Indian Drama
North American Indian Thought and Culture
North American Theatre Online
North American Women's Drama
North American Women's Letters and Diaries
Opera on Video
Oral History Online
The Romantic Era Redefined
Scottish Women Poets of the Romantic Period
The Sixties: Primary Documents and Personal Narratives, 1960 to 1974
Smithsonian Global Sound for Libraries
Social and Cultural History: Letters and Diaries Online [combined
    index to seven separate database collections]
Social Theory
South and Southeast Asian Literature
Theatre on Video
*Twentieth Century Advice Literature: North American Guides on Race,
    Gender, Sex, and the Family*
Twentieth Century North American Drama
Underground and Independent Comics, Comix, and Graphic Novels
Women and Social Movements in the United States
Women and Social Movements International
World History in Video: English-Language Documentaries

Full descriptions of these databases are available at http://alexanderstreet
.com/products.

Gale Digital Collections

17th and 18th Century Burney Collection Newspapers
19th Century British Library Newspapers (Parts I and II)
19th Century U.S. Newspapers
19th Century U.K. Periodicals Series I: New Readerships
19th Century U.K. Periodicals Series II: Empire
Archives Unbound [scores of digitized archival collections]
British Literary Manuscripts Online, c. 1660–1900
British Literary Manuscripts Online, Medieval and Renaissance
Conditions and Politics of Occupied Western Europe, 1940–1945
Declassified Documents Reference System
Eighteenth Century Collections Online (Parts I and II)

Gale Newsvault [cross-searches multiple full-text databases of U.K. periodicals and newspapers with some coverage of U.S. newspapers]

The Making of Modern Law: Legal Treatises, 1800–1926

The Making of Modern Law: Primary Sources, 1620–1926

The Making of Modern Law: Primary Sources II, 1763–1970

The Making of Modern Law: Trials, 1600–1926

The Making of Modern Law: U.S. Supreme Court Records and Briefs, 1832–1978

The Making of the Modern World Parts I: The Goldsmiths'-Kress Collection, 1450–1850

The Making of the Modern World Part II: 1851–1914

The Middle East Online Series I: Arab-Israeli Relations, 1917–1970

The Middle East Online Series II: Iraq 1914–1974

Northern Ireland: A Divided Community, 1921–1972

Post-War Europe: Refugees, Exile and Resettlement, 1945–1950

Public Life in Contemporary Argentina

Sabin Americana, 1500–1926

Slavery and Anti-Slavery: A Transnational Archive

Sources in U.S. History Online: Slavery in America

Sources in U.S. History Online: The American Revolution

Sources in U.S. History Online: The Civil War

State Papers Online—Part I, The Tudors: Domestic, 1509–1603

State Papers Online—Part II, The Tudors: Foreign, 1509–1603

State Papers Online—Part III, The Stuarts: Domestic, 1603–1714

State Papers Online—Part IV, The Stuarts: Foreign, 1603–1714

Testaments to the Holocaust

Women, War & Society, 1914–1918

Full descriptions are available at http://gdc.gale.com/products-by-name/.

ProQuest Chadwyck-Healey Digital Collections

Acta Sanctorum and Patrologia Latina Database

African-American Biographical Database

African-American Poetry, 1760–1900

American Drama, 1714–1915

American Poetry [1600–1900]

Colonial State Papers [British]

Digital National Security Archive [40 collections, 1945–]

Documents on British Policy Overseas [1898–]

English Drama [1280–1915]

English Poetry [600–1900]
German Literature Collections
Gerritsen Collection of Women's History Online, 1543–1945
John Johnson Collection: An Archive of Printed Ephemera
Literature Online [600–current]
Parliamentary Papers
Twentieth-Century African-American Poetry
Twentieth-Century American Poetry
Twentieth-Century Drama
Twentieth-Century English Poetry

Descriptions of these collections are available at www.proquest.com/en-US/products/default.shtml.

ProQuest History Vault: This is a new project intended to digitize dozens of microfilm collections originally published by University Publications of American (UPA) (see Microform Special Collections, below). An overview of the modules being made available can be found by searching "ProQuest History Vault" in Google or Bing. Current online collections include:

Vietnam War and American Foreign Policy (1960–1975)
American Politics and Society from Kennedy to Watergate (1960–1975).

SPECIAL COLLECTIONS ONLINE: FREE WEBSITES

Library of Congress American Memory—the Library of Congress is one of the largest providers of free, full-text content on the Internet. More than 140 of its collections on American history are available, including pamphlets, maps, photos, manuscripts, sound recordings, and motion pictures; full descriptions of all the collections are online at www.loc.gov (click on the American Memory icon). Note, however, that the digitized sources consist of only of copyright-free materials; in most cases this means they were produced or published prior to 1923.

Library of Congress E-Resources Online Catalog is a listing of (as of this writing) nearly 400 websites selected by LC experts, in all subject areas; these are freely available full-text collections mounted by institutions other than LC itself. The list is maintained at http://eresources.loc.gov/search~S9/m?SEARCH=Free. It can also be found via http://eresources.loc.gov/under the heading "ALL Free Resources."

OAIster is a subscription database available in the OCLC FirstSearch system; it is a listing of freely available full-text sources from more than

1,100 open archive collections. Direct links to the sources are given. More than 23,000,000 items are cataloged, including digitized books and articles, images, audio files, born digital texts, and films.

The European Library website at www.theeuropeanlibrary.org provides links to free digital collections mounted by dozens of European national libraries.

MICROFORM SPECIAL COLLECTIONS

Of the high-quality, commercially available special collections—which are often prepackaged whole libraries on particular subjects—many more exist in microformats than can be found online. ("Microformat" can refer either to micro*film*, which is spooled on reels, or to micro*fiche*, which are separate sheets, each containing dozens of miniaturized text pages.) Frequently these sets include thousands of individual books, journals, government documents, archival records, or other primary sources. In most cases there is a printed (or online) guide to the individual items within the set, and the guide itself may be discoverable as a cataloged record in the library's OPAC—but the thousands of items within the collection will not be individually listed in the OPAC. You usually have to find the guide to gain any overview of what lies within the microform collection. Often such guides are cataloged under the *LCSH* forms **[Subject]—Microform catalogs** or **[Subject]—Bibliography**.

A helpful solution to this problem—i.e., that the guide to a set may appear in your OPAC, but not the individual titles it lists—is sometimes available through the *WorldCat* database. If you already know an individual title that you want, a *WorldCat* search will often turn it up even if it appears within a large microform collection—and the *WorldCat* record, further, will provide the specific reel number (or fiche number) for that title within the collection that contains it.

Many researchers are initially deterred from using microforms because they mistakenly assume that photocopies on paper cannot be made from them; such copies, however, are easy to make—and many libraries now also have machines that enable you to digitally scan images directly to a flash drive. It is unfortunately becoming more common for students who are accustomed to nothing but digital formats to simply disregard resources that are available only in microform sets due to the relative inconvenience of viewing them. But graduate students, in particular, who look for and exploit these resources will often have a major advantage in doing their dissertations for two reasons: they will probably be finding relevant sources overlooked by others in their field, and the assemblage of thousands of relevant records in one collection, often including primary sources or ephemera not otherwise accessible, can greatly speed and deepen their research. In Chapter 9 I discussed the great advantage that accrues to one's research if a published subject bibliography can be found; all the greater is that advantage if the bibliography is accompanied by the actual texts of the items it cites, assembled all in one place. There are a great many dissertations waiting to be done using these microform collections.

Let me just mention details of four such sets before providing larger lists of comparable titles:

> *Confederate Imprints* (Gale) on 143 microfilm reels includes 6,188 items that contain anything from religious sermons and tracts to treasurers' reports of the New Orleans municipal government to the journal of the Mississippi secession convention.
>
> *Early American Medical Imprints* (Gale) on 105 microfilm reels contains more than 1,600 books, pamphlets, broadsides, and theses published between 1668 and 1820, with 36 periodicals included as well.
>
> *French Political Pamphlets* (Gale) on 86 microfilm reels assembles approximately 6,000 pamphlets published from 1547 to 1648.
>
> *Utopian Literature, Pre-1900 Imprints* (ProQuest) on 1,990 microfiche contains 462 titles, in a range of European languages, from 1500 to 1899.

Many other microfom collectons exist; in what follows I have categorized them by their publishers.

GALE CENGAGE LEARNING PRIMARY SOURCE MEDIA

Primary Source Media (a subsidiary of Gale) offers more than 430 microform sets, each containing hundreds or thousands of sources on its particular topic. A small sample of the titles of these sets will indicate their range and importance:

> *African-American Baptist Annual Reports, 1865–1990s*
> *American Natural History, 1769–1865*
> *Anti-Slavery Collection*
> *Books of the Fairs* [i.e., world's fairs]
> *Business History Collection*
> *Chronicles and Documents of Medieval England, c. 1150–c. 1500*

Cinema Pressbooks of the Major Hollywood Studios

City Directories of the United States

Civil Rights and Social Activism in the South

Conquistadors: The Struggle for Colonial Power in Latin American, 1492–1825

County and Regional Histories and Atlases

Darwin, Huxley and the Natural Sciences

Dreyfus Affair in the Making of Modern France

Early American Medical Imprints, 1668–1820

Early American Orderly Books, 1748–1817

Early and Central Middle Ages, c. 650–c. 1200 AD: The Manuscript Record

English Stage after the Restoration, 1733–1822

European Music MSS Before 1820

European Women's Periodicals

First Three Centuries of Appalachian Travel

French Political Pamphlets, 1547–1648

Gay Rights Movement

History of Education

History of Photography

History of the Pacific Northwest and Canadian Northwest

History of Women

Immigrant in America

Incunabula: The Printing Revolution in Europe, 1455–1500

International Population Census Publications

The Internment of Japanese Americans

Iroquois Indians: A Documentary History

Latin American History and Culture

Literature of Theology and Church History in the United States and Canada

Making of Modern London

Medieval and Renaissance Manuscripts

Mexican Pamphlet Collection, 1605–1888

Middle East: A Documentary Resource: Arab-Israeli Relations, 1917–1970

Music Manuscripts

Native America, A Primary Record

On Color: The Faber Birren Book Collection

Oscar Wilde Collection

Plains and the Rockies: 1800–1865

Popular Stage: Drama in Nineteenth Century England

Published Records of the American Colonies

Russian Archives
Russian Revolutionary Literature
Slavery, Source Material and Critical Literature
Spanish Civil War Collection
Testaments to the Holocaust
Travels in the Confederate States
Travels in the New South, 1865–1955
Travels in the Old South, 1607–1860
Travels in the West and Southwest
Twentieth Century Composers
Utah and the Mormons
Viennese Theatre, 1740–1790
*Voices from Wartime France, 1939–1945: Clandestine Resistance and
    Vichy Newspapers*
Warner Brothers Screenplays, 1930–1950
Western American Frontier History, 1550–1900
Western Books on Asia
Witchcraft in Europe and America
Women's Lives: American Women Missionaries and Pioneers Collection

The full list of all the Primary Source microform collections, with descriptions and downloadable copies of their individual Guides, is online at http://microformguides.gale.com/GuideLst.html. Note the "Browse by Subject" option.

PROQUEST MICROFORM COLLECTIONS: UMI, CHADWYCK-HEALEY, AND UPA

UMI (formerly University Microfilms International) is a subsidiary of ProQuest that offers hundreds of microfilm collections: some are topically arranged libraries or compilations of sources; others are collections of the papers or writings of particular individuals or corporate bodies. More than 450 alphabetical listings are given on the UMI Research Collections at www.proquest.com/products-services/; type "UMI research collections" in the search box. Among these are the following:

American Labor Unions
Black Abolitionist Papers, 1830–1865
History of the Cinema
Early English Books
English Linguistics, 1500–1800
Food, Cookery, and Catering Microfiche Library

Health Care
Index to Illustrations of Shakespeare's Plays [17,000 cards reproduced]
Jewish Sheet Music
New York Public Library Artists Files [1.5. million clippings]
The History of Nursing
Photographic Views of New York City
Quaker Women's Tracts
Regimental Histories of the American Civil War
Salem Witchcraft
Utopian Literature, Pre-1900 Imprints
World War II through the American Newsreels, 1942–1945
Yugoslav Civil War

Chadwyck-Healey, another ProQuest subsidiary, offers 170 similar microform collections, among them:

American History and Culture
Archives of British and American Publishers
Archives of the Soviet Communist Party and Soviet State
Black Biographical Dictionaries, 1790–1950
British and Irish Biographies
Charles Dickens Research Collection
Portraits of Americans

Further listings can be found within the ProQuest.com website.

UPA, yet another subsidiary of ProQuest, offers more than a thousand microform collections; you can readily skim the whole list online—with full texts of their finding aids—if you Google the phrase "UPA Microform Collection Guides"; here is only a tiny sampling of these collections:

American Primers
American West: Overland Journeys, 1841–1880
Black Workers in the Era of the Great Migration, 1916–1929
Communist Activity in the Entertainment Industry
Confidential U.S. State Department Central Files [multiple countries]
Early Photography Books
Film Journals
Grassroots Women's Organizations
Indian Removal to the West, 1832–1840
Indian Wars of the West and Frontier Army Life, 1862–1898: Official Histories and Personal Narratives
Korean War Studies and After-Action Reports

Latin American Pamphlets
Motion Picture Catalogs by American Producers and Distributors, 1894–
    1908
Murray's Handbooks for Travellers
New England Women and Their Families in the 18th and 19th Centuries
Occupation of Japan
Oil and the Energy Crisis
Political Pamphlets from the Indian Subcontinent
Records of Antebellum Southern Plantations from the Revolution through
    the Civil War
Southern Women and Their Families in the 19th Century
Trade Catalogs from the Avery Library at Columbia University
Voices from Ellis Island: An Oral History of American Immigration
Women in the U.S. Military
Yiddish Children's Literature

Further information on all these collections is available at the "Collection Guides" website mentioned above.

Although there is a trend to digitize sets that already exist in microformats, the vast majority of these sets do not have full-text online counterparts (although many of their Guides are online). The annual *Guide to Microforms in Print* (De Gruyter Saur) lists all microforms, but the large prepackaged collections, such as those just sampled, get buried within its listings for hundreds of thousands of individual titles of books, journals, government documents, and newspapers that are also available in microform. The two best ways into these collections, in terms of identifying which ones exist, are to look at the various vendors' websites given above and to consult these printed volumes:

> *Microfilm Research Collections: A Guide* (2nd edition), edited by
> Suzanne Cates Dodson (Meckler Publishing, 1984). This is an
> extensively annotated list of 376 collections. Most of these do
> not have online versions; they can usually be located through
> *WorldCat* searches for either the title of the collection itself,
> or the title of the printed guide accompanying the collection.
> Graduate students who discover any of these collections will
> have found troves of material that are simply ignored by most
> other scholars.
>
> *An Index to Microform Collections*, edited by Ann Niles (2 vols;
> Meckler Publishing, 1984, 1988). Volume 1 is a listing of all
> of the individual items in 26 of the collections in the Cates

Dodson *Microfilm Research Collections* volume above, with cumulative author and title indexes. Volume 2 extends coverage to 44 additional collections, many of which are not listed at all in the Cates Dodgson volume.

Both volumes identify many collections that are now out of print, often because their microfilm publishers have gone out of business—in many cases without being bought out by any larger company intent on digitizing the collections. These older "out-of-print" microfilm collections are just sitting in large research libraries, waiting to be rediscovered by enterprising grad students who can think outside the box of the digital world.

The best way to find out which ones are available to you locally is to talk to the librarians or curators at your research institution. You can also search the names of collections within the *WorldCat* database, but you have to be careful: some libraries will own the printed guides to collections without owning the microforms themselves. For the libraries that actually own the latter, however, the *WorldCat* record shows a little icon representing a microfiche card.

One additional microform set that is not generally regarded as a separate collection is the aggregate of American and Canadian doctoral dissertations (and some master's theses) available from ProQuest/UMI. More than 2 million of these works are available for sale from the vendor. The Library of Congress is the only institution that owns nearly all of the American (not Canadian) dissertations on microfilm or microfiche; all of them can be read there for free. Some researchers have justified trips to the Library just to use this collection, as the cost of ordering many individual titles from ProQuest/UMI may be greater than that of a plane ticket to Washington. (It is a very common misconception to believe that most dissertations are subsequently published as books; copies of the vast majority are available *only* from ProQuest UMI.) The company has, however, digitized the texts of most of the works since 1997, and offers downloadable (but not e-mail-able) PDFs to any libraries that subscribe at the full-text level.

Another equally amazing set not usually regarded as one aggregation is the collection of National Technical Information Service (NTIS) reports on microfiche. These are millions of research studies funded by the U.S. government. Again, the Library of Congress is the only facility that owns all of them, for free reading onsite; however, about 700,000 are now available online through the subscription database *National Technical Reports Library* (see next section).

GOVERNMENT DOCUMENTS

The term "document" is synonymous with "publication"; it can refer to just about any format, including books, magazines, newsletters, reports, pamphlets, broadsides, hearings, maps, prints, photographs, posters, kits, and websites. Also included are many finding aids and reference sources such as catalogs, indexes, directories, dictionaries, and bibliographies.

The United States federal government—with whose publications this section is primarily concerned—also produces films, sound recordings, and microforms. Today many federal agencies produce postings on Facebook, Twitter, and YouTube and send out e-mail alerts, RSS feeds, and e-newsletters.

The range, variety, and depth of coverage of these materials are amazing. They are particularly thorough in scientific and technological areas, and in all of the social sciences, especially regarding issues of public policy. Agriculture, business, commerce, communications, culture, economics, education, employment, energy, environment, foreign affairs, health, history, homeland security, housing, law, military affairs, politics, social services, and transportation are all very well covered. (You can browse publications in a wide variety of subject areas at http://bookstore.gpo.gov/subjects/index. jsp.) In using government documents, you can ask almost the same questions—and expect to find answers—as you can in using the more well-known research resources.

The main publisher of U.S. government documents is the Government Printing Office (GPO). In recent years, however, this agency has made a concerted effort to produce fewer materials in paper format and to publish most of its output directly on the Web. In addition, in those cases in which the GPO formerly published printed materials for other federal agencies, it now encourages those agencies to publish their own offerings directly on their own websites.

In looking for *current* information from the U.S. government, then, the Web is the first place to check, at the following sites.

USA.gov is the government's official Web portal. It provides direct access to many thousands of government titles, full text, and links to further information on individual agencies' own websites:

- By agency: www.usa.gov/Contact/By_agency.shtml
- By topic: www.usa.gov/Contact/By_topic.shtml

This is always the first place to look. **Search.USA.gov** provides a search box that indexes millions of government web pages.

FDsys (Federal Digital System) is a major source for current online government publications: www.gpo.gov/fdsys.

An important point is that the government's electronic archives, in most cases, do not nearly cover the range of its older paper publications that have never been digitized. These latter hard copies are nonetheless freely available at nearly 1,250 Selective and Regional government depository libraries located around the country. (These are all listed at USA.gov.) The 49 Regional depository libraries essentially contain full retrospective sets of *all* federal publications from the GPO. The Selective depositories, as their name indicates, can pick and choose which publications they wish to receive; they can also choose, individually, how long they will retain what they receive. (Continued funding for depository libraries is very much at issue, but one or another government website will provide current information.)

FedStats (www.fedstats.gov) provides direct links to statistical data from more than 100 agencies.

U.S. Census Bureau (www.census.gov) is particularly valuable for its "Subjects A–Z" listing of live links to statistical publications: www.census.gov/main/www/a2z.

NTIS National Technical Information Service (www.ntis.gov/search/index.aspx) searches 2 million bibliographic records for nonclassified federally funded research studies, copies of which can be ordered through the website. (These are generally non-GPO publications.)

Since it is almost impossible to speak systematically of the subjects of government documents, let me offer only a brief menu of titles, simply to suggest how surprising their range and variety is. A recent trip to the GPO bookstore in Washington found these titles on display, many of which are hardcover books of hundreds of pages:

> *Are We Prepared? Four WMD Crises That Could Transform U.S. Security*
>
> *Armed Groups: Studies in National Security, Counterterrorism, and Counterinsurgency*
>
> *A Basic Guide to Exporting: The Official Government Resource for Small and Medium-Sized Businesses* (10th ed., 2008)
>
> *Biosafety in Microbiological and Biomedical Laboratories* [5th ed.]
>
> *Black Americans in Congress: 1870–2007*
>
> *Breaking the Mold: Tanks in the Cities*
>
> *The Condition of Education: 2010*
>
> *Controversies in the Determination of Death: A White Paper by the President's Council on Bioethics*

Cosmos and Culture: Cultural Evolution in a Cosmic Context
Critical Thinking and Intelligence Analysis
Drugs of Abuse
Exploring the American West, 1803–1879
An Eye for History: The Paintings of William Henry Jackson
The FBI: A Centennial History, 1908–2008
Field Artillery
The Healthy Woman: A Complete Guide for All Ages
A History of Army Communications and Electronics
A History of Dentistry in the U.S. Army to World War II
A History of Innovation: U.S. Army Adaptation in War and Peace
How Tobacco Smoke Causes Disease
Improving Law Enforcement—Intelligence Community Relationship
Interrogation: World War II, Vietnam, and Iraq
Medical Aspects of Chemical Warfare
Monitoring Stem Cell Research
National Lakes Assessment: A Collaborative Study of the Nation's Lakes
The Navy SEAL Nutrition Guide
Neptune's Table: A View of America's Ocean Fisheries
Nisei Linguistics: Japanese Americans in the Military Intelligence Service
    during World War II
Patriots of Color
A Photographer's Path: Images of National Parks near the Nation's Capital
Promoting Effective Homicide Investigations
Reclamation: Managing Water in the West
Restorative Commons: Creating Health and Well-Being through Urban
    Landscapes
Rogue Wave: The U.S. Coast Guard on and after 9/11
Spinoff 2009 [i.e., spinoff benefits of the Space Program]
The Sun, the Earth, and Near-Earth Space: A Guide to the Sun-Earth
    System
Terrorism Research & Analysis Project (TRAP): A Collection of Research
    Ideas, Thoughts, and Perspectives [Vol. 1]
The U.S. Army and the Media in Wartime: Historical Perspectives
United States Senate Catalogue of Graphic Art
War Surgery in Afghanistan and Iraq
Wings in Orbit: Scientific and Technical Legacies of the Space Shuttle,
    1971–2020
Women in Congress: 1917–2006
The Women's Army Corps: 1945–1978
The Woody Plant Seed Manual

The World Cruise of the Great White Fleet
World Factbook: 2010

A good site for browsing the range of current publications, arranged in more than 140 subject categories, is http://bookstore.gpo.gov/subjects/index.jsp. Beneath the tip of this iceberg of current publications, however, lies a vast array of older titles such as the following:

The African Mosaic: A Library of Congress Resource Guide for the Study of Black History and Culture
Library of Congress Music, Theatre, Dance: An Illustrated Guide
Literary Recordings: A Checklist of the Archives of Recorded Poetry and Literature in the Library of Congress
The Star of Bethlehem [Library of Congress Bibliography]
The Tradition of Science: Landmarks of Western Civilization in the Collections of the Library of Congress
The Tradition of Technology: Landmarks of Western Technology in the Collections of the Library of Congress
A Descriptive List of Treasure Maps and Charts in the Library of Congress
Doing Research at the Library of Congress: A Guide to Subject Searching in a Closed Stacks Library (2nd ed.)
Backyard Bird Problems
The Bark Canoes and Skin Boats of North America
Ducks at a Distance: Waterfowl Identification Guide
Falconry
Fifty Birds of Town and City
Migration of Birds
Artillery through the Ages
A Barefoot Doctor's Manual
Camper's First Aid
Catalog of Federal Domestic Assistance
Dietary Guidelines for Americans, 2010
Diplomatic Hebrew
The Education System of Switzerland
Family Folklore: Interviewing Guide and Questionnaire
Fermentation Guide to Potatoes
Guide to High Speed Patrol Car Tires
Guide to the Study and Use of Military History
The Hammered Dulcimer in America
Handbook of North American Indians
How Basic Research Reaps Unexpected Rewards

How to Buy a Christmas Tree
Low Cost Wood Homes for Rural America: Construction Manual
The Martian Landscape [with 3-D viewer]
Miro: Selected Paintings
Modern Written Arabic
The Naval War of 1812: A Documentary History (2 vols.)
NOAA Diving Manual
Occupational Diseases: A Guide to Their Recognition
Occupational Outlook Handbook
An Office Building Occupant's Guide to Indoor Air Quality
Polish Genealogy and Heraldry
Protect Your Family from Lead in Your Home
Raising a Small Flock of Sheep
Rotorcraft Flying Handbook
The Science of Fingerprints
ATF Arson Investigative Guide
Selling to the Military
Sex and the Spinal Cord Injured
The Ship's Medicine Chest and Medicine Chest at Sea
Small Scale Beekeeping
Soil Taxonomy
Soldier's Manual and Trainer's Guide: Broadcast Journalist
Special Operations Forces Medical Handbook
A Study of Global Sand Seas
A Study of Lumber Used for Bracing Trenches in the United States
Substance Abuse in Popular Movies & Music
Survival, Evasion, and Escape
The Translation of Poetry
Treaties in Force
Underground Railroad: Official National Park Handbook
Wildlife Portrait Series

Many of these publications are themselves but the tip of a subject iceberg—whenever you find one document on a subject that interests you, you can usually assume that there are many others waiting to be discovered. The Government Printing Office and other federal agencies publish thousands of titles each year. Most, however, do not stay in print indefinitely—as with commercial publications, many are for sale only for a few years, after which they can be found only in libraries' collections of government documents.

If you have not used government documents before, you almost have to make a leap of faith to start looking for them, but the probability is that you will be pleasantly surprised. (Students who use documents will almost invariably find that none of their classmates has found the same sources.)

A number of reasons account for the general neglect of government publications by academic and other researchers; let me extend a few points made at the beginning of this chapter:

- Although government websites are crawled by Internet search engines, they face the customary problem that hits within them are likely to be overlooked because they are crowded out of the first two or three displayed pages.
- Although the government spends millions of dollars a year to publish these materials, it spends comparatively little to advertise them. Some enterprising private companies such as Hein Online and ProQuest republish documents online, with better indexing—which is perfectly allowable, since virtually nothing printed by the GPO or any other federal agency is copyrighted—but such efforts pick up only a fraction of what is available.
- Libraries that own large collections of government documents often shelve them separately rather than integrate them into the general collections. This is done because the best access to documents is provided by their own special indexes and catalogs, which are keyed to Superintendent of Documents (SuDocs) call numbers rather than Library of Congress or Dewey Decimal numbers; and the alphanumeric patterns of SuDocs numbers are such that they cannot be interfiled with such traditional shelf-arrangement schemes. The result is that you will not find documents through two of the major avenues of subject access to the library's books: the computer catalog and shelf browsing. (Even in its own library department a documents collection cannot be browsed very efficiently because the SuDocs scheme arranges items according to the agencies that produced them and not according to the subjects of the documents. This is the difference between an archival scheme of arrangement and a subject classification scheme.)
- Documents are not covered by the most commonly used OPACs, databases, or indexes.
- Documents are not sold in most bookstores and do not usually appear in the popular online services such as Amazon or bn.com.

• Courses in government publications are not required in library schools. One result is that not all librarians themselves are aware of their potential. This is unfortunate for researchers, because you probably won't be referred to documents in the first place unless you chance upon someone with experience in using them.

For those who wish to undertake systematic research in U.S. government documents, there are a variety of databases and printed indexes that have different strengths and weaknesses and that must therefore be used in combination.

Catalog of U.S. Government Publications is searchable at http://catalog.gpo.gov; it includes entries for publications going back to 1976, with hotlinks to full texts (when available). The pre-1976 records will be entered eventually. The same site includes a link to *MetaLib*, which searches additional publications from many other agencies' own websites. The corresponding printed index is the *Monthly Catalog of U.S. Government Publications*, sets of which are still required for searches of the pre-1976 documents. In either format, this is the "umbrella" index to government publications, excluding NTIS reports (for which, see below). For earlier decades of coverage you will want to use the *Cumulative Subject Index to the Monthly Catalog of United States Government Publications 1900–1971* (15 vols., Carrollton Press, 1973–1975) and the *Cumulative Subject Index to United States Government Publications 1895–1899* (2 vols., Carrollton Press, 1977). There is also a *Cumulative Title Index to United States Public Documents 1789–1976* (16 vols., U.S. Historical Documents Institute, 1971–1979) and a *United States Government Publications Monthly Catalog: Cumulative Personal Author Index 1941–1975* (5 vols., Pierian Press, 1971–1979). A cumulative approach through corporate author or agency name is provided by volumes 606–624 of the *National Union Catalog: Pre-1956 Imprints*, which segment has also been republished as a separate set. The *Public Documents Masterfile* from Paratext (below) is particularly good in searching material from these early decades. The *WorldCat* database is also useful, but it does not supersede the printed sources in either coverage or accuracy—the database has some very sloppy, inconsistent, and duplicative records and cannot be relied on for complete coverage of documents. Several other indexes and catalogs for historical approaches are ably discussed in Joe Morehead's *Introduction to United States Government Information Sources* (Libraries Unlimited, 1999), which, admittedly, is becoming dated but which remains the bible for historical searches in documents. A good companion volume is Jean L. Sears and Marilyn K. Moody's *Using Government Information Sources: Electronic and Print*, 3rd ed. (Oryx Press, 2001).

Public Documents Masterfile is a subscription database from Paratext; it indexes the vast majority of U.S. government documents from 1774 to date. It incorporates many of the print sources mentioned above, along with a variety of others:

- *American State Papers* 1789–1838 (full-text links to LC's *American Memory*)
- Ames: *Comprehensive Index to the Publications of the United States Government* 1881–1893
- *Annals of Congress* 1789–1824 (full-text links to LC's *American Memory*)
- *Annual Report of the Smithsonian Institution, Author-Subject* 1848–1961
- *Catalogue of the Public Documents of the 53rd to the 76th Congress* 1893–1940
- *Checklist of United States Public Documents* 1789–1909
- *Compilation of the Messages and Papers of the Presidents* 1789–1897
- *Congressional Globe* 1833–1873 (full-text links to LC's *American Memory*)
- *Cumulative Subject Index to the Monthly Catalog of United States Government Publications* 1895–1976 (Carrollton Press)
- *Cumulative Title Index to the Monthly Catalog of United States Government Publications* 1789–June, 1976
- *ERIC (Educational Resources Information Center) Records* 1965– (with full text links)
- *Farmers Bulletin* 1889–1984
- Greely: *Public Documents of the First Fourteen Congresses* 1789–1817 (full-text links to LC's *American Memory*)
- Hickcox: *Monthly Catalog of U.S. Government Publications* 1885–1894
- *International Public Documents* 1960–
- *Journals of the Continental Congress* 1774–1789
- Maclay: *Sketches of Debate in the First Senate of the United States* 1789–1791
- *Monthly Catalog/Catalog of Government Publications* 1976– (some full-text links)
- *Monthly Catalog Subject Indexes with Page/Entry Numbers* 1895–1976
- Poore: *Descriptive Catalogue of the Government Publications of the United States* Sept. 5, 1774–March 4, 1881
- *Popular Names of U.S. Government Reports* 1821–1981
- *Public Documents Held by the Library of Congress* 1860–
- *U.S. Congressional Serial Set* (Readex) 1817–1994

- *Register of Debates* 1824–1837 (full-text links to LC's *American Memory*)
- *SciTech Connect (Office of Scientific and Technical Information, DOE)* 1943–

Though it is not itself a full-text database, *Public Documents Masterfile* includes links to full texts in Open URLs and in Google Books, as well as links to the Readex subscription database for the full text of the *U.S. Congressional Serial Set* (1817–1994).

ProQuest Congressional: ProQuest now owns Congressional Information Service (CIS), and this database includes all of the CIS indexing of U.S. congressional publications:

- Congressional bills and resolutions (1789–)
- Committee prints and miscellaneous publications (1830–)
- Congressional Record and its predecessors (1789–)
- Congressional Research Service (CRS) reports (1916–) [see Chapter 8]
- Hearings (1824–)
- House and Senate documents (1817–)
- House and Senate reports (1817–)
- Legislative histories (1969–)
- Serial Set maps (1789–)
- Serial Set (1789–)

Statutes at Large (public laws), the *United States Code*, and the *Code of Federal Regulations* are also searchable, as are campaign finance reports, financial disclosures, and personal profiles of Members of Congress. This database, while adding much additional material, is also a cumulation of a variety of print indexes which are likely to be available in many libraries that may not have the online versions:

> ***CIS Index.*** This is the best index to U.S. congressional publications—House and Senate hearings, committee prints, reports, and documents—as well as legislative histories for all Public Laws from 1969 forward.
>
> ***CIS US Congressional Committee Hearings Index***, providing coverage for the years 1833–1969.
>
> ***CIS Index to Unpublished US House of Representatives Committee Hearings***, providing coverage for the years 1833–1968.
>
> ***CIS Index to Unpublished US Senate Committee Hearings***, providing coverage for the years 1823–1976.
>
> ***CIS US Congressional Committee Prints Index***, providing coverage from the early 1800s to 1969.

> *CIS US Serial Set Index*, providing coverage for tens of thousands of miscellaneous congressional reports and documents from 1789 to 1969.
>
> *CIS Index to US Senate Executive Documents and Reports*, providing coverage from 1817 to 1969.

The database version is configured in a way that does not provide a one-to-one correspondence to all of these print indexes, but all of their contents are indeed accessible through one or another of the subscription modules. All of these print indexes are also keyed to microfiche sets of the actual documents, and the full texts of these same documents are also now available in the *ProQuest Congressional* database if libraries choose to subscribe to the full-text modules. (For example, the texts of congressional hearings are in a separate database, **ProQuest Congressional Hearings Digital Collection** [1824–present], and full texts of Congressional Research Service reports are also separate, in **ProQuest Congressional Research Digital Collection** [1830–present]). Remember that not all library subscriptions are identical. But also remember that the printed indexes and microfiche sets of documents are probably still available in libraries that don't have full online access.

ProQuest provides a separate but related database in **ProQuest Legislative Insight**. This is a legislative history source for U.S. public laws at the federal level; its coverage goes far beyond the "Legislative histories" component of *ProQuest Congressional*. It provides full texts of the laws themselves as well as all related documents: related bills, *Congressional Record* sections, hearings, reports, documents, prints, CRS reports, and presidential signing statements (even though courts ignore the latter). About 18,000 histories covering laws as far back as 1929 are included at present; additions will be made both prospectively and retrospectively.

Printed indexes to executive branch publications, with corresponding sets of microfiche documents, are also available:

> *CIS Index to US Executive Branch Documents*, in two sets covering **1789–1909** and **1910–1932**; both cover executive documents not printed in the U.S. Serial Set.
>
> *CIS Index to Presidential Executive Orders and Proclamations*, covering 1789 to 1980.

These two indexes (with microfiche) are not yet digitized.

It will be useful to step back a moment and focus specifically on U.S. congressional committee hearings, because they are very rich sources of information for those researchers who have the initiative to seek them out. The U.S. Congress has an astonishing range of oversight interests and responsibilities that generate detailed inquiries; these investigations monitor all areas of U.S. society and world relations. Most people are aware, simply from newspaper and Web coverage, of Congress's investigations of such specific matters as the Madoff financial scandal, the 2009 Fort Hood shootings, or the BP oil spill and, more generally, hearings held on the progress of various wars, on the federal deficit, Social Security, dependency on foreign oil suppliers, climate change, drug abuse in sports, nuclear plant safety, foreign policy directions, veterans' affairs, and so on; however, the many hearings it conducts on smaller issues are underpublicized and underutilized.

The value of hearings is that they assemble experts and interested parties on all sides of an issue to testify on the current state of the problem and to recommend specific courses of action. (Of course, they can also be manipulated for political purposes. One is reminded of the famous line spoken by Claude Rains in *Casablanca*: "I'm shocked, *shocked*....") Moreover, Congress has the power of subpoena to compel witnesses to appear—a very powerful investigative tool not available to newspaper and media reporters. Hearings frequently include extensive documentary material in appendices in support of witness's testimony—documents that themselves may have been subpoenaed.

The overviews provided by hearings are often not available anywhere else. Some examples of recent hearings include:

For-Profit Colleges
Native Language and Culture-Based Education
Social Media Communications in Disasters
Financial Literacy
Rare and Neglected Pediatric Diseases
Marine Mammals in Captivity: What Constitutes Meaningful Public Education
Smokeless Tobacco: Impact on the Health of Our Nation's Youth and Use in Major League Baseball
Childhood Obesity
Cyprus' Religious Cultural Heritage
Crimes against America's Homeless
Protecting Student Athletes from Concussions
Is Brooklyn Being Counted? Problems with the 2010 Census
China's Policy toward Spiritual Movements
Press Freedom in the Americas
Video Laptop Surveillance

Aggressive Sales Tactics on the Internet
Body Building Products and Hidden Steroids
Contraband Cell Phones in Correctional Facilities
Aquatic Nuisance Species
Religious Organizations and Global Warming
Breeding, Drugs, and Breakdowns: The State of Thoroughbred Horseracing
and the Welfare of the Thoroughbred
Chinese Seafood: Safety and Trade Issues
On Thin Ice: The Future of the Polar Bear
Near-Earth Objects (NEOs)
Sex Crimes and the Internet
Crimes against Americans on Cruise Ships
Review Colony Collapse Disorder in Honey Bee Colonies across the U.S.

Hearings from earlier years include:

Assessing the Impact of Nasal Radium Treatments
Violence in Video Games
Status of the African Elephant
The Nursing Shortage
Methamphetamine and Date Rape Drugs
Mold: A Growing Problem
Under the Influence: The Binge Drinking Epidemic on College Campuses
The Role of Basic Research in Economic Competitiveness
Life on Mars?
Contaminated Frozen Strawberries in School Lunches
Shaping Our Response to Violent and Demeaning Imagery in Popular
Music
Medical and Psychological Impact of Abortion
Samoan White-Collar Crime
Hearing on the Rights of Artists and Scholars to Freedom of Expression
and the Rights of Taxpayers to Determine the Use of Public Funds
Atlantic Swordfish Oversight
Public Safety Issues Surrounding Marijuana Production in National Forests
New Research on the Potential Health Risks of Carpets
Breastfeeding in the U.S.
The Effects of Traffic Radar Guns on Law Enforcement Officers
Sex and Violence on TV
Effect of Pornography on Women and Children

As should be obvious from even these very brief lists, congressional committee hearings provide rich materials for both advanced scholarship and student term papers. Researchers who browse through the listings in either *ProQuest Congressional* or the printed CIS indexes will have an advantage in covering topics that their classmates will overlook entirely. *Thousands* of topics are covered by hearings every year.

ProQuest Statistical Insight. The U.S. federal government is also one of the best sources for statistics on any subject imaginable; even better, ProQuest has combined a thorough index to federal statistics with two other indexes that cover statistics from nonfederal U.S. sources and international organizations. The combined database is *ProQuest Statistical Insight*; it is a merger (and continuation) of three different indexes from CIS:

American Statistics Index (ASI), which is the best index to *every* statistical table, list, or publication from all U.S. federal government sources (executive, legislative, or judicial) since 1973, with full texts online since 2004.

Statistical Reference Index (SRI) covers statistics produced by state and local governments, universities, trade and industry bodies, think tanks, pollsters, and nonprofit organizations. Coverage is from 1980; full texts online from 2007 forward.

International Index to Statistics (IIS) covers sources from the United Nations, European Union, Organization for Economic Cooperation and Development, Organization of American States, and about a hundred other international agencies since 1983, with full texts online from 2007 forward.

These three titles can still be found in print format in many libraries, and they are keyed to microfiche sets of the actual documents they index (not all of which are online). Both the combined database version and the individual print indexes enable you to search by a variety of very useful category indexes (e.g., By Age, By City, By Country, By Disease, By Educational Attainment, By Income, By Individual Company or Institution, By Industry, By Marital Status, By Occupation, By Race and Ethnic Group, By Sex, By State, By ZIP Code), which greatly facilitates finding comparative figures. Through these sources you can find answers to such questions as "What value do consumers place on local newspaper websites?"; "How many Americans use Twitter or other social media sites for political information?"; "What is the level of tomato production in Chile, Italy, or Mexico?"; "How many hours per day do Americans devote to various activities (By Age, By Sex, etc.)?"; "What are the operating performance rankings of the top power plants in the U.S.?"; or "What are the causes of homelessness in various geographical areas?"

ProQuest Government Periodicals Index provides ongoing coverage of more than 160 federal periodicals back to 1988; most of these are not indexed elsewhere. These various *Bulletins, Digests, Journals, Reviews,* and *Quarterlies* provide a good window into the concerns of scores of agencies.

Data-Planet Statistical Datasets is a subscription database that enables users to merge various statistical datasets and interactively create tables, charts, or maps to order. It covers governmental, public domain, and licensed commercial sources. Graphical displays showing such things as these can be created "on the fly" (some of these examples come from the company's promotional material):

- The unemployment rate matched to the prime rate
- Employment data by county
- Federal Assistance Awards under 600 programs by state, county, type of recipient, and program
- The amount of money spent by consumers in Columbia, OH, on their pets
- Graduation rates of athletes, by institution
- Presidential election data at the county level
- Income by zip codes
- Economic stimulus spending under the American Recovery and Reinvestment Act, by type of project, state, county, and zip code.
- Mortgage loan applications and outcomes, by lender, county, census tract, borrower characteristics, reasons for denial.

No other database allows so many different data sets (5,000 and growing) to be crossed, mapped, charted, or graphed against each other.

Statistical Abstract of the United States, an annual volume, is a smorgasbord of statistical information on thousands of subjects—population, births and deaths, marriages, health, education, law, geography, elections, finances and employment, veterans affairs, labor and employment, income, prices, science, agriculture and forestry, environment, energy, construction, trade, transportation, banking, arts and recreation, foreign commerce and aid, and international statistics, all of which topics are but the tips of icebergs of data. From 1878 through 2012 it was published by the U.S. Census Bureau; from 2013 forward, by ProQuest (both print and online via subscription).

NTIS Database (National Technical Information Service): The National Technical Information Service (NTIS) is a federal agency within the U.S. Department of Commerce; its function is to systematically round up and make available to the public all nonclassified federally funded research reports and studies. Most of the studies are not free however;

they must be purchased because NTIS works on a cost-recovery basis. A free *index* to NTIS products is available at www.ntis.gov/search/index.aspx; ProQuest offers the *NTIS Database*, a subscription service for libraries with different indexing capabilities. These indexes cover 2 million research studies in 350 subject areas back to 1946. About 30,000 new reports are added every year.

NTIS studies cover virtually all subject areas in science, technology, and social sciences; there is even surprising coverage in the humanities as well. You can expect to find a government-funded research report on just about anything. There are studies of air pollution, anchor chains, astronomy, chemistry, drug abuse, educational philosophy, environment, energy, food contamination, foreign military forces, Greenland's ice cap, health care, junction transistors, leadership, macaque monkeys, military sciences, money laundering, personnel management, poisonous animals and insects, quark models, rape in the military services, seafloor spreading, sex behavior, terrorism, and garbage collection in Machala, Ecuador. There is even a study of one of Lord Byron's poems—it was done as a master's thesis at one of the military service academies. All master's theses from these academies are included since federal money paid for them. (Studies of Shakespeare and Dickens can also be found here.)

The vast majority of these millions of NTIS reports are not depository items in documents collections. Copies of all documents can be ordered from NTIS. (The Library of Congress is the only library that owns a full set of virtually all NTIS reports, which onsite researchers can read for free.) The **National Technical Reports Library** is a separate subscription database from the NTIS itself; as described earlier, it indexes the same reports but also contains the full texts of more than 700,000 of them.

Digital National Security Archive (ProQuest) is a collection of more than 100,000 declassified documents relating to U.S. foreign and military policy from World War II to the present. The documents are grouped in 40 collections—more are planned—assembled by teams of scholars and experts. The Archive's website lists its current topics of interest:

1. Afghanistan: The Making of U.S. Policy, 1973–1990
2. Argentina, 1975–1980: The Making of U.S. Human Rights Policy
3. The Berlin Crisis, 1958–1962
4. Chile: U.S. Policy toward Democracy, Dictatorship, and Human Rights, 1970–1990
5. China and the United States: From Hostility to Engagement, 1960–1998

6. CIA Covert Operations: From Carter to Obama, 1977–2010
7. Colombia and the United States: Political Violence, Narcotics, and Human Rights, 1948–2010
8. The Cuban Missile Crisis, 1962
9. The Cuban Missile Crisis Revisited: An International Collection of Documents, From the Bay of Pigs to the Brink of Nuclear War
10. Death Squads, Guerrilla War, Covert Operations, and Genocide: Guatemala and the United States, 1954–1999
11. El Salvador: The Making of U.S. Policy, 1977–1984
12. El Salvador: War, Peace, and Human Rights, 1980–1994
13. Iran: The Making of U.S. Policy, 1977–1980
14. The Iran-Contra Affair: The Making of a Scandal
15. Iraqgate: Saddam Hussein, U.S. Policy and the Prelude to the Persian Gulf War, 1980–1994
16. Japan and the United States: Diplomatic, Security, and Economic Relations, 1960–1976
17. Japan and the United States: Diplomatic, Security, and Economic Relations, Part II, 1977–1992
18. Japan and the United States: Diplomatic, Security, and Economic Relations, Part III, 1961–2000
19. The Kissinger Telephone Conversations: A Verbatim Record of U.S. Diplomacy, 1969–1977
20. The Kissinger Transcripts: A Verbatim Record of U.S. Diplomacy, 1969–1977
21. The National Security Agency: Organization and Operations, 1945–2009
22. Nicaragua: The Making of U.S. Policy, 1978–1990
23. Peru: Human Rights, Drugs and Democracy, 1980–2000
24. The Philippines: U.S. Policy during the Marcos Years, 1965–1986
25. Presidential Directives on National Security from Harry Truman to William Clinton (Part I)
26. Presidential Directives on National Security from Harry Truman to George W. Bush (Part II)
27. South Africa: The Making of U.S. Policy, 1962–1989
28. The Soviet Estimate: U.S. Analysis of the Soviet Union, 1947–1991
29. Terrorism and U.S. Policy, 1968–2002
30. The United States and the Two Koreas from Nixon to Clinton (1969–2000)
31. U.S. Espionage and Intelligence, 1947–1996

32. U.S. Intelligence and China: Collection, Analysis, and Covert Action
33. The U.S. Intelligence Community after 9/11
34. The U.S. Intelligence Community, 1947–1989
35. U.S. Intelligence on Weapons of Mass Destruction: From World War II to Iraq
36. U.S. Military Uses of Space, 1945–1991
37. U.S. Nuclear History: Nuclear Arms and Politics in the Missile Age, 1955–1968
38. U.S. Nuclear Non-Proliferation Policy, 1945–1991
39. U.S. Policy in the Vietnam War, Part I: 1954–1968
40. U.S. Policy in the Vietnam War, Part II: 1969–1975

The individual collections usually contain thousands of pages of primary source material obtained from the federal government through Freedom of Information requests. The National Security Archive itself is a nongovernmental organization with offices in Washington, DC; it has much more material available to onsite researchers than is available digitally. Further information is available at its website, www.gwu.edu/~nsarchiv/index.html.

Declassified Documents Reference System (Gale) is a subscription database with full texts of more than 75,000 previously classified government documents obtained from presidential libraries. Coverage is primarily from post–World War II through the 1970s—i.e., the Cold War and Vietnam War eras—but there is also some earlier and later material. Foreign and domestic events (e.g., the civil rights and anti-war movements) are covered. The database's self-description lists the following types of material covered:

- National Security Council policy statements and memoranda and meeting materials
- CIA intelligence memoranda and studies
- Presidential and cabinet correspondence
- White House Confidential File materials
- Trade treaties, studies and analyses
- Cabinet meeting materials and correspondence
- Presidential conferences and visits
- FBI surveillance and intelligence correspondence and memoranda
- Joint Chiefs of Staff papers
- U.S. government analyses and studies on international socioeconomic issues
- U.S. briefing materials for meetings with foreign heads of state and government officials

- FBI documents on American political personalities, events, and crises
- Full texts of letters, instructions, and cables sent and received by U.S. diplomatic personnel

Maps, charts, and aerial photographs: the federal government produces thousands of such materials; the best overview is the website www.usa.gov/Topics/Maps.shtml. (See also Chapter 14.)

Foreign Broadcast Information Service (FBIS) Daily Reports, 1974–1996 (ProQuest) and *Dialog Professional* (ProQuest), which includes the former *World News Connection* (1994–), are two full-text subscription databases providing English language translations of foreign newspapers, periodicals, and broadcast media.

How to Get It: A Guide to Defense-Related Information Sources is a 500-page directory last published in print in 1998; it is freely available online at www.dtic.mil/dtic/tr/fulltext/u2/a346513.pdf. It is occasionally extremely useful if you need to identify and locate old federal documents. It is especially good at explaining report numbers—if all you have is a citation with such a number, this guide will tell you what the number means, which agency produced it, and whom to contact for a copy of the report. The contacts listed in a 1998 volume are, of course, frequently outdated, but if you have the name of the older agency you can often find its current incarnation via the Web.

Index to Current Urban Documents (ILM Corporation) is, according to its website www.urbdocs.com, a subscription database that "contains more than 31,000 reports generated by local government agencies, civic organizations, academic and research organizations, public libraries, and metropolitan and regional planning agencies from more than 500 major cities in the United States and Canada." The core collection is made up of fiscal (budget and financial reports) and architecture and planning documents at the city, county, and regional levels. The *Index* also provides information for "all urban-related issues, from hazardous waste disposal to arts in the community." The database currently includes indexing and full texts from 2000 forward; retrospective coverage back to 1972 is provide by the printed *Index to Current Urban Documents*; the corresponding documents are in a microfiche set.

The Complete Guide to Citing Government Information Resources, 3rd ed. (Congressional Information Service, 2002), is a useful supplement to the standard style manuals, many of which do not adequately deal with government documents.

All in all, documents are much like other special collections in that, usually, you just have to make a leap of faith into the various sources that index them. If you lack prior experience in this area, it probably won't occur to you to think of such sources at all, and yet they cover as many subjects, in as much depth, as the more widely known databases and indexes. Most researchers who venture into this territory are surprisingly well rewarded for their efforts.

ARCHIVES, MANUSCRIPTS, AND PUBLIC RECORDS

Unpublished primary sources fall into two classes: archives or manuscript collections that have been assembled in special historical repositories, and sources that are still with the people or agencies that originally created or received the records. Many primary sources, including manuscripts, have now been published and can be identified through the usual library search mechanisms for published material, whether in printed, microform, or online formats. Many "documentary editions" of important American individuals and organizations published by the National Historical Publications and Records Commission and others are listed at:

www.archives.gov/nhprc/projects/publishing/catalog.pdf
www.archives.gov/nhprc/projects/publishing/alpha.html
www.archives.gov/nhprc/projects/statesterritories/http://
documentaryediting.org/projects/editions.html

The focus of this section, however, will be primarily on identifying *un*-published sources.

Research in archives or historical manuscript collections is, in several important ways, unlike research in books or journals in libraries (although databases containing previously unpublished manuscripts tend to blur the lines). Sources within conventional libraries—e.g., books—are comparatively well cataloged and indexed, and there is subject access to each individual item. This is usually not the case with unpublished manuscript or archival sources—there may be broad subject access (via a "finding aid" to a collection) to boxes or folders of items, but not specific subject access to the individual papers or documents within the containers. One reason for this is that many unpublished sources are meaningful only within the context of the other items in the group in which they are stored. Another reason is that the preparation of finding aids to manuscript collections is very labor intensive—the basic sorting of an individual's papers may take months in itself—and so archivists cannot spend the time needed to describe and catalog each of the individual letters, notes, or other papers within a collection.

The strategy for working with such materials involves, broadly speaking, three levels of searching:

1. Identifying relevant collections.
2. Examining manuscript registers/finding aids, or archival inventories, for the particular groups documents you wish to examine. These will provide at least a listing, with or without annotations, of folders or boxes within collections but, again, not to the individual items. The finding aids themselves will tend to be arranged according to the original order in which the collections were assembled by their creators, or they may be arranged chronologically if the archivists had to create their own order from an unsorted mass of manuscripts. Many finding aids are now digitized online (see below); many others exist only as printed guides, available only onsite at the locations of the physical collections.
3. Browsing through the actual documents. In the physical repositories that you may have to visit, the documents will be grouped according to who wrote or received them or which agency produced them—often regardless of what the subject(s) of the individual paper(s) may be. In online collections, you may be able to search either finding aids or actual documents, depending on the coverage or indexing practice of the particular database.

At the first level of searching, several specific free websites, subscription databases, and printed guides will help you to identify which collections exist, and where they are located.

National Union Catalog of Manuscript Collections (NUCMC) (pronounced "nuckmuck" by librarians) began in 1959 as an ongoing set of printed volumes, published by the Library of Congress, identifying whose unpublished papers are located in which repositories in the United States. The printed set of 29 volumes ceased publication in 1993; it lists approximately 72,300 collections in more than 1,400 repositories. Entries after 1993 were folded into the *WorldCat* database—but *WorldCat* extended its coverage of *NUCMC* entries retrospectively back to 1986. Thus, the *NUCMC* entries from 1959 through 1985 are not digitized in *WorldCat* (although they are in *Archive Finder*). Manuscript records in *WorldCat* are not confined to those reported by repositories in the United States; coverage now extends throughout the world, although North American collections predominate. The *NUCMC* database (a subset of *WorldCat*) can be searched freely at www.loc.gov/coll/nucmc/oclcsearch.html; this online version includes approximately 116,000 collections in 1,800 repositories.

Chadwyck-Healey has published two cumulative printed indexes to most of the older, printed *NUCMC* volumes: *Index to Personal Names in the National Union Catalog of Manuscript Collections, 1959–1984* (2 vols., 1988) and *Index to Subjects and Corporate Names in the National Union Catalog of Manuscript Collections, 1959–1984* (3 vols., 1994).

Archive Finder is a subscription database from ProQuest; it is an index to well over 200,000 collections of manuscripts and primary source materials in more than 5,600 repositories in the United States, the United Kingdom, and Ireland. The database includes all the entries in the printed *NUCMC* back to 1959. (It does not have all of the additional OCLC coverage, however.) In addition, it provides name and subject indexing of 72,000 collections whose finding aids are published in a separate, ongoing microfiche set, the *National Inventory of Documentary Sources in the United States*; and also indexing of the 47,000 collections whose finding aids appear in another ongoing microfiche set, the *National Inventory of Documentary Sources in the United Kingdom and Ireland* (see below for descriptions). Links to the full texts of more than 6,000 finding aids are included. Additional reports of collections are included insofar as repositories choose to send them in.

ArchiveGrid is a subscription database available from OCLC; its contents are not included in *WorldCat*. It is an index to nearly a million collections of personal papers, historical collections, and family histories held in thousands of repositories around the world. It includes the texts of about 50,000 finding aids from about 200 of the contributing institutions. Its coverage overlaps with *Archive Finder*, but *ArchiveGrid* covers additional collections and also provides those full texts of finding aids.

Repositories of Primary Sources is a free website maintained by the University of Idaho. (Its URL has changed over the years, but it can be found easily via Google or Bing by typing its name in quotation marks.) It is a listing of 5,000 websites that describe holdings of archives, manuscripts, historical photographs, and primary sources from all over the world. It is arranged (and searchable) only by geographical location, not by subjects or individuals' names—i.e., you cannot search all 5,000 collections simultaneously, looking for a particular needle in the haystack.

Archives Library Information Center is a free website maintained by the National Archives at www.archives.gov/research/alic/reference/state-archives.html. It provides directory information with links and other contact information for all state-level archives in the United States.

SearchSystems *Free Public Records* (http://publicrecords.search-systems.net/) is a listing of 55,000 websites for public records from U.S., Canadian, and some other countries' agencies. (You have to be careful here—there are many advertisement links to fee-based sites. But the original website at least provides direct contact information for the various records offices.)

Although Google, Bing, Yahoo!, and Wikipedia are not the emphasis of this book, they are all sometimes very useful for finding locations for manuscript collections of either individuals or organizations (e.g., search for "Firstname Lastname" and "archives" or "papers" or "collection").

In addition to websites and subscription databases, a number of printed sources are often quite useful in manuscript or archival sleuthing; some have online subscription versions. Several relevant printed directories have been mentioned already in the section in Chapter 11 on "Determining Which Libraries Have Special Collections on Your Subject." (Clear lines cannot be drawn regarding libraries' special collections: they may be composed primarily of books or manuscripts—or other formats [maps, photographs, etc.]—or they may include multiple forms, both published and unpublished).

If you are trying to locate someone's unpublished papers and you cannot find them in *NUCMC* or *WorldCat* or *Archive Finder*, you still have several other sources to check—sources that usually work. *American National Biography*, both in print and in a subscription database (Oxford University Press; www.anb.org), is the standard biographical encyclopedia for prominent deceased Americans; its individual articles always contain a bibliography of sources on the person, and these bibliographies will identify where the person's papers are located (if they exist). (A major collection of the papers of Member of Congress Edith Green [1910–1987], for example, is recorded in *American National Biography* but is not listed in either *NUCMC* or *Archive Finder*.) A similar situation exists with the *Oxford Dictionary of National Biography* (Oxford University Press, www.oxforddnb.com), also available in print or online; it covers British and Canadian individuals and others connected to the British Empire.

Another excellent source for locating the papers of individuals (and some corporate bodies) is the ongoing *Dictionary of Literary Biography* (Gale). It currently has more than 370 volumes covering authors worldwide, from all time periods, as well as associated subjects (collectors, publishing houses, etc.). Each article within the set identifies where the papers of the subject are located. A subscription version is also available, as either *Dictionary of Literary Biography* or *Dictionary of Literary Biography Complete Online*—the latter also includes the texts of the extra printed sets *Dictionary of Literary Biography Yearbook* (ca. 23 vols.) and *Dictionary of Literary Biography Documentary Series* (ca. 50 vols.). This *Documentary* set reprints primary source documents. (Volume 263 of the "regular" *DLB* series is *William Shakespeare, A Life Record: A Documentary Volume*; this is the best compilation, at more than 300 pages, ever assembled of primary sources on The Bard.)

Two older British publications are still useful. The *Index of English Literary Manuscripts* (Mansell/Bowker) is a listing of authors and manuscript locations; Volume 1 covers 1450 to 1625; Volume 2, 1625 to 1700; Volume 3, 1700 to 1800; Volume 4, 1800 to 1900. The second is *Location Register of Twentieth-Century English Literary Manuscripts and Letters: A Union List of Papers of Modern English, Irish, Scottish, and Welsh Authors in the British Isles*, 2 vols. (G. K. Hall, 1988).

For access to unpublished U.S. federal agency records, which often include individuals' papers, the best starting point is the website of the National Archives and Records Administration (NARA) at www.archives .gov. A set of printed volumes, the *Guide to the Federal Records in the National Archives of the United States*, 3 vols. (National Archives and Records Administration, 1995), is available in many libraries; it is also online, with updates at www.archives.gov/research/guide-fed-records/. The *Guide* describes the various Record Groups held by the National Archives; these groups of government "filing cabinet" records are arranged not by the subject of the individual documents but rather according to the agency or bureau that produced them. If you wish to find out which agencies' records have material on your subject, the NARA website will certainly be of use, but you also have to use some imagination in thinking of how the federal government would have become involved with your area of interest, for (with some exceptions) there aren't any subject or name indexes to the records. For this reason alone your best access will come from working with the archivists, who will have a better sense of what types of things, or whose papers, can be found in the various agencies' documents. This same rule applies at other repositories: use the expertise of the staff as much as you can and be sure that they understand clearly—and not just in vague, general terms—what you are *ultimately* trying to research. Although many guides to archival and manuscript collections are now appearing on the Web, and in subscription databases, direct contact with the archivists onsite is still a very important element in this kind of research.

The British equivalent of NARA is the National Archives, holding official governmental records for England, Wales, and the United Kingdom; this agency combines the former Public Records Office and the Historical Manuscripts Commission. Its website is www.nationalarchives.gov.uk. The National Archives of Ireland's site is www.nationalarchives.ie/; the site for Scotland is www.nas.gov.uk.

The second level of searching is done through archival inventories or manuscript registers; usually these are locally produced finding aids. Each will describe a particular collection with an introductory note followed by a listing of the collection's contents down to the box or folder level. Most of these inventories and registers are themselves unpublished, although there is now an effort among major archives to put their finding aids online. The largest online source with full texts of finding aids is *ArchiveGrid*, but again, Google, Bing, Yahoo!, and Wikipedia are also useful. An excellent printed list of finding aids can be found in Donald L. De-Witt's 479-page *Guide to Archives and Manuscript Collections in the United States: An Annotated Bibliography* (Greenwood Press, 1994); it lists more than 2,000 inventories, checklists, and registers (at this second level), as well as repository guides at the first level. (Many of these have been digitized since the appearance of this book.) DeWitt has also compiled the 459-page *Articles Describing Archives and Manuscript Collections in the United States: An Annotated Bibliography* (Greenwood Press, 1997). Each volume has an excellent subject index, and together they may bring to your attention many collections and articles describing them in depth that you would not find through web searches.

Chadwyck-Healey, a subsidiary of ProQuest, publishes ongoing microfiche collections of the finding aids of a variety of manuscript collections in the United Statesand the the United Kingdom. All of these finding aids are *indexed* in the *Archive Finder* database, but (as of this writing) the full texts of the guides themselves are available only in the microfiche collections. The U.S. set is the *National Inventory of Documentary Sources in the United States*, which has three components: Part 1, *Federal Records* (including the National Archives, Presidential Libraries, and Smithsonian Institution Archives); Part 2, *Manuscript Division, Library of Congress*; and Part 3, *State Archives, State Libraries, State Historical Societies, Academic Libraries and Other Repositories*. (Note that the holdings of the National Archives, and of the many state archives, are not covered by NUCMC.) The British microfiche set is the *National Inventory of Documentary Sources in the United Kingdom and Ireland*, containing more than 14,000 unpublished finding aids from more than 120 libraries and records offices. These sets do not publish the actual manuscripts located in these repositories (either U.S. or U.K.); rather they give you the finding aids and manuscript registers *of* the collections. Some of the same finding aids that are published in these Chadwyck-Healey microfiche sets are now directly searchable on the websites of the various repositories themselves.

As helpful as the inventories and registers may be, only at the third level of research—reading through the documents themselves—can you really know what is in a collection. Although much manuscript material is being published online through repositories' websites, the vast majority of manuscript material can be read only onsite when you actually visit the particular collection that interests you. The reason for this is that copyright restrictions apply to unpublished manuscripts as well as to books (with the exception of most records produced by government agencies); legal restrictions prohibit the wholesale republication of most manuscripts. So you still have to go, in many cases, to physical repositories. And you cannot do archival or manuscript research quickly; you must be prepared for much browsing and many dead ends before you come to any nuggets. Plan your time accordingly.

If you do plan a site visit, it is especially important to read as many secondary or published sources as you can on your subject *before* you look into the unpublished sources. The reason is that the latter, unlike book collections, are—again!—not cataloged or arranged by subject. This means that you will have to have in advance a rather clear idea of what you are looking for in order to recognize it when you're browsing. It is especially useful to know the names of any people connected with your area of interest; names are easy to look for in records. If you are planning a research trip, it is a good idea to e-mail or write the archives in advance, stating what you are interested in and asking for suggestions on what to read before you come in personally. Advance contact with the local archivists is highly desirable for other reasons as well: some collections may be stored offsite and entail delayed retrieval, and some may have restrictions on access requiring written permissions. There may also be local restrictions on photocopying, scanning, or digital photography; it is best to find these things out before a visit.

Once you are at the repository and are looking through the boxes or folders of manuscripts and documents, it is essential that you use only one file folder of material at a time within a box, maintain the order of the folders within a given box, and carefully preserve the original order of manuscripts as you find them within each folder. Always replace in correct order any individual item you remove to photocopy or photograph, and never mix items from various boxes or folders. The individual papers are not individually cataloged or recorded, so if you misplace an item it may be permanently lost for other researchers. Remember, too, to make a careful record in your notes of the box and folder title or number in which the documents are located within a collection. A good pattern is: Container number, Collection title, Repository division, Repository name. (This is *very* important—my colleagues in Manuscripts tell me that people frequently forget where they saw something and then often have to make a special return trip to check a citation, especially when they have used a lot of collections in many repositories.)

As with the other two levels, some of this third-level material—the actual records, not just finding aids—is now appearing on the Internet. An example is the *Online Archive of California*, a site that leads to tens of thousands of digital images of primary sources on the history of that state, at www.oac.cdlib.org.

Research in public records—those that are still with the agency that produced or collected them and not yet sent to an archival repository—is another very valuable avenue of inquiry for studying individuals, businesses, and government itself. A good guide to finding such records is *The Investigative Reporter's Handbook: A Guide to Documents, Databases, and Techniques* by Brian Houston and Investigative Reporters and Editors, Inc., 5th ed. (Bedford/St. Martin's, 2009).

Other useful sources for locating manuscript or archival records are discussed in Chapter 14 in the sections on Biography, Business Sources, Genealogy and Local History, and Primary Sources.

It should be obvious at this point that few researchers would get very far into special collections (subscription databases, free websites, or microforms), government documents, or archival/manuscript sources if left only to the most widely used Web search engines or the most popular subscription databases—you must actively seek out these collections. This will often mean making a leap of faith that the effort will be worthwhile, but you should give it a try anyway—the results could be spectacular.

CHAPTER 14

Special Subjects and Formats

ALTHOUGH THE VARIOUS GENERAL METHODS OF SEARCHING discussed so far are all applicable in any subject area, some topics present unusually complex arrays of research materials and require more particular overviews of individual sources. Those discussed in this chapter have proved themselves useful in providing answers to many specialized inquiries.

BIOGRAPHY

Two excellent starting points for biographical information on individuals, prominent or obscure, living or dead, worldwide, are *Biography and Genealogy Master Index* and *Biography in Context*. Both are subscription databases from Gale Cengage. The former is a cumulative index to more than 13.6 million biographical sketches in more than 1,600 biographical dictionaries and "Who's Who"–type publications, with hundreds of thousands of new citations added each year. It is not a full-text database, but if you have a person's name it will tell you where he or she is written up. (A printed set of this *Index*, with ongoing supplements, also exists.) *Biography in Context*, in contrast, is a full-text database with actual biographical articles; but it is much smaller in scope. Its articles are taken from more than 350 periodicals and newspapers and more than 170 reference sources.

EBSCO offers two important biographical databases. *Biography Past and Present* is a combination of indexes formerly produced by the H. W. Wilson Company, covering more than a million biographical articles, books, obituaries, memoirs, interviews, and other sources back to 1946. *Biography Reference Bank* is an index and full-text source providing online versions of *Current Biography, World Authors,* and the biographical content of *Junior Authors & Illustrators,* as well as indexing of other sources.

World Biographical Information System (De Gruyter) is another subscription database indexing all of the individual names in thousands of old biographical encyclopedias and other reference works; it is especially strong in its coverage of foreign-language sources. It currently lists information on more than 6 million people from the eighth century B.C. to the present, with 8.5 million full-text articles from a wide range of national/ethnic *Biographical Archive* indexes that are available individually, with corresponding microfiche sets. (These microfiche sets provide the full texts for the database, but not all of the fiche sets have yet been digitized.) These sets (in both printed and database formats) include the following:

African Biographical Archive
American Biographical Archive
Arab-Islamic Biographical Archive
Archives Biographiques Françaises
Achivio Biografico Italiano
Archivo Biográfico de España, Portugal e Iberoamérica
Australasian Biographical Archive
Baltisches Biographisches Archiv
Biografisch Archief van de Benelux
Biographical Archive of the Middle Ages
Biographisches Archiv der Antike
Biographisches Archiv des Christentums
British Biographical Archive
Canadian Biographical Archive
Cesky biograficky archive a Slovensky biograficky archive
Chinese Biographical Archive
Deutsches Biographisches Archiv
Griechisches Biographisches Archiv
Indian Biographical Archive
Japanese Biographical Archive
Jüdisches Biographisches Archiv
Korean Biographical Archive
Polskie Archiwum Biograficzne
Russisches Biographisches Archiv und Biographisches Archiv der Sowjetunion
Scandinavian Biographical Archive

South-East Asian Biographical Archive
Südosteuropäisches Biographisches Archiv
Türkisches Biographisches Archiv
Ungarisches Biographisches Archiv

A full subscription to the *World Biographical Archive* database would search all of these at the same time; it enables you to search not just by the name of an individual but also by years of birth or death, and by individual occupations or subjects (using all of the variant language terms in the particular sets) or broad occupational classifications (using English language categorizations). The searchable subjects include terms such as "murder victim," "accomplice to murder," "fire-eater," "photographer," and "embezzler"; the indexing terms, however, are not applied consistently or uniformly.

There are, of course, many free biographical websites beyond Wikipedia and Biography.com; a good overview of the others can be found at the *Internet Public Library* www.ipl.org; just type "biography" into the search box. *Refdesk* also points to many free websites at www.refdesk.com/factbiog.html.

The standard biographical encyclopedia for biographies of deceased Americans is *American National Biography* (Oxford University Press), which exists both as a multivolume print set and as a subscription database (www.anb.org). Its predecessor, the printed *Dictionary of American Biography* (*DAB*) (Scribners, 1928–1996), is not superseded, however, since it has many biographies not picked up or revised by the later set. The *DAB* is full-text available in *Biography in Context*. The comparable (although much larger) biographical encyclopedia for deceased individuals from the British Isles, or those who lived in territories formerly connected to the Empire (and some others connected to Britain), is the *Oxford Dictionary of National Biography*, which is also available both in print and online via subscription (www.oxforddnb.com). (The British encyclopedia includes even legendary figures such as King Arthur and Robin Hood.) Both the American and British databases can be searched by occupations, realms of renown, or fields of interest as well as by sex, ethnicity, religious affiliation, and so on. Cambridge University Press produces a comparable 9-volume *Dictionary of Irish Biography*.

The *National Cyclopedia of American Biography* (James T. White Co., 1892–1984) is a 63-volume set that is especially good for picking up noteworthy people who are otherwise neglected by history books (e.g., business executives, lawyers, military officers, clergy). The articles are based on questionnaires sent to the families of the subjects, or to the subjects themselves, so they should generally be regarded as authorized or approved by the biographees. Not all of the names in the *National Cyclopaedia* are directly indexed in *Biography and Genealogy Master Index*— the latter, however, indexes *Biography Index*, which in turn indexes the *National Cyclopaedia*. What that means in plain English is that you cannot rely on *Biography and Genealogy Master Index* to provide direct references to all of the *Cyclopaedia* articles; if you are looking for an American, you still have to check the printed *Index* volume of the *Cyclopaedia*.

If these sources don't cover the individuals you want, the many full-text databases of newspapers are often useful; they frequently contain not just obituaries but regular articles containing information of biographical interest. Genealogical databases and websites are also useful. (See the Genealogy and Local History and Newspapers sections below.) The large, foreign-language national encyclopedias of various countries can also turn up biographical information not accessible elsewhere.

Another good source is Robert B. Slocum's two-volume *Biographical Dictionaries and Related Works* (Gale Research, 1986, 2nd ed.), which is well described by its subtitle: *An International Bibliography of More Than 16,000 Collective Biographies, Bio-bibliographies, Collections of Epitaphs, Selected Genealogical Works, Dictionaries of Anonyms and Pseudonyms, Historical and Specialized Dictionaries, Biographical Materials in Government Manuals, Bibliographies of Biography, Biographical Indexes, and Selected Portrait Catalogs.* Each entry is annotated, and all are categorized by country/subdivision and by vocational area. This set can alert you to biographical dictionaries not indexed by either *Biography and Genealogy Master Index* or *World Biographical Information System*.

Old city directories, such as those published by the R. L. Polk Company, can sometimes be used to construct mini-biographies of individuals. Among the questions they can often answer are: Is the individual married? If so, what is the spouse's name? If a widow, what was the husband's name? Who else resides at the same address? Who are the neighbors? What is the individual's occupation, and where is he or she employed? Is the individual a "head of house" or a resident? Retrospective searching of earlier volumes can also indicate how long an individual has been employed at a job, what his previous jobs or business associations were, how long the person has resided at an address, who were previous neighbors, and so on. (Researchers who want to milk old directories to the last drop should study pages 158–160 of Harry J. Murphy's *Where's What: Sources of Information for Federal Investigators* [Quadrangle/New York Times Book Company, 1976]; Murphy quotes a previous publication listing about 50 questions that the old city directories can answer.) The drawback is that Polk directories are no longer published for large cities; they are mainly good for small towns and suburbs—or for older decades of the large cities. The various directories now published tend to be strictly "criss-cross": you have to start out with either a phone number or an address, and the directory will give you the names connected with either (without any biographical or occupational information). Note that Google offers somewhat similar capabilities for current phone numbers, although, as of this writing, the service is usually clogged with unwanted advertisements and commercial sites. The subscription databases *Reference USAGov* (InfoUSA) and *Mergent Intellect* (Mergent) provide excellent criss-cross information without all the clutter.

BOOK REVIEWS

Many book reviews lie beyond the coverage of Amazon.com. Virtually all of the commercially available databases that cover journal articles—whether from ProQuest, EBSCO, Gale, Thomson Reuters, et al.—have search features that enable you to "limit" your search to only book review formats. Many of these same databases provide full texts of the reviews themselves. *Book Review Digest Plus* (EBSCO) is a popular source among students; it covers all of the reviews picked up by more than 5,000 journals since 1983 (more than 2 million citations, with more than 270,000 full text). *Book Review Index Retrospective* extends coverage back to 1905 (with fewer sources covered in these earlier decades). *Book Review Index Online* (Gale) indexes more than 5 million reviews of more than 2.5 million book titles as far back as 1965, with links to hundreds of thousands of the reviews in full text.

A good source for older book reviews (going back more than a hundred years) is *Periodicals Index Online*, indexing more than 6,000 periodicals back to the seventeenth century. Retrospective decades are also covered by the *Science Citation Index* (1900–) and *Social Sciences Citation Index* (1900–), both of which are included in *Web of Science*—if libraries choose to subscribe to these components. (The *Arts & Humanities* component of the *Web* goes back only to 1975.) They not only cover book reviews directly, they enable you to see if any book has been cited in the footnotes of any of the thousands of journals covered. Some of these citations may provide substantive discussions of a book, even if not formally a "book review" of it.

In earlier discussions I warned about overreliance on federated or "discovery" searching of multiple databases at the same time, because many of the files may use entirely different subject descriptor terms, but searches for book reviews are a good use of federated search capabilities, whether in ProQuest, EBSCO, Gale, or other aggregations of databases.

For scholarly purposes the *IBR-Online* (De Gruyter) subscription database is good for identifying reviews in multiple languages worldwide in social sciences and humanities fields. The electronic version indexes reviews in more than 6,800 journals back to 1985; the printed version *Internationale Bibliographie der Rezensionen wissenschaftlicher Literatur/International bibliography of book reviews of scholarly literature* goes back to 1971.

Two excellent sources for scholarly reviews of older books are the printed sets *Combined Retrospective Index to Book Reviews in Scholarly Journals 1886–1974*, 15 vols. (Carrollton Press, 1979–1982) and *Combined Retrospective Index to Book Reviews in Humanities Journals 1902–1974*, 10 vols. (Research Publications, 1982–1984). To date, neither is available online. I have found many reviews listed in these two sets that I could not identify in any database.

Note that book reviews are generally not the best sources for students who want literary criticism or scholarly analyses of individual books, stories, plays, or poems. This is because such reviews are always contemporary with the first publication of the sources that are reviewed and usually lack historical perspective. (See the section on Literary Criticism, below.)

BUSINESS SOURCES

The Web is now the first place to check for at least basic information about individual companies, nonprofits, organizations, or industries, since so many corporate bodies maintain their own websites. These are other good starting points, however, beyond such individual sites, for providing overviews of Internet resources:

- *Business Reference Services* is a free website maintained by the Science, Technology and Business Division of the Library of Congress at www.loc.gov/rr/business. A subsection listing many free Internet resources, by titles and subject, is at www.loc.gov/rr/business/beonline/beohome.html.
- *Internet Public Library* at www.ipl.org provides another good list of free websites in its "Business and Economics" section.
- Rutgers University Library maintains a website listing business information resources, some of which are available only to Rutgers students, but also including about 3,000 Internet sites available to anyone. The website is at http://libguides.rutgers.edu/business.

In spite of the myriad business information sources on the free Internet, the best sources are provided by subscription databases available only through libraries. Among these are the following:

ABI/INFORM Complete (ProQuest), ***Business Abstracts with Full Text*** (EBSCO), and ***Business Source Complete*** (EBSCO) are three of the best databases with full-text articles from business journals and other sources. See the descriptions in Chapter 4.

ALA Guide to Business and Economics Reference (American Library Association, 2011; ca. 500 pages) is another printed volume that provides a good starting point for business inquiries. It lists and minutely categorizes both Internet and print sources and provides directory information on organizations and associations.

Business Monitor International (Business Monitor International) is a huge subscription database covering tens of thousands of full-text business sources. It can be searched by country, by market, by company, or by industry. The 179 country reports provide political, economic, outlook, and SWOT (strengths, weaknesses, opportunities, and threats) analyses. Market reports are frequently more than a hundred pages long. Company reports focus on multinational enterprises. Rankings of industries and 5- and 10-year forecasts are included.

Encyclopedia of Business Information Sources (Gale, annual) is one of the directories included in the *Gale Directory Library* database; it also exists in a printed volume form that is in some ways easier to look through. It is a listing of electronic and print sources, websites, and people contacts listed alphabetically under more than 1,100 very specific subjects, such as:

> Advertising Specialties, Building Materials Industry, Chemical Marketing, Dismissal of Employees, Economic Indicators, Financial Ratios, Grocery Business, Honey Industry, International Monetary Fund, Job Hunting, Knit Goods Industry, Landscape Architecture, Men's Clothing Industry, Narcotics, Office Furniture Industry, Packaging, Quality Control, Relocation of Employees, Sexual Harassment in the Workplace, Technology Transfer, Uniforms, Vending Machines, Women's Clubs, Yarn, and Zoning. Under each heading, insofar as sources are available, the following are listed: General Works, Abstracts and Indexing Services, Almanacs and Yearbooks, Bibliographies, Biographical Sources, CD-ROMs, Directories, Encyclopedias and Dictionaries, Financial Ratios, Handbooks and Manuals, Internet Databases, Online [i.e., subscription] Databases, Periodicals and Newsletters, Price Sources, Research Centers and Institutes, Statistics Sources, Trade and Professional Associations, and Other Sources.

Phone numbers, web URLs, and e-mail addresses are usually provided. This *Encyclopedia* is often a good starting point for getting an overview of important resources in any area of business, even at very specific levels—something that is often hard to see when one goes directly to the large business databases.

Gale Business Insights: Global (Gale) is a subscription database covering more than 7,000 business magazines, journals, and newsletters (with full texts of most) and a variety of other sources including millions of investment research and brokerage reports. Domestic and international companies and associations are covered. The database's self-description lists its features:

- More than 2 million investment research/brokerage reports
- Thousands of detailed financial reports (including fundamentals data and comparison tools)
- More than 1,200 business executive video interviews for classroom learning
- More than 1,000 unrestricted case studies
- More than 2,500 market research reports
- Hundreds of country economic reports
- More than 1,000 SWOT reports (updated quarterly)
- More than 3,500 full-text periodicals
- Nearly 25,000 industry reports
- Nearly 11,000 company histories published by Gale (*International Directory of Company Histories*)
- More than 43,400 articles from *Market Share Reporter* published by Gale
- More than 65,000 articles from *Business Rankings Annual* published by Gale
- More than 2,200 corporate chronologies
- More than 2,000 additional reference articles published by Gale
- Nearly 70,000 associations
- Thousands of interactive live charts for economic and business indicators
- 193 detailed country profiles (with deep links to related content and statistical data)
- Nearly 500,000 detailed company profiles (with deep links to related content and statistical data)
- More than 600 in-depth industry profiles (with deep links to related content and statistical data)

Gale Directory Library (Gale Cengage) is a composite subscription database that searches all of 16 different Gale directories, singly or in combination:

- *Consultants and Consulting Organizations Directory*
- *Directories in Print*
- *Directory of Special Libraries and Information Centers*
- *Encyclopedia of Associations—International Organizations*
- *Encyclopedia of Associations—National Organizations of the U.S.*
- *Encyclopedia of Associations—Regional, State and Local Organizations of the U.S.*
- *Encyclopedia of Business Information Sources*
- *Encyclopedia of Government Advisory Organizations*
- *Gale Directory of Databases*
- *Gale Directory of Publications and Broadcast Media*
- *Government Research Directory*
- *International Research Centers Directory*
- *National Directory of Nonprofit Organizations*
- *Publishers Directory*
- *Research Centers Directory*
- *Ward's Business Directory of U.S. Private and Public Companies*

An interesting feature of this database is that it also enables you to search backfile editions of these directories, if that component of the database has been purchased by your library.

Hoover's (Dun & Bradstreet) is another good subscription source for business researchers. Its *Company Information* component provides detailed information on 85 million public, private, and international companies; *Industry Analysis* covers more than 900 industries. The data on companies include (according to the database's self-description) "Company overview, Company history, Officers and board members, Competitors, Products and operations, Auditors, Rankings, Related industry information, Historical financials, and Industry analyses."

Kompass (Kompass North America) is a full-text subscription database with information on more than 3 million companies in more than 60 countries, covering company activity, products and services, trade names, and executives and members of corporate boards—about 40 data fields are searchable per company in a wide variety of industries: Agriculture and food, Extraction industries, Utilities and waste management, Manufacturing, Chemicals/pharmaceuticals/plastics, Building and civil engineering, Information technology, Wholesale and distribution, Transport and storage, Business services (marketing, financial, insurance, legal), Technical services/R&D/training, Telecommunications/news/media, Leisure/entertainment/hospitality, Repair and maintenance, Health care/social services, and Public administration/associations. Company phone numbers are provided, and it is possible to send an e-mail Request for Quotations through this database. *Kompass* is more than just a database with company information; it is also tool for direct business-to-business communications worldwide.

LexisNexis and **Factiva** are huge full-text databases covering much business information; see the descriptions of these files in Chapter 5.

Leadership Library and **Carroll Publishing Company directories** both provide extensive directory information for companies and individuals; see Chapter 12.

Mergent Archives (Mergent) is a subscription database with several components, among them all *Moody's Manuals* digitized since 1909 and hundreds of thousands of historical annual reports from more than a hundred countries as far back as 1925. The company also offers many other huge business databases: *Mergent Bond Viewer, Mergent Intellect, Mergent WebReports,* and *Mergent Online.* Full descriptions can be found at the company website, www.mergent.com.

Plunkett Research, Ltd. (Plunkett Research) provides analyses of companies, market research reports, and industry statistics and trends. Its reports can be purchased through its website at www.plunkettresearch.com.

PrivCo (PrivCo Media) is a subscription database providing much hard-to-find information on more than 225,000 privately held companies, primarily in the United States and Canada, that bring in more than $10 million in annual revenues; it also provides data on more than 12,500 private market investors. The database covers financial statements, venture capital funding deals, mergers and acquisitions, private equity deals, family ownership breakdowns, bankruptcies, and related topics; it is updated daily.

ReferenceUSAGov (InfoUSA) is a subscription database that has several components; individual libraries can choose which parts they wish to subscribe to. Its "Business Databases" section contains several subsections:

- *U.S. Businesses* (14 million)—information includes Business Profile, Industry Profile, Location Map, Business Demographics, Management Directory, Company News, Stock Data, Business Expenditures, Historical Data, Uniform Commercial Code (UCC) Filings, Nearby Businesses, Reports on Competitors, and Brands and Products. (Not every category here will be filled in for every business.)
- *Canadian Business* (1.5 million)
- *OneSource* (International Companies and Executives by Title)

- *U.S. New Businesses* (4 million)
- *U.S. Healthcare* (855,000 physicians and dentists)

Its "Consumer Databases" section also has several parts:

- *U.S. Standard White Pages* (89 million residents)
- *U.S. Consumers/Lifestyles* (address/phone information on 260+ million consumers)
- *Canadian White Pages* (12 million households)
- *U.S. New Movers/Homeowners* (300,000 weekly)

The data in *ReferenceUSAGov* is collected from a variety of sources including Yellow and White pages, corporate annual reports, SEC 10K filings, Chamber of Commerce directories, and other public listings. Businesses can be searched not just by company name but also by name or title of chief executives, assets, sales volume, location, number of employees, and year established. (I have heard from more than one professional business researcher that the Dun & Bradstreet *D&B International Business Locator* database is "riddled with mistakes"; the information in *ReferenceUSAGov* is more consistently reliable, although the financial data provided there for private companies are generally estimates.)

In researching any individual company it is useful to approach the task with some basic distinctions in mind, which may not be obvious to those just starting out in this area. The first thing to do is to situate the firm into one of four categories: those that sell stock and are *publicly owned*; those that don't sell stock to the public and are *privately held*; those that are *nonprofit* organizations; and those that are *foreign-owned*. Private companies are not required to disclose as much information on their operations as are public companies; the databases and websites (above) may have much less information on them, especially if they are small or locally owned. Another distinction to keep in mind is that information can be of two general types: what the company says about itself, and what others say about it. The former is contained in annual reports, in filings with governmental regulatory agencies, and on companies' websites. For the latter you will want to read articles in business (or other) magazines, journals, newsletters, and commercially prepared research reports and analyses—many of them full text online via the various databases listed above.

In researching company histories, specifically, there are a few shortcuts to be aware of. In addition to the above databases there is the *International Directory of Company Histories* (Gale), which is available as an ongoing series of printed volumes (more than 140 so far) and as a subscription database, available individually and also included in the *Gale Virtual Reference Library*. It provides 3- to 5-page histories of public, private, foreign, and international companies, with listings of additional sources for further reading. Of course, for companies not covered by this *International Directory*, many of the databases listed above will be useful. A good researcher's trick in doing company histories is first to find the founding date of the firm (often provided in standard directories such as *Standard & Poor's Register* or *Ward's Business Directory*), then to check for articles in business journals or local newspapers at important anniversary years for the company (especially their twenty-fifth, fortieth, and fiftieth years); often there will be write-ups on a company's history at these points. For very old firms founded in the United States between 1687 and 1915, Etna M. Kelley's *The Business Founding Date Directory* (Morgan & Morgan, 1954), available in research libraries, may be helpful; its *Supplement* (1956) covers foundings up to 1933.

The best guide for job hunters is the annual *What Color Is Your Parachute?* by Richard Nelson Bolles (Ten Speed Press). Although there are tons of Internet sites for job hunters, the basic advice offered by this book still provides a crucial insight that is otherwise easily lost in the shuffle: first, decide where you want to be, then get to know the person or persons who can hire you—so that they know *you* personally. (This really does work much better than sending out scores of résumés or relying on want ads or posted job vacancies. I've gotten three jobs myself—including my current one—by following what this book says to do.)

The field of business research is *very* large—the sources discussed elsewhere in this book on statistics, newspapers, associations, and country studies will also be relevant. When you are doing work in this field, don't just go to the open Web, or even just to the subscription databases listed above; be sure to talk to the business reference librarians at your library, too, and ask them for other suggestions. And seek out people to talk to who actually work at the particular businesses you're interested in.

COPYRIGHT STATUS INFORMATION

The Harry Ransom Center at the University of Texas at Austin, along with the University of Reading, maintains the WATCH (Writers Artists and Their Copyright Holders) website at http://tyler.hrc.utexas.edu/; this is a directory of sources providing information on the copyright holders for works by writers, artists, and "prominent figures in other creative fields." It will not tell you the copyright status of individual works, but it may help in directing you to the people who hold the rights. The Copyright Clearance Center at www.copyright.com is another site to check. The copyright slider website at www.librarycopyright.net/digitalslider/ offers an easy mechanism for navigating the changes in U.S. copyright law for works published at different time periods. As helpful as these sites may be, there is simply no easy way to determine the copyright status of all books, journals, or photographs. The only overall source for this information is the Copyright Office at the Library of Congress (www.copyright. gov), but its older card catalog files are not all online as of this writing. Searches of the manual catalogs can be done for free by onsite researchers; those done by Copyright staff cost $165 per hour with a two-hour minimum. Information on British copyright regulations can be found at the British Library website www.bl.uk/copyright.

COUNTRY STUDIES

Europa World (Taylor & Francis) is both a printed annual 2-volume set and a subscription database. For each country in the world it provides a lengthy "Introductory Survey" covering recent history, government, defense, economic affairs, and education, followed by a "Statistical Survey" with tables covering Area and Population, Health and Welfare, Agriculture, Forestry, Fishing, Mining, Industry, Finance, External Trade, Transport, Tourism, Communications Media, and Education. A "Directory" section then provides either a description or, in some cases, the full text of the country's Constitution; this is followed by names, titles, and contact information for current top government executives and legislators. Extensive contact information is then given for political organizations, religious groups, the press, publishers, broadcasting and communications companies, financial institutions, trade and industry groups, transport companies and departments, and tourism contacts.

The Economist Intelligence Unit Ltd. (EIU) produces databases that go into much greater detail about individual countries (and cities) in a variety of heavily used subscription databases, such as:

EIU CountryData
EIU MarketIndicators & Forecasts
EIU CityData
EIU Country Reports & Country Profiles

The China database, unlike the others, allows the creation of statistical tables on the fly (e.g., Energy consumption in China, by Province).

GENEALOGY AND LOCAL HISTORY

The best book for genealogists to start with is Val D. Greenwood's *Researcher's Guide to American Genealogy* (Genealogical Publishing Company, revised irregularly). *The Source: A Guidebook to American Genealogy* (Ancestry, 2006, 3rd ed.) is also excellent. Doing genealogical research is not a matter of simply typing names into large databases—although that's part of it. Although the current edition of the Greenwood book is more than a decade old, and therefore does not cover many Internet sites, it is nonetheless required reading if you want to trace your family history because it will alert you to the range of questions that you need to ask in the first place.

Cyndi's List (www.cyndislist.com) is the best starting place on the Internet; it categorizes and indexes more than 300,000 free websites of genealogical interest. It is particular useful because users can submit new links themselves and report broken ones, so it is effectively updated continually by a very large and active community of researchers.

Another free website is *familysearch.org* (Church of Jesus Christ of Latter Day Saints); it provides both full-text information and links to other online sources.

There are three excellent subscription databases to genealogical sources; these are likely to be available through local libraries and will provide access to many important sources not freely available on the open Internet. The first is *Ancestry Library Edition* (ProQuest); it provides full-text search capabilities in more than 8,600 international sources of genealogical interest (censuses, court records, parish registers, military records, grave registers, birth and death records, land office registrations, newspaper and magazine articles, obituaries, ships' passenger lists, tax lists, school yearbooks, etc.). *Billions* of individual names can be searched; coverage is particularly good for the United States and the United Kingdom. A free website, *Ancestry.com*, is mainly useful for providing just enough information to induce you to subscribe individually if you don't have access to the *Library* edition through your local library.

The second database is *HeritageQuest Online* (ProQuest), which searches not just U.S. Census records but also people and places described in more than 28,000 published family histories and local histories. One important subset of the file is *PERSI*, or *Periodical Source Index*, which is an index to more than 6,500 local history and genealogy periodicals in English and French (Canada) going back to 1800. You can search for individual names or subjects (keywords in article titles). This index covers many important historical sources not elsewhere indexed; its coverage of American history at the local level is astonishingly good.

It should be used routinely by historians to supplement the *America: History and Life* database from EBSCO. Other files in *HeritageQuest* include *Freedmen's Bank Records* and *Revolutionary War Records*, as well as private relief actions and memorial petitions included in the U.S. Serial Set.

The third database is *Fold3: History & Genealogy Archives* (EBSCO), formerly called *Footnote*, which provides full-text material from the U.S. National Archives, including many digitized city directories. It is especially good for military records. A version that allows some free searching is at www.fold3.com, but at a certain level of searching you have to subscribe.

Often material on particular families or individuals can be found in local or county histories; two good listings of these are P. William Filby's *A Bibliography of American County Histories* (Genealogical Publishing Company, 1985) and Arthur P. Young's *Cities and Towns in American History: A Bibliography of Doctoral Dissertations* (Greenwood, 1989). Many county histories are also full-text searchable through the subscription database *Accessible Archives* (from Accessible Archives, Inc.).

Another good approach to local history is through old fire insurance maps. The subscription database *Digital Sanborn Maps 1867–1970* (ProQuest) reproduces more than 660,000 maps of more than 12,000 American cities and towns. The Sanborn company produced unusually detailed maps of urban areas; they can often show you who owned the land on which you now live, where your ancestors lived in a given city at the time of the map (some cities have as many as seven maps published at different times), how many rooms each building had, the number of windows, the kind of roof and the materials the walls were made of. (Such data were important for fire insurance purposes.) You can use these maps to identify which businesses were located in a community (when and exactly where), the location and denomination of churches in particular neighborhoods, and where the grocery stories, banks, hotels, and saloons were. These maps can shed light on the characteristics of the neighborhoods in which your ancestors lived and how the areas the changed over the years. (The database reproduces the original maps held in the Library of Congress; the LC website provides a list of the maps that exist, at www.loc.gov/rr/geogmap/sanborn/.)

ILLUSTRATIONS, PICTURES, AND PHOTOGRAPHS

The Internet provides a number of large, freely searchable archives of photographs and illustrations. Among the first sites to check are these:

- Google's Images site (click on Images along the top of the search page)
- Bing.com; click on Images
- Yahoo.com; click on Images
- Altavista.com; click on Images
- Flickr.com (widely used for sharing images)
- Visual collections at www.davidrumsey.com/collections/
- Fagan Finder Image Search Engines at www.faganfinder.com/img/
- The Library of Congress's Prints and Photographs Online Catalog at www.loc.gov/pictures/
- The New York Public Library's Digital Gallery at www.nypl.org/collections

Many photographs can be found in relevant books, too, and the *Library of Congress Subject Headings* system has a number of standard subdivisions that are useful for zeroing in on them:

[Subject heading]—Caricatures and cartoons
—Illustrations
—Pictorial works
—Portraits

In searching for older books, also try two additional subdivisions that formerly appeared under names of places:

[Name of place]—Description—Views
—Description and travels—Views

Many of the citations discoverable through the many subscription databases will also note whether a journal article is accompanied by illustrations.

Facts on File publishes a wide variety of three-ring loose-leaf binders with copyright-free illustrations, pictures, diagrams, charts, and maps, all intended for easy scanning or copying. Among these titles are:

African-American Experience on File
American History on File
Animal Anatomy on File
Chemistry Experiments on File
Comparative Religions on File
Earth Science on File
Environmental Issues on File
Forensic Science Experiments on File
Geography on File

Government on File
Health on File
Historical Maps on File
Outline Maps on File
Physics Experiments on File
Science Experiments on File
Timelines on File
Weather and Climate on File

The thousands of specialized encyclopedias that exist are also frequently useful for pictures or illustrations (see Chapter 1), as is the technique of doing focused browsing in subject-classified books in the library's stacks (Chapter 3).

LITERARY CRITICISM

Two good overviews of sources available to students of literature are James L. Harner's *Literary Research Guide: An Annotated Listing of Reference Sources in English Literary Studies* (Modern Language Association, 2008, 5th ed.) and James K. Bracken's *Reference Works in British and American Literature* (Libraries Unlimited, 1998, 2nd ed.).

The first source that students often go to for literary criticism is the subscription database *MLA International Bibliography* (EBSCO, Modern Language Association), which is the largest online index to literary criticism journals. Sometimes this is combined with a search of *JSTOR* for full-text articles. Either way will provide "something quickly"—which may be adequate for undergraduate purposes, but not for more in-depth study. One major problem with *MLA* is that its results will be spotty due to very inconsistent indexing in the database (e.g., not all of the articles on Captain Ahab are findable by searching "Moby Dick"). *JSTOR* is fine as far as it goes, but it does not cover nearly the full range of journals containing literary criticism. Better overviews of the critical literature can usually be found by finding a published bibliography devoted to the particular author, then checking its index for the particular story, play, or poem you have in mind. (The Bracken volume mentioned above is particularly good in identifying such bibliographies.)

For example, a student who wishes to find analyses or John Donne's "Death Be Not Proud" (*Holy Sonnet 10*) will find seven articles on it by searching "Death Be Not Proud" in the *MLA*. (The same researcher would probably miss an additional article findable via "Holy Sonnet 10"—another example of inconsistent indexing.) If the student checks her library catalog under **Donne, John, 1572–1631—Bibliography**, however, she may find three compilations by John R. Roberts, *John Donne: An Annotated Bibliography of Modern Criticism, 1912–1967; John Donne…1968–1978;* and *John Donne…1979–1995* (University of Missouri Press, 1973 and 1982; Duquesne University Press, 2004). The first lists 5 articles about the sonnet; the second, 16; the third, 35.

Similarly, a student interested in Edgar Allan Poe and cryptography would get different results looking in the *MLA International Bibliography*, on the one hand, and in either J. Lesley Dameron and Irby B. Cauthen's *Edgar Allan Poe: A Bibliography of Criticism 1827–1967* or Esther F. Hyneman's *Edgar Allan Poe: An Annotated Bibliography of Books and Articles in English 1827–1973*, on the other. In this case, the online resource serves to update the latter published bibliographies—but it does not include everything listed in them.

A neglected but occasionally very useful index to 146 printed bibliographies of literary criticism is Alan R. Weiner and Spencer Means's *Literary Criticism Index*, 2nd ed. (Scarecrow Press, 1994). This source enables you to search for articles on particular plays, poems, novels, and short stories and frequently leads to citations not indexed anywhere online. (It is probably not necessary for undergraduates to use this index; but grad students who wish to do comprehensive literature reviews should consult it.)

If you wish to avoid the morass of postmodern and deconstructionist criticisms of a particular work and are looking for insights on what it might actually tell you about life, a good shortcut is provided through the old Prentice-Hall *Twentieth Century Interpretations* series. Look in your library's catalog under the title phrase *Twentieth Century Interpretations of [Title of Work]*. Within the brackets you can enter such titles as *A Farewell to Arms, The Crucible, Doctor Faustus, Gray's Elegy, Julius Caesar, Moby Dick, Oedipus Rex, Pride and Prejudice*, etc. There are about a hundred volumes like this, each about 120 pages long, and each presents an excellent collection of scholarly analyses.

Another comparable series is Prentice-Hall's *Twentieth Century Views*. These volumes tend to have titles of the format *[Name of Author]: A Collection of Critical Essays*. A good entry into the contents of this series is an obscure but useful volume entitled *Reader's Index to the Twentieth Century Views Literary Criticism Series, Volumes 1–100* (Prentice-Hall, 1973). This reproduces the index pages from the end of each volume in the series. It thus offers a way to find predeconstructionist articles on particular topics connected with authors (as opposed to particular works), such as "Negative capability in Keats," "Inscape and instress in Hopkins," "Irony in Mann," and "Puritan influences on Hawthorne." (As with published bibliographies, you can in effect do Boolean combinations of "specific topic AND particular author" in this printed source.)

You can easily find either of these series in your library's computer catalog by combining the phrase "Twentieth Century" with either the name of a literary work or the name of the literary author.

Three newer series published by Chelsea House are *Modern Critical Views* (each volume of which is entitled with the name of a literary author, e.g., *Alice Walker* or *Homer*); *Major Literary Characters* (each with a title such as *Hester Prynne* or *Huck Finn*); and *Modern Critical Interpretations* (each with the title of a particular works such as *Jane Eyre* or *The Scarlet Letter*). All three of the Chelsea House series have Harold Bloom as their general editor. This makes online searching easy: just combine "Bloom" and "author" (or "title" or "character") to find if there is a volume relevant to your interest.

G. K. Hall has published more than 250 volumes in two comparable "Critical Essays" series; these can be found by searching for titles of the form *Critical Essays on [Name of Author]* or *[Title of Literary Work]*.

The largest online source for full-text literary criticism is the subscription database *Literature Criticism Online* (Gale). It contains the full texts of several sets that are separately available and that collectively have more than 1,800 volumes:

- *Contemporary Literary Criticism*®
- *Twentieth-Century Literary Criticism*®
- *Nineteenth-Century Literature Criticism*®
- *Shakespearean Criticism*
- *Literature Criticism from 1400 to 1800*
- *Classical and Medieval Literature Criticism*
- *Poetry Criticism*
- *Short Story Criticism*
- *Drama Criticism*
- *Children's Literature Review*

My own experience with the database, however, is that its page-viewing software is extremely clunky, and since many of its articles are more than a hundred pages long, they are very difficult to read online. The database version is most useful as an index to the various paper-copy sets, which are much preferable for reading.

Another good subscription database is *Literature Resource Center* (Gale). It includes biographical and critical articles and a variety of other sources, among them:

- Articles on more than 146,000 authors from the print series *Contemporary Authors, Contemporary Authors New Revisions,* and *Dictionary of Literary Biography*
- More than 850,000 articles from nearly 400 magazines and journals
- Tens of thousands of articles that are *selected* from the various sets covered fully by *Literature Criticism Online* (above).
- Full-text articles from more than 500 journals
- Links to thousands of websites

If you are looking more for full texts of literary works themselves, rather than critical articles about them, the best database is *LitFinder* (Gale), which includes:

- 135,000+ full-text poems
- Indexing and publication information on another 820,000 poems
- 7,000+ full-text short stories and novels
- 4,000 full-text literary essays
- 2,000 full-text speeches
- 1,700 full-text plays
- Author biographies and photographs

Literary Reference Center and *Literature Reference Center Plus* (EBSCO) are somewhat comparable to the Gale databases in that they provide full texts of both literary works themselves and critical/biographical studies. Overviews of their contents may be found at the EBSCO website www .ebscohost.com/academic/literary-reference-center-plus.

Yet another good database covering literature is *MagillOnLiterature-Plus* (Salem Press), which includes 35,000 analyses of individual works (novels, short stories, poems, plays, essays, philosophical works) plus biographies and bibliographies, but not texts of the literary or philosophical works themselves.

Perhaps the most important thing for an undergraduate to keep in mind when doing an analysis of a literary work, however, is that quite possibly no research at all is required, or even desired, by the professor. Often the purpose of such assignments is to stretch your own analytical and critical powers rather than your research abilities. One problem with critical articles is that much of what you find simply won't be worth reading. (This was already the case nearly 40 years ago when I was getting my own Ph.D. in English; it is questionable that the situation has improved much since then.) Few things are more frustrating to a student than expending a great deal of effort tracking down and reading critical articles, and then finding they don't give you any particular "keeper" insights; the time involved would often be more profitably spent devising your own analyses.

MAPS

For most everyday purposes of getting from point A to point B, the "Maps" search options within Google or Bing and GPS location devices are eminently suitable. For academic or other research purposes, however, a number of other resources are preferable, both for their coverage that is nondigitized to begin with and for the convenience factor of not having to view large maps formatted to be viewable on small computer screens. Scholars who are writing for publication may also prefer to cite printed copies of the map sheets they have used, if only because their online equivalents have a way of changing their URLs—or vanishing entirely.

Good starting points on the Web for finding maps of any area, as well as historical and thematic maps, are the following:

- The German site *Die Welt der Karten* at www.kartenportal.ch/
- *Western Association of Map Libraries Map Librarians' Toolbox* at www.waml.org/maptools.html
- Map collections at the Library of Congress at www.loc.gov/rr/geogmap/and the Geography & Map Reading Room's *Guide to the Collections* at www.loc.gov/rr/geogmap/guides.html
- *David Rumsey Map Collection* at www.davidrumsey.com/about
- *Map History* at www.maphistory.info
- Maps from U.S. federal government sources, found via www.usa.gov/Topics/Maps.shtml
- *UK Map Collections* at www.cartography.org.uk

The printed set *Inventory of World Topographic Mapping*, compiled by Rolph Böhme (English language editor, Roger Anson), 3 vols. (London and New York: International Cartographic Association and Elsevier Applied Science Publishers, 1989–1993), continues to be the best overview source for the history of mapping in each country; it also provides lists of map scales and map series for each. Historical listings may be found in Thomas Chubb's *The Printed Maps in the Atlases of Great Britain and Ireland: A Bibliography, 1579–1870* (Homeland Association, 1927; reprinted, Martino Publishing, 2004) and *A List of Geographical Atlases in the Library of Congress, with Bibliographic Notes*, 9 vols. (Martino, 1997). The *World Directory of Map Collections* edited by Olivier Loiseaux (541 pages; Saur,

2000) and *Guide to U.S. Map Collections* edited by Christopher J. J. Thiry (511 pages; Scarecrow Press, 2006, 3rd ed.) are useful directories.

The *Maps on File, Historical Maps on File,* and *Charts on File* compilations of copyright-free illustrations from Facts on File are also useful (see the above section on Illustrations), and probably can be found in local libraries.

NEWSPAPERS

The most important databases providing full texts of newspapers include the following (many of which are described in Chapters 4 and 5):

- *ProQuest Newsstand* (current U.S. newspapers)
- *ProQuest International Newsstand* (current newspapers worldwide)
- *ProQuest Historical Newspapers*
- (Other ProQuest newspaper databases: *Ethnic Newswatch, GenderWatch, ProQuest Historical Black Newspapers,* and *ProQuest Historical American Jewish Newspapers*)
- *African Newspapers* (1800–1922; Readex)
- *African American Newspapers 1827–1998* (Readex)
- *Accessible Archives Complete* (Accessible Archives)
- *America's Historical Newspapers, 1690–1922* (Readex)
- *Chronicling America* (Library of Congress)
- *Factiva* (Factiva)
- *Financial Times Historical Archive 1886–2006* (Gale)
- *Gale News Vault* (Gale), with full texts of thousands of British newspapers and periodicals back to the seventeenth century, and about 250 U.S. newspapers from the nineteenth century
- *Google News Archive*
- *Illustrated London News Historical Archive 1842–2003* (Gale)
- *Latin American Newpapers* (1805–1922; Readex)
- *LexisNexis* (LexisNexis)
- *National Index to Chinese Newspapers & Periodicals* (1833–; Shanghai Wenda Information Co.)
- *NewspaperArchive* (Heritage Archives), covering thousands of titles (primarily American) worldwide back to the 1600s
- *17th–18th Century Burney Collection Newspapers* (Gale)
- *Sunday [London] Times Digital Archive 1822–2006* (Gale)
- *19th Century British Library Newspapers* (Gale)
- *19th Century U.S. Newspapers* (Gale)
- *South Asian Newspapers* (1864–1922) (Readex)
- *The [London] Times Digital Archive 1785–1985* (Gale)

One of the biggest mistakes made rather routinely by researchers is to assume that they've "covered" all newspapers relevant to their topic by simply having done a search in only one or two of these databases (usually mentioning ProQuest—without paying attention to the scope of their local library's ProQuest subscription—or *LexisNexis*). Each of the above databases, however, contains full texts not available elsewhere; a combination of searches is almost always required if comprehensive coverage is desired.

Further, there are thousands of newspapers on microfilm that have not been digitized at all, especially for the years 1923 and after. If you don't find what you need through the databases, be sure to ask your librarians if other newspapers exist on microfilm, covering the cities and time periods you want. The best listing of existing U.S. newspapers, with library locations, is provided by the free website *U.S. Newspaper Directory*, 1690–present, at http://chroniclingamerica.loc.gov/search/titles/.

Many indexes to small-town newspapers exist in unpublished form throughout the United States in libraries, newspaper offices, and historical and genealogical societies. The best guide to these is Anita Cheek Milner's *Newspaper Indexes: A Location and Subject Guide for Researchers*, 3 vols. (Scarecrow Press, 1977–1982).

The databases and websites listed above in the Genealogy and Local History section will also provide indexing, and often full texts, of many other newspapers, or sometimes sections (e.g., obituaries) within them.

An excellent guide to the literature on American newspapers in general is Richard A. Schwarzlose's *Newspapers: A Reference Guide* (Greenwood Press, 1987).

PRIMARY SOURCES

Many term paper assignments nowadays are given with the specification that students should "use primary sources" in their research. To judge from the questions that come to a library reference desk, this admonition seems in many cases to mean "don't confine your search to sources on the open Internet sources [read: Google and Wikipedia]—use the library, too." The problem is that many teachers themselves do not realize what can (or cannot) be found in libraries that lies beyond the reach of Google. Their assignments are thus often more than a little confusing, because millions of primary sources are indeed directly available, full text, on the open Internet; and saying "use primary sources" does not guarantee any use of real libraries. So, right off the bat, it would be helpful for teachers and professors to specify more clearly what they have in mind by specifying "primary sources"—and for students to ask for such clarification.

In a sense, every chapter of this book so far has discussed sources that would identify, if not provide direct access to, primary sources. Several shortcuts, however, are worth repeating.

First, specialized subject encyclopedias frequently include Appendices (sometimes an entire volume) specifically reprinting the most important primary sources relevant to their subject coverage (see Chapter 1).

Second, the *Library of Congress Subject Headings* system (see Chapter 2) provides several subject subdivisions that can be used to zero in immediately on primary sources that have been published in book form. If you first find the right heading for your topic (e.g., **Civil rights movements**; **World War, 1939–1945**; etc.), you can then look for these subdivisions in a browse display, or enter them directly into a Boolean combination (see Chapter 10) with the heading:

Sources
Diaries
Personal narratives (or just **Narratives** if entered into a Boolean
    combination)
Correspondence
Interviews
Quotations
Collections
Pictorial works

When I am doing such searches myself I usually add the following keywords into the combination:

Document? [to include titles with the words "Documentary" or
    "Documents"]
Eyewitness?
Oral [to pick up "oral history" accounts]

Theoretically, documentary histories and eyewitness accounts should already be included under the format subject subdivisions listed above, but oversights in cataloging are not unknown. **Oral history** is actually an *LCSH* heading in its own right (not a subdivision of other topics), but "Oral" as a keyword within a Boolean combination would pick up both that heading and any use of the term in a title or subtitle.

You may find that you cannot combine all of these elements in one Boolean command without overloading your library catalog's search software—e.g., "'**World War, 1939–1945**'AND (**Sources** OR **Diaries** OR **Narratives** OR **Correspondence** OR **Interviews** OR **Quotations** OR **Collections** OR '**Pictorial works**' OR document? OR eyewitness? OR oral)." If you break the search into smaller units of combination, however, you'll still get the results you want. Remember, too, that using *browse displays* of subdivisions under LC subject headings is a very effective way to spot most of these terms if you cannot remember them, as well as to notice other standard subdivisions that may be of use (e.g.,—**Songs and music**, which can alert you to resources that could readily be considered primary literature in some contexts). Look also for the subdivision **Bibliography** (see below).

A third tip is that many large collections of primary sources have already been assembled in a variety of subscription databases (e.g., *American Civil War Letters and Diaries*, or *Oral History Online*) or microform sets (e.g., *Anti-Slavery Collection* or *Early American Medical Imprints 1668–1820*) (see Chapters 4 and 13). The individual items in these collections will usually not be cataloged by library OPACs, nor will they be adequately identifiable by federated searches of multiple databases simultaneously.

A fourth tip is that many published bibliographies (see Chapter 9) exist, such as the following, that readily identify primary sources:

- *American Diaries: An Annotated Bibliography of Published Diaries and Journals*, 2 vols., by Laura Arksey, Nancy Pries, and Marcia Reed (Gale Research, 1983–87).
- *British Diaries: An Annotated Bibliography of British Diaries Written between 1442 and 1942*, by William Matthews (P. Smith, 1967).
- *And So to Bed: A Bibliography of Diaries Published in English*, by Patricia Pate Havlice (Scarecrow, 1987).

These all have useful subject indexes that connect the diaries to various historical events or periods. When you are searching an OPAC, then, be sure to include **Bibliography** as one of the terms in your Boolean combinations.

QUOTATIONS

Unverified, garbled, and misattributed quotations are floating around the Internet by the thousands. There is no simple way to deal with all of these cases, but among the many available compilations of quotations, the two best starting points are these:

- *Respectfully Quoted*, edited by Suzy Platt (Library of Congress, 1989; reprinted by Congressional Quarterly, 1992, and Dover Publications, 2010. [The Dover edition omits the editor's name.]) This 520-page book was compiled by the Congressional Research Service at the Library of Congress; it is one of CRS's jobs to make sure that quotations used by members of Congress are both accurate and accurately attributed.
- *The Yale Book of Quotations*, edited by Frank R. Shapiro (Yale University Press, 2006). This is a 1,067-page compilation, with verified attributions.

STANDARDS AND SPECIFICATIONS

A useful group of sources that are likely to be available in libraries are the various *Architectural Graphic Standards* from John Wiley & Sons; they are all revised irregularly:

Architectural Graphic Standards
Architectural Graphic Standards, Student Edition
Architectural Graphic Standards for Residential Construction
Interior Graphic Standards
Landscape Graphic Standards
Planning and Urban Design Standards

The first one is a basic source providing diagrams and standard measurements of such things as tennis courts, horseshoe pits, swimming pools, door frames, fireplaces, etc. It even diagrams the profiles of major species of trees, listing their average heights and spreads.

If you need to obtain a technical, engineering, industrial, military, or governmental standard, a good overview website is provided by the Science, Technology & Business Division of the Library of Congress at www.loc.gov/rr/scitech/trs/trsresources.html. This site provides further links (under "IHS Global") to the American National Standards Institute (ANSI), the Institute of Electrical and Electronic Engineers (IEEE), the Society of Automotive Engineers (SAE), and Underwriters Laboratory (UL), as well as to the International Organization for Standardization (ISO) and a score of other national and international websites for standards.

Another good starting point is the National Institute of Standards and Technology (NIST) at www.nist.gov with links to national standards bodies all over the world, as well as to international standards organizations.

STATISTICS

The most useful general compendium of statistics on all sorts of things is the annual *Statistical Abstract of the United States*, published by the U.S. Census Bureau up through 2012 and by ProQuest thereafter. Another large collection of federal statistics online is search at the FedStats website, www.fedstats.gov. The UK National Statistics website is www.statistics.gov.uk/hub/index.html; the Canadian site is www.statcan.gc.ca/; the site for Australian statistics is www.abs.gov.au/.

Several compendia are good for historical data:

- *Historical Statistics of the United States, Earliest Times to the Present: Millennial Edition*, 5 vols. (Cambridge University Press, 2006); an online subscription version is also available.
- *Historical Statistics of the States of the United States: Two Centuries of the Census 1790–1990*, compiled by Donald B. Dodd (Greenwood Press, 1993).
- *International Historical Statistics: The Americas, 1750–2000*, 5th ed., by B. R. Mitchell (Palgrave Macmillan, 2003).
- *International Historical Statistics: Europe, 1754–2000*, 5th ed., by B. R. Mitchell (Palgrave Macmillan, 2003).
- *International Historical Statistics: Africa, Asia & Oceania, 1750–2002*, 4th ed., by B. R. Mitchell (Palgrave Macmillan, 2003).
- *British Historical Statistics*, by B. R. Mitchell (Cambridge University Press, 1988; reprinted 2011).
- *Historical Statistics of Canada*, 2nd ed., edited by F. H. Leacy (Statistics Canada, 1983).
- *Australians, Historical Statistics*, edited by Wray Vamplew (Fairfax, Syme & Weldon Associates, 1987).
- *New Zealand: A Handbook of Historical Statistics*, by G. T. Bloomfield (Macmillan/G.K. Hall, 1984).
- *Historical Statistics of Japan*, 2 vols., edited by Japan Statistical Association (Tokyo: Nihon Tokei Kyōkai, Heisei 18 [2006]).
- *The Arab World, Turkey, and the Balkans 1878–1914): A Handbook of Historical Statistics*, by Justin McCarthy (Macmillan/G.K. Hall, 1982).
- *The Value of a Dollar: Prices and Incomes in the United States, 1860–2009*, 4th ed., by Scott Derks (Grey House Pub., 2009)
- *The Inflation Calculator* (for U.S. dollars) at http://westegg.com/inflation.
- *MeasuringWorth* at www.measuringworth.com.

The most extensive ongoing subject indexes to statistical publications worldwide are the databases *ProQuest Statistical Insight* and *Data-Planet Statistical DataSets* (see Chapter 13). Both are also good sources for historical statistics.

Polling the Nations (ORS Publishing) is a subscription database of public opinion polls with full texts of a half-million questions and responses from more than 14,000 surveys conducted since 1986 in the United States and more than a hundred other countries.

Statistical Warehouse (RegionalOneSource) is another pay-per-view database somewhat like *ProQuest DataSets*, which enables you to create charts or graphs on the fly from a wide variety of cross-searchable sources; it is described at http://statisticalwarehouse.com.

Rankings of various sorts can be found in sources such as these; you have to check individual titles for their most recent editions:

- *Places Rated Almanac* (Places Rated Books)
- *Retirement Places Rated* (John Wiley & Sons)
- *World Retirement Places Rated* (Places Rated Books)
- *Cities Ranked and Rated: More Than 400 Metropolitan Areas Evaluated in the U.S. and Canada* (John Wiley & Sons)
- *State Rankings* (CQ Press)
- *Crime State Rankings* (CQ Press)
- *Education State Rankings* (CQ Press)
- *Health Care State Rankings* (CQ Press)
- *City Crime Rankings* (CQ Press)
- *Educational Rankings Annual* (Gale Cengage)

Other good compendiums include the United Nations *Statistical Yearbook* and its *Demographic Yearbook*. The *UNESCO Statistical Yearbook* ceased publication after its 1999 issue.

A particularly good reference book is *Statistical Sources: A Subject Guide to Data on Industrial, Business, Social, Educational, Financial, and Other Topics for the United States and Internationally* (Gale Cengage, revised irregularly). It is an extensive listing of more than 1,500 organizations, printed sources, databases, and websites from more than 210 countries, with specific contact information (phone and FAX numbers, e-mail addresses, mailing addresses, and URLs) categorized under more than 30,000 very specific topics (e.g., Aggravated Assault, Dairy Products-Consumption, Farm Mortgage Loans, Silk Production, Vanuatu—Postal Service). It's often a very useful starting point.

The Inter-University Consortium for Political and Social Research at the University of Michigan is a nonprofit organization that maintains the world's largest archive of machine-readable data files in the social sciences; both current and historical data sets are available (via fees or subscriptions) in manipulable formats. Its home page is at www.icpsr.umich.edu.

TABULAR DATA

Many of the statistics sources listed above either present data or enable data to be presented in tables and charts. A particularly useful subset of data in such formats is provided by the Chemical Rubber Company (CRS) of Cleveland, Ohio; it publishes more than 50 handbooks that present tabular reference data in such fields as chemistry and physics, mathematics, optics, probability and statistics, microbiology, nutrition and food. The best avenue into this bewildering maze of data is the printed *Composite Index for CRC Handbooks*, 3rd ed. (Taylor & Francis, 1992), which is a cumulative index to more than 300 of the CRC handbooks. The full-text subscription database *CRCnetBASE* (Taylor & Francis Online) includes all of the handbooks plus several thousand other CRC publications.

TESTS (PSYCHOLOGICAL AND EDUCATIONAL)

Two excellent sources that outline your options for finding published or unpublished tests are websites from the American Psychological Association and the Educational Testing Service:

- The American Psychological Association publishes a subscription database *PsycTESTS* that comprehensively indexes relevant tests and measures.
- The Educational Testing Association provides links to many sources on educational tests at www.ets.org/tests_products.

A good overview in book form is *Tests: A Comprehensive Reference for Assessments in Psychology, Education, and Business*, by Taddy Maddox, 6th ed. (PRO-ED, Inc., 2007).

It is sometimes also possible to find full-texts of tests included as appendices to doctoral dissertations that have made use of them. (Note, however, that discovering a test appended to a dissertation does not automatically mean that you are entitled to use it; you will probably still have to seek out its author[s] or publisher for the necessary permission.)

TRANSLATIONS

The easiest way to find out if a foreign-language book has been translated into English is to look under the original author's name in *World-Cat*, the old *National Union Catalog: Pre-1956 Imprints*, or the subscription database *Books in Print Global* (Bowker).

Another good source for identifying translations of books since 1979 is UNESCO's *Index Translationum* website; its URL is lengthy, but a Google or Bing search for "Index Translationum" will bring it up quickly. Printed volumes of this title cover from 1932 to 1940, with a gap from April 1940 to 1947, then resuming for 1948–1986. There is a 2-volume *Cumulative Index to English Translations 1948–1968* (G.K. Hall, 1973), covering that portion of the *Index Translationum*.

In the humanities, a series from Boulevard/Bable, Ltd. in London is sometimes useful; it includes:

The Babel Guide to Brazilian Fiction: Fiction in Translation (2001)
The Babel Guide to Dutch & Flemish Fiction in English Translation (2001)
The Babel Guide to Hungarian Literature in English Translation (2001)
The Babel Guide to Scandinavian and Baltic Fiction (2001)
The Babel Guide to German Fiction in English Translation: Austria, Germany, Switzerland (1997)
The Babel Guide to French Fiction in English Translation (1996)
The Babel Guide to Italian Fiction in English Translation (1995)
The Babel Guide to the Fiction of Portugal, Brazil & African in English Translation (1995)

Good subject headings to look for in library catalogs are of this form:

[Name or Subject]—Translations into English [or **French, German**, etc.]

Dialog Professional (ProQuest) is a subscription database that now incorporates *World News Connection* as a component; the latter offers ongoing English translations of foreign media sources (broadcast and print) from 1997 forward. *Foreign Broadcast Information Service (FBIS) Daily Reports* (a subscription database from Readex) provides coverage from 1974 to 1996. *World News Connection* includes what used to be called the *Joint Publications Research Service (JPRS)* series of indexes to, and translations of, foreign newspaper articles. Retrospective paper-copy indexes covering a microfiche set of documents are the *Bibliography-Index to Current U.S. JPRS Translations,* vols. 1–8 (1962–1972); *Bell & Howell Transdex* (1975–1983); and *Transdex* (1984–1996).

CHAPTER 15

Reference Sources: Types of Literature

S O FAR WE HAVE BEEN CONCERNED MAINLY TO DELINEATE THE options for pursuing *research* questions rather than *reference* questions. The former are more open-ended, in the sense of not having definite right or wrong answers. For example, "What information is there on land reform in seventeenth-century China?" or "What is available on U.S.–Israeli relations after the Six-Day War?" are research questions in the sense that I'm using the term. The major concerns with this type of inquiry involve, first, getting a reasonably good overview of "the shape of the elephant," such that you can be confident you haven't overlooked any major sources, and second, gaining some reasonable assurance that you are not wasting time re-inventing the wheel in duplicating research that has already been done. Reference questions, in contrast, are those looking for a specific bit of information—for example, "What is the height of the Washington Monument?" or "Who won the Oscar for Best Actor in 1932?"—and that have a more ascertainable "right" answer.

RECAP OF WAYS TO APPROACH RESEARCH QUESTIONS

In dealing with research questions, the overall point of the discussion so far is that there are eight different methods of subject searching available through research libraries:

- Controlled vocabulary subject heading or descriptor searches
- General or focused browsing of subject-classified full texts
- Keyword searches
- Citation searches

- Related record searches
- Searches through published bibliographies
- Using people sources
- Truncations, combinations, and limitations of search elements[1]

Browsing classified full texts in library bookstacks and using published (and usually copyrighted) subject bibliographies are techniques that cannot be done via computers—the texts and bibliographies I'm referring to are precisely the bulk of library records that are not digitized to begin with. Since the copyright law is still in effect, most books published in 1923 and afterward cannot legally be digitized and made freely readable online.

Each method of searching is potentially applicable in any subject area; each has distinct advantages and disadvantages (both strengths and weaknesses); and each is capable of turning up information that cannot be reached by the other seven. Information that lies in a blind spot to any one method of searching, however, usually lies within the purview of one or more of the other means of inquiry.

Knowledge of these few distinct search techniques—with an understanding of the advantages and limitations of each—will enable most researchers to increase substantially the range and efficiency of their investigations in any subject area. Knowing this framework of options is much more practically and immediately useful than simply having guidelines on "how to think critically about websites." The latter, of course, is important, but in many cases—and in *all* cases of scholarly research—it is even more important to know the options for getting beyond free Internet sites in the first place, especially if the sole means of subject access to them is algorithmic relevance ranking of guessed-at keywords.

PROBLEMS EXPERIENCED BY MOST RESEARCHERS

Most scholars, unfortunately, do most of their research within very limited frameworks of perception; they too often act as though their research options consist only of the following:

1. Doing keyword searches in Google (or other search engines) on the Internet
2. Looking at footnotes in sources they already have
3. Communicating with a small circle of acquaintances (never including reference librarians)
4. General browsing in only one or two areas in library bookstacks

Those in the sciences skip number (4) entirely and inflate (3) excessively. Further,

- Very few researchers use databases, catalogs, or indexes efficiently because they so frequently search under the wrong terms to begin with (mistakenly assuming that keywords are conceptual category terms and searching under too-general rather than specific terms).
- They are familiar with only a very small range (primarily a few databases such as *JSTOR*, *LexisNexis*, and some undefined segments of ProQuest) of the thousands of subscription sources that exist outside the open Internet.
- They have never been told about search methods that don't rely on the prior verbal specification of search terms and that, instead, allow systematic recognition of terms that cannot be guessed at in advance.
- They have never had the *Library of Congress Subject Headings* system explained to them, and many are now burdened with library OPACs incapable of showing either cross-references or browse-displays, without which the *LCSH* system cannot work.
- The only library-related instruction they have received consists of high-level overviews of either the Dewey Decimal or the Library of Congress classification schemes, but they have never been told that browsing in bookstacks is a function of first finding the right subject headings in the OPAC.
- They have had almost no education at all in search techniques other than simply typing keywords into the first search box they see. The mistaken instructional assumption is that keyword searching is self-evident and does not need to be explained. To the contrary, however, it does have to be explained just as much as controlled vocabulary searching—or citation searching, related record searching, etc. Without such explanation, not only do students assume that keywords are category terms, they also routinely do their searches with no understanding of word truncation, use of Boolean operators and parentheses, or even use of quotation marks for phrase searching.[2]

Familiarity with the outline of eight search techniques sketched above, however, will enable most researchers to get beyond these limitations and gain an overview of essentially the full range of options available in any research inquiry; it will also assist them in achieving a sense of closure in making estimates of what options remain to be pursued.

TYPE-OF-LITERATURE SEARCHING

The framework of techniques available for research questions, however, is not fully adequate to deal with reference questions. A ninth method of searching is frequently preferable here:

- Type-of-literature searches

This kind of searching is based on the fact that within any subject or disciplinary field, certain distinctive types of reference sources can predictably be expected to exist. By "reference sources" I mean those that either point the way into the core literature contained in books, journals, reports, dissertations, etc., or those that summarize, abstract, compile, digest, or review it. Reference sources tend to be those forms of publication that are simply consulted rather than read from beginning to end.[3] These various types of sources form a discernable and predictable structure within the literature of any academic subject area, and a foreknowledge of the existence of this structure can enable you to quickly find the most efficient paths of inquiry, each tailored to answering certain types of questions. Without an ability to focus on one type of literature rather than another, searchers frequently become overwhelmed by way too much retrieval across way too many irrelevant sources.

VARIANT CONCEPTUAL MODELS

An important qualification is in order: the line between open-ended research and specific-fact reference questions is often rather blurry. In general, however, it is useful to distinguish the two; as a reference librarian I find that in pursuing research questions it is usually best to think in terms of the first eight methods of searching listed above, while in pursuing the fact questions it is often best to think in terms of searching types of literature. (I have crossed this line several times in this book, however—the discussions of encyclopedia articles, literature review articles, bibliographies, and union lists are essentially focuses on particular types of literature.)

In other words, you can think of two different conceptual frameworks here, "methods" and "types," each applicable in any subject area, or you can regard the "types" framework itself as an additional, ninth method of searching within a single "methods" model. I prefer the latter. This distinction, however, may be more of a concern to instructors who are trying to structure a class on research techniques than to anyone else. In my own class presentations I discuss the first eight methods alone.

In any event, don't lose sight of the overall point: the multipart "methods" model is itself a radically different conceptual framework from the "Internet model" of a single search box supposedly covering "everything" simultaneously.

SPECIFIC TYPES OF LITERATURE

Even though the Internet is indeed the first source to which people turn for reference-type facts, it is still very useful for serious researchers to grasp the structure of *printed* reference sources defined by types of literature. You can reasonably expect to find any of these forms of publication within a wide range of very different subject areas:

- *Almanacs.* These are fact books and compendiums of miscellaneous information. They are particularly good for answering questions having to do with statistics, awards, brief summaries of news events, historical data, dates and anniversaries, geography, city and county data, sports, weights and measures, flags or other insignia, and so on.
- *Atlases.* These are compendiums of maps or tables that graphically display information not just on geopolitical matters but also on subjects such as crop production, spread of diseases, military power balances, climate variation, ecological conditions, status of women, literacy levels, population trends, soil conditions, occupational distributions, area histories, trade patterns, and the like.
- *Bibliographies.* These are listings of citations (often with annotations) to books, journal articles, conference papers, dissertations, reports, and so on, on particular subjects. They are especially useful in historical or literary research, as they frequently include references to works that are overlooked by computer databases, or buried indiscriminately with huge retrievals. Their arrangement, too, often provides an overview of the structure of a topic, which cannot be duplicated by computer printouts.
- *Catalogs.* These provide listings of merchandise, art objects, publications, equipment, parts and supplies, and so forth that are located at particular places or that are available in a particular market niche; they often provide descriptive details, specifications, and prices.
- *Chronologies.* These present facts arranged by the time sequence of their occurrence. Often chronologies present parallel listings that display the temporal contexts of different areas of study (e.g.,

politics, arts, technology, religion) simultaneously, so that a reader may correlate the events of one area with contemporaneous, earlier, or later developments in other subject areas.

- *Computer databases and websites.* These information sources exist in all subject areas and allow interactive searching, always by keywords and often by other methods of inquiry as well. The main distinction is that commercially published databases are not freely available to everyone on the open Internet.

- *Concordances.* These are word lists associated with particular texts (usually literary, philosophical, or religious classics) that enable researchers to determine exactly where any particular word or words appear within the text.

- *Dictionaries.* These reference sources provide an alphabetically arranged list of words with definitions, pronunciations, etymology, scope of usage, and so on. Often they contain biographical and geographical information. The term "dictionary" is often synonymous with "encyclopedia," referring simply to an alphabetical (rather than a systematic) arrangement of entries, regardless of their length.

- *Directories.* These provide information for identifying or locating individual people, organizations, or institutions in various geographical or subject areas. They list names, addresses, telephone and FAX numbers, e-mail addresses, and Web pages.

- *Encyclopedias.* The purpose of an encyclopedia is to summarize established knowledge in a given subject area and to provide a starting point for more extensive research; it seeks to provide an overview of a subject written for nonspecialists (unlike a review article). Note that encyclopedias specialized in a particular subject area still tend to be written with a nonspecialist audience in mind. An encyclopedia may be contrasted to a treatise, which attempts to provide all knowledge on a subject in a systematic (rather than an alphabetical) arrangement and which may be written for specialists rather than laypeople. Encyclopedias can usually be counted on to have detailed keyword indexes that will reveal more of their contents than can be found through the simple alphabetical arrangement of their articles.

- *Gazetteers.* These are alphabetical dictionaries of geographic place names; entries often include data on the history, population, economic characteristics, and natural resources of the places listed. They are also useful for identifying which larger geopolitical units a smaller locale is part of (e.g., they will tell you which county a town is in—often of great interest to genealogists.)

- *Guides to the Literature.* The literature of any subject area may be thought of in terms of different levels. *Primary literature* deals directly with a particular problem or concern, presenting contemporaneous original testimony from participants, observations by witnesses, or records about it or creative expressions of it. *Secondary literature* is generally comprised of both scholarly analyses and popularizations of the primary literature. *Tertiary literature* consists of reference works (the various types of literature: dictionaries, encyclopedias, handbooks, etc.) that identify, point out, summarize, abstract, or repackage the information provided by the other two levels. Guides to the literature ideally seek to provide an intellectual structure that orients a researcher to the most important sources at all three levels of literature for a given subject. In practice, however, many such guides fall short of this mark and present instead bibliographies of only the tertiary reference works for their field.

- *Handbooks and manuals.* These are a type of reference source intended to be easily transportable for actual use "in the field" rather than just in libraries. They are related to encyclopedias and treatises in that they try to provide the principles and important facts of a subject area and they can be arranged alphabetically or systematically. Their major distinction from these other forms is their emphasis on practice, procedures, and "how-to" directions for producing actual results rather than just intellectual understanding. Also, they tend to be much more concisely written, again, so as to be more easily carried about in field situations.

- *Newsletters.* There are current awareness sources, providing up-to-date information in fields that tend to develop or change with some rapidity. They can appear daily, weekly, or monthly.

- *Review articles.* These should not be confused with book reviews. They are articles that appear in journals, annuals, or essay anthologies that seek to provide a "state-of-the-art" or "state-of-the-situation" literature review and critical assessment or overview of a particular subject. Unlike encyclopedia articles, they are usually written for specialists, and so may assume familiarity with technical or occupational jargon. They also include bibliographies or footnoted references that seek to be comprehensive rather than merely selective. Review articles, too, tend to place a greater emphasis on the current state of a subject, whereas encyclopedia articles tend to emphasize historical aspects.

- *Treatises.* Like encyclopedias, these try to present a comprehensive summation of the established knowledge of a particular subject; unlike encyclopedias, however, they tend to be arranged systematically, according to the distinctive features of the subject, rather than alphabetically; they also tend to be written for specialists rather than laypeople.
- *Union lists.* These are location devices; they enable researchers who have already identified specific sources to determine which libraries actually own a copy of the desired works.
- *Yearbooks.* This type of literature seeks to provide a historical record of, and usually an evaluative commentary on, the year's development in a particular field. Often they will include a chronological list of events or developments within the field for the given year. Such annuals sometimes provide a more permanent and better-indexed cumulation of the updating information contained in newsletters.

Advance knowledge of the existence of this structure of reference source options can greatly increase the efficiency of your searches by enabling you to focus your inquiries to begin with on only the type(s) of literature most likely to answer them. For example, a researcher who wants to know "What was going on in Virginia in 1775?" could do a search for relevant journal articles in *America: History & Life*, specifying "1775" in the database's Historical Period limiting box, but the result would be list of more than 1,800 articles. Similarly overwhelming retrievals result from searches of full-text newspapers of the time. An OPAC search for the heading **Virginia—Chronology**, however, is likely to turn up James A. Crutchfield's *The Grand Adventure: A Year-By-Year History of Virginia* (Dietz Press, 2005), which provides a much more manageable overview.

What makes types of literature so important is that their existence is *predictable* within all subject areas. Even if you know nothing in advance of the subject content of a disciplinary area, or any specific titles within it, you can still move around efficiently within its reference literature by focusing your inquiries on only the few types that are most appropriate to your interest. You can thereby eliminate from your search hundreds of sources that are not formatted in ways that will get you directly to what you want. For example, consider the arrangement of C. D. Hurt's *Information Sources in Science and Technology* (346 pages; Libraries Unlimited, 1998); the first three sections of its Contents are structured as follows:

1—Multidisciplinary Sources of Information

Guides to the Literature
Bibliographies
Abstracts and Indexes
Encyclopedias
Dictionaries
Handbooks
Serials
Directories
Biographical Directories
Theses and Dissertations
Meetings
Translations
Copyrights and Patents
Government Documents and Technical Reports
Internet Guides
Web Sites

2—Biology

History
Guides to the Literature
Abstracts and Indexes
Encyclopedias
Dictionaries
Handbooks
Treatises
Directories
Web Sites

3—Botany

Guides to the Literature
Bibliographies
Abstracts and Indexes
Encyclopedias
Dictionaries
Handbooks
Directories
Web Sites

Essentially the same few type-of-literature breakdowns are used in 21 different subject areas (Zoology, Astronomy, Chemistry, Environmental Sciences, General engineering, Civil Engineering, Health Sciences, etc.).

While no one can possibly remember the 1,542 individual sources described in Hurt's book, anyone with a bit of training can remember the much smaller number of *types* of literature that can be expected to exist, no matter what subject is being researched. The predictability of this format structure within any topic area, again, allows many inquiries to be much more immediately focused, with fewer wasted steps, and accomplished without the searcher having to wade through massive retrievals of term-weighted irrelevancies.

It is the predictability of this structure across *all* disciplines that often makes types of literature the focus of information literacy or bibliographic instruction classes. The types of literature all by themselves will always provide at least one kind of initial and readily discernible "shape" to the literature of any subject area, in a way that will alert you to look for multiple important parts of "the elephant" that would not otherwise fall within your initial purview. Note, however, that these types apply only to reference sources—the tertiary literature of a subject that lists, summarizes, or describes its primary and secondary literature. Compare the table of contents of the Hurt bibliography above to that of the Remini/Rupp bibliography on Andrew Jackson in Chapter 9. Both are themselves tertiary-level bibliographies, but one lists the (predictable) types of tertiary reference works, whereas the other presents a listing of (unpredictable) individual primary- and secondary-level sources.

Some of the types of reference literature—"abstracts and indexes," for example, whether electronic or print—are themselves geared much more toward answering research rather than reference questions; so, again, the line between inquiries that can be handled by "methods of searching" and "types of literature" is not hard and fast. Both models of predictable search options can sometimes be used for either research or reference inquiries.

STRUCTURING QUESTIONS BY PREDICTABLE FORMAL PROPERTIES OF RETRIEVAL SYSTEMS

The overall point here is that if you understand the trade-offs and the strengths and weaknesses of all of the different methods of searching and types of literature, then just from this knowledge of the formal properties of the several retrieval systems, you can ask much better questions to start with. Further, even without having any prior subject knowledge or knowing any specific sources, titles, or databases in advance, you can also have much better expectations of finding answers than if you start out with only a knowledge of a few particular subject sources or an uncritical faith in the capabilities of keyword searching in Google or Bing or Yahoo!. You can map out a strategy on a formal level before looking at any particular sources by making such distinctions as these:

- This question requires overview information of an unfamiliar topic, and so two predictable types of reference sources, encyclopedias and literature review articles—wherever they may be found—are desirable.
- This question allows "takes" from multiple different disciplinary perspectives, and so the examination of encyclopedia articles on it from multiple different fields is desirable.
- This question requires the comparison of selective bibliographies from *several* encyclopedia articles to see if they overlap in recommending sources that are probably "standard" (or at least particularly important).
- This question would be best addressed by another predictable type of literature, a published bibliography with sources compiled, vetted, and annotated by an expert, which will enable me to recognize a whole group of relevant citations whose keywords I cannot adequately specify in advance in a computer search.
- This question requires a predictable arrangement of books in classified order, rather than just a catalog of superficial OPAC records arranged either alphabetically by subject headings or in class number order—i.e., I need *depth* of access to the individual paragraphs and pages of books' contents, and I don't want to limit my purview to only digitized copyright-free texts, or to mere snippets of post-1922 books.
- This question requires a predictable arrangement of books categorized by subject, regardless of the keywords they use, rather than a ranking of sources based on the frequency of the few relevant keywords I can think of—i.e., I need *recognition* access to a carefully delimited group of full texts whose keywords I cannot guess in advance.
- This question requires a predictable browse list of subject headings with subdivisions that will map out, in a single roster, the whole range of aspects of a subject (topical, chronological, geographical, format) as well as cross-references to other related topics, in a way that will enable me to recognize whole clusters of relevant sources whose keywords I could not anticipate—i.e., I need menus showing me how the *LCSH* subject categories

themselves are related to each other before I look at any of the actual book records they bring together.

- This question demands databases or indexes that predictably allow keyword access rather than just subject heading or descriptor approaches.
- This question requires databases that predictably allow citation searches to find subsequent relevant sources in addition to the previous sources listed in footnotes.
- This question requires databases that predictably allow related record searching to bring to my attention relevant sources using keywords I cannot think of in advance.
- This question requires a database that predictably allows citation search or related record results to be further limited by the specification of keywords within results that are otherwise connected only by their footnote linkages.
- This question requires talking to some expert who can cut through the clutter, get me oriented, alert me to "crackpot" positions in unfamiliar subject areas, and otherwise provide answers or directions not readily discoverable by computer or print sources.
- This question requires the use of printed bibliographies, catalogs, and indexes that have never been digitized and that cover earlier literature not noticed by computer databases or websites.
- This question requires the use of union lists or databases that will tell me who owns a copy of a particular source that is not available online and is also not owned by my local library.
- This question requires the use of a database that will predictably enable me to limit its output to subject coverage within a certain historical time frame, no matter when the articles discussing it were published—i.e., I need a database that will allow limitation by historical period rather than by date of publication.
- This question requires a full-text database that will predictably allow me to limit to the document type "Obituary" so I won't have to look through every article that mentions a person's name in any context.
- This question requires a database that will allow word truncation, Boolean combinations, and parentheses in order to combine all the terms I want in proper relationships to each other.
- This question requires that I first cut down a prospectively immense body of reference literature into a much smaller and more manageable number of types of sources, so that I can identify and pursue only those that are likely to provide the most on-target results.

Again, it is possible to form scores of *a priori* "framing" observations like this that entail a combined knowledge of both methods of searching and types of literature that will predictably be available in any subject area. Simply knowing the *kinds* search techniques and sources that are always available will make you more proficient in finding specific instantiations of them geared toward whatever particular inquiry you may be pursuing. Having this mental framework is much more useful than having prior subject knowledge in most research inquiries. (Subject knowledge is indeed important in some—not all—instances; hence, "people sources" are indeed included as part of the frame.)

Note especially that having such a range of conceptual and procedural options available will give you much better results than having only the commonly assumed single option that might be stated as:

- This question requires keyword searching in a single search box that will give me, through computer relevance ranking and federate searching, all I need from all sources that exist, in the first three screens of retrievals.[4]

Students who have experience with only this option are, I find, usually hungry to be shown the many preferable alternatives—especially if they are working on something that matters to them.

Having a prior knowledge of the different methods of searching and types of literature will also enable you to eliminate whole areas of options with which you might otherwise waste time (e.g., in trying to use either computer or print sources when the information you need is most likely to exist in some person's head; in trying to use databases rather than classified bookstacks when the needed information is likely to exist only at the page or paragraph level within printed, copyrighted books that haven't been digitized; in trying to use Internet search engines or even Wikipedia for overview perspectives when multiple published encyclopedia or literature review articles are preferable.) That knowledge also can, and does, eliminate the retrieval of hundreds of thousands of irrelevant sources having the right words in the wrong contexts or in wrong formats of records.

THE STUDY OF INFORMATION

It is this foreknowledge of the predictable formal properties of the several retrieval options—no matter what the subject area—that usually makes good reference librarians much more efficient in finding the best information quickly, uncluttered by irrelevancies, than even full professors in a given subject area.

Students in a particular academic subject area usually learn its information resources from a particular list they are given to study. The result is that they often learn a few individual "trees" without perceiving the overall arrangement of the forest or the variety of methods available for getting through it, whether by walking, riding, flying over, swinging from branch to branch, or burrowing underneath. The training of reference librarians, on the other hand, is more from the top down than from the bottom up. They first learn the options than can be expected in *any* forest—here the analogy is not perfect—and the various ways of moving around in it. They learn the overall methods of searching and types of literature that predictably exist in *any* subject area; they thereby usually gain an understanding of the full range of options for finding information even—or rather, especially—in unfamiliar subjects areas. (Most questions are such that neither the questioner nor the librarian has sufficient prior subject knowledge in the area.) The librarians may not understand the content of the discipline in which they are searching as well as professors within it, but the librarians will probably have a better grasp of the range of options for finding the content, which is a distinct and different skill.

The study of the categorization, arrangement, storage, and retrieval of information is a discipline unto itself; it is called library and information science. Those whose acquaintance with it is minimal should be wary of assuming that they are doing fully efficient research on their own, for there will always be more options in searching than they realize. (Many of the same people would also be well advised to progress well beyond the naïve assumption that the intellectual scope of librarianship extends only to the creation of Dewey Decimal numbers.) The moral of the story is brief: the more you know about what your options are, the better the searcher you will be, but remember to ask for help, since the probability is that you are missing a great deal if you work entirely on your own. (A very good time to ask for help is when you are about to change the scope or the subject of your paper because you can't find the information you need to support the paper you really want to write.)

SPECIFIC SOURCES FOR IDENTIFYING TYPES OF LITERATURE IN ANY SUBJECT AREA

So, then, how do you actually find the particular types of literature within the subject area of your interest? Librarians have a few major aids enabling them to identify the type-of-literature structures within any given field. The first two can be considered basic sources; the others, updates. They are:

1. *Guide to Reference* (American Library Association). This is a subscription database with annotated entries for about 16,000 reference sources in all subject areas. It succeeds the 2,020-page printed *Guide to Reference Books* (ALA), 11th edition, edited by Robert Balay. Most libraries retain the printed version, however, as its format allows easier scanning and recognition of nearby entries and categories of sources than does the database, which requires continual back-and-forth clicking on links.

2. *The New Walford Guide to Reference Resources. Volume 1: Science, Technology and Medicine* (2005). *Volume 2: The Social Sciences* (2008). *Volume 3: Arts, Humanities and General Reference* (2013). This is similar in scope to the ALA *Guide to Reference* in providing annotated entries to reference sources (including websites) arranged by types of literature, but it has more of an emphasis on British sources.

3. *ARBAonline* (Libraries Unlimited). This subscription database lists virtually all reference books published in the United States since 1997. (The corresponding printed set, *American Reference Books Annual: ARBA*, extends back to 1970.) The distinctive feature of this source is that it provides a detailed review of each work listed. It is helpful to use *ARBA* in conjunction with *Guide to Reference* (above).

4. The library's own online catalog. Subject headings within the OPAC are often followed by form subdivisions that correspond to the various types of literature; for example:

[LC Subject Heading]—Atlases
                         —Bibliography
                         —Case studies
                         —Catalogs
                         —Charts, diagrams, etc.
                         —Chronology
                         —Concordances
                         —Dictionaries
                         —Directories
                         —Discography
                         —Encyclopedias

—Film catalogs
—Guidebooks
—Handbooks, manuals, etc.
—Illustrations
—Indexes
—Manuscripts—Catalogs
—Maps
—Periodicals—Bibliography
—Periodicals—Bibliography—Union
lists
—Periodicals—Indexes
—Photograph collections
—Photographs
—Pictorial works
—Posters
—Quotations
—Statistics
—Tables
—Textbooks
—Union lists
—Yearbooks

The predictability of this kind of "form" cataloging enables researchers to identify quickly new instances of familiar types of literature within any subject area, because their library's catalog will be updated daily.

The above sources enable researchers to find types of literature primarily in monographic or printed-book formats. Remember, however, that many other types of literature exist within journal and report literature; these include such forms as book reviews, literature reviews, database reviews, software reviews, film reviews, editorials, letters to the editor, editorial cartoons, obituaries, curriculum guides, and bilingual materials (see Chapter 10). Many of the thousands of subscription databases enable you to specify such formats within the literature they cover. Researchers are always well advised to look at the Advanced search screen for whichever database they select and to actively look for the form-limit options (often hidden in drop-down menus) before typing in any keywords.

The various distinctions among methods of searching and types of literature obviously provide much to remember. An easy way to keep the outline of options in front of you would be to use the table of contents of the present volume. Remember that all of these options potentially apply to virtually any subject.

Perhaps the most important point overall, however, is the observation with which this book began: if you want to do serious research, it is highly advisable not to confine your searches to the open Internet alone. The information universe of the future, no matter how its contents may change and grow, is best understood in terms of unavoidable trade-offs among *what, who*, and *where* restrictions. The free Internet itself will never include everything available in real research libraries until such time as human nature itself changes in the direction of selfless benevolence and all writers, artists, and creators forgo the advantages of intellectual property to voluntarily contribute their work products to the good of a socialist whole, accepting recompense at levels determined by bureaucratic formulas rather than by marketplace forces of supply and demand. History has not been kind to social systems based on the assumption that all (or even most) human beings will act in this manner. Within the world of learning, however, history has also witnessed the creation of a marvelous mechanism for protecting the rights of authors while also making the universe of knowledge freely available to anyone who will travel to certain locations. I hope this book will lead to a more efficient use, and a greater appreciation, of that mechanism: bricks-and-mortar research libraries.

Wisdom and Information Science

THERE ARE BOUNDARY RESTRICTIONS OF *WHO*, *WHAT*, AND *WHERE* on the information that can be made freely available to researchers, and these restrictions necessarily prevent the open Internet from providing "all" information freely to anyone, anywhere, at any time. These boundaries are created primarily by copyright laws and legal site license and password limitations that are just a much an unavoidable part of the information world as is computer technology itself. It is also the case that the higher levels of learning in our culture—knowledge, understanding, and wisdom as contrasted to data, information, and opinion—are conveyed primarily by book-length texts (either print or electronic in format) of sufficient amplitude to convey large perspectives integrating wide ranges of information into coherent frameworks of exposition or narration.

The means of discovering, evaluating, and bringing to bear those large frameworks themselves is not something that can be accomplished by computer algorithms, no matter how sophisticated they may be. A justification of that claim will require an analysis of the nature of wisdom and of what it entails that eludes Internet search mechanisms.

It is indeed generally taken for granted that there is a hierarchy in levels of learning, from data to information and opinion, to knowledge and understanding, with wisdom often placed at the top of the sequence. I think there is an important qualification to that positioning: as conventionally understood, wisdom seems to have one foot on the hierarchical ladder and another off to the side. It usually does entail cognition of a sort—i.e., an intellectual apprehension of the *true*—and also at a level of comprehension above that of "understanding." In this sense, what I'll call "cognitive wisdom" does indeed occupy the space at the top rung of the ladder. But wisdom as a whole does not reduce to "cognitive" (or "intellectual" or "speculative") because it also entails the habit of willing the good in conduct—a crucial aspect separate from any of the ladder's intellectual steps. The moral component ideally surrounds or envelops the ladder, but experience shows that it may also be lacking even when all of the cognitive steps from data up to the top are present.

This aspect of wisdom consists in the habit of living, or at least striving to live, according to the virtues. A traditional list of these would include prudence, justice, fortitude, and temperance, if not faith, hope, and charity or compassion as well. It is this ethical aspect that often leads observers to note that many people who have little formal education—and who may also live within widely variant religious, agnostic, or atheistic creeds—nevertheless live wisely or sagely,[1] while, conversely, many who have great knowledge or understanding of particular subjects are nonetheless foolish in the practical conduct of their own lives.

The possession of wisdom as a whole, however, does not simply reduce to acquiring the habit of acting on moral values such as prudence, justice, or compassion; it also entails an intellectual insight of being able cognitively to discern a reasonably justifiable grasp of the ultimate structure of the "forest" (i.e., the universe and our experience of it) amid the myriad "trees" of data—opposed, at least, to mistaken views assumed by those who are recognizably ignorant, unwise, shortsighted, or foolish or opposed to views that, playing out over time in the laboratory of history, have repeatedly led to disastrous consequences of war, genocide, oppression, or large-scale misery and injustice.

The achievement of wisdom, both cognitive and moral, entails considerations of "what needs to be brought to bear on the question at hand" that cannot be captured by any relevance-ranking keyword searches. The reason is obvious: the same data and information can be framed very differently according to different belief systems. Such systems themselves are variable according to their cognitive assumptions of what is the ultimate source of meaning. A list of only a few candidates for providing that ultimate ground for meaning would include the Biblical God, the Qur'anic Allah, the pantheistic One, the Void (or nonbeing/nonexistence), Marxist dialectical materialism, matter and energy, mathematical elegance, endless cosmic cycles or multiverses, Platonic Forms, Aristotelian form and matter, Darwinian evolutionary success and genetic diffusion, sustainable environmentalism, societal conventions based on power relationships, one's own self or will, one's family or tribe or social group, the interaction of *yin* and *yang*, sexual fulfillment—and many others.

There seem to be some important considerations that are not entirely arbitrary—while also being not "provable" one way or the other, either—entailed in the acceptance of one ultimate intellectual framework or ordering principle in comparison with another:

- Does the proposed framework explain or account for the universe having a "big bang" beginning? Does the principal of Ockham's razor (accepting a simpler explanation in preference to multiplying assumptions) apply to this choice itself, or does that principle operate only within the frame of a "post-bang" universe?
- Does the frame accept or deny (as illusory) the experience of human free will?
- Does it account for the correspondence of pure mathematics to physical reality, and for the power of mathematical discoveries, independently arrived at, not only to predict physical outcomes but even to direct attention to the existence of otherwise unsuspected properties of the physical world?[2]
- Does it account for the elegance or beauty of that correspondence, as in its many and complex symmetries?
- Does it account, in quantum physics, for the status of an observer whose own characteristics are not explained by the variables or coordinates of the system observed, and does it account, in mathematics, for the parallel Gödelian insight that a finished mathematical system cannot account for the outside status of its observer either (whose outside status enables him to discern additional truths *of* the system not provable *within* the system)?[3]
- Does it accord relationships (e.g., mathematical, causal, moral, economic, political) a reality or ontological status comparable to entities? That is, are such relationships objectively discoverable, or are they, rather, created by the mind and imposed (with inevitable baggage of power interests) on perceptions of a fundamentally unstructured and unknowable reality?
- Does it accord to intellectual coherence itself, in addition to correspondence to physical conditions, a role in indicating truth?
- Does it admit or deny any reality to moral obligation prior to societal conventions or contracts?
- Does it see one's connection to the ultimate ground of meaning—whatever it may be—as one of "relationship to" or "identity with"?
- Does it regard that ultimate ground as personal or impersonal?

- Does it regard a spiritual life after death as a reality or as mere wishful thinking?

Quite obviously no computer "relevance ranking" can bring to bear any of these concerns in patterning which configuration of information is preferable to the alternatives. Disagreements about such matters, however, are not without consequences.

I will not presume to make a case here for any one of the above "ultimates" over the others—they are not all mutually exclusive in any event—but I would point out that the cognitive choice or even tacit assumption of any one of them entails moral value assumptions that are not universally shared by the others. These values in turn serve to frame not just perceptions of what counts to begin with as relevant data and information, but also to contribute in forming the networks of coherence criteria by which the data and information become accepted as adequately integrated knowledge or understanding. The same data and information can be received through multiple different lenses or filters that change, block, or highlight what is perceived as "relevant," particularly when judgments leading to actions are required. One has only to look at current social debates on gun control, immigration, assisted suicide, or government/corporate responsibilities to see that such problems can never be resolved by information retrievals created by computer algorithms underlying Internet (or other) search boxes. The "relevance" of data and information determined by algorithms working on specified keyword search terms cannot determine the relevant cognitive frameworks or moral values by which the data and information are to be integrated. Any such incapacity is an incapacity to convey wisdom.

There are particular dangers lying in the fact that "information" (as well as opinion) tends to be mistaken as either knowledge or understanding and that the "relevance" of information determined by algorithms can be uncritically taken as "value-neutral" in the sense of somehow floating above partisan concerns and not characterized by distorting filters or selectivity imposed by the algorithms themselves. Bluntly, the concealed proposition would be something like "since the algorithms cannot impose values shaped by any particular worldview framework of meaning, their determination of 'relevance ranking' in what they retrieve can simply be taken as 'objective.'"

Internet searching, however, does impose a framework of its own in determining what is "relevant" to any inquiry, and that frame might best be described as a kaleidoscope view. In a kaleidoscope one sees many individual small pieces of colored glass that are indeed arranged in patterns or larger structures, often of great complexity, but the patterns and structures themselves are quite unstable, and the change in position of even one or two individual pieces can bring about cascades that radically alter the overall view. The analogy is not perfect here, but it is nonetheless readily confirmable that Google, Bing, Yahoo!, or other Internet searches on the same terms can bring about results that are substantially different among themselves, and even within each system the retrievals will vary not only from one day to the next but even from one minute to the next. The turning of the Internet kaleidoscope never stops. One might well ask, then, "Are the first three screens of any Internet retrieval reliably indicative of the truth of the subject?"

The relative stability of the top positioning of Wikipedia articles within algorithmic rankings is especially problematic in conveying the concealed proposition that this source itself is "above the fray" in *its* objectivity. Granted, there is no better mechanism available on the Internet for providing general overviews of what I have called "the shape of the elephant" of the many subjects it covers, but the Wikipedia's shaping itself is variable, very frequently unsupported by adequate documentation, and often lacking in comparative perspectives. Further, no encyclopedia-length article is ultimately as intellectually anchored as a scholarly book-length text. Wikipedia is generally good for what it does at the levels of data and information, but it, too, cannot convey the relevance of large worldview perspectives on the subjects it treats of. The danger here is its conveyance of the concealed proposition that such larger perspectives are routinely *ir*relevant to the information at hand.

There is thus an unarticulated assumption that the avoidance of any particularly specified worldview framework provides intellectual objectivity or moral neutrality, but this very assumption subliminally conveys its own worldview—that the shifting kaleidoscopic arrangement of data and information *is* the best determinant of meaning that can be appealed to. This perspective itself, however, needs to be compared to the other frames based on quite different assumptions of what is the best or ultimate determinant of meaning.

This is where wisdom comes into play in ways that cannot be reached by computer algorithms: wisdom is the mechanism by which we determine what counts as evidence to begin with according to overarching or ultimate standards of truth, goodness, and beauty. And those standards themselves are not matters of mere opinion, but can be judged by the range and adequacy of which considerations (as only partially suggested by the above list) they take into account as requiring explanation to begin with.

Once more: no computer algorithm can bring to bear any of these large and unavoidable framing assumptions determining the "relevance ranking" of information retrievals.

If nothing else, such considerations should reasonably restrain those of us in the information profession from claiming too much for what we can actually deliver in furthering the goals of either formal education or informal human learning in general. Grandiose assertions that either "all information" or even "all knowledge" can be conveyed electronically (and immediately) stumble badly, to begin with, at the lower levels of the learning hierarchy: our best algorithms cannot distinguish either understanding or knowledge from information or opinion; further, they are oblivious to the choice of one or another ultimate ordering principle, the selection of which has profound consequences in shaping our responses to, and evaluations of, both new situations and new information. Indeed, that choice has a major influence in framing what we judge to be worth attending to right from the start in defining what we accept *as* knowledge or understanding.

Emerson once wrote, "it is not observed...that librarians are wiser men than others." If I may paraphrase the sage of Concord, "it is not observed that either librarians or information scientists are wiser people than others." This is particularly true if we regard the goal of our profession as achievable by providing "one-stop" access to "all" information at once—i.e., by breaking down the boundaries of carefully crafted disciplinary "silos" and asserting that "a single search" box backed by algorithmic relevance ranking of keywords is all that we need to provide. Such a belief—and such a practice—would be deadly to the conveyance of the higher levels of learning that our culture requires. If we as a profession wish to promote scholarship at its highest levels, perhaps even those approaching the achievement of wisdom, we cannot rely on either Internet content or search mechanisms alone to do the job for us. We have to provide real alternatives, not only covering important sources that lie in blind spots to Internet searching, but also in also in providing access to those sources in ways that enable recognition of what cannot be specified in advance. Real libraries staffed by knowledgeable librarians and curators *are* that alternative.

APPENDIX B

Scholarship vs. Quick Information Seeking

THROUGHOUT THIS BOOK I HAVE TRIED TO MAKE A CASE THAT there are substantive differences between scholarly research and quick information seeking. A spectrum of continuities exists between the two, of course, and Google and Wikipedia, which are very often quite adequate for the latter pursuit, have their place in scholarship as well. But they cannot show you "the shape of the elephant" of relevant sources in the same ways, or to the same extent, as the approaches discussed in this book.

It may be useful to articulate more specifically some of the differences between the two types of research[1]:

- Scholars seek, first and foremost, as clear and as extensive an *overview* of *all* relevant and important sources as they can achieve.
- Scholarship is necessarily iterative, proceeding in successive steps that change depending on feedback provided by previous steps; it cannot all be done "seamlessly" through "one-stop" single search boxes, nor can it be done by progressively refining initial sets if those sets themselves have been created with the wrong keywords to begin with.
- Scholars are especially concerned that they do not overlook sources that are unusually important, significant, or standard in their field of inquiry.
- Scholars especially wish to avoid wasting effort, or "re-inventing the wheel," by duplicating research that has already been done.
- Scholars wish to be aware of cross-disciplinary and cross-format connections relevant to their work—but they also do not wish

to be misled by "seamless" searches whose many trade-offs and blind spots are concealed from them by impenetrable "under-the-hood" programming. (They especially wish to avoid searching so many different sources at the same time that the resultant retrievals are overloaded with thousands of irrelevant "noise" or "junk" hits.)

- Scholars wish to find current books on a subject categorized with prior books on the same subject, so the newer works can be perceived in the context of the existing literature—not just in connection with the much smaller subset of titles that happen to be currently in print.

- Advanced scholars also wish for similar categorizations of English and foreign language books—i.e., they want subject searches to retrieve relevant materials in all languages together, so that a worldwide context of resources on their subject can be easily discerned. They do not wish to be straitjacketed within retrieval systems that are good *only* for finding English-language sources.

- Scholars particularly appreciate mechanisms that enable them to *recognize* highly relevant sources whose keywords they cannot think up in advance to enter into a blank search box. (Such recognition is often a function of prior conceptual categorization of keyword-variant sources, rather than relevance ranking of only those sources containing the exactly specified keywords.)

- Although they are more cognizant of the need for diligence and persistence in research, and of the requirement to check multiple sources, and of the need to look beyond the "first three screens" display of any retrievals, scholars also wish to avoid having to sort through huge lists or displays—from *any* source—in which relevant materials are buried within inadequately sorted mountains of chaff.

An equally important general observation is that scholars really do want these things even if they do not explicitly articulate them in response to user surveys that have not asked the right questions to begin with.

Notes

Chapter 1

1. The editor's introduction to *Mrs. Byrne's Dictionary*, by her ex-husband, is famous among bibliophiles: "Working alone and without government support (or even comprehension) she managed to assemble the six thousand weirdest words in the English language. Nobody asked her to do it because nobody thought such a thing was possible. In fact, I asked her *not* to do it."

Chapter 2

1. "Fewer added entries are required and no more than one or two subject headings need be added to the core record." (Willy Cromwell, "The Core Record: A New Bibliographic Standard," *Library Resources & Technical Services*, 28 [October, 1994], p. 422.)

Chapter 3

1. David H. Shayt, quoted in the *Washington Post*, July 5, 1992, p. C8. A copy of the illustration Shayt found appears with his remarks.
2. Thomas Mann, "The Principle of Least Effort" and "Bibliography," in *Library Research Models* (Oxford University Press, 1993). The same book provides numerous other examples of information that can be found only by direct examination of subject-categorized books.

Chapter 4

1. At least three such services are currently available: EBSCO Discovery Service, Primo Central, and Summon Article Finder.

2. Descriptions are taken from the EBSCO website at www.ebscohost.com.

3. The database descriptions are largely taken from the ProQuest home page at www.proquest.com.

4. This list is derived from the company's online brochure at http://support .dialog.com/publications/dbcat/dbcat2010.pdf.

5. Descriptions are taken from the Gale Cengage website at www.gale.cengage .com/catalog/facts.htm.

6. Descriptions are taken from the online information pages available to subscribers of the FirstSearch system.

7. A study by John Martin and Alan Gilchrist, *An Evaluation of British Scientific Journals* (ASLIB, 1968), once found that in the *Science Citation Index*, citing authors abbreviated *Proceedings of the Institute for Electrical Engineers* 24 different ways.

Chapter 5

1. This points up another persistent problem with copy cataloging available in the OCLC system: catalogers at smaller libraries are not in a position to see the range of new books being published in any given subject area, and so may tend to assign broad subject headings to books because their own collections are not large enough to require finer distinctions. The broad headings they use then get picked up without review by larger libraries, which should be making finer "specific entry" distinctions.

2. See http://about.jstor.org/service/early-journal-content.

3. I am most grateful to Alistair Morrison, Director of Product Planning at LexisNexis Academic Library Solutions, for his help in sorting out a very complicated can of worms here, and for permission to take descriptive information from company sources, among them:

   http://academic.lexisnexis.com
   http://wiki.lexisnexis.com/publib
   http://wiki.lexisnexis.com/schools

   The continued existence of these specific URLs is in doubt, however, since much of LexisNexis has recently been acquired by ProQuest; but ProQuest.com should remedy the situation.

4. Descriptions in the section are derived from the company's website, www .heinonline.org/.

Chapter 6

1. Descriptions of *the Web of Science* products are derived from their printed sets and from their home page at http://wokinfo.com/products_tools/multidisciplinary/ webofscience/.

Chapter 11

1. Beall, J., et al. "The Proportion of NUC Pre-56 Titles Represented in OCLC WorldCat." *College & Research Libraries*, 66, 5 (September, 2005), 431–435; and DeZelar-Tiedman, C. "The Proportion of NUC Pre-56 Titles Represented in the RLIN and OCLC Databases Compared: A Follow-Up Study to the Beall/ Kafadar Study." *College and Research Libraries*, 69, 5 (September, 2008), 401–406.

2. I cannot resist referring researchers to the reference to a disgruntled note, famous among reference librarians, recorded in the *Pre-'56 NUC* in the entry for James Wolveridge's *Speculum Matricis* (vol. 671), and the bibliographic ghost recorded in entry NP0576549 (vol. 471), which is not owned by the University of Oregon. Similar peculiarities add dashes of color to otherwise stodgy reference works in other areas. The way to tell if your library has the first (1980) printing of the *New Grove Dictionary of Music and Musicians* is via the presence of a decidedly unconventional spelling of the word "fugue" in vol. 7, p. 782, column 1, line 2. The obscenity is corrected in subsequent printings. Also in the 1980 *New Grove* set, two hoax entries slipped past the editors, for the fictitious composers Guglielmo Baldini and Dag Henrik Esrum-Hellerup; in later printings these spaces are filled by illustrations. A hoax entry also appears in the 1971 edition of *Music since 1900*, entered under 27 April 1905; subsequent printings reproduce the entry with an explanatory disclaimer note. In the *Congressional Record* of September 27, 1986, p. S14050, col. 1, a memorandum in support of a bill to outlaw indecent communications by means of telephone includes a full-paragraph transcription of a dial-a-porn message, thereby making the *Record* itself a printed means of indecent communication. Chapter 42 of Niels Horrebow's *Natural History of Iceland* (London: A. Linde, 1758), entitled "Concerning Owls," reads "There are no owls of any kind in the whole island." The "rights" statement of Hillel Schwartz's *The Culture of the Copy* (Zone Books, 1996) vents explicitly the secret wishes of many authors; it reads:

> All rights reserved under the International and Pan-American Copyright Conventions. No part of this book may be reproduced, replicated, reiterated, duplicated, conduplicated, retyped, transcribed by hand (manuscript or cursive), read aloud and recorded on audio tape, platter, or disk, lipsynched, stored in a retrieval system, or transmitted in any form or by any means, including genetic, chemical, mechanical, optical, xerographic, holographic, electronic, stereophonic, ceramic, acrylic, or telepathic (except for that copying permitted by Sections 107 and 108 or U.S. Copyright Law and except by reviewers for the public press who promise to read the book painstakingly and all the way through before writing their reviews) without prior written permission from the Publisher.

Finally, male readers will wince, and some feminists cheer, at the singular particulars of the death of the son and heir of Sir John Hussey

Delaval, later created Baron Delaval, as succinctly recorded in G. E. Cokayne's *Complete Peerage*, vol. 4, p. 139, note (b).

Chapter 12

1. *Following the Equator*, vol. 1 (vol. 5 of *The Writings of Mark Twain*), epigraph to chapter 11, p. 125 (1897; reprinted 1968).
2. Here as elsewhere in this chapter I am passing along some of the savvy of *Washington Post* reporter Joel Achenbach.
3. See "The Peloponnesian War and the Future of Reference" at www.guild2910 .org/Pelopponesian%20War%20June%2013%202007.pdf. It is a copyright-free paper, so simply googling its title (in quotation marks) will also bring it up.

Chapter 15

1. Other techniques such as original observation and analysis, controlled experimentation, site examinations, and statistical surveying or sampling are beyond the scope of this book.
2. An August 22, 2011, paper on *Inside Higher Ed*, "What Students Don't Know," effectively explodes the myth of the "digital native." The open-source article appears quickly in Google if a search is done on its exact title, in quotation marks.
3. For a much more extensive, and technical discussion of reference sources see my article on "Reference and Informational Genres" in the *Encyclopedia of Library and Information Sciences*, 3rd edition (CRC Press, 2010), vol. 6, pp. 4470–4480.
4. A librarian colleague once e-mailed me to ask for a copy of a previous edition of this book; she said some of the academics in her school were teaching this, and she wanted to hit them over the head with my book. I sent her a hardcover copy.

Appendix A

1. The point here is similar to that recognized by the drafters of the United Nations Universal Declaration of Human Rights. As Jacques Maritain, one of the drafters, wrote, "It is related that at one of the meetings of a UNESCO National Commission where human rights were being discussed, someone expressed astonishment that certain champions of violently opposed ideologies had agreed on a list of those rights. 'Yes,' they said, 'we agree about the rights *but on condition that no one asks us why.*'"—Jacques Maritain, "Introduction," p. 9, in *Human Rights: Comments and Interpretations: A Symposium edited by UNESCO* (London and New York: Allan Wingate, [1949]; reprinted, Westport, Conn.: Greenwood Press, [1973]).
2. "For example, complex numbers were invented and the theory of them deeply investigated by the early nineteenth century, a mathematical development

that seemed to have no relevance to physical reality. Only in the 1920s was it discovered that complex numbers were needed to write the equations of quantum mechanics. Or, in another instance, when the mathematician William Rowan Hamilton invented quaternions in the mid-nineteenth century, they were regarded as an ingenious but totally useless construct. Hamilton himself held this view. When asked by an aristocratic lady whether quaternions were useful for anything, Hamilton joked, 'Aye, madam, quaternions are *very* useful—for solving problems involving quaternions.' And yet, many decades later, quaternions were put to use to describe properties of subatomic particles such as the spin of electrons as well as the relation between neutrons and protons. Or again, Riemannian geometry was developed long before it was found to be needed for Einstein's theory of gravity. And a branch of mathematics called the theory of Lie groups was developed before it was found to describe the gauge symmetries of the fundamental forces."—Stephen Barr, "Fearful Symmetries," *First Things*, 206 (October, 2010), 35.

3. Hume's *An Enquiry Concerning Human Understanding* is an interesting example of an observer's status, in light of its famous concluding paragraph:

> When we run over libraries, persuaded of these principles, what havoc must we make? If we take in our hand any volume; of divinity or school metaphysics, for instance; let us ask, *Does it contain any abstract reasoning concerning quantity or number?* No. *Does it contain any experimental reasoning containing matter of fact and existence?* No. Commit it then to the flames: for it can contain nothing but sophistry and illusion.

> According to these criteria Hume's *Enquiry* itself would have to be committed to the flames: it is not a book of abstract reasoning concerning quantity or number, nor one of scientific measurement or experiment. The unarticulated assumption of the author is that his own observer status enables him to present truths about the "closed" materialistic world-system he sees that cannot themselves be measured or quantified within it. If this is the case, however, then there is a tacit recognition that another kind of knowledge, the philosophical, can produce truths not provable by mathematical analysis or experimental scientific methods.

Appendix B

1. This list is largely derived from the more extensive discussion of these issues in my open-source paper "The Peloponnesian War and the Future of Reference, Cataloging, and Scholarship in Research Libraries" at www.guild2910 .org/future.htm.

Index

When multiple page references are listed, page numbers of the major discussion are in *italics*.